Maturity and Stagnation in American Capitalism

Maturity and Stagnation in American Capitalism

Josef Steindl

with a new introduction by the Author

MATURITY AND STAGNATION IN AMERICAN CAPITALISM
Josef Steindl

Published in agreement with Monthly Review Press, New York for publication and sale only in the Indian Subcontinent (India, Pakistan, Bangladesh, Nepal, Maldives, Bhutan & Sri Lanka)

First Published in India 2011

ISBN 978-93-5002-147-7

Published by
AAKAR BOOKS
28 E Pocket IV, Mayur Vihar Phase I, Delhi 110 091
Phone : 011 2279 5505 Telefax : 011 2279 5641
info@aakarbooks.com; www.aakarbooks.com

Printed at
Mudrak, 30 A, Patparganj, Delhi 110 091

CONTENTS

PART I

PRICES, COSTS AND PROFIT MARGINS

PART II

THE ACCUMULATION OF CAPITAL

LIST OF TABLES

LIST OF FIGURES

INTRODUCTION

The first (1952) edition of this book appeared at a time which could not have been less propitious for its success. Neoclassicism reigned in the economics profession. The advanced industrial countries had begun to establish full employment, rapidly rising living standards, and international cooperation; and in this atmosphere of confidence an analysis of the dismal experience of 1929-1939 seemed to be out of place. More recently, since the worms have been creeping out of the welfare state, the mood may be different. However that may be, I have been convinced by friends, and especially by Paul Sweezy, to have the book reprinted with all its faults, seeing that I am much too lazy to rewrite it. It is only fair, however, that I should try to give an account of (a) what has happened on the economic scene since the interwar period, and why; and (b) how far my ideas have changed and what I consider to be wrong in this book today.

On the first point, I am much helped by the fact that Michal Kalecki treated just this question in an admirable paper. [1] How did it come about that American capitalism, seemingly very sick before 1939, had become vigorous again, providing high levels of effective demand and employment? The answer is (at least in part): vastly increased public expenditures provided additional effective demand, although these outlays were not deficit-financed, but in large part financed by taxation of profits. The reference made in this context is usually to Haavelmo's principle; but Haavelmo refers to an average income earner, taxpayer, and saver, whereas Kalecki distinguishes wage earners and profit receivers, and in this way makes it obvious that the expansion occurs only to the extent to which the tax hits the profits and not mass consumption.

The principle can be illustrated by the following simple model. Profits are the sum of investment (after deduction of government saving, import surplus, and workers' savings), capitalists' consumption, and profit taxes:

$$P = I + C + T \qquad (1)$$

We assume that profits and wages are the only forms of income, and that wages are linked to the national product by a linear relation:

$$W = \alpha Y + \beta Z \, , \qquad Y \leqslant Y^* \tag{2}$$

in which βZ represent the overhead wage costs, here regarded as a fixed proportion of the capital stock Z, to which they are in reality only loosely linked. The relation (2) is constrained by the capacity limit Y^*. Thus profits are:

$$P = Y - W = (1 - \alpha) \; Y - \beta Z$$

or as a fraction of national product,

$$P/_Y = 1 - \alpha - \beta Z/_Y = I/_Y + C/_Y + T/_Y \tag{3}$$

$$(Y \leqslant Y^*)$$

This means that the marginal profit ratio $1 - \alpha$ equals the sum of the average profit ratio and the overhead ratio. The latter depends, of course, on the utilization of capacity and varies inversely with it, subject to the constraint of the capacity barrier. There is thus a minimum to the overhead ratio.

The marginal profit ratio $1 - \alpha$ is difficult to derive empirically because we do not have adequate data on capital and capacity to estimate equation (3). For the present analysis, we assume that α and β are given. β is determined by the cost structure, α by market power ("degree of monopoly"). The ratio $\frac{1-\alpha}{\alpha}$ can be regarded as a markup (this, it is true, is a markup reckoned on wages alone, whereas in commercial practice the markup is reckoned on direct wages plus materials).

Given $1 - \alpha$ and β, the investment (minus government saving, import surplus, and workers' savings), capitalists' consumption, and profit taxes will determine the degree of utilization and the overhead ratio. An increase in public expenditure financed by profit taxes will thus be paid out of reduced overheads as long as there is available capacity and manpower. [2]

The table on the facing page shows the increase in profit taxes in the United States over the prewar level. As a proportion of private GNP at factor prices, corporate taxes in the high employment period 1951-1957 were 5 percent above the prewar level. If we add taxes on non-wage personal incomes, and on the other hand take into account the fact that government deficits were smaller than before the war, we find that an increase of nearly 5 percent in the profits-before-tax ratio must be attributed to fiscal policy. In accordance with this reasoning, the

PERCENT OF PRIVATE GROSS NATIONAL PRODUCT AT FACTOR COST [3]

	1929-38	1951-57	1951-71
Corporate taxes	1.49	6.60	5.60
Personal taxes on nonwage incomes [4]	1.73	3.59	3.40
Profit taxes	3.22	10.19	9.00
Government dissaving	2.28	0.17	0.57
Total	5.50	10.36	9.57
Increase over prewar		4.86	4.07
Corporate profits after tax	4.07	7.45	6.89
Gross private domestic investment	11.28	19.30	18.61
Foreign balance	0.94	0.91	0.77

overhead ratio must have correspondingly decreased, if the marginal profit ratio $1 - \alpha$ remained unchanged.

Thus, if the overhead ratio had been (to put it rather arbitrarily) 40 percent before the war, it has been reduced by 1/8 on account of fiscal policy, which means that with unchanged α, utilization must have increased by 14 percent over prewar levels on that account. (The assumption of constant α and β plays only the role of *ceteris paribus* in this analysis.) In other words, a substantial rise in utilization of capacity should have been expected as a result of the heavy increase in public expenditure (mainly on arms); and if capacity has increased in step with manpower and productivity, the utilization of available manpower should have been increased to the same extent as that of capacity.

Since utilization—as I contend in this book—has an influence on investment, there is a further effect of heavy public expenditure: a permanent addition to the rate of private investment as a consequence of the higher utilization. This addition to the rate of private investment has in fact materialized (as a ratio of private GNP, the rate is 8 percent above prewar), but it is probably only in part due to the utilization factor. There is another reason for it: the stream of commercially exploitable innovations arising as a by-product of the development of military technology and research since the last war. Atomic power, electronic computers and automation, jet aircraft, electronics, miniaturization of equipment, bulldozers, the materials technology resulting from space research have all stimulated investment. The civilian application of military technology is facilitated by the fact that it is often done by the same concerns.

In this book (Chapter X) I denied that innovations stimulate investment. I was impressed by the long intervals between the emergence of a scientific idea and its actual exploitation in industry (examples given by Bernal), and I did not appreciate the fact that business would not touch a new thing unless it was sufficiently advanced. There lay my error: those ideas (e.g., new products) which are sufficiently advanced, which can be exploited without too much delay and risk, and which somehow appeal to the businessman's mind are scarce indeed, and their emergence in each case is a powerful inducement to invest.

The advent of massive Research and Development programs since the last war has not really changed this basic situation: most of it would not be done without the government (almost two-thirds of all R & D in the United States is government financed), and industry is in general not prepared to engage in ventures which do not promise quick results. War has often been a stimulus to technical progress in the past, but never has this influence been so overwhelming as today. This is because modern war is more thoroughly science-based than any other human occupation, and modern military men are fully science-conscious.

In a purely economic sense both public expenditure and research might be channelled into other uses, but the workings of our political institutions seem to make this exceedingly hard. Thus Rosa Luxemburg's view that capitalism can only thrive by war has a very timely ring in our ears.

There are still other elements in the postwar situation which are new. The big corporations generally have spread their activities to several lines each. Impediments against the flow of funds between industries would therefore play no role today. This again favors investment. Other developments are the shortening of the construction period, and the expansion of consumers credit; the first especially is bound to have had some effect on both trend and cycle.

From this excursion into the recent past let us return to history. My data are from Kuznets, and although much more are now available, they remain the basis for my contention that the growth rate of private wealth had declined for a long time before it stagnated in the 1930s. My confidence is based on the data of GNP: its rate of growth declined, and since savings as a proportion of GNP did not increase, the slowing down of wealth accumulation is only too plausible.

The decline, according to Goldsmith, mainly though not entirely reflects the slowing down of population growth. [5] This sounds very natural, but in default of a secret planner, who brings this correspondence about? Presumably it is thought that families with fewer children spend less; I think it very likely that they spend everything on better education, etc., for the fewer children. And it seems to me more natural that investment should continue until labor shortages appear and should then perhaps turn to replacement of older equipment to save labor, etc. But even if the decline in accumulation were due in part to the population trend and not to other causes, its consequences are no less problematic: is a smooth adjustment to such a decline in accumulation to be taken for granted?

In order to deal with such questions I needed an analysis of cost, price, distribution, and investment which showed the links between these elements in a new light.[6] The gist of my analysis is contained in Chapters V, IX, X, and XII. On the whole the theoretical basis on which I build is Kalecki's economic dynamics, which form a fairly complete system that is only somewhat open at the "long-term" end. [7]

My modifications in this system are as follows:

I regard profit as a differential rent accruing to the large agglomerations of risk capital. If we want to draw up a schedule in which firms are arranged in ascending order according to their cost, we must of course presuppose a certain capacity use for each of them: I select the "planned capacity utilization" which is what firms on the average of boom and slump would regard as desirable. Accordingly, the profit which will be shown as a differential rent on this schedule is not necessarily the actual one: it is the profit which would be realized at planned capacity. Let us call this *capacity profit*.

The schedule mentioned is clearly quite different from the profit function (equation (3) above), which relates actual profits to capacity utilization. (This difference corresponds to the difference between "realized" and "produced" surplus value in Karl Marx's terminology.) To the extent to which utilization changes, a greater or smaller proportion of capacity profit will be realized.

If the capacity profit retained in an industry, multiplied by a factor of indebtedness, exceeds investment in the industry as determined by the increase in effective demand, then a certain tension and competitive pressure is set up. This will lead to squeezing out of competitors on the margin of existence, until the desired utilization of capacity is restored and, as a necessary by-product, the capacity profit of the industry is reduced.

My theory embodies two crucial hypotheses:

(1) Firms wish to establish a planned degree of utilization over a number of years (boom and slump). They will push out competitors to obtain this result if the process is not too costly.

(2) If utilization is below the desired level, this acts as a deterrent to investment.

These assumptions are not present in Kalecki's system, in which utilization is a purely passive variable.

The differential rent or capacity profit schedule will be continuously subject to two opposite influences. Successful innovations will give some of the firms a differential advantage and increase the total capacity profit. On the other hand, diffusion of innovations will reduce the differential advantages again.

The competitive mechanism of reestablishment of a planned degree of capacity utilization will, for the economy as a whole, lead to an adjustment of long-term capacity profits to the level of investment (taking due account of retention of profits and the indebtedness ratio). This mechanism, however, operates more and more imperfectly as the power and influence of oligopoly increases, because cut-throat competition becomes too costly. A decline in investment will then lead to lower utilization, which will react on investment again.

Oligopolistic firms, in recent times, have had more and more recourse to other forms of competition: (1) Sales outlays: this method may at least enable them to increase their share in the market.[8] (2) Product innovation: really new products enable firms to transcend the given market and find the open field for expansion which they are seeking. (3) Direct investments abroad may again offer an escape from the narrow oligopolistic situation.

Sales outlays and product innovation relieve the tendency to underconsumption set up under oligopoly, but the third way makes it worse.

My theoretical analysis was to help in explaining, first, why the growth rate of private capital ever started to decline (primary fall); and, second, why the decline continued. Since, in fact, there are strong reasons for a "cumulative process" of declining growth, this second question should perhaps be: why did not the downward process proceed more quickly? (Because of the development of capital markets which counteracted the consequences of the decline in the profit rate as long as they expanded. But when a saturation of this process was reached, there remained the permanent weight of high "rentier saving.")

I explained both the primary and the secondary decline as a consequence of the growth of oligopoly and its tendency to raise capacity profits or to keep them rigid. The secondary fall has other reasons also—the rigidity of rentier saving. In this context I used two arguments which need sorting out:

(1) Oligopoly brings about a maldistribution of funds by shifting profits to those industries which are reluctant to use them. This argument presupposes impediments to the flow of funds between industries which today can hardly exist with the multibranch activities of large firms, but which for all that might have been present in the nineteenth century.

(2) Oligopoly leads to a decline in the degree of utilization, either by a tendency to increase markups or by a rigidity of the markup in face of a decline in investment. This second argument only requires the hypothesis that with one and the same profit rate, a lower degree of utilization will induce less investment than a higher degree of utilization.

It should be stressed that the second argument in no way depends on maldistribution or immobility of funds. It is not a question of reduced effectiveness of funds in producing investment which might be remedied by a freer flow of funds, but rather of the investment opportunities offered by a particular industry, which will be inadequately exploited if utilization is low. I may add that the second argument is the important one. I was perhaps only creating difficulties for myself by bringing in the first argument at all.

A third line of argument, not contained in this book, does not depend on oligopoly, but on the growth of big business generally. It says that the preference for safety increases with size, and that profit is bartered for safety, with a resulting reluctance to go into debt and a consequent weakening of the incentive to invest.

To explain the primary decline, however, I am ready today to admit a possibility which I denied in my book: that it might be the result of exhaustion of a long technological wave begun with the Industrial Revolution and reaching its eclipse with the maturity of the railway age. A technological wave is a diffusion process of a higher order, in which an idea or principle (e.g., the steam engine) spreads to various applications, and in which economic consequences such as migration, urbanization, etc., ensue.[9]

It is obvious, however, that the whole course in time of this process would depend on familiar economic factors. Not only is the diffusion of consumer durables, like motor cars, dependent on the level of income and its advance, but equally the diffusion of new equipment and production methods depends on effective demand. In other words, the all-important timing and speed of the process depends on ordinary economic variables like income, demand, utilization, profits retained, interest rates, finance, markets, etc.

This kind of technological development would preferably be integrated into our economic concepts. But economists have no concepts and no measurements for technological development. We are helpless before it. It was thus a kind of instinctive movement with which I swept the whole thing under the carpet. Today I can only say that although innovations do generate a trend (Kalecki), mere reference to the technological development in itself does not yield a very satisfactory explanation of the secular decline of accumulation. What I tried to do is to look into all the other factors first.

The attempt at mathematical formulation (Chapter XIII) leaves me deeply dissatisfied, because it does not reproduce my theory adequately. Most readers will prefer to skip it. Some may, however, be interested in my aim of integrating trend and cycle theory, a task which few—apart from Kalecki—have wanted to face. Unfortunately I failed in this because I disregarded Kalecki's warning that a self-continuing stable trend would come about only through innovations or other exogenous factors.

Postscript

Since I wrote the above pages three years ago the scene has changed once again, and I should perhaps write another introduction to explain why the cheerful extroverted era of growth has apparently come to an end. The reasons are (1) the reduction of tension between the superpowers; (2) the increase in tension within the capitalist countries, largely as a consequence of full employment and growth; and (3) the emergence of environment, raw material, and energy problems, again stemming from rapid growth.

For some time the political and psychological basis of the postwar boom has been sapped by such developments as these: public spending in the United States as a ratio of GNP decreased under Nixon (when for demographic reasons it ought to have increased!); the competition in technology, Research and Development, and education unleashed by Sputnik has flagged; the development in these fields has been dominated instead by the internal reaction against intellectuals and youth after the student unrest of 1968; the cooperation between the capitalist powers has broken down—witness their political incapacity to resolve the endemic international currency problem; the internal stresses of groups contending for shares in the national income have shown themselves as inflationary; instead of placating the masses by a steady increase in living standards, the aim has become to dampen their spirits by unemployment, which hits hardest at those who are considered to be the most unruly elements. The arguments against full employment have got the upper hand in the councils of the powers, and thus we witness stagnation not as an incomprehensible fate, as in the 1930s, but stagnation as a policy.

—Josef Steindl
Vienna, June 1976

1. Michal Kalecki, "The Economic Situation in the United States as Compared with the Pre-War Period," in *The Last Phase in the Transformation of Capitalism* (New York: Monthly Review Press, 1972).
2. For the functioning of this mechanism see M. Kalecki, "A Theory of Commodity, Income, and Capital Taxation," in *Selected Essays on the Dynamics of the Capitalist Economy* (Cambridge, 1971).
3. Private Gross National Product is GNP minus the government civil and military wage bill.
4. Figures for 1929-38 are based on Frane and Klein, *Review of Economics and Statistics* (1953), p. 335. For 1951-71, personal taxes not withheld (*Statistical Abstract of the United States*). This item is, of course, not an exact measure of noncorporate profit taxes, but it may be taken as an approximation.
5. Raymond Goldsmith, *A Study of Saving in the United States*, Vol. 1, p. 87.
6. My efforts at integration in this respect have been noted by G. Becattini in his introduction to *Maturità e ristagno nel capitalismo americano* (Torino: Paolo Boringhieri, 1960).
7. In his last major work (*Economic Journal*, 1968) Kalecki laid great stress on his view that the theory of investment, especially in its application to the long run, was the most difficult problem of economic theory, and a satisfactory answer to it was still lacking.
8. See Paul A. Baran and Paul M. Sweezy, *Monopoly Capital* (New York: Monthly Review Press, 1966), Chapter 5.
9. Baran and Sweezy, *Monopoly Capital*, Chapter 8.

MATURITY AND STAGNATION IN AMERICAN CAPITALISM

Part I

PRICES, COSTS AND PROFIT MARGINS

I. The Theory of Imperfect Competition

1. *Some Critical Observations*

To the detached observer the theory of imperfect competition in its present state appears somewhat of a paradox. Its basic concept has, with good reason, been condemned as unrealistic.[1] Indeed, it hardly needed an extensive enquiry to establish that business men are not acquainted with the concept of marginal revenue. The position is much worse, in so far as we know that they *could* hardly ever form a reasonable estimate of it, even if they wanted. This view is shared by some who have made an outstanding contribution to the theory: Mrs. Robinson thinks that for the explanation of the profit margin we must probably have recourse to historical accident or ' conventional views among business men as to what is reasonable '.[2] Indeed ' it seems that economic science has not yet solved its first problem—what determines the price of a commodity ? '[3]

And yet the chief lessons which ' imperfect competition ' is intended to drive home are undoubtedly correct. In fact, it was conceived with the intention of taking account of realities neglected by earlier economists, and in this sense it has been successful. But when one tries to demonstrate it to a new student one is struck with the difficulty of explaining something true, important, and relatively simple, in a way which seems abstruse and complicated.

The didactic difficulty suggests that our analytical apparatus may not be the best conceivable one for the purposes in hand. This feeling of dissatisfaction is given more concrete shape in the following points which are very general and briefly put, because their aim is not criticism as such, but rather the search for an alternative approach.

(*a*) In contrast to the old doctrine of perfect competition, modern price theory is full of indeterminacy. The most elementary problems—the consequences of an increase in demand, of the appearance of new sources of supply, or new products—do not admit of an unambiguous answer, unless very specific assumptions are introduced. In itself this would be no cause for blame; the facts just happen to be complicated. But the analytical apparatus in hand is not such as to stimulate empirical research which would lead to an elimination of this indeterminacy; its concepts are singularly unfruitful, because they are not designed to stimulate empirical investigation,

[1] R. L. Hall and C. J. Hitch, Price Theory and Business Behaviour, *Oxford Economic Papers*, No. 2.

[2] J. Robinson, *An Essay on Marxian Economics*, p. 94.

[3] *Op. cit.*, p. 95.

but rather casuistic speculation. An outstanding example of this is the theory of oligopoly.

(*b*) The concept of uncertainty plays hardly any essential role in the existing theory. This is surprising since we should expect the entrepreneurs, if they make estimates of elasticities at all, to be very uncertain about them. Moreover, the relevant market conditions (demand curves) must in many cases relate to the future and thus constitute uncertain estimates made by the entrepreneur. Attempts have certainly been made to take these factors into account, but they have not led to any fundamentally new approach. In other fields of economic theory, however, the concept of uncertainty has come to play a much more fundamental role. In the theory of money, the concept of uncertainty is the very basis for the explanation of cash holdings and liquidity preferences. Nobody seems to have thought of applying similar ideas to the holding of excess capacity.

In general, one may feel also that the whole theory of prices and imperfect competition is not linked up sufficiently closely with certain other parts of economic theory, in particular the theory of investment.

(*c*) The most familiar characteristic of certain monopolistic practices (cartels, price leadership) is price rigidity. It is surprising that the theory lends itself so badly to its explanation. An explanation is offered, but only by departing from the principle of maximisation of profits: price rigidity, so runs the current explanation, is due to the *disutility* involved for the entrepreneur in the task of price adjustment.[1] A supplementary principle has thus to be introduced in order to explain one of the most striking features of monopoly. But one would have liked the explanation of it to flow as naturally and easily from the theory as does the 'point of Cournot' (the output which maximises profits).

(*d*) The great virtue of the imperfect competition theory is that it explains the existence of excess capacity in a state of equilibrium. For this it relies on the assumption of an excess of price above marginal cost, which in the range of approximately full capacity use and beyond (where marginal cost is equal to, or higher than, average cost) must mean 'abnormal' profits; then on the further assumption that free entry *tends* to eliminate abnormal profits, it follows logically that imperfect competition must create excess capacity.

The problem does not end there, because we have still to explain how the entrepreneur chooses plant of a particular capacity. This question is treated by means of the concept of long run cost curves.[2] These are derived from the short run cost curves for various types of plant of different capacity on the following principle. The long run cost curve is the locus of *equilibrium points* on the short run cost curves of the various types of plant of different capacity. The equilibrium points are determined by the condition that short run and long run variations (*i.e.* a change in capacity use and a change in size of plant)

[1] J. R. Hicks, *Econometrica*, 1935. T. de Scitovszky, *Journal of Political Economy*, 1941.

[2] See R. F. Harrod, Doctrines of imperfect competition, *Quarterly Journal of Economics*, 1934.

at these points must involve the same change in cost, *i.e.* short run and long run marginal cost must be equal; for, if short run marginal cost, for example, were higher than long run marginal cost, it would be profitable to reduce the degree of capacity use and simultaneously increase the capacity of the plant. The long run average cost curve will be tangential to the short run average cost curves to satisfy the above conditions. The long run cost curve having been thus determined, we can find the size of plant chosen by the entrepreneur, if we know the individual demand curve. By dint of reasoning analogous to that used earlier on, it can be shown that free entry will again tend to reduce profits and that the plant chosen will therefore be smaller than the optimum sized plant, and that, in addition, its capacity will not be fully used.

None of the above arguments, however, can help us to explain excess capacity in those industries where free entry cannot be assumed with any degree of realism. This applies to all those industries in which a very great part of the output is produced by one or a few firms and in which entry of new competitors is difficult owing to heavy capital requirements and large scale of operations—in a word, typical oligopolistic industries. It may be noted that the threat of *potential* new entrants, which in all these cases may still be present, cannot have the same consequences as the actual entry of new competitors. Whereas the latter creates excess capacity, higher costs, and perhaps higher prices, the mere threat of potential competition in an oligopolistic situation should have no such result; it should rather tend to keep prices lower than they would be without this threat. Thus, in all these numerous cases of oligopolistic industries the above explanation of excess capacity does not apply. Excess capacity would appear, in these cases, only if the demand curve by chance happened to be in a position where maximisation of profit involves excess capacity.[1] In an expanding market, however, the demand curve would shift to the right, and excess capacity would tend to disappear.

There might still be a possible method of explaining excess capacity even in these cases. It might simply be said that the average cost of producing with a larger equipment and a certain amount of excess capacity is lower than with a smaller equipment at full capacity, in other words, the *long* run cost curve is declining. If, however, the demand curve shifts sufficiently to the right (owing to an expanding market) then the optimum size of equipment should be reached. In some of the expanding industries of oligopolistic character (steel, cement in U.S.), the big firms hold many plants, so that they could choose optimum size for a new plant without creating over-capacity. They might have difficulty in just achieving optimum capacity, no more and no less, but we are then left wondering why there is, in fact, always a bias towards excess capacity rather than the opposite.

We conclude that in expanding industries where free entry is considerably restricted, the existence and prevalence of excess capacity is not easy to

[1] Harrod, *loc. cit.*

explain with the help of the usual analysis of imperfect competition, unless this excess capacity is always regarded as arising entirely through disequilibrium.

2. *Statistics of Excess Capacity*

Yet what evidence there is suggests a general prevalence of excess capacity even in the boom, and not excluding expanding oligopolistic industries.

An investigation of excess capacity in U.S.A. manufacturing and other industries in 1925–29 has been made by the Brookings Institution.[1] 'Capacity' of an industry is there defined as the output which it could turn out with the length of the working day and number of shifts ordinarily in use in the industry, and with a proper standard of plant maintenance (*i.e.* taking account of necessary shut-downs for repairs, etc.). Seasonal variations are taken account of in the calculation of this '*practically attainable capacity*'. Plants which are shut down have been excluded, so that they do not count as excess capacity. The capacity so defined[2] is thus lower than the 'rated capacity' usually given by trade statistics and based on technical estimates. The Brookings Institution found that on the average in 29 branches of manufacturing, the degree of capacity utilisation was 80 per cent in 1925–29, and 83 per cent in 1929.[3] I quote figures for the degree of utilisation in 1929 in *expanding* industries: automobiles 85 per cent; automobile tyres 76 per cent; rolled steel products 81 per cent; tin plate 74 per cent; wire 74 per cent; chlorine and allied products 90 per cent; newsprint (U.S. and Canada taken together) 84 per cent. The industries quoted are all of the oligopolistic type with considerable restriction on free entry.

It is of interest to follow up the change in degree of utilisation in the years before 1929. We find that there were a number of industries in which expansion was going on at that time, and in which the degree of capacity use was *decreasing* during this expansion up to 1929: the capacity was increased ahead of demand. This applies to the following industries (which, again, are 'oligopolistic'): automobiles, automobile tyres, Portland cement, newsprint (United States and Canada combined), wire (see Table 1). In some of them—newsprint, cement—the capacity still increased in 1930, after the boom had broken, and in steel the expansion of capacity continued up to 1932 (see Table 2). Apparently, the expansion of capacity was not brought about by the entry of new competitors, but rather by the existing firms.

These facts are valuable for our argument, because, in contrast to the uncertainty of capacity estimates for a given year, the *changes* in the degree of utilisation referred to are quite incontestable facts. It is possible to give special reasons in all cases for this development: In the automobile industry, the shutting down of Ford in 1927, which gave his competitors an opportunity to expand. In Portland Cement, technical improvements (more

[1] *America's Capacity to Produce*, Washington, 1934.
[2] *ibid*, p. 23 seq.
[3] p. 307.

efficient large scale equipment was built in the 20's). In newsprint, the capacity increase occurred in Canada (in U.S. production was actually decreasing), so that there was partly a *shift* in production. But we must consider Canadian and U.S. newsprint industry economically as one whole.

The data show that a fair amount of excess capacity is not unusual in oligopolistic industries, in which the mechanism of free entry cannot be supposed to work. It is, of course, not legitimate to assume that the excess capacity existing in these industries in 1929 is necessarily *equilibrium* excess

TABLE 1

DEGREE OF UTILISATION OF CAPACITY

	Automobiles			*Automobile tyres*	
	Production in thousands	% of theoretical capacity	% of practical capacity	Production number in millions	% of practical capacity
1919	1934	88	—	32.8	—
1920	2227	86	—	32.4	—
1921	1682	63	—	27.3	60
1922	2646	84	—	40.8	88
1923	4180	94	108	45.4	74
1924	3738	74	85	50.8	82
1925	4428	82	101	58.7	91
1926	4506	68	81	60.0	88
1927	3580	46	68	63.7	85
1928	4601	55	80	75.4	87
1929	5622	66	85	69.8	76

Wire

	Wire-drawing departments of rolling mills			*Wire Industry outside rolling mills*			*Total Wire Industry*
	Theoretical capacity	Production	% utilised	Theoretical capacity	Production	% utilised	% of theoretical capacity
	(Millions of tons)			(Millions of tons)			
1923	3.5	2.4	69	1.5	1.1	72	70
1925	3.7	2.4	65	1.4	0.9	63	64
1927	3.7	2.3	62	1.5	1.0	68	64
1929	4.1	2.7	65	1.8	1.0	57	63

	Newsprint (U.S. and Canada combined)			*Portland Cement*		
	Practical capacity	Production	% utilised	Practically obtainable capacity	Production	% utilised
	(Thousands of tons)			(Million barrels)		
1919	2178	2178	100	120.8	80.8	67
1920	2412	2388	99	124.4	100.0	80
1921	2675	2033	76	122.7	98.8	81
1922	2780	2530	91	124.3	114.8	92
1923	2836	2751	97	137.6	137.5	100
1924	3161	2845	90	148.8	149.4	100
1925	3317	3052	92	164.5	161.7	98
1926	3756	3568	95	183.0	164.5	90
1927	4252	3572	84	193.0	173.2	90
1928	4633	3799	82	207.1	176.3	85
1929	4906	4121	84	220.1	170.6	78
1930	5251	3781	72	229.5	161.2	70

Source:
Cement: Monthly Labor Review, Oct. 1941.
All other: *America's capacity to produce.*

TABLE 2

UTILISATION OF CAPACITY IN THE STEEL INDUSTRY (STEEL INGOTS)

	Rated capacity [1]	Production	% utilised
	(Millions of gross tons)		
1920	55.6	42.1	76
1921	57.4	19.8	35
1922	58.4	35.6	61
1923	58.6	44.9	77
1924	59.4	37.9	64
1925	61.1	45.4	74
1926	57.8	48.3	84
1927	60.0	44.9	75
1928	61.5	51.5	84
1929	63.8	56.4	89
1930	65.2	40.7	62
1931	69.0	25.9	38
1932	70.3	13.7	20
1933	70.2	23.2	33

Source :
Steel Ingots : U.S. Steel Corporation, T.N.E.C. Papers Vol. 3.

capacity. It may well have been due to disequilibrium, and also the rise in excess capacity observed in years of expanding markets might have been due to disequilibrium. It might have been an *unintended* increase in excess capacity. There is even much to say in favour of the idea that the increase in excess capacity in the years before 1929 was unintended and ' unplanned '. But on a reasonable judgment we should say that not *all* of the excess capacity observed in these industries in 1929 was due to disequilibrium and a certain part of it was probably accepted as normal by the manufacturers in those industries. Equilibrium excess capacity, we should say, is just as ordinary in oligopolistic industries as in others. We cannot expect, however, that the relative degree of this excess capacity is as great as under ' pure imperfect competition '. The entrepreneurs in oligopolistic industries have probably a much greater fear of excess capacity and are inclined to aim at a higher degree of utilisation than entrepreneurs in other industries.

We have still to discuss the question how far the concept of '*practical capacity*' as used in the investigation of the Brookings Institution, corresponds to the *optimum capacity*, which is the output at which average costs are a minimum for the given plant or firm. It is this optimum capacity which is relevant in a theoretical sense. Unfortunately it is not possible to give a simple and direct answer to this question. A number of cost investigations have been made on the basis of cost data of individual enterprises over a series of years, showing the relation of cost to output. The result of these investigations is, broadly speaking, that over the range of output levels which have occurred in the firms studied, total cost is a linear function of output, and marginal cost is therefore constant.[2] The cost studies relate to steel and

[1] Capacity of January 1 each year. The decrease in 1926 is due to readjustment of data; the figures before and after 1926 are therefore not comparable.

[2] These studies thus confirm the assumption made by M. Kalecki *Essays in the Theory of Economic Fluctuations*.

steel products (the United States Steel Corporation), cement, hosiery and a leather belt shop.[1] The range of output levels covered does not, however, reach up to rated capacity, and thus the studies fail to show at which point the 'optimum capacity' is situated. In most cases it is not indicated what degrees of utilisation the output levels represent. In the steel study we are told that the output levels covered by the (annual) data range between 18 per cent and 90 per cent of (rated) ingot capacity;[2] for the steel finishing section, the upper limit of utilisation reached must have been lower, because finishing capacity is always higher than steel ingot capacity.

There is one study for the cement industry which gives at least a partial indication of the development of cost up to 'practically obtainable capacity'. This study is based on the comparison of a number of plants and shows the labour cost in man-hours for different levels of utilisation of capacity. The figures reproduced below (Table 3) show that cost in man-hours per unit decreases up to the level of 'practically obtainable capacity'.[3]

TABLE 3

LABOUR COST OF PORTLAND CEMENT

Practically obtainable capacity utilised.	Labour Cost in man-hours per Unit of Output (Index)
100%	100.0
80%	108.6
60%	120.8
40%	140.4
20%	181.4

The evidence is again not completely conclusive, because cost other than labour cost might begin to rise earlier although this is far from plausible.

We may hazard, however, an answer to our question on the basis of some general considerations. In the few cost investigations made there is, up to the levels of utilisation reached in a boom, no sign of 'decreasing returns'. It seems that, in order to provide a reason why marginal cost should rise, exceptional circumstances must be adduced, e.g. prolongation of the working time for the employed labour force beyond the customary hours, so as to necessitate overtime payment; reduction in the length of useful life of equipment due to omission of repairs and maintenance, as a consequence of continuous operations without temporary shut-downs; waste of raw material, faulty work, and damage to machines arising from a speed up of operations beyond the limit which ensures a smooth co-ordination of the process of production.

It would appear that these factors begin to operate only at the level of *practical capacity*, which is defined as the output achieved with normal length of working time, with sufficient shut-downs to allow for repairs and mainten-

[1] U.S. Steel Corporation, *TNEC Papers*, Vol. 1; K. Ehrke, *Die Übererzeugung in der Zementindustrie*, Jena 1933; Joel Dean, *Relation of Cost to Output of a leather belt shop*, National Bureau of Economic Research 1941; *Statistical Cost functions of a hosiery mill*, University of Chicago Press 1941. See also *Cost Behaviour and Price Policy*, National Bureau of Economic Research 1943.

[2] U.S. Steel Corporation TNEC Papers Vol I, p. 309.

[3] Works Progress Administration *National Research Project Report* M. 3; *Monthly Labor Review*, October, 1941.

ance, and without disturbance of the smooth running of the production process. We should thus expect that marginal cost will probably not rise until practical capacity has been reached but that it will then rise sharply. The point of minimum average cost, or optimum capacity is therefore probably near the practical capacity. That means that the figures of excess capacity as given by the Brookings Institution (provided that they have succeeded in estimating practical capacity correctly on their own definition) are relevant indications of excess capacity for our purposes.

In concluding this paragraph we might ask what entrepreneurs' own opinions about excess capacity are. They tend to deny its existence or to make light of it, because they feel themselves attacked on account of the waste involved in excess capacity (although their answer might, much more reasonably, be that if there is unemployment of labour anyway this waste has its compensations). According to a study submitted by the U.S. Steel Corporation[1] in 1939, 'capacity in the steel industry is not excessive'. The study explains the existing unused finished steel capacity by two factors: (1) demand is fluctuating and the industry must have sufficient capacity to take care of a boom; (2) demand is distributed between diverse types and qualities of output which require separate facilities, and this distribution of demand between types cannot be correctly foreseen. Therefore, a reserve capacity is necessary to take care of possible shifts in the pattern of demand.[2]

Although these points in themselves could hardly explain, for example, the expansion of steel capacity from 1929 to 1932, they are worth keeping in mind.

3. *A Reconsideration of Older Price Theories*

Alfred Marshall's theory of competitive prices follows the pattern of the Ricardian theory of differential rent. The price is equal to the cost of the marginal producer who appears in the guise of the 'representative firm'. Ricardo's idea was simple and useful. In its Marshallian application to industry it has degenerated into a short run theory, and thereafter it has disappeared in the whirlpool of highly sophisticated modern analysis.[3] Would it not be possible, dialectically speaking, to re-establish it on a higher plane?

Once the assumption of perfect competition has been dropped, there arise three main difficulties, which make the explanation of price by the cost of a marginal producer impossible.

(*a*) The net profit margin of the marginal producer is not known. With Marshall it is determined by 'normal profits'. But in industries where entry is difficult owing to big capital requirements, little substance can be given to the concept of normal profits.

[1] *T.N.E.C. Papers*, Vol. I. Some Factors in the Pricing of Steel, p. 404.

[2] It is partly due to this fact that the rolling mill capacity has been about 14 per cent greater than the steel capacity. (*America's Capacity to Produce*, p. 264).

[3] It is significant that Chamberlin eliminated cost differences by his 'heroic assumptions' (which imply that no cost differentials exist), and Mrs. Robinson by capitalising the differential rents.

(*b*) The degree of utilisation of capacity of the marginal producer is not known. Thus his costs per unit are not determined, and his gross profit margin could not be calculated even if the net profit were given.

A similar difficulty is that of the selling costs (*e.g.* advertising expenditure) which a marginal producer might incur. They, too, are not determined by technical data, and destroy, therefore, the simplicity of the original concept of the marginal producer's cost.

(*c*) The products in an industry are heterogeneous, and prices and costs are therefore not comparable. But even if these products happen to be technically and physically homogeneous, the prices charged by the various firms need not be the same, as their products, though physically the same, are from the consumer's point of view different, owing to the attachment of customers to certain firms. Thus, there is no uniform price in the industry which can be explained by the condition of the marginal producer alone. The price structure is rather more complicated, and we have to explain the relation of prices charged by various firms to the price of the marginal producer.

Similarly, selling cost and degree of capacity utilisation may vary within the industry, so that the net profit margins of the intra-marginal producer will be determined not by technical cost advantages alone, but also by the factors mentioned.

We propose to deal with these points in the following chapters, turning first to the question of excess capacity.

II. The Concept of Excess Capacity

1. In speaking of the degree of utilisation of capacity or the degree of excess capacity in what follows, we do not mean the excess capacity which establishes itself currently according to the varying state of demand; rather we mean the excess capacity which is involved in a long run equilibrium of the sort described earlier on.

It is surprising that this equilibrium excess capacity should never have been dealt with in the same way as other forms of idle reserves, for example, stocks of commodities, or balances of money. It would then have to be explained as a reserve held in anticipation of future events, or in view of some existing uncertainty. If we can find plausible reasons to assume that producers, including the marginal producer, deliberately hold excess capacity, then we can easily show that costs and prices will be driven above the competitive level, and the usual picture of an industry under imperfect competition will be realised.

But for what reasons should producers deliberately hold excess capacity? The first reason suggests itself very easily by the existence of fluctuations in demand. The producer wants to be in on a boom first, and not to leave the sales to new competitors who will press on his market when the good time is over.

But there is a deeper and more general reason. Any producer who sets up a new plant knows that for a certain initial period (which we must not imagine too short) he will be able to get only a restricted market, because of the attachment of customers and all the other well-known factors. He will nevertheless choose his capacity so as to leave comfortable room for a greater output, because he hopes to be able to expand his sales later. This hope is founded on the well-established experience that the *growth of the market* (or of his ' goodwill ') *is a function of time*. Whatever he might do within a restricted period in the way of advertisement, price cuts, or by whatever method, he will not be able to increase his sales above a certain level; whereas with the lapse of time the mere existence of the firm will bring a gradual extension of goodwill; and advertisement and other methods of stimulating sales will only gradually bring results as time goes by. This ' law of accumulation of goodwill ' is essential for our explanation. That it is plausible will hardly be contested. It is striking that Marshall who devoted so much attention to the time factor in the case of supply somehow failed to notice its full implications on the side of demand.

But, it will be asked, why is it not possible for the producer to expand his capacity step by step as his market grows ? The reasons for this are obviously the indivisibility and durability of plant and equipment. Only if plants were more easily divisible and the economies of large scale did not exist, or, alternatively, if plants were scrapped and rebuilt at shorter intervals, could adjustment of capacity proceed evenly. This possibility exists, to some extent, for the community as a whole, where an expansion of output can be made possible by a gradual extension of capital equipment. But the individualism of a competitive system does not permit this solution. Each of the competing producers wants to take part in an eventual expansion of sales, and not to have it snatched away by new competitors. If no general expansion of sales is to be expected, the individual producer who enters the industry nevertheless hopes to gain business in the course of time at the expense of others who will be leaving the industry. If an industry is shrinking, the logical solution from the point of view of the community would be to shut or eliminate some plants and concentrate output in the remaining ones. The competitive system is reluctant to adopt this solution; each producer clings to a share in the output so as not to lose his ' goodwill '. Thus, a *planned* and deliberate reserve of excess capacity is at all times held by most producers, with good reason from their point of view, even though a part of it, at least, is waste from the point of view of the community.

The deliberate holding of excess capacity cannot, however, be regarded entirely as a competitive waste. Like other types of reserves (for example, inventories) it accounts for the elasticity which the system shows, in ordinary times, in face of rapid changes of effective demand. This elasticity, due to the existence of an ample margin of reserves in labour, material, equipment and inventories, is one of the most striking characteristics of capitalism (at least in modern times) except in war and post-war conditions. It is this elasticity which makes it possible for the trade cycle to operate as it does, *i.e.*

as large fluctuations in the volume of real income. On the whole, it seems that the system is always very much on the safe side with regard to its available reserves, and the hypothesis of deliberate holding of capacity reserves would explain that.

The deliberate holding of a certain amount of excess capacity as a consequence of the policy of 'building ahead of demand' is clearly shown for example in electricity generation. As the Brookings study explains 'the large machines represent capacity equal to one, two or three years' growth of the system load. Thus, while the load grows gradually, the capacity grows by sudden steps and for many months after each new installation the utility has an increased margin of unused capacity ...'[1] In this example, the concept of a deliberate reserve appears very realistic, because we can see how it is quantitatively determined, we might almost say calculated, on the basis of certain data. Certainly, when we generalise this type of explanation, the concept of planned excess capacity becomes much more vague: how much excess capacity an entrepreneur holds with the hope of increasing his market in some way or other (either on account of growing demand or at the cost of competitors) will be a matter of his own subjective judgment and mood. But it would seem that the explanation can be generalised so as to apply to the less obvious cases too.

2. The approach outlined above puts the reasoning of the imperfect competition theory, as it were, upside down. Instead of explaining the existence of excess capacity in a state of equilibrium by excessive profit margins, it explains these excessive profit margins by the deliberate holding of excess capacity.

The present approach, however, shares with the alternative one the interest in the problem of utilisation, and it goes perhaps farther in this direction. It resolutely puts the concept of excess capacity and degree of utilisation in the centre of the analysis. Once this concept comes into the limelight, there appear several problems which are, however, not entirely of our own making.

We have talked about 'planned' excess capacity, and the qualification implies that there is also a different excess capacity—*undesired excess capacity* as we may call it. The necessity for such a distinction does not arise from our peculiar approach, but exists in any case. What corresponds to it in the traditional analysis is the distinction between excess capacity *in equilibrium*, and excess capacity arising merely through the absence of equilibrium. The first type can exist and continue with given demand conditions, and full adjustment to these conditions; the second type can only arise from unanticipated shifts in the demand curve for the industry as a whole. The second type of excess capacity is of course possible also under perfect competition.

The question arises: how do we distinguish in practice between the two types of excess capacity? By what criterion can we tell one from the other?

Economic intuition tells us, in the first place, that the 'undesired'

[1] *America's capacity to produce*, p. 331–2.

excess capacity is temporary. It arises through unanticipated changes in demand, and it should disappear as soon as we can assume an adjustment to have taken place. Over a longer period, including a full trade cycle, some of the unforeseen changes in one and the other direction will cancel out; and the remaining secular development, we might perhaps assume, will be anticipated. It would follow then that over the average of a trade cycle the planned degree of utilisation will be approximately the actually observed degree of utilisation. Our first line of intuition leads us to identify planned or equilibrium excess capacity with actual long-run excess capacity.

On closer examination this idea proves wrong. There is no good reason why a state of disequilibrium, with undesired excess capacity, should not persist. For practical purposes, disequilibrium may be permanent.

We have to ask: in what way, by what mechanism, is the adjustment of the supply side to shifts in demand conditions brought about? In the traditional analysis this happens by entry and exit of competitors. This mechanism may be effective under certain conditions. In those conditions we should then conclude that if there is no net entry or exit into the industry the actual long-run excess capacity probably corresponds more or less to the desired excess capacity. If there is a net entry or exist we might conclude that excess capacity is above or below the desired level. On this argument it is quite possible that undesired excess capacity may exist for a longer time, together with a continuous stream of 'exits'; but by and large we might consider that we have defined at least a range of the desired excess capacity by pointing to the actual excess capacity realised over a long period in these conditions. It may be noted that the planned excess capacity, in terms of this mechanism, will be approximately realised only for an industry as a whole, not necessarily for individual firms.

Under different conditions, however, which will in reality often obtain, the mechanism of entry and exit cannot be supposed to work. An adjustment of supply conditions to shifts in demand can only be obtained then by quickening or slowing the pace of investment by existing firms in the industry, if necessary by *dis*investment. This type of adjustment need not be successful in establishing an 'equilibrium' or planned excess capacity. For one thing, whenever actual *reduction* of equipment is needed to restore an equilibrium capacity, it will take a long time because it has to wait for equipment to wear out. What is much more important, however, is this: supposing an equilibrium could in this way be obtained for a single industry, it does not follow that it can be obtained for the economy as a whole. The type of adjustment assumed, if it is performed by many industries, will react on the demand side, and this may render it impossible for an equilibrium to be obtained. The degree of utilisation actually obtaining in the long run, we must conclude, is no safe indication of the *planned* level of utilisation.

We find, then, that we possess really no general criterion for distinguishing between planned and undesired excess capacity. Logically we can expect to find it only in the reactions of entrepreneurs to the degree of utilisation.

The preceding discussion has already implicitly suggested the idea that undesired excess capacity, or in general any deviation from the level of planned utilisation, will affect the rate of investment in the industry in question.

That, in itself, does not mark out any particular level of utilisation as the desired one. But this question is less important than the general idea to which this discussion has led : namely that investment activity will be a function of the degree of utilisation.

3. In addition to the theoretical questions just mentioned, there arise various conceptual problems with regard to utilisation and excess capacity. Utilisation is defined as production (which we regard, for simplicity's sake, as equal to sales) divided by capacity :

$$u = \frac{S}{H}$$

and excess capacity (whether planned or undesired) is then simply $1 - u$.

How do we measure capacity ? Ultimately this is a matter of convention. The type of question to be answered is : how much more *can* this factory produce than that one, or how much more *can* the industry produce in this year as compared with an earlier year ? If we have any convention for measuring capacity which can be applied consistently so as to make possible (*a*) comparison over time and (*b*) comparison between firms and perhaps, assuming certain price relations, also between industries, then we should be on firm ground. Unfortunately the statistics in this field are lacking precisely in such conventions, and in clear concepts which are consistently applied. In principle there is no reason why they should not be worked out, just as they have been in other fields such as national income statistics.

Traditional economic analysis would lead us to think that capacity is more than an arbitrary convention. There is one particular basis for measuring it, namely the point of minimum average cost, which indicates the 'optimum' use of capacity (which would be realised in the long run, under perfect competition). This point would seem, theoretically, the obvious basis for measuring capacity. This is quite true. But in practice the determination of this point is not unambiguous. The 'optimum' capacity is not constant for a given physical equipment, because it depends also on organisational factors. Among these are the length of the normal working week and the shift system in use, and the productivity of labour, in so far as it may vary without any change in equipment, but as a result solely of a change in intensity of work. What is to be regarded as capacity will be left to convention. Comparing two plants with different shift systems, shall we say the double shift plant has a greater capacity, or that it has a higher planned utilisation ? Similarly, if we make comparisons in time, a reduction in the normal working week may be regarded as a reduction in capacity, and a corresponding increase in capital intensity. Or else, if we regard capacity as constant for a given physical equipment, we may say that planned utilisation has decreased.

Again, the same doubt arises for variations in productivity with given physical equipment.

It is not always certain how existing statistics of capacity are to be interpreted in this respect. On the whole it is likely that capacity is regarded as constant with given physical equipment. Changes in the factors mentioned must show their effect then in the planned degree of utilisation. On the other hand there is no reason why we should not equally well regard the changes in the working week etc., as a corresponding change in capacity. The historical reduction in the working week would then appear as a tendency of capital intensification, which was counteracted, on the other side, by a tendency to reduced capital intensity as equipment became cheaper in relation to capacity, a tendency which seems to have played some role in recent decades.

The measurement of utilisation can be facilitated if we start, not from output capacity, but from *input capacity*. Taking the input of labour (we could equally well start with inputs of materials or energy), we can determine the input-capacity of a given equipment in the same way as we did for the output capacity, and by comparison with the actual input of labour we obtain the utilisation. Changes in productivity of labour would leave this measure unaffected. The input capacity can, moreover, be much more directly compared as between different industries. Input capacity as applied not to a given physical equipment, but to a given investment in terms of real value, corresponds to the concept of capital per man. In practice this method of measuring capacity and utilisation has been little used.

Of considerable importance in industrial practice is, however, the measurement of utilisation on the basis of machine hours. 'Capacity' is here measured in terms of the maximum possible number of hours for which the machine can be operated during the year. The number of actual machine hours, divided by the possible number of machine hours, gives the measure of utilisation. This definition avoids the complications arising from heterogeneity of production.

One difficulty is common to all methods of measuring utilisation. In order to establish the capacity of a plant we have in practice to confine our attention to one particular piece of equipment which forms a decisive bottleneck and as it were occupies a strategic position in the plant (ring spindle, loom, paper machine). In some industries it is rather difficult to find the particular type of equipment which occupies this strategic position in the plant. In those industries there are indeed great difficulties in applying any measure of utilisation. These difficulties, however, are probably not greater than those encountered in the application of almost any other economic concept.

III. Price Rigidity

Empirical studies of prices show that in 'price regulated' industries prices are characteristically rigid.[1] 'Price regulation' in the present sense

[1] *TNEC Monograph No. 21*: Monopoly and Competition in American Industry *Mon. No. 1*: Price Behaviour and Business Policy.

includes not only cartel agreements, but also price leadership. In fact, in practically all oligopolistic industries, where a few big firms exercise a dominating influence on the prices, price rigidity obtains.

The rigidity means that prices change less frequently and that the amplitude of price movements in the trade cycle is much smaller than in the 'non-price regulated' industries. In fact, rigid prices often show hardly any influence of the trade cycle. The reluctance of firms in those industries to cut prices even in a deep slump is notorious.

What is the explanation? One would expect that the *relative* increase of rigid prices as compared with unregulated prices in a slump would make the oligopolistic industries lose sales, owing to a shift in demand induced by the price differential. One would also expect that an estimate of the elasticity of demand, if at all, is more nearly possible in an oligopolistic industry, where the price leader has only to consider the demand curve for the industry as a whole.

The answer which the industrialists themselves almost invariably give to this question is very simple. They are convinced that the price elasticity of demand for their products is very small, and that any price cut would lead only to a relatively small increase in the quantity sold.

A particularly good example is steel. Steel producers hold that the demand for their product is largely determined by the state of trade. As the cost of steel is only a fraction of the ultimate cost of investment goods or consumers goods, into which it goes, the demand for these goods is hardly affected by any reductions in steel prices. Direct substitution of other raw materials plays only a limited role, so that demand is thought to be inelastic.[1]

The statistical evaluation of the elasticity of demand for steel has shown that the steel producers' view is correct.[2] According to this calculation, which was based on yearly data for 1919 to 1938, the elasticity of demand for steel was between 0.3 and 0.4. Even taking into account all the possible errors and weaknesses of any such calculation, it seems to have definitely established an elasticity of demand below one. In other words, any decrease in steel price would bring a reduction of the total value of sales. The marginal revenue is negative.

If such are the assumptions of the entrepreneurs, and if these assumptions, moreover, are quite correct, what becomes of the theory of monopoly? According to that we should have expected that the price leader in the steel industry would have *raised* the price long ago, to such an extent as to make the marginal revenue positive and equal to marginal cost. We can only conclude that steel producers, even in so far as they know *something* about the marginal revenue, do not care to act solely on this knowledge.

The case of steel is an extreme example, but the *a priori* considerations which lead us to expect a low elasticity of demand apply in a great number of

[1] *Monopoly and Competition* p. 124.

[2] U.S. Steel Corporation *TNEC Papers Vol I*: A statistical analysis of the demand for steel.

other industries. In any case, however, the entrepreneurs, wherever they have the opportunity to ' regulate ' prices, seem to assume that price elasticity of demand is low. ' The reduction of prices in an effort to increase volume often seems to them as, at best, an uncertain adventure at a time when undue hazards should be avoided.'[1] How are we to explain, then, that entrepreneurs in these ' price regulated ' industries do not actually increase prices ? The situation is aptly described by Messrs. Hall and Hitch in the picture of an imaginary *kinked demand curve*, which is inelastic for a price reduction and elastic for a price increase.[2]

A natural explanation suggests itself if we again introduce the time element. It can be argued that in the short run the demand for the products of an industry is very inelastic, because the possibilities of substitution for other products are very limited. The substitution of one consumer's good for another, for example, rayon for silk, or rayon staple for wool, is a process which takes considerable time. The consumers are attached to the product of a particular industry in a much greater degree than to that of a firm. A whole series of traditions and prejudices has to be changed until a considerable shift of demand can occur, and propaganda continuing over a long period will often be necessary. In the case of producers' goods a similar role will be played by technical traditions and inertia, and by quite objective technical difficulties, which make substitution again dependent on the lapse of time. The substitution may require changes in outlay and equipment which cannot be quickly effected and which must be decided on permanently. Just as in the case of the individual firm, the growth of the market of an industry is, therefore, dependent on time.

We conclude that in the short run the demand for the products of an industry is in most cases probably very inelastic, whereas in the long run this is less likely to be the case. This provides the explanation for the imaginary ' kink ' in the demand curve. Prices are determined with a view to long run demand conditions, and short run changes, which are not thought to be of a permanent character, do not induce any change in price. Price reductions in slumps do not stimulate demand, and price increases in face of a temporary boom may be disturbing for the long run development of demand. A 'rigid ' price policy is the natural consequence. Price rigidity in the short run does not preclude considerable long run changes, as is shown by the example of rayon, where there was a long run price decrease from 1927 on, accompanied by an expansion of the market.

The fact that in the long run the competition of other industries must be taken into account is, however, only one factor which prevents the price leader, cartel, or monopolist from fixing his prices at a higher level than he does at present. In the case of steel, even the long-run elasticity of demand is probably low, so that on considerations of elasticity alone we might well expect the industry to fix prices higher than they do. Another important

[1] *TNEC Monograph No 1*. Price Behaviour and Business Policy, p. 36.
[2] Cf. Price Theory and Business Behaviour. *Oxford Economic Papers, No 2.*

factor is the danger of new entry. The restriction of entry into an industry —apart from the case of legal restrictions such as patents—is a relative factor, depending largely on the rate of profit earned in the industry. If prices, and consequently profits, are sufficiently high, entry of new competitors into an industry becomes feasible even where capital requirements are great. The price in oligopolistic industries is therefore fixed on a level which just keeps potential competitors out; or, in other cases, it may be fixed at a level which is sufficient to squeeze out some existing competitors, whose markets the price leaders want to take.

Consideration of the danger of free entry again makes short-run price changes appear unprofitable. In a slump, the danger of new entrants coming in is very much reduced, and there is therefore no reason for price reduction except if existing firms are to be squeezed out. In a boom, on the other hand, the danger of new entry increases, and the price leaders will therefore tend to refrain from exploiting the favourable market situation. The policy of short-run price stability commends itself therefore, also on these grounds.

To sum up : Price rigidity in oligopolistic industries is a phenomenon which the traditional theory of imperfect competition, with its strong accent on the concept of elasticity of demand, is particularly ill-designed to explain. The usual explanation is that entrepreneurs in such industries (the price leaders, or the participants in an open or tacit agreement) do not take the trouble to maximise their profits. But this explanation is rather artificial and does not go to the root of the matter. What business men themselves say—and it seems that they are right—is that it would be quite useless to alter prices in response to short-run changes in demand, because the short-run elasticity of demand is very low. It may be different in the long run, when consumers' habits, or methods of production, can be sufficiently changed to alter the demand for a consumption good or a producers' good in response to a price change. This shows the importance of the time element on the demand side which we have already stressed in connection with the problem of ' planned excess capacity '.

It is quite likely, however, that even in the long run, in many cases, the elasticity of demand is too low to be relevant, in practice, for the determination of prices. What prevents oligopolistic industries from charging higher prices than they actually do is probably the fear of new entry into the industry, rather than any considerations of elasticity of demand.

We are thus led to question altogether the usefulness of the concept of elasticity of demand for the explanation of prices. We shall in the following chapters attempt to discuss the various problems of price formation, and even the problem of selling cost, without making use of the elasticity of demand. We shall make much use of another concept, however, namely that of cost differentials between different firms, which have an important bearing on the intensity of competition, and therefore on the formation of prices.

IV. The Importance of Cost Differentials

1. The present chapter is largely devoted to some evidence concerning the importance of differences in cost in one and the same industry, particularly in connection with differences in size. The existence of considerable cost differentials is of crucial importance for the theoretical analysis of price formation, and it is worth while to offer some evidence on this point, even at the cost of burdening the argument with technical details. (The reader who is prepared to accept the statement on its face value, and wants to avoid technical details, may well omit this chapter.)

That cost differentials in one and the same industry are large, larger than many economists probably would have expected, and that such marked differentials occur frequently among the industries investigated, appears to be a well-founded result of Mr. Rostas' painstaking analysis of a number of British industries.[1] In the following we shall try to obtain some (though rather less elaborate) evidence with regard to the United States. It will be based on the *Census of Manufactures* for 1939. This permits us to calculate wage cost as a proportion of value added for various size classes of plants. The variations in this proportion will be taken as an indication of differences in labour cost. More directly, we are interested in the differential profits, and this may be measured by comparing the share of gross profits in value added. But this ratio of gross profits to value added is of course the complement to unity of the ratio of wages to value added, and we shall therefore be content to analyse this last mentioned ratio.

An appreciation of the statistical material concerning size must, however, be preceded by the discussion of a peculiar statistical problem. We can measure the size of establishments in various ways. Two measures of size, value of gross output per establishment and number of workers per establishment, are used in the Census of 1939. A third measure, capital employed per establishment, would on theoretical grounds be the most satisfactory. Now it so happens that the particular measure which we employ will have a decisive influence on the results obtained. This circumstance has not received sufficient attention hitherto, but it is brought sharply to light by the data of the 1939 Census. If we investigate, for example, the relation between size and gross output per worker, we get two apparently contradictory results (Tables 4 and 5, Fig. 1). Where establishments are classified according to value of output, the output per worker increases steadily with size of establishment. Where establishments are classified according to number of workers, the output per worker, on the contrary, decreases with size although in a less regular fashion; in the higher size classes, except the last one, there is again an increase of output per worker.

The apparent contradiction is merely the result of a 'spurious' correlation. It can easily be demonstrated that if output per worker is uncorrelated with size in the first case when size is measured by output, then a nega-

[1] L. Rostas, *Productivity, Prices and Distribution in Selected British Industries.*

tive—and spurious—correlation must obtain in the second case, where size is measured according to number of workers. Similarly, it can be demonstrated that if output per worker is positively correlated with size in the first case, it must, under certain conditions, be negatively correlated with size in the second case. We can visualise how this will happen. Imagine that establishments are classified according to value of output, and that the distribution is represented in a scatter diagram, the abscissa measuring size, and the ordinate output per worker. Imagine that there is a positively inclined regression line, and around it a cluster of points, which are dispersed rather widely in the vertical direction. Now if we change the classification of size, measuring it according to number of workers per establishment, we must redistribute the points in the scatter diagram. Each point will be shifted to the left by a proportion which depends on its ordinate—because the number of workers per plant is equal to output per plant divided by output per worker. The greater the ordinate of a point with a given abscissa, therefore, the more it is shifted to the left. If the correlation were perfect it would only mean that the regression line would become steeper. But as the points are widely dispersed above and below the regression line, the points above it will receive a stronger pull to the left than the points on the regression line, or below it. The effect is thus that *in relation to the regression line* the points above it, representing unusually 'productive' plants, will be pulled towards the left, and the points below it, representing unusually 'unproductive' plants, will be pulled to the right. The cluster of points round the regression line will thus be subject to a pull in two directions which will distort it. Provided that the dispersion of points in the vertical direction is great enough, the regression line will be turned over so as to obtain a negative slope. This result is obviously more easy to obtain if the regression line happens to be steep at the outset.

To demonstrate this mathematically we shall measure all the variables concerned on a logarithmic scale, which will make the calculation easier, and which anyhow recommends itself because the correlation involved becomes more nearly linear when logarithms are used. Thus we use the following notation:

Y = log of value of output per worker.

X = log of value of output per establishment.

$X-Y$ = log of number of workers per establishment.

Using the corresponding small letters to denote the deviations from the mean, we can write r_1 for the coefficient of correlation between X and Y and b_1 for the regression coefficient of Y on X, where

$$r_1 = \frac{S(xy)}{\sigma_x \sigma_y}; \quad b_1 = r_1 \frac{\sigma_y}{\sigma_x}.$$

The coefficient of correlation between Y and $X-Y$ and the regression coefficient of Y on $X-Y$, denoted by R_1 and B_1 respectively, are determined as follows:

$$R_1 = \frac{S(xy)-S(y^2)}{\sigma_y \sigma_{x-y}} = \frac{r_1\sigma_x - \sigma_y}{\sqrt{\sigma_x^2+\sigma_y^2-2r_1\sigma_x\sigma_y}} = \frac{r_1^2-b_1}{\sqrt{r_1^2+b_1^2-2r_1^2 b_1}} \tag{1}$$

$$B_1 = \frac{r_1\sigma_x\sigma_y-\sigma_y^2}{\sigma_x^2+\sigma_y^2-2r_1\sigma_x\sigma_y} = \frac{b_1(r_1^2-b_1)}{r_1^2+b_1^2-2b_1 r_1^2}. \tag{2}$$

It can now easily be seen that if X and Y are uncorrelated, a spurious correlation arises between X and $X-Y$. If $r_1 = 0$,

$$R_1 = -\frac{\sigma_y}{\sqrt{\sigma_x^2+\sigma_y^2}} \qquad B_1 = -\frac{\sigma_y^2}{\sigma_x^2+\sigma_y^2}. \tag{3}$$

The degree of this spurious correlation depends obviously on the dispersion of Y in comparison with the dispersion of X.

Now we can find the condition under which a positive correlation between Y and X will involve a negative correlation between Y and $X-Y$. This condition, from (1), is

$$r_1^2 < b_1.$$

From the data it appears that in fact r_1 is positive and the regression line of Y on X, is very approximately, linear (Table 4 and 5, Fig. 1). The graphical representation is rendered somewhat difficult by the fact that we should have to plot *means of logarithms* of the variables output per plant and output per worker, whereas the data available are only the means of output per plant for each class interval (abscissa), and the mean output per worker for each size class (ordinate), *on the natural scale*. On the abscissa no large error is involved by taking the logarithm of the means instead of the means of the logarithm, for each class interval. On the ordinate it is different; we can do nothing else but plot the logarithm of the means on the ordinate, but it must be stressed that the picture obtained does not represent the true regression lines of the logarithmically measured variables (Fig. 1). It can, however, enable us to form an idea of the shape of these regression lines. The correlation between X and Y does seem to be linear to some approximation. The slope in reality may be different from that on the graph, but it will still be positive and show an approximately linear correlation.

The correlation between Y and $(X-Y)$—between output per worker and size as measured by number of workers per plant—presents a rather more complicated picture (Fig. 1). As size increases, the mean output per worker falls first, then increases (in the medium range of size) and finally declines again in the highest size classes. The correlation is decidedly non-linear. By and large it appears that the overall tendency of the curve is to *fall*, so that the correlation is in fact the opposite of what it was in the first case. This would be explained by the algebraical demonstration above. What requires

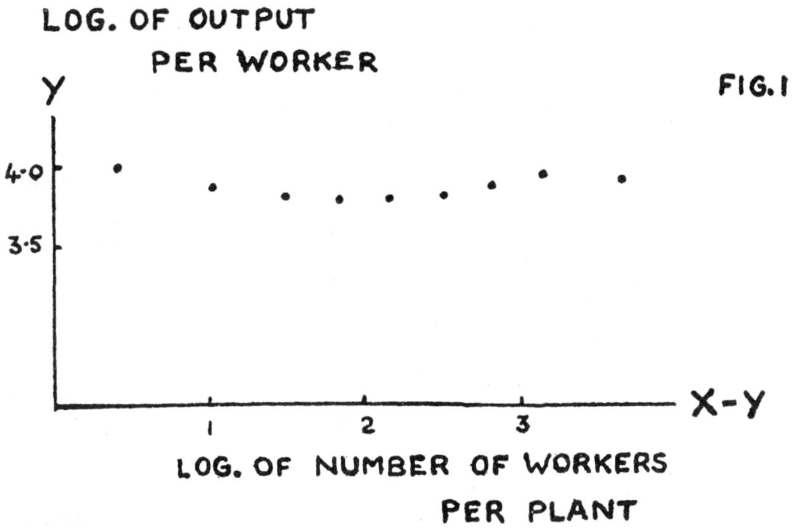

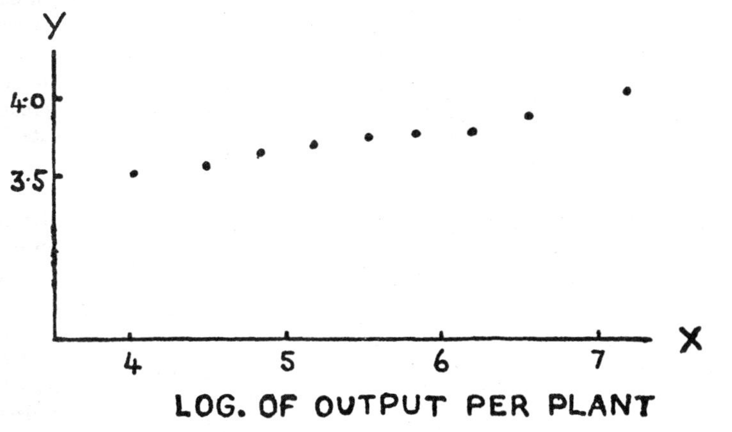

FIG. 1. *The relation between gross value of output per worker and size of establishment in manufacturing*. The ordinates represent the logarithm of the average gross output per worker in various size classes. Data from Tables 4 and 5.

TABLE 4

PRODUCTIVITY AND SIZE (CENSUS OF MANUFACTURES 1939)

Establishments classified by value of product

Value of product in 1000 $	No. of establishments	Value of product per establishment	Ditto, logarithm	Wage earners per establishment	Value of product per wage earner $	Ditto, logarithm	Value added per wage earner $	Wages as % of value added
5— 19.9	60593	11235	4.05057	3.13	3591	3.55522	2088	38.0
20— 49.9	42083	32167	4.50741	7.78	4135	3.61648	2290	39.7
50— 99.9	25490	71066	4.85166	15.29	4649	3.66736	2454	39.0
100— 249.9	24718	158628	5.20038	31.08	5103	3.70783	2523	38.5
250— 499.9	13066	354120	5.54915	64.23	5513	3.74139	2583	38.2
500— 999.9	8706	701923	5.84629	119.25	5886	3.76982	2713	37.9
1000—2499.9	6088	1524304	6.18307	240.35	6354	3.80305	2923	37.7
2500—4999.9	2013	3437122	6.53620	449.17	7652	3.88378	3496	34.9
5000 and over	1473	15017720	7.17660	1335.25	11247	4.05104	4180	35.4
All establishments ..	184230	308544		42.81	7208		3130	36.8

TABLE 5

PRODUCTIVITY AND SIZE (CENSUS OF MANUFACTURES 1939)

Establishments classified by number of wage earners

No. of wage earners per establishment	No. of establishments	Wage earners per establishment	Ditto, logarithm	Value of product per establishment	Value of product per wage earner $	Ditto, logarithm	Value added per wage earner $	Wages as % of value
no wage earners	8315			65374				
1— 5	75930	2.67	0.42651	26939	10074	4.00320	4371	24.4
6— 20	49015	11.07	1.04415	83615	7552	3.87806	3362	30.8
21— 50	23646	32.34	1.50974	219042	6772	3.83072	3027	34.1
51— 100	11908	71.25	1.85278	461855	6482	3.81171	2940	35.4
101— 250	9458	155.70	2.19229	1002245	6437	3.80868	2902	36.6
251— 500	3653	347.38	2.54080	2230629	6421	3.80760	2838	38.6
501—1000	1495	685.15	2.83579	4946892	7220	3.85854	3044	38.5
1001—2500	634	1478.13	3.16971	12499101	8456	3.92717	3340	39.1
2501 and over	176	4684.84	3.67069	37094179	7918	3.89862	3374	45.4
All establishments ..	184230	42.81		308544	7208		3130	36.8

further explanation, however, is the *non-linearity* of the correlation, the peculiar wave-like shape of the regression line. In fact, if the original correlation between Y and X were a *normal* correlation then we should expect with certainty that the new correlation between Y and $(X - Y)$ should be *linear*, too. We know, however, from the data, that the correlation between Y and X can by no means be a normal correlation. This is because the distribution of plants according to X, *i.e.* among size classes, is strongly skewed, with a great part of the plants contained in the lowest size classes. The correlation surface will thus not show the elliptic contour map which obtains in the case of a normal correlation, but it will be truncated on the left. We have no direct evidence on the distribution of plants according to Y, the output per worker. We might guess that this distribution is asymmetrical, probably negatively skewed, for any given size of plant X. The correlation between Y and X is thus certainly not normal, because the distribution in the direction of X is certainly positively skewed and the distribution in the direction of Y is probably also asymmetrical. This seems to be the explanation of the non-linearity of the correlation of Y and $(X - Y)$.

The apparent contradiction between the two correlations obtained by measuring size in two different ways can thus be explained on statistical grounds. In fact, it is really not a contradiction at all that we should obtain different results by measuring size in the two different ways.

There is, however, a more fundamental question. We have implied that the result obtained when measuring size by output is genuine, and the other result is merely a distorted reflection of the true relationship between size and output per worker. But what is the justification for regarding the correlation between X and Y as genuine, and the other correlation as spurious? In other words, is it correct to measure size by value of output for our purpose?

This is an economic, not a statistical question. One way of answering it is to call to our aid additional facts, obtained in other, non-statistical, ways, which are in agreement with one, and in contradiction to the other of the two statistical results obtained. Now industrial experience and the testimony of engineers very strongly suggest that economies of large scale are very important, that a considerable increase in output per worker is obtained by technical methods which involve a great scale of production. On the other hand, leaving fairly exceptional cases aside, there is no corresponding experience of technical facts which suggest that the co-operation of a smaller number of workers in a productive unit brings about greater output per head. There are, at best, only some vague ideas about a possibly greater efficiency of the smaller entrepreneur, which hardly carry any weight as compared with the technical facts mentioned. This would seem to settle the issue in favour of the positive correlation between output per worker and output per plant.

There is still another way of looking at the question. We can consider the issue within the wider framework of economic theory, and ask which of the relations, that between Y and X, or that between Y and $X - Y$, is *relevant*.

A relation between two quantities will be theoretically relevant if important conclusions follow from it, or rather from the fact that these quantities are positively, negatively, or not at all correlated, as the case may be. A relation will, on the contrary, be irrelevant if it does not make any great difference to our conclusions about the working of the economic system whether the two quantities are positively, negatively, or not at all correlated.

Now from the economic point of view the really significant measure of size is neither output nor number of workers, but the amount of capital employed in a plant. What we want to know is whether plants which are greater *in terms of capital* have on the average a greater output per worker. This is the decisive question because we know that command or control over a certain sum of capital is the rarer the greater the sum. If, therefore, greater capital employed per plant means greater productivity, the consequence is —given certain further assumptions which we cannot go into at the moment[1]— that command over big sums of capital secures competitive advantages not open to those who do not command so much capital.

The relevant relation is therefore that between productivity and capital per plant. The other relations, in which different measures of size are employed, are in themselves not important. That, for example, high productivity is associated with a small number of workers per plant is *in itself* not interesting. To conclude from it that ' small plants are more productive ' would certainly be nonsense, because we know from our previous analysis that among plants with the same output and capital invested those which have higher productivity tend to be classified as small, if size is measured by number of workers.

The measurement of size which we should like best, on economic grounds, is thus *capital per plant*. Unfortunately the data for this purpose are not available. We shall have to be content with the measurement by output per plant. This does not come to the same as the measurement by capital, because plants with the same amount of capital invested may have different outputs on account of different utilisation and different capital intensity. (In homogeneous industries the last mentioned factor is probably not important.) But output will at least give a measurement of size which is independent of the productivity of labour in the particular plant, and is thus the best substitute for the measurement of size by capital.

2. On theoretical grounds we expect that the share of wages in value added will decline with size, because output and value added per man increase owing to large scale economies, and although wages per man also increase with size this increase is not sufficiently strong to offset the increase in productivity. How far can this hypothesis be confirmed by actual data ?

As mentioned already we have no classification of establishments by capital employed. All we can do is to use the classification of plants according to output, and try to draw what conclusions we can from this material.

It must be noted that the picture obtained is only a distorted reflection,

[1] See my ' Small and Big Business '.

in so far as many of the industries in the Census are far from homogeneous. Therefore irregularity in the behaviour of the share of wages need not surprise us.

There is another factor to be taken into account if we want to appreciate the results correctly. The *wages* given in the Census do not include any remuneration of small working proprietors and their family members. In many cases the smaller plants will show a low share of wages on this account mainly. Furthermore, work given out is not reckoned as wages although it is not always excluded from value added. In certain industries it will be mainly small and medium plants which will give out work to home workers, and irregular behaviour of the share of wages is to be expected in these cases.

In some industries production up to a certain size is negligible, and the figures given for the smaller size classes have little relevance. Sometimes practically all plants are in the highest size class, and no conclusion can be drawn.

The share of wages in value added has been calculated for 87 industries which have been selected mainly for their size and importance (Table 6). The industries have been numbered so that we can refer to them by their number in the text.

The results are as follows: there are 17 industries in which the share of wages declines over practically the whole range (minor irregularities excepted) These are industries Nos. 4, 9, 12, 16, 18, 21, 25, 31, 32, 36, 40, 48, 56, 58, 63, 64, 69. No further comment is required, except that they belong to the most diverse types of industry. There are 41 other industries in which we can see a clear trace of the negative correlation (industries Nos 2, 5, 6, 10, 13, 14, 15, 17, 19, 20, 22, 23, 26, 27, 28, 30, 35, 37, 39, 41, 42, 43, 45, 46, 47, 50, 51, 57, 59, 61, 67, 71, 75, 77, 78, 79, 82, 83, 85, 86, 87). The picture of these industries is not quite uniform. In some cases the negative correlation is there in the medium range, and both ends of the distribution show the opposite tendency (for example, blast furnaces, machine tools). In some cases it is only the lower end of the distribution which appears distorted (for example, candy and confectionery, cigars, women's dresses made in contract factories). In a few other cases there is a complicated picture of two 'waves', such as in book-binding. In all these industries, however, the negative correlation appears partly reflected in the data.

Of the remaining industries 7 have to be discarded as evidence, because the great bulk of production is in the highest size class (industries Nos. 11, 55, 66, 73, 76, 80, 81). There remain 14 industries which suggest a positive correlation (3, 7, 33, 34, 38, 44, 49, 52, 53, 62, 70, 72, 74, 84), four which show no tendency either way (8, 24, 54, 68) and four which are altogether irregular (1, 29, 60, 65). All these cases 'adverse' to the theory are worth reviewing in detail. A number of them belong to the iron, metal and machinery industries: structural steel, wirework n.e.c., forgings, steam fittings, hardware, alloys, stamped goods, metal working machinery, radio and phonographs. All these groups seem to be very heterogeneous, composed of very

TABLE 6

WAGES AS A PERCENTAGE OF VALUE ADDED IN DIFFERENT SIZE CLASSES OF MANUFACTURING PLANTS

Selected manufacturing industries in U.S. (1939)

Where size classes have been *grouped* the figures for the group are in italics, and the classes merged in the group indicated by X.

E. = Number of establishments. V.A. = Value added ('000 $). % = Wages as % of value added.

Industry		Size of plant as measured by value of product in thousands of $: 5 to 19.9	20 to 49.9	50 to 99.9	100 to 249.9	250 to 499.9	500 to 999.9	1000 to 2499.9	2500 to 4999.9	5000 & over
1. Agricultural Machinery (except Tractors)	E	75	58	51	46	31	22	16	12	6
	V.A.	386	1077	2111	3798	5716	9328	12273	23143	30793
	%	46.1	30.6	32.0	40.9	37.3	32.2	45.0	36.6	43.3
2. Aircraft and Parts including Aircraft Engines	E.	17	11	16	21	16	15	13	6	10
	V.A.	125	239	809	2188	3644	7288	14027	14436	140491
	%	46.4	37.2	59.5	60.2	53.3	44.5	45.6	49.7	40.4
3. Alloying and Rolling and Draining of Non-ferrous Metals except Aluminium	E.	13	13	18	23	27	28	21	21	24
	V.A.	74	169	421	1217	2972	6162	10732	25148	117275
	%	18.9	30.8	21.6	24.7	28.0	31.1	32.7	35.3	34.7
4. Biscuit, Crackers and Pretzels	E.	92	54	43	38	35	34	44	11	5
	V.A.	548	960	1644	3325	6883	12277	39792	53314	(X)
	%	48.0	41.7	40.6	33.3	32.0	29.2	25.5	19.1	(X)
5. Blast Furnace Products	E.	..	..	..	1	7	3	11	25	34
	V.A.	..	..	..	(X)	876	289	4017	18951	62949
	%	..	..	..	(X)	42.7	56.8	34.2	29.4	33.1
6. Bookbinding and related Industries	E.	541	292	131	93	32	24	16	2	1
	V.A.	4720	6956	6915	10488	7224	10565	16761	*8532*	(X)
	%	39.5	41.2	43.0	42.8	36.9	39.5	45.3	28.6	(X)
7. Books, Printing without Publishing	E.	153	178	158	128	46	20	4	2	1
	V.A.	1173	3844	7361	12608	10395	8289	3398	*8576*	(X)
	%	36.7	39.2	40.0	42.3	45.7	48.0	48.5	51.9	(X)
8. Bread and other bakery products (except biscuit, crackers and pretzels)	E.	9798	4804	1499	1003	453	306	151	27	2
	V.A.	52009	69798	50355	80612	87222	120542	120605	*62454*	(X)
	%	38.0	41.4	42.4	41.6	39.8	39.5	41.4	41.8	(X)
9. Brick and hollow structural tile	E.	158	183	188	213	46	11	1	..	..
	V.A.	1326	4498	9761	23241	11166	*5692*	(X)	..	..
	%	52.0	49.9	51.6	47.3	43.7	44.3	(X)	..	..

TABLE 6 (*continued*)

Industry		Size of plant as measured by value of product in thousands of $								
		5 to 19.9	20 to 49.9	50 to 99.9	100 to 249.9	250 to 499.9	500 to 999.9	1000 to 2499.9	2500 to 4999.9	5000 & over
10. Candy and other confectionery products	E.	375	294	188	171	96	74	29	21	4
	V.A.	1977	4166	5745	11082	14561	22780	19719	31969	15027
	%	35.6	34.6	35.6	36.9	35.8	32.1	34.7	28.5	28.9
11. Cane sugar refining	E.	..	..	1	1	..	1	3	1	20
	V.A.	..	..	(X)	(X)	..	*67*	*1528*	(X)	54399
	%	..	..	(X)	(X)	..	98.5	18.7	(X)	29.1
12. Canned and dried fruits and vegetables (including canned soups)	E.	446	410	323	391	208	123	68	31	7
	V.A.	1831	4968	8237	22087	26047	31908	35703	38096	62186
	%	43.4	38.5	34.7	33.6	33.6	33.4	31.5	30.9	15.8
13. Carpets and rugs, wool	E.	1	2	4	2	3	5	12	7	7
	V.A.	(X)	*24*	*262*	(X)	789	1431	9483	14800	52483
	%	(X)	87.5	44.7	(X)	43.4	58.9	43.3	33.3	37.7
14. Cars and car equipment—railroad, street, and rapid-transit	E.	12	19	23	23	13	14	23	5	11
	V.A.	102	395	948	1793	2042	4485	15584	7904	31467
	%	68.6	77.5	81.9	81.0	81.2	75.5	64.6	39.9	43.7
15. Cast-iron pipe and fittings	E.	1	1	5	13	17	20	12	4	1
	V.A.	(X)	(X)	*281*	1238	3533	8093	12346	11573	(X)
	%	..	..	70.5	53.6	78.7	60.7	42.6	35.1	..
16. Cement	E.	..	1	..	10	11	51	80	7	..
	V.A.	..	(X)	..	767	2605	24508	80413	15789	..
	%	..	..	..	42.5	34.2	27.0	24.5	25.9	..
17. Chemicals not elsewhere classified	E.	48	46	40	99	92	67	71	38	42
	V.A.	279	773	1513	7131	15573	21737	51737	63428	308946
	%	41.9	24.8	18.7	27.8	24.8	25.4	23.5	22.9	18.2
18. Cigarettes	E.	6	..	3	..	2	2	1	..	21
	V.A.	25	..	56	..	*1096*	(X)	(X)	..	225501
	%	36.0	..	30.4	..	14.7	..	..	..	11.5
19. Cigars	E.	318	92	45	50	29	24	26	9	5
	V.A.	1638	1599	1723	4249	5862	8615	21487	14957	21374
	%	48.1	53.4	54.0	50.2	46.1	43.5	44.0	41.0	35.0

TABLE 6 (*continued*)

Industry		Size of plant as measured by value of product in thousands of $								
		5 to 19.9	20 to 49.9	50 to 99.9	100 to 249.9	250 to 499.9	500 to 999.9	1000 to 2499.9	2500 to 4999.9	5000 & over
20. Coats, suits, and skirts (except fur coats) made in contract factories	E.	259	383	172	25	5	2	..	..	..
	V.A.	2807	11708	10827	2856	2108	(X)	..	..	..
	%	71.7	76.8	76.6	73.6	69.4	..	..	..	..
21. Coats, suits and skirts (except fur coats)—made in inside factories or by jobbers engaging contractors	E.	136	204	183	282	173	99	36	6	1
	V.A.	748	3093	5103	16058	19544	20789	15646	*6070*	(X)
	%	44.9	42.4	40.7	42.0	40.1	37.5	38.5	23.7	..
22. Communication equipment	E.	54	39	29	40	23	16	17	6	3
	V.A.	392	763	1263	3873	4348	6910	17475	15270	92683
	%	37.0	34.6	41.5	41.8	40.4	39.3	41.6	34.7	26.8
23. Cotton broad woven goods	E.	15	21	26	60	95	168	193	61	22
	V.A.	82	403	1014	4918	15715	57128	135810	108725	114536
	%	85.4	47.6	44.5	56.2	62.6	57.3	60.7	48.2	38.7
24. Cotton yarn	E.	17	6	21	60	115	85	38	5	2
	V.A.	114	63	655	4930	18132	25100	23588	*11708*	(X)
	%	61.4	69.8	49.6	53.4	55.1	51.0	53.9	55.8	..
25. Creamery butter	E.	338	908	1027	762	281	143	45	2	..
	V.A.	795	4848	10151	16575	13996	16251	*10854*	(X)	..
	%	35.2	30.4	29.6	25.6	23.5	22.0	23.0	..	..
26. Dyeing and finishing cotton, rayon, silk, and linen textiles	E.	53	73	51	83	72	64	52	14	6
	V.A.	477	1687	2468	8409	16179	24920	42110	22348	12097
	%	44.4	43.2	48.3	51.4	47.0	46.4	47.1	50.5	41.2
27. Electrical Appliances	E.	22	24	21	11	21	15	12	4	8
	V.A.	135	368	780	766	3389	5837	10407	9103	56830
	%	32.6	36.1	32.1	32.6	35.8	37.8	37.1	29.6	26.0
28. Enamelled-iron sanitary ware and other plumbers' supplies (not including pipe and vitreous and semi-vitreous china sanitary ware)	E.	29	49	32	45	43	36	18	5	2
	V.A.	194	849	1287	4308	7876	12965	18140	(X)	*27329*
	%	34.5	36.3	37.3	40.6	48.0	45.8	43.7	..	38.5

TABLE 6 (*continued*)

Industry		Size of plant as measured by value of product in thousands of $								
		5 to 19.9	20 to 49.9	50 to 99.9	100 to 249.9	250 to 499.9	500 to 999.9	1000 to 2499.9	2500 to 4999.9	5000 & over
29. Fabricated structural steel and ornamental metal work, made in plants not operated in connection with rolling mills	E.	249	236	167	233	135	66	39	8	5
	V.A.	1638	4358	5934	16057	20974	18097	22231	9405	13537
	%	41.5	40.3	38.9	36.9	37.7	38.1	43.5	35.9	66.9
30. Flat glass	E.	..	3	4	2	2	5	10	3	8
	V.A.	..	53	*498*	(X)	(X)	*2690*	10852	5512	48935
	%	..	41.5	34.7	..	..	48.9	44.8	49.0	30.5
31. Flour and other grain-mill products	E.	738	498	276	221	142	103	110	39	16
	V.A.	2310	4007	4726	8385	11544	14876	36376	28313	33345
	%	30.5	27.6	22.1	20.3	21.8	19.7	20.0	19.1	17.0
32. Footwear (except rubber)	E.	89	90	101	161	179	205	197	44	4
	V.A.	490	1543	3614	13079	31149	71904	146437	64369	13649
	%	59.0	55.7	57.1	58.0	57.2	53.7	52.1	53.2	43.8
33. Forgings, iron and steel—made in plants not operated in connection with rolling mills	E.	13	26	25	44	36	38	21	3	1
	V.A.	87	514	971	4001	6948	14095	17656	*8637*	(X)
	%	37.9	48.8	41.8	40.1	39.9	43.5	43.7	43.3	..
34. General commercial (job) printing	E.	5533	2221	930	586	190	93	29	11	2
	V.A.	38195	44875	40504	56237	41107	39512	24169	*39003*	(X)
	%	33.9	38.0	40.5	40.1	42.2	43.5	49.5	44.8	..
35. Generating, distribution and industrial apparatus, and apparatus for incorporation in manufactured products, not elsewhere classified	E.	86	78	59	94	48	54	43	16	13
	V.A.	545	1453	2408	7963	9313	21254	42001	*198198*	(X)
	%	36.9	38.3	33.7	36.4	38.1	34.4	33.7	37.6	..
36. Glass containers	E.	1	..	2	2	8	15	31	8	10
	V.A.	(X)	..	277	(X)	1541	6411	29845	19425	40879
	%	..	..	53.4	..	46.8	41.5	37.3	37.3	30.0

TABLE 6 (*continued*)

Industry		Size of plant as measured by value of product in thousands of $								
		5 to 19.9	20 to 49.9	50 to 99.9	100 to 249.9	250 to 499.9	500 to 999.9	1000 to 2499.9	2500 to 4999.9	5000 & over
37. Gray-iron and semisteel castings	E.	230	237	210	256	236	62	23	6	1
	V.A.	1858	5500	10006	26447	29426	26004	18920	*12585*	(X)
	%	54.2	55.6	58.6	58.1	52.5	55.3	52.0	46.3	..
38. Hardware not elsewhere classified	E.	90	74	56	74	61	39	30	6	4
	V.A.	625	1536	2408	6675	12710	15940	26771	11505	15533
	%	37.3	34.2	38.4	39.5	38.6	41.9	44.4	39.8	50.4
39. Hosiery—fully-fashioned	E.	25	53	62	114	100	73	54	15	3
	V.A.	171	866	2319	10109	20173	28209	44093	30196	19910
	%	80.1	72.3	63.5	62.4	61.0	62.5	67.4	65.7	64.0
40. Hosiery—seamless	E.	51	57	73	101	63	63	21	3	1
	V.A.	347	1023	2587	8425	11320	23175	15200	*9313*	(X)
	%	67.4	61.7	65.4	61.5	59.3	61.7	52.9	50.3	..
41. Household furniture, except upholstered	E.	366	347	225	287	184	123	52	7	1
	V.A.	2461	6422	9202	24715	35161	43883	38943	*12651*	(X)
	%	47.4	49.7	49.5	49.4	47.8	46.2	49.5	51.3	..
42. Industrial machinery, not elsewhere specified	E.	118	116	108	119	62	23	26	6	1
	V.A.	897	2445	4802	12056	13120	9310	24010	*21023*	..
	%	38.9	40.2	37.7	38.4	31.8	37.1	38.0	31.7	(X)
43. Internal-combustion engines	E.	4	8	6	11	10	6	14	6	9
	V.A.	30	95	283	1006	2158	1575	13074	10963	27719
	%	56.7	74.7	56.5	41.6	32.3	43.6	38.4	37.1	37.4
44. Leather: tanned, curried, and finished—regular factories or jobbers engaging contractors	E.	18	24	20	71	30	56	77	35	4
	V.A.	101	323	530	4289	3502	13724	39868	37869	6781
	%	33.7	39.6	44.2	38.4	42.8	44.8	45.5	50.7	52.5
45. Machine-shop products, not elsewhere classified	E.	717	537	309	266	138	83	54	17	4
	V.A.	5657	11079	13674	24299	28847	35050	47712	34132	18391
	%	41.4	41.4	38.3	37.4	33.6	36.8	35.8	29.0	55.9

TABLE 6 (*continued*)

Industry		Size of plant as measured by value of product in thousands of $								
		5 to 19.9	20 to 49.9	50 to 99.9	100 to 249.9	250 to 499.9	500 to 999.9	1000 to 2499.9	2500 to 4999.9	5000 & over
46. Machine-tool and other metal-working-machinery accessories, metal-cutting and shaping tools, and machinists' precision tools	E.	252	236	190	174	54	27	19	2	..
	V.A.	2288	6122	10416	19605	14125	13034	*28631*	(X)	..
	%	45.6	49.9	51.2	48.2	43.7	46.3	35.8	..	..
47. Machine tools	E.	13	20	19	42	21	36	29	10	10
	V.A.	100	477	820	4257	4229	17804	36641	25770	64079
	%	38.0	39.8	44.6	50.1	46.2	39.4	38.6	37.4	41.9
48. Malt liquors	E.	22	35	76	123	120	95	85	36	13
	V.A.	173	781	3687	14156	30334	48092	91422	83954	90580
	%	42.8	33.2	27.1	22.8	19.2	18.7	16.6	16.3	15.4
49. Meat packing, wholesale	E.	100	148	187	301	209	178	167	78	110
	V.A.	292	929	2357	8152	13360	22083	44722	41410	288483
	%	28.4	30.3	30.0	30.1	29.6	28.5	30.1	37.1	41.2
50. Mechanical power-transmission equipment	E.	31	28	28	45	25	27	18	7	9
	V.A.	235	583	1384	4927	6050	12537	19216	15799	59195
	%	45.5	37.9	42.9	38.8	37.8	40.1	38.6	35.5	34.8
51. Men's and boys' shirts (except work shirts), collars, and nightwear—made in inside factories or by jobbers engaging contractors	E.	39	54	55	97	84	74	40	5	1
	V.A.	232	761	1716	6227	11978	19350	23058	*10361*	(X)
	%	55.6	47.4	52.7	46.5	50.4	54.1	50.9	46.2	..
52. Men's and boys' suits, coats and overcoats (except work clothing)—made in contract factories	E.	430	271	188	165	22	1	1	..	..
	V.A.	4228	8098	12525	22976	8886	(X)	(X)	..	..
	%	65.7	73.9	76.4	80.9	76.2	..	..	..	..
53. Men's and boys' suits, coats and overcoats (except work clothing)—made in inside factories or by jobbers engaging contractors	E.	115	230	201	375	220	112	78	30	10
	V.A.	564	2787	4461	19266	26648	26992	50220	44871	31195
	%	33.2	33.4	34.0	44.3	44.9	43.1	47.5	52.4	44.6

TABLE 6 (*continued*)

Industry		Size of plant as measured by value of product in thousands of $								
		5 to 19.9	20 to 49.9	50 to 99.9	100 to 249.9	250 to 499.9	500 to 999.9	1000 to 2499.9	2500 to 4999.9	5000 & over
54. Metalworking machinery and equipment, not elsewhere classified	E.	19	24	22	39	22	21	20	10	1
	V.A.	163	525	1019	4063	4963	9895	17283	*26315*	(X)
	%	31.3	31.2	41.4	41.4	39.2	40.9	42.7	35.7	..
55. Motor vehicles, motor-vehicle bodies, parts and accessories	E.	171	193	127	143	80	73	71	44	152
	V.A.	1207	3370	4722	12177	12794	25122	55530	71064	1133385
	%	47.5	46.1	44.9	42.2	41.6	38.6	43.0	48.9	49.6
56. Oven coke and coke-oven products	E.	..	1	..	3	5	3	26	26	19
	V.A.	..	(X)	..	*137*	608	674	10211	25973	46944
	%	..	(X)	..	70.8	53.5	32.9	49.3	39.0	34.0
57. Paints, varnishes and lacquers	E.	214	24	140	233	133	113	59	22	9
	V.A.	1100	3298	4076	14978	20376	35696	43325	31904	34639
	%	27.2	17.9	16.4	17.7	16.5	15.2	14.6	17.0	20.0
58. Paper and paperboard mills	E.	4	18	26	70	100	136	173	80	31
	V.A.	25	286	1076	5677	16189	42774	114599	116720	103409
	%	52.0	57.7	49.4	44.4	42.5	38.7	36.5	34.5	32.8
59. Paperboard containers and boxes not elsewhere classified	E.	154	247	257	287	190	108	78	17	..
	V.A.	1096	4814	10043	23757	30348	32964	43302	22547	..
	%	41.8	45.9	41.5	40.8	38.5	36.1	35.7	36.6	..
60. Petroleum refining	E.	27	33	27	42	53	46	96	63	98
	V.A.	141	313	689	1649	3869	7721	34518	45997	432965
	%	27.7	40.9	22.5	23.0	28.2	17.2	20.0	21.9	25.0
61. Photographic apparatus and materials and projection equipment (except lenses)	E.	40	32	21	26	14	10	10	2	5
	V.A.	254	666	868	1986	2459	3200	9714	*72196*	(X)
	%	40.2	40.8	38.0	28.4	24.7	28.8	29.0	27.3	(X)
62. Planing mills not operated in conjunction with sawmills	E.	856	800	643	490	181	74	29	3	..
	V.A.	5344	12980	21833	32069	26878	21685	17825	4363	..
	%	48.5	44.9	43.5	40.0	40.4	45.3	50.1	57.2	..

TABLE 6 (*continued*)

Industry		Size of plant as measured by value of product in thousands of $								
		5 to 19.9	20 to 49.9	50 to 99.9	100 to 249.9	250 to 499.9	500 to 999.9	1000 to 2499.9	2500 to 4999.9	5000 & over
63. Primary smelting and refining of non-ferrous metals	E.	..	1	..	..	2	2	7	14	37
	V.A.	..	(X)	..	..	(X)	*602*	3869	15223	117309
	%	..	(X)	..	..	(X)	56.3	40.0	43.0	25.6
64. Pulp mills	E.	..	11	10	25	27	41	49	28	3
	V.A.	..	151	322	1496	3098	10105	26180	32730	8034
	%	..	68.2	48.1	55.8	56.7	44.4	43.2	38.7	22.1
65. Radios, radio tubes and phonographs	E.	35	38	28	37	14	20	23	19	10
	V.A.	232	564	1220	3171	2552	6683	17094	35905	62599
	%	34.9	30.9	35.6	35.4	30.8	32.8	39.8	37.5	35.1
66. Rayon and allied products	E.	..	..	..	..	1	4	3	5	17
	V.A.	..	..	..	..	(X)	*1733*	3353	11015	152506
	%	..	..	..	..	(X)	37.5	48.5	55.6	33.9
67. Refrigerators, domestic (mechanical and absorption), refrigeration machinery and equipment, and complete air-conditioning units	E.	50	81	48	51	26	18	17	7	11
	V.A.	328	1394	1595	4126	4353	6067	13956	8600	87764
	%	39.6	33.6	45.7	33.6	34.7	31.9	35.8	34.1	39.1
68. Sawmills, veneer mills, and cooperage-stock mills, including those combined with logging camps and with planing mills	E.	3802	1632	719	682	267	169	97	21	2
	V.A.	24535	30175	29106	60055	53134	71628	84238	*60054*	(X)
	%	53.2	49.3	46.9	49.3	52.4	55.4	53.7	51.7	(X)
69. Sheet-metal work not specifically classified	E.	392	364	203	182	76	27	14	4	..
	V.A.	2752	6789	8062	14683	11629	7568	8010	6866	..
	%	42.8	42.4	38.0	36.7	36.1	34.2	28.5	22.0	..
70. Shipbuilding and ship repairing	E.	71	88	62	82	38	31	15	8	11
	V.A.	572	1889	2703	8299	8585	14305	15690	16638	105291
	%	51.4	56.0	55.0	57.3	56.3	55.0	58.3	54.6	62.6

TABLE 6 (*continued*)

Industry		Size of plant as measured by value of product in thousands of $								
		5 to 19.9	20 to 49.9	50 to 99.9	100 to 249.9	250 to 499.9	500 to 999.9	1000 to 2499.9	2500 to 4999.9	5000 & over
71. Soap and glycerin	E.	63	58	34	45	15	14	10	9	16
	V.A.	356	812	1110	3170	2303	3911	7342	14795	107832
	%	22.8	21.8	19.5	16.8	13.5	14.1	17.3	14.8	12.5
72. Stamped and pressed metal products (except automobile stampings)	E.	146	136	115	113	64	47	24	8	2
	V.A.	1056	2591	4611	9724	11861	17806	18665	*22941*	(X)
	%	37.4	41.4	40.5	40.2	41.3	41.7	41.9	44.2	..
73. Steam engines, turbines and water wheels	E.	..	1	4	4	2	2	2	2	1
	V.A.	..	(X)	*223*	383	(X)	*1474*	(X)	*13119*	(X)
	%	..	..	35.9	72.6	..	31.5	..	42.1	..
74. Steam fittings, regardless of material	E.	28	35	20	20	21	19	21	4	3
	V.A.	201	752	810	3148	4813	7907	20054	11401	25232
	%	32.3	28.7	33.7	29.5	37.6	35.8	35.9	35.5	48.6
75. Steel castings	E.	1	7	12	29	34	44	24	10	3
	V.A.	(X)	*215*	609	3464	8447	20038	22299	22136	13027
	%	..	37.7	48.3	46.6	47.9	48.3	52.3	41.6	41.1
76. Steel works and rolling mills	E.	2	..	4	8	5	19	47	46	122
	V.A.	(X)	..	*152*	498	879	8378	35365	77209	1025067
	%	..	..	57.9	70.1	52.0	44.6	52.1	48.4	49.7
77. Stoves, ranges, water heaters, and hot-air furnaces (except electric)	E.	53	66	58	87	72	48	47	15	3
	V.A.	375	1270	2401	8128	14907	18177	39582	30157	10955
	%	39.7	34.8	41.6	40.0	42.7	43.2	40.5	31.2	32.8
78. Tableware, pressed or blown glass, and glassware not elsewhere classified	E.	11	8	18	16	18	17	15	8	4
	V.A.	74	193	914	1882	4923	8535	15391	20910	17463
	%	51.4	65.8	56.2	60.0	55.7	57.2	37.2	34.7	44.2
79. Tin cans and other tinware not elsewhere classified	E.	17	25	20	35	29	25	51	29	17
	V.A.	101	434	714	2422	4240	7425	28698	32354	47183
	%	49.5	38.0	40.9	42.4	39.9	36.2	31.3	27.5	26.7
80. Tyres and inner tubes	E.	..	1	1	2	3	4	5	6	31
	V.A.	..	(X)	(X)	*152*	426	1010	2803	5995	220986
	%	..	..	..	44.1	46.7	32.1	42.3	43.7	38.6

TABLE 6 (*continued*)

Industry		5 to 19.9	20 to 49.9	50 to 99.9	100 to 249.9	250 to 499.9	500 to 999.9	1000 to 2499.9	2500 to 4999.9	5000 & over
		Size of plant as measured by value of product in thousands of $								
81. Tractors	E.	3	1	1	4	3	3	3	1	11
	V.A.	(X)	(X)	*62*	203	322	758	*4478*	(X)	112501
	%	..	..	50.0	51.7	38.2	35.9	43.3	..	42.1
82. Upholstered household furniture	E.	151	216	142	202	91	42	6	3	..
	V.A.	905	3412	5205	14634	15432	13386	*9772*	(X)	..
	%	44.6	46.8	46.2	48.4	49.9	47.1	47.0	..	..
83. Wire drawn from purchased rods	E.	1	3	2	8	7	19	26	22	7
	V.A.	(X)	61	*67*	755	1287	5828	19526	32810	16193
	%	..	47.5	39.3	38.4	44.3	40.9	40.0	39.9	35.6
84. Wirework not elsewhere classified	E.	183	137	92	101	78	36	34	8	..
	V.A.	1201	2505	3721	8819	14083	13378	26125	14035	..
	%	35.9	38.6	34.9	39.5	38.2	41.0	40.5	56.4	..
85. Women's and misses' dresses (except house dresses)—made in contract factories	E.	282	760	381	62	5	..	..	..	..
	V.A.	3496	25224	23967	7707	1240	..	..	..	..
	%	74.0	76.5	75.9	75.1	70.8	..	..	..	..
86. Women's and misses' dresses (except house dresses) made in inside factories or by jobbers engaging contractors	E.	92	186	197	380	296	203	63	0	..
	V.A.	558	2896	6390	27694	38280	47890	22637	10351	..
	%	48.6	47.4	46.9	45.3	40.8	35.8	34.0	38.7	..
87. Woollen and worsted manufactures—regular factories or jobbers engaging contractors	E.	27	26	36	80	85	126	137	46	20
	V.A.	166	447	1185	5298	13581	34875	75007	56183	76221
	%	51.2	50.1	56.5	56.3	48.8	53.8	51.2	44.4	53.5

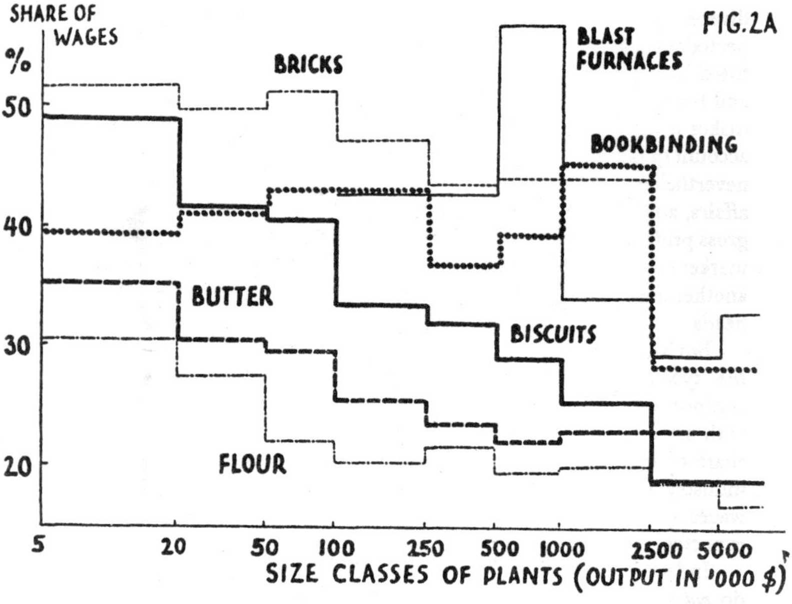

SHARE OF WAGES
%
FIG. 2A
50
40
30
20
BRICKS
BLAST FURNACES
BOOKBINDING
BUTTER
BISCUITS
FLOUR
5
20
50
100
250
500
1000
2500
5000
SIZE CLASSES OF PLANTS (OUTPUT IN '000 $)

SHARE OF WAGES %
FIG. 2B
50
40
30
20
GLASSCONTAINERS
MACHINE TOOLS
ELECTRICAL APPLIANCES
PAINTS
CEMENT
SOAP
5
20
50
100
250
500
1000
2500
5000
SIZE CLASSES OF PLANTS (OUTPUT IN '000 $)

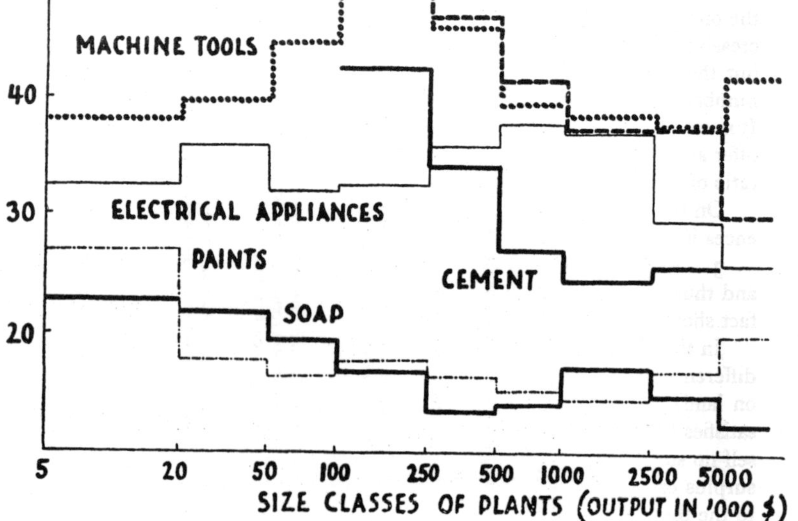

FIGS. 2A and 2B. *Percentage share of wages in value added in different size classes : selected manufacturing industries.* (Size of establishment is measured by gross value of output, plotted on a logarithmic scale.) Data from Table 6.

diverse types of industries. This may account for a good deal of the unexpectedness of the result. The bulk of the remaining adverse cases is constituted by printing, certain clothing industries, leather, timber, meat packing and bread. In all these cases small scale production plays a large role. This makes it likely that the data have been much distorted by the failure to take account of unpaid family labour and home work in small establishments. It is nevertheless possible that these data do reflect to some extent the true state of affairs, and that bigger establishments do not have a differential advantage in gross profits—or even have a disadvantage owing to imperfection of the labour market—in these industries. They may quite likely have an advantage in another form, through cheaper distribution and consequently lower overheads.

But we must be careful not to attribute the increasing share of wages to *the type* of industry. Several types of textile and clothing industry conform quite closely to the prevailing pattern of a decreasing share of wages with size. While the two printing industries (7 and 34) show an increasing share of wages, the closely related and in many ways similar book-binding industry gives a different picture. Bread shows no dependence of the share of wages on size, but the closely related biscuit industry conforms to the expected negative correlation.

Indeed it is an important result of these calculations that in general they do *not* suggest that particular types of industries conform to any particular pattern. Out of the 80 industries which can be used, 58 suggest a negative correlation, 22 suggest a positive correlation or independence. But we do not find a consistent tendency of certain types of industries to belong to the one or to the other group. Large scale economies in production and increasing gross profit margins do not seem to be confined to certain industries, but they make their appearance in the most diverse fields. A considerable number of exceptions do occur, and at least part of them are probably genuine. It must be remembered that economies in purchase and distribution may still offer an advantage to larger units in these cases, which is not reflected in the ratio of wages to value added.

On the whole the data confirm the widespread importance of cost differences in favour of the larger establishments.

3. As differences in cost and profit margins between different plants—and thus presumably between different firms—play a considerable role, this fact should be given its due place in a theory of cost-price relations.

In the classical theory of differential rent, as formulated by Ricardo, cost differences provide the explanation for a surplus (in the specific case, the rent on land). The crucial concept of the theory is the *marginal producer*, who satisfies two conditions: (1) he is the highest cost producer, (2) he has himself no surplus, *i.e.* the price equals his cost. Under these conditions, all the surplus can be explained by the cost differentials. It is, of course, essential to the theory, that the margin is variable: which of the producers is at the margin is determined by the extent of the demand. Costs are also recognised to be variable, at least in the long run, although the existence of cost differentials as such is taken for granted as a fundamental assumption (scarcity of the better land).

These last points have to be stressed particularly when we come to apply the theory to industrial conditions. The 'margin' is particularly variable here. Not only average costs, but also cost differentials, are liable to change. But it is possible to assert, here too, that cost differentials *as such* are of a permanent character. The reason for this is the relative scarcity of big units of capital, which explains why only a limited number of enterprises can make use of the most productive methods, and that, side by side with them, less productive methods are always in use. The scarcity of 'big capital' is by no means invariable—as the scarcity of fertile land in the rather unrealistic textbook case is. On the contrary, big capitals may increase in number and extent. At the same time the opportunities for securing differential cost advantages are not fixed: they are ever changing with the process of technical innovation. Thus there is a complicated process in which the actual 'margin' is in a sense the result rather than the starting point of the analysis. None the less, the fact of systematic cost differentials in favour of the larger units remains as a permanent feature.

If profits are to be explained as a surplus arising from these systematic cost differentials, the concept of a marginal producer is essential.

We may start from the idea that in any industry there is, either *actually*, or *potentially*, a competitive pressure. If this pressure is actual, and sufficiently acute, it will mean a struggle for survival, in which probably the highest cost producer will be eliminated. In this sense we may always call the highest cost producers in an industry the marginal producers. This is a very wide interpretation of the concept of marginal producer. In many industries the marginal producer in this sense of the term will be making considerable profits, which means that the competitive pressure mentioned above is not actual. It may, however, become so under certain circumstances. As long as it is only potential and the marginal producer enjoys a profit, the differential rent theory will obviously be insufficient to explain the level of profits in the industry. The profit of this marginal producer will have to be itself explained, a task which we relegate to a later chapter (Chapter VII).

There are, however, a good many other industries in which the competitive pressure is very acute, and in which there are a number of firms struggling at the margin of existence. In practice this will probably apply to industries where there are many small firms. We call small firms those which can be started and run with a moderate amount of capital. The number of people who can command such a moderate amount of capital is rather greater than the opportunities which are open to firms of this size. These small firms will be competing strongly with each other, and this competition will never allow their remuneration to exceed a certain maximum, at least of we take the average of profits and losses over a business cycle. Now we must, of course, take into account that the costs and profits of small firms are widely dispersed. Quite a number of them enjoy tolerable or even good profits ; others never cover their cost. That these deficit firms are always present in large numbers can be easily explained. Once a firm exists it will carry on as long as it can cover its ' cash-expenses ', that is, expenses which have to be currently met, and could be avoided by closing down. It need not, therefore, cover expenses like depreciation, and may even sell inventories below their cost. The firms which incur losses of this type sooner or later fail, but their place is taken by new ones, who similarly operate at the very margin of existence. Any increase in competitive pressure in the industry will drive out some of these deficit firms and prevent their replacement by new ones; any relaxation of competitive pressure will increase the length of their life, and increase the number of similar high cost firms. We could thus regard these firms as the marginal producers, defined as those which just cover their cash-expenses. The *gross profits* of all other firms could then be treated as differential rents.

We may, however, choose another approach. If we consider *small firms as a group*, good ones and bad ones together, they will on the average probably just ' break even ' : they will cover their cost (on the average of good and bad years) and they will get a remuneration corresponding roughly to the salary which the entrepreneur could get as an employee, with practically no remuneration for his own capital. If we accept this assumption then the group of small firms together can be treated as ' the marginal producer '. They will be marginal in the sense that their net profit is zero—they just cover their cost. The net profit margins of all other producers can then be treated as differential rents in relation to this marginal producer. We are here applying the term marginal producer obviously in a more narrow sense than before, when it was simply the ' highest-cost producer '. To give it a name we might say that the marginal producer is here a ' normal profit producer ' or a ' normal profit firm ', meaning the average of small firms which together have zero net profit.

Now this would seem to be only just good enough for a practical approximation. We can, however, round off the concept quite neatly for theoretical purposes. In fact, the group of smallest firms in an industry where competitive pressure is acute will exactly conform to the conditions described, *i.e.* have a zero net profit, provided only that we define it properly : we must set the limit to the group of smallest firms just wide enough to make their profits on the average zero. With any increase or slackening of competitive pressure the limit of the group will change : the group which constitutes the normal profit firms will be variable. If, for example, all small firms in the usual sense of the word are eliminated, and the competitive pressure is still acute in the industry, then medium firms may become 'normal profit firms '. On the other hand, a considerable slackening of competitive pressure might make even the smaller firms so profitable as a group, that they cease to be ' normal profit firms ', but this case is rather unlikely for the reasons mentioned before.

' Normal profit firms ' are thus by definition a group which has on the average zero net profits, subject to the condition that it must be the smallest firms in the industry. Provided that competitive pressure is acute there will always be such a group of normal profit making firms, even if it is difficult to point them out exactly in practice. It follows that under this condition it is possible to treat all the net profits in the industry as differential rents. At the same time we realise that our problem is only beginning here. The question is how the differential rents are determined, and what regulates the competitive pressure within the industry which is the very force which determines who are to be the marginal, normal profit making producers. It is this question to which we now have to turn.

V. The Pattern of Competition Within an Industry

(a) *The case of an industry with plenty of small producers*

We shall now consider the problem of costs, prices and profit margins for an industry as a whole. In the present paragraph we shall deal with an industry in which the marginal firms are 'small firms', and in which there is a sufficient number of such small firms to account for more than a negligible proportion of the industry's total output. In accordance with the empirical evidence, we assume that owing to economies of large scale the gross profit margin increases if we pass from the lowest to successively higher size classes of firms. For the lowest size class we may assume 'normal profits' as long as it is composed of 'small firms', which require a modest amount of capital and are therefore subject to strong competition by newly entering firms. We have then to discuss the relation of prices, selling cost, and quality of products of the various firms to those of the marginal firm.

The problem is complicated by the fact that there is not a uniform price in the industry which corresponds to the cost of the marginal producer. There is rather a *structure* of prices, corresponding to the different qualities and types of the product. Moreover, even for one and the same quality different firms may charge different prices. The profit margins of intra-marginal firms are thus not determined solely by their differential cost advantage alone, but by other factors as well. In addition, it is of course clear that the 'margin' itself is shifting, either by the elimination of high cost firms, or by the possible entrance of even higher cost firms.

The aim of our analysis is to explain how profit margins in an industry are determined. In dealing with this problem some general guiding principles will be observed. First it must be realised that this is a *long term* problem. We are not interested, therefore, in adjustments which occur over one or two years, as a consequence of boom or slump conditions, but in the trend of development. This implies, secondly, that we cannot base ourselves on the narrow 'static' assumption of given technical methods; on the contrary, we shall take account of the effects of continuing technical progress and cost reductions as an essential part of the development.

Lest the reader be in any confusion about the relative importance of the various assumptions made in what follows, we shall state the two most important ones at the beginning. It is assumed, first, that firms invest only in their own industry. The full rigidity of this assumption will not be maintained to the end, but it will be held throughout that entrepreneurs consider in the first instance investment in their own industry, and depart from this practice only for very strong reasons. Secondly, it is assumed that the increase in entrepreneurial capital of a firm—that is, share capital plus reserves in case of a joint stock company, or entrepreneurs' private capital in case of a private business—is an important inducement for the entrepreneur to invest. The increase of this entrepreneurial capital takes place ordinarily by retaining part of the profits in form of saving, and we shall call this process *internal accumulation*. Thirdly, we assume that the rate of growth of the market is given for the industry as a whole, and can be regarded as a datum.

It is in the nature of the argument that it is not altogether easy to present, and we have to start with a rather sketchy outline.

If there are firms which owing to large scale economies, or, more generally speaking, owing to the adoption of any cost-reducing technical innovations, have greater gross profit margins, and greater net profit margins, than the marginal firms, they will often have a natural tendency to expand relatively to other firms. The reason is that firms with greater profit margins—if we may assume that this also implies a greater profit rate[1]—will accumulate internal funds, and will accumulate them at a rate which is the greater, the greater is their differential advantage. The marginal firms, if they are earning only normal profits, will presumably not accumulate at all, as a group. This internal accumulation will lead the advantageously placed firms to expand, owing to the fact that their first line of investment is in their own industry. This expansion, be it noted, can proceed without increasing the relative share of these firms in the industry. If the rate of expansion of the industry, as a whole, owing to a favourable development (a positive long-term trend) of demand for its products, is at least as great as the expansion to which the favourably placed firms are driven by their internal accumulation, then the share of the latter in their industry will not increase. The share of the small firms will be kept up by a corresponding increase in their number, to make up for their non-existent internal accumulation.

If, however, the rate of internal accumulation of the favourably placed firms, as determined by their differential advantage, is such as to push their expansion *beyond* the rate at which the industry as a whole expands, they will have to secure a greater relative share in the market. To do this, it will be necessary for them to make a special *sales effort;* for, if they sell at the same prices as other firms, provide products of the same quality, and advertise to the same extent, the chances are that they will capture only a proportionate share of the expanding market. They will, therefore, either sell at lower prices than the marginal firms, or engage in quality competition, that is produce

[1] The greater profit margin will mean greater profit rate only if it more than compensates for a possible increase in the ratio of capital to output. For a discussion on this point, see my 'Small and Big Business', Chapter III.

better products which presumably cost more, and sell them at the same price as the marginal firms. Or else they will proceed to advertise or make other sales expenditure on a heavier scale than the marginal firms, which will presumably mean that their sales expenditure per unit of sales will be higher than with the marginal firms.[1]

The first two forms of the sales effort will mean that the differential advantage in the *gross* profit margin, and consequently also in the *net* profit margin, will be reduced. The greater advertisement will reduce the differential advantage in the *net* profit margin only. Thus the sales effort will reduce the differential advantage in the *net* profit margin of the large firms as determined by the technical possibilities of large scale economies in production, distribution and administration. It can, on the other hand, never eliminate these advantages, because they are the very cause of the large firms wanting to expand more quickly, and therefore of the sales effort. We may say that the sales effort which is defined as the sacrifice in the form of reduced prices, or increased production cost, or increased sales cost, per unit of sales, is a function of the desired rate of increase of sales of the large firms in relation to the rate of increase of sales of the industry as a whole, because a greater increase in the large firms' relative share of the market calls for a greater sales effort. The rate of expansion of the large firms depends, however, on the rate of internal accumulation of these firms, which, in turn, depends on their profit margin. Thus, given the rate of expansion of the industry, if the profit margin of some large firms increases above a certain level owing to new technical innovations which allow them to reduce their costs, there will ensue, *via* an increased internal accumulation, an increased sales effort by these firms.

So we conclude that the sales effort will have the tendency *partly* to offset an increase in profit margins brought about by a decrease of costs of some large firms through technical innovations and other methods of increasing productivity adopted by them.

We must now consider the special case which will arise if the internal accumulation of large firms surpasses a certain critical level. The cause of such an increase in internal accumulation would be the adoption of new technical methods which would reduce the costs and increase the profit margins of these large firms, because they could not be adopted by all firms, especially not by small firms. The critical level of which we are speaking is the maximum rate of expansion of large firms, which, given the rate of expansion of the industry, is consistent with an undiminished *absolute* share of the other firms. If the large firms expand at a quicker rate than that indicated by this level, the other firms' *absolute* share must necessarily diminish. There will then be *absolute concentration*, *i.e.* an elimination of a certain number of existing firms.

[1] We have, it is true, to consider the possibility that larger firms may advertise more effectively with the same expenditure per unit of sales, which would be just a case of large scale economies in advertising.

How will this elimination come about? It can only happen if the large firms' sales effort becomes so intensive that other firms are actually losing sales, and are therefore forced to cut prices or increase cost by quality competition and more intensive advertisement. The firms with the highest cost or the lowest financial resilience, which are likely to be found predominantly among the small firms, will not be able to stand the strain and will be forced out of business. It must be stressed that the elimination of firms discussed here is not the temporary elimination which occurs during the slump in every business cycle and which is reversed again in the following boom. We are dealing essentially with a long run phenomenon, and therefore with an elimination which may occur either in boom or slump, but which is *not* reversible, because the price-cost relations established do not permit the re-entry of similar firms.

If the process of elimination of some existing firms is to come to an end, so that a new 'equilibrium'—in the sense that there is no absolute concentration—is reached, then the condition mentioned earlier on has again to be satisfied, *i.e.* the rate of expansion of the expanding firms must again be within certain limits. We should say that the rate of expansion of those expanding firms, multiplied by the proportion which their sales constitute in the sales of the industry as a whole, must not exceed the rate of expansion of the whole industry. If the expansion of these firms depends on their rate of internal accumulation, and this in turn depends on their profit margins, then we must conclude that our condition imposes a limit on the profit margins in the industry. The price-cost adjustment which brought about the process of absolute concentration must have brought about also a reduction of the average profit margins in the industry which had been temporarily raised by cost reductions of the favourably placed firms. These latter firms will probably not have destroyed the additional differential advantage acquired by the new innovations entirely by their sales effort, but they will have brought down the average profit margins in the industry, at the expense of other firms, to a level which makes the rate of internal accumulation of all firms again consistent with the rate of growth of the industry.

The argument—which at this stage remains necessarily sketchy—can be represented in graphical form (Fig. 3). Imagine that the total output of the industry is plotted on the abscissa, and that the ordinate measures the average unit cost at which each small part of the output is produced.[1] The output of the various firms is arranged in the declining order of their costs, exactly in the manner of the rent theory. (We have to assume a very large number of firms to be able to work with continuous curves.) The cost curve for the industry will then be described by *CD*. For each small part of the output the price at which it is sold may also be plotted on the ordinate. As the price is not the same for the whole industry, but tends to be lower, the lower the cost of the firm, we get a declining price curve *DE*. The decline of the price curve will

[1] We are assuming that costs are calculated on the basis of the 'planned' degree of utilisation.

not be as strong as that of the cost curve. Consequently the *profit margin*, which is the difference between the two curves, will be increasing with decreasing cost. The sales effort will be measured by *EF* if we assume a homogeneous product. The total profit margin in the industry will then be the area *CDE*. Now assume that the 'progressive firms' reduce their cost.

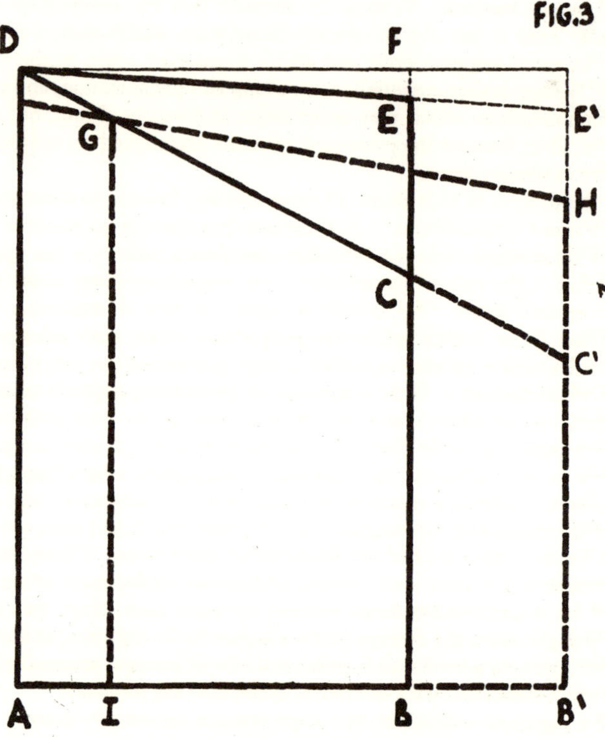

FIG. 3. *The squeezing of the profit margin.*

For simplicity's sake let us assume that this cost reduction affects only additional capacity which they build to satisfy an expanding demand in the industry. The industry's output will thus increase from *AB* to *AB'*, and the unit cost of this new output will be lower than the cost of any of the other output. If we imagine the price curve to be prolonged to *E'*, then the profit margin on the new output will increase up to *C'E'* for the last lot. We must conclude that the average profit margin, in proportion to cost or to price, in the industry has increased. Now according to our argument, if this increase surpasses a certain level, *i.e.* if it leads to more internal accumulation in the industry than can be used for the purpose of expansion of the industry as a whole, then a competitive struggle sets in. The price of the lowest cost producer is reduced from *B'E* to *B'H*, and the price pressure is passed on successively to the higher cost producers, so that the whole price curve *DE'*, is shifted downwards to *GH*. This involves an elimination of the highest cost producers *AI*. As a result, the profit margin will be the area *C'GH*. This need not be the same, in proportion to cost, as the original profit margin *CDE*,[1] but it will be certainly less than the profit margin *C'DE'*.

The graphical illustration serves to bring out the interaction of two fundamental factors: the cost reductions by progressive firms, which tend to increase the profit margin; and the explosive force of an excessive internal accumulation which leads to elimination of high cost firms, and tends to reduce the profit margin again.

This description of the competitive struggle consequent upon cost reductions achieved by some firms is plausible in the light of what we know of the development of capitalism. We know that in most industries productivity has continuously increased and costs have been reduced by technical innovations, etc.[2] We know also that some firms have been leading in this process. In the following we shall refer to these firms which initiate new methods as 'progressive firms'. They need not necessarily be the largest firms, and it is possible that their methods may be imitated by some other firms later; but it is essential that not all firms are capable of adopting these methods. We know finally that, by and large, prices have been to a large extent adapted to costs. If they had not been, we could not fail to notice a continuous and considerable divergence between the cost of labour and raw materials on the one hand and the value of the product on the other hand, and consequently a strong tendency of the share of labour in the distribution of the product to fall. This tendency has not been generally observed, and the described mechanism of competition is a plausible explanation. Nor is this anything new. Rather less well-known, however, is the relation between the rate of expansion of the industry, the rate of internal accumulation and the profit margin, which the preceding analysis suggests. We have to examine this relation somewhat more closely. The contention was that an increased profit margin in an industry will lead to an increased rate of internal accumulation; and that this in turn will lead to an increase in output capacity, which, if it is greater than the expansion of the industry's sales, must lead to 'absolute concentration'.

The connection between profit margin and rate of internal accumulation of a firm is fairly straightforward. If the profit margin increases owing to the adoption of new technical methods which give a differential cost advantage then the *profit rate* on the capital employed will also increase, unless there is a

[1] Because the ratio of capital to output in the industry may have increased as a result of the adoption of the new methods, so that a greater profit margin will be necessary to give the same rate of profit as before.

[2] See S. Fabricant, *Employment in Manufacturing Industries, 1899–1937*.

rise in capital intensity which compensates for the increase in profits. If the profit rate on the capital employed increases, then the *net* profit rate (exclusive of interest paid) on the entrepreneur's funds will also increase, unless there is a change in the proportion of capital borrowed, which we shall later show to be unlikely. If the net profit rate on entrepreneurs' funds increases, we may assume that the proportion saved out of profits increases too.[1] It follows that the increase in the profit margin, except in so far as it is compensated by an increased capital intensity, will lead to an increase in the rate of internal accumulation.

At this point it is necessary to clarify the concept of net profit margin. The net profit margin can, in fact, change for two quite different reasons: either because of a change in utilisation of capacity, with an otherwise unchanged structure of costs and prices; or the net profit margin can change at a *given level of utilisation of capacity*. The latter type of change will take place, for example, if gross profit margins change, while overhead costs at any given level of utilisation of capacity remain constant. We shall have to be very careful not to confuse the two types of change in net profit margins. It was clear from the context that in the preceding argument we have always talked about the second type of change. In order to avoid confusion, we shall in future always use the term '*net profit margin at a given level of capacity utilisation*'.

We now have to see how the increased internal accumulation can cause the firm to expand. The increase in funds need not lead to a corresponding expansion of equipment, if the ratio of capital assets to own funds (the gearing ratio) is changed. Again, the expansion of equipment need not mean a corresponding change in production capacity, if the capital intensity is changed. And finally, the resulting change in sales depends on whether the degree of utilisation is changed. This can be illustrated by very simple algebraical equations. Let us define the gearing ratio as the ratio of capital assets to the firm's own capital where capital assets include all capital invested in the business, but not holdings of bonds, and own capital includes share capital plus reserves in the case of joint stock companies, and private capital in the case of non-incorporated firms. Then it is clear that

$$\textit{capital assets} = \textit{own funds} \times \textit{gearing ratio}$$

Let us define the ratio of capital assets to output per annum at full use of capacity as Capital Intensity. Then we can see that

$$\textit{Capacity Output} = \textit{Capital Assets} \times \textit{Reciprocal of Capital Intensity}$$

Let us define Utilisation of Capacity as the ratio of sales to capacity output. Then

$$\textit{Sales} = \textit{Capacity Output} \times \textit{Utilisation of Capacity}$$

If these equations are combined we obtain the following relation.

[1] In accordance with the assumption made by M. Kalecki that capitalists' saving, in proportion to their capital, is a (positive) function of the rate of profit. See *Studies in Economic Dynamics*, p. 52.

Sales = Utilisation of Capacity × Reciprocal of Capital Intensity × Gearing Ratio × Own Funds

or in algebraical terms :

$$s = u \cdot \frac{1}{k} \cdot g \cdot C \tag{4}$$

where s = sales

u = degree of capacity utilisation

k = capital intensity

g = gearing ratio

C = entrepreneur's capital

If a change takes place in the above magnitudes, then the relation must still hold.

Let us adopt the following notation :

α = proportionate rate of internal accumulation.

g' = proportionate change in gearing ratio (ratio of capital assets to the firm's own funds).

k' = proportionate change in capital intensity (ratio of total capital invested to output capacity).

u' = proportionate change in utilisation of capacity (ratio of sales to production capacity).

R = proportionate rate of expansion of sales.

Then we can write

$$(1+R) = (1+u')\frac{1}{1+k'}(1+g')(1+\alpha). \tag{5}$$

If we choose the time period sufficiently small, so that the proportionate changes are small, then (as the products of R, u', etc., become negligibly small) we can write with good approximation :

$$R = u' - k' + g' + \alpha. \tag{6}$$

The above equations, and therefore also the last one, can be applied to an industry as a whole provided it is in ' equilibrium '—in the sense that there is no absolute concentration going on. The equation for the industry is then obtained simply by adding up the equations for individual firms. If, however, elimination of firms has been going on over the period considered, then we can apply this equation to the firms *remaining* at the end of the period. The proportionate increase in the sales of these remaining firms (R') results then from two factors : the proportionate increase in the sales of the whole industry, R, and the proportion of the eliminated firms' sales to the industry's sales, c. We can write, therefore,

$$(1+R') = (1+R)(1+c). \tag{7}$$

If we apply equation (6) to the remaining firms, we must replace R by

R' in this equation; but as R', according to the relation just given, is approximately equal to $R+c$, we obtain

$$R = u' + g' - k' - c + \alpha. \tag{8}$$

In our previous analysis the contention was that for all firms taken together the rate of internal accumulation is limited by the rate of expansion of the industry, on the assumption that the firms invest only in the same industry. That is to say that, if progressive firms by introducing innovations and therefore reducing their cost and increasing their profit margins bring about an increase of profit margins in the industry as a whole, and therefore an increase of the rate of internal accumulation α, *above* the level which is just sufficient to finance the required expansion of the industry, then an explosive force will make itself felt: the progressive firms will drive out weak firms, so as to gain room for their own expansion. This can be easily described in terms of equation (8): the (temporary) increase in α above the equilibrium level will be compensated by the appearance of a positive c, a certain rate of elimination of existing firms. If the system is to return to equilibrium, *i.e.* if absolute concentration is to cease again after a while, then the item c must become zero, and α must return again to the 'equilibrium level'. That means that the average level of profit margins in the industry which had been temporarily raised by cost reductions of progressive firms, must be gradually reduced again by a competitive struggle of which the 'absolute concentration' is only one aspect.

The decisive contention is that *in equilibrium* the rate of internal accumulation is determined largely by the rate of expansion of the industry. From equation (6) it is seen that this connection holds good, unless there are compensating changes in the factors g', k' or u', which would make it possible for α to grow with a given rate of expansion R of the industry. Are such compensating effects likely to take place ?

With regard to capital intensification, this possibility must at once be admitted. If the rate of capital intensification k' rises permanently to a higher level, in other words, if the increase of capital per unit of output capacity proceeds more *quickly*, then α may increase correspondingly. Capital intensification provides an outlet of funds in the industry, just like the expansion of the industry does.

What about compensating changes in the other items ? The most obvious possibility is a fall in the gearing ratio, which might offset an increase in α. In other words, the rate of internal accumulation might increase without corresponding increase in investment, if the additional funds are used to repay debts, or to invest in bonds which comes to the same, and thus to reduce the gearing ratio.

Whether this will happen or not depends entirely on the profitability of new investment and on the risks connected with it. If new investment opportunities are available at constant or increasing rates of profit then there is no reason why the gearing ratio should fall; it might even increase. On the other hand, if the profit rate on new investment is decreasing then the gearing ratio might fall. Now the situation which we are envisaging is that of an expanding industry in which firms which already enjoy a differential cost advantage manage to bring about further cost reductions by making use of technical innovations. These cost reductions make it possible for them to engage in a sales effort so as to enlarge their market, while still retaining some of the differential cost advantage due to the new innovations, sufficient to increase their rate of profit. This presupposes that the enlarging of their market by a sales effort (price reductions, etc.) is not too difficult, which in general can be supposed if there are a sufficient number of firms with high cost, which can be squeezed out of the industry easily by the sales effort. Given these assumptions, it is safe to say that the firms carrying through the innovations will be induced to expand investment in proportion to their increased internal accumulation, rather than repay debts and reduce the gearing ratio. In fact, the differential advantage brought about by the new innovations has a dual function: on the one hand it provides the funds for greater investment: the internal accumulation ' pushes forward the barriers set to investment plans by the limited accessibility of the capital market and increasing risk '.[1] On the other hand, it provides sufficient, or even increased, profitability for new investment, because the reduction in production cost provides the means for overcoming the ' barrier of imperfect competition '.

It is true that to the increased profit rate of our progressive firms there must ultimately correspond a reduction in profit rates of other firms. This is because the ultimate result of the competition must be a reduction of the rate of internal accumulation of all firms (after elimination of the superfluous firms) to the former level, consistent with the given rate of expansion of the industry. Thus the profit rate for all firms together, assuming the propensity to save for different firms to be equal must also be at the same level as before. An unchanged profit rate for all firms on balance is however sufficient to make it likely that the average gearing ratio will not fall.[2]

It remains to consider the degree of utilisation of capacity. The progressive firms which make use of new methods may increase their ' planned ' degree of excess capacity, but not to an extent which could offset their increased accumulation. It is utterly unlikely that they would merely ' invest in excess capacity '. There is, however, a possibility that the other firms could experience an ' unplanned ' reduction in their degree of utilisation.

In the first instance, they are bound to do so, because the sales effort of the progressive firms tends to take away sales from all other firms. There are, generally speaking, two possibilities. In the one case the sales pressure coming from the progressive firms is distributed over all firms, and their reaction to it is passive endurance, so that they all experience a fall in utilisation of capacity. In this case an ' absolute concentration ' is not altogether

[1] M. Kalecki, *Studies in Economic Dynamics*, p. 61.

[2] All that is required for my argument could really be proved on the less stringent assumption that an increase in internal accumulation will not be *fully* offset by a reduction of the gearing ratio; it will thus stimulate investment, though the gearing ratio need not remain constant.

certain, and will in any case be slow. In the other case, the sales pressure coming from the progressive firms leads to greater efforts on the part of all but the weakest of the remaining firms, who in their turn cut prices, improve quality, etc. The sales pressure is thus passed on and concentrated on the marginal firms who are in this way eliminated. Whether the second alternative will materialise depends on the existence of sufficient cost differentials between the firms.[1] In the type of industry which we assume here this condition is realised; there are varying degrees of competitive advantage between firms, expressed by the varying magnitude of their net profit margin at a given level of capacity utilisation. We assume, therefore, that by elimination of a sufficient number of marginal firms the remaining firms succeed in re-establishing their 'planned' level of capacity utilisation. Thus we conclude that under the conditions assumed here changes in capacity utilisation are not likely to provide an outlet for an increased internal accumulation.

The conclusion which emerges from this picture of the 'ideal' pattern of competition in an industry is the following: the rate of internal accumulation is limited by the rate of expansion of the industry and the rate of capital intensification. The net profit margin at given levels of capacity utilisation (given the propensity to save) is therefore also limited by these factors. This applies to conditions where the process of absolute concentration is already over, as we have up to now supposed. If, however, new innovations and therefore cost reductions are again made, the process of concentration may well continue. As long as it does, there is a further 'outlet' for internal accumulation. It will be further determined, therefore, by the extent to which existing firms and their equipment are continuously eliminated.

So far we have only demonstrated that there is an *upper limit* to internal accumulation, and consequently to the profit margin at given utilisation. But will this upper limit be reached? This depends on additional factors. If there is a fairly steady and not inconsiderable technical progress in the industry, and if the rate of expansion is not too great, then it follows that the average profit margin will rise, up to the limit permitted by the above considerations. Continuous cost reductions introduced by progressive firms, and spreading to other firms, but not to the small firms which are for technical reasons unable to apply them, will increase the average profit margin to the possible maximum. On the other hand, if the rate of expansion of the industry is exceptionally great, the internal accumulation within the industry may become insufficient to finance the expansion. The competitive pressure will relax and marginal firms will increase their profits above the level of 'normal profits'. As a consequence new firms will be drawn into the industry. In this case the average profit margin will obviously not reach the

[1] See M. Kalecki, The Supply Curve under Imperfect Competition, *Review of Economic Studies*, Vol. III (1940), p. 101.

maximum determined by the rate of expansion, because part of the expansion will be accounted for by newly entering firms and by an increase in the degree of utilisation.

The case just considered shows that it will not always be possible to restore and maintain a given 'planned' degree of capacity utilisation. If the expansion of the market is very quick, then utilisation will increase above the planned level. In order to get the ideal case of a constant (long-run) degree of utilisation we must really suppose that there is always a latent tendency for excess capacity to appear, owing to a continuous emergence of new profit differentials which tend to increase internal accumulation in the industry, and thus push the growth of equipment ahead of the growth of the market; and we must further suppose that this tendency for excess capacity to appear is continuously offset by aggressive competition which eliminates undesired excess capacity as soon as it appears. This is certainly a very special case, but one of considerable theoretical interest.

The conclusion is then that the rate of internal accumulation and consequently the net profit margin at given levels of capacity utilisation will *tend* to a (maximum) level determined by the rate of growth of the industry, the rate of capital intensification and the rate at which existing production capacity is being eliminated. This amounts to saying that the share of net profit at given utilisation in the product is determined in such a way as to provide sufficient funds for the investment in the industry. This is a surprising conclusion, and it must at once be stressed again, that it does not apply to the short run. It would not apply to the changes taking place over a boom or a slump where the degree of capacity utilisation is obviously the elastic factor. It would only apply in the long run, that is, in statistical terms, to the trend values of the various factors, or to the secular development. Nor have we as yet said anything about how generally applicable this pattern of competition is in reality.

It is, however, appropriate here to make a few general points. Firstly, our analysis has brought out the connections between competition and accumulation of capital, which were familiar to classical economists and to Karl Marx, but which have been lost sight of in recent times.

Secondly, it provides us with a theory of concentration. I have tried elsewhere[1] to explain the process of 'absolute concentration' and its inevitability by assuming *a priori* that the share of profit in the product is limited, and the rate of profit therefore cannot increase in the course of capitalist development. On this assumption the necessity for absolute concentration was easy to demonstrate. But this sort of reasoning puts the cart before the horse. The present analysis shows that the limitation to the share of profits is itself the consequence of the aggressive, dynamic character of internal accumulation, which at the same time brings about the 'absolute concentration'. Absolute concentration and limitation on net profit margins at given levels of utilisation are really only two aspects of the same thing,

[1] Risk and Capitalist Enterprise, *Oxford Economic Papers*, No. 7.

and the cause of both is the competitive pressure of the internal accumulation of funds.

The pattern of competition in an industry which we have described is thus not without interest, but how far does it correspond to reality?

The most restrictive of the assumptions which we have made is that in the industry concerned there are small marginal producers with only 'normal' profit, which therefore can be squeezed out relatively easily by a sales effort of the progressive firms. It is necessary to assume, too, that these small marginal producers account for more than a negligible share in the output, as compared with the share of the firms which expand, otherwise they would all too soon disappear. These assumptions are most essential, because on them depends the possibility of the 'progressive' firms increasing their investment at constant or increasing rates of profit.

(b) *The case of an industry where entry is difficult*

In reality, there will be many industries where the marginal producers—those with the highest cost—have 'abnormal' profits. Such a situation seems *a priori* quite likely where the marginal producers are producing on a scale, and require capital equipment of a type, which makes it necessary for each of them to have substantial capital, more than what we call 'small firms' require. In these circumstances it becomes much more difficult to squeeze out some of the marginal producers. Imagine that this should happen by a price cut. The marginal firms can always offset the effects of a price cut on the part of the progressive firms by an absolute price cut of the same order. The absolute price difference between the two groups of firms will then be the same as before, and if we assume that the imperfection of competition, the ease with which the products of the two groups of firms are substituted for each other by the customers, depends on the *absolute difference* in prices, then the competitive situation is clearly the same as before, *i.e.* the sales effort of the progressive firms will have been nullified, and the division of sales between them and the marginal firms will remain unchanged.[1] The price cut of the progressive firms must therefore be greater than the net profit margin of the marginal firms at the level of capacity utilisation which the latter regard as normal, in order to make it impossible for these marginal firms to nullify the sales effort of the progressive firms.

In addition we have to remember that, as the marginal firms in our case are not small, they will often have a certain measure of financial resilience, and hence a greater staying power than small firms would have. The sales effort required would thus be considerable and unless the cost reductions achieved by the 'progressive' firms are very great, the process of squeezing out would involve a considerable reduction of profit margins and profit rates

[1] The assumption that substitution depends on the *absolute* price difference between firms is rather arbitrary. If imperfection is due to transport cost it will hold good; in other cases, it may be rather the *relative* price difference which matters. As long as the price differences between firms are not large, it will, however, make no great difference whether we work with absolute or relative price differences.

in the industry. This means, however, that it will not happen, because the profit incentive for expansion of equipment will be missing. The sales effort required for expansion would be so big that it would more than offset the differential advantage secured by innovations.

The situation is not likely to be fundamentally different if the sales effort is by way of advertising or quality competition. In both cases the marginal firms can retaliate, because their profit margin gives them sufficient room to increase advertising, or improve quality in their turn. The sales effort required will therefore again be considerably greater than in the case of the 'ideal pattern' and unless the cost reductions achieved by innovations of the progressive firms are very big, the squeezing out competitors and the simultaneous squeezing of the net profit margin at given levels of utilisation will not happen, because it would lead to a reduction of the profit rate even for the progressive firm.

We conclude that in this case the working of competition as previously described is considerably impaired; it may work again only after the differential advantage of progressive firms has reached a certain limit which enables them to afford the sales effort required for squeezing out marginal competitors. This possibility is of considerable practical importance. It means that the process of absolute concentration and squeezing of profit margins characteristic of the 'ideal pattern of competition' *can* work also in an industry where the marginal producers are not 'small' in the usual sense of the word. Medium, or even fairly big firms might thus be reduced to the level of 'normal profits', if the competitive pressure in the industry is strong enough, that is, if the progressive firms achieve a sufficiently big cost differential. Normal profits are thus not exclusively the characteristic of small firms, but marginal firms in any industry may be brought into the same position, provided only that the competitive pressure is strong enough. It is clear, however, that where marginal firms are fairly big, it will take some time until the differential cost advantage of progressive firms reaches the point at which it becomes possible to exert a serious pressure on these marginal firms. Up to that point the net profit margins at given levels of utilisation in the industry are free to rise, independently of the determining factors of growth and capital intensification. The increased internal accumulation will in this case lead to a reduction of the gearing ratio.

This case is realised most clearly in oligopolistic industries where each of a few producers accounts for a substantial share of the market. It does not matter whether there is a number of small firms besides, if all together they only account for a small part of the total output. The profit rates in all the big firms will be 'abnormal' and, compared with their absolute level, the difference in the profit margins of the individual firms will often be less important. In any case, these big firms are likely to have a certain financial strength and the struggle for elimination would also for this reason be extremely prolonged and costly. For this reason the internal force of competition, due to internal accumulation, *in general* will not work at all in these industries to keep net profit margins at given level of utilisation down to a limit.

We must, however, now introduce a new factor. We have hitherto assumed that all investment is done within the industry. But it is possible that the funds accumulated by firms are used to establish new enterprises in other industries. Thus an outlet for the funds for investment in capital equipment is found. Simultaneously we find then that in each industry there is a competition from new funds entering the industry from outside, setting up new enterprises, and in this way affecting the price structure. How strongly will the influence of this type of competition work to keep profit margins limited ?

The crucial question here again is the incentive to invest. Let us take first the possibility of new entry in one of the above mentioned oligopolistic industries. The difficulty is at least as great as that of expansion by one of the existing firms at the expense of the others. The magnitude of the ruling profit margins is a measure of the height of the wall which has to be scaled by the competitive sales effort of the newly entering firm, if it wants to eliminate existing firms. If, on the other hand, the incoming firm merely shares the market with the others, there will be a reduction in utilisation of capacity, and profit rates will decline on this account, but the net profit margins at given levels of utilisation of capacity will remain unchanged. There will be no squeezing of profit margins in this sense. The level of existing profit rates in an oligopolistic industry is therefore far from being a measure of the profitability to be expected for investment by a new firm. Unless the new firm can secure very considerable differential advantages from new innovations, the profit rate to be expected will be considerably lower and the incentive to invest is therefore weak. In general, the prospects for competition by outside capital in such an industry, and consequently for squeezing of profit margins, are rather limited, though they still exist.

What about the possibilities of outside capital funds entering ' competitive ' industries, where there are marginal producers with normal profits only ? If the ' surplus ' funds accumulating in oligopolistic industries find their way into those other industries, they might squeeze profit margins there, and thus the pattern of competition might still in some way work for the economy as a whole. Although entry of outside funds into these ' competitive ' industries is much easier than into oligopolistic industries, there is still a more general difficulty involved. The factor of imperfect competition works even more strongly against the setting up of a new firm than against the expansion of an existing one. It is more difficult for a firm to start from scratch and build up a market, than it is for an existing firm to expand. Above all, it needs considerable time, and in the interval the new firm will not make profits, but even incur losses. The necessity of waiting for a market to be built up can be avoided, if in the first instance an existing firm and its equipment is taken over, which requires payment for the goodwill, but at least saves time. This in practice seems indeed the most frequent way by which entrepreneurial funds enter a new industry. In any case a substantial additional sales cost is required for a new firm, and that impedes the flow of entrepreneurial funds between industries. This factor justifies the assumption which has been made at the start, that entrepreneurs prefer in the first place to invest in their own industry. It is a factor which weakens the incentive to invest outside one's own industry. To this has to be added the additional risk which faces entrepreneurs entering an industry with which they are not familiar.[1]

Summarising, we may say that in industries where the marginal producers have 'abnormal' profits, the competitive effect of the internal accumulation is considerably impaired, owing to the magnitude of the sales effort required to push out marginal producers. The internal accumulation therefore tends to exceed the amount required for expansion of capital equipment in these industries. The flow of the 'surplus' funds into other industries is impeded by the additional effort required for entering new lines which weakens the incentive to invest for the owners of these funds. The automatic limitation of the rate of internal accumulation, and thus of the profit margins at given levels of utilisation of capacity by the rate of investment is seriously disturbed. Oligopoly is grit thrown into the mechanism of competition previously described.

VI. Selling Cost and Quality Competition

1. In the preceding chapter selling costs have been dealt with only in one of their aspects. They have been considered as one of the methods by which more efficient producers try to gain a larger share of the market at the expense of their weaker rivals, and have been treated as an alternative to the method of price cutting. This is, however, not the only aspect of selling costs. It is fairly certain that there are many industries in which all producers incur selling costs, including those which are, as it were, struggling at the margin of existence. From this it appears that selling costs may be part and parcel of the cost of the marginal producer, which determines the price, or rather the system of prices, in the industry. We have, therefore, to consider the problem of selling costs in more detail.

Selling cost is a theoretical concept, and to ascertain it statistically is not an easy and straightforward matter. What statistics and cost accounting of entrepreneurs offer us directly is rather the *cost of distribution*, a much wider concept. It includes all the costs of distributing and selling, as opposed to producing, the commodity or service in question. The Census of Business of the United States, for example, includes in distribution cost of manufacturers the pay of employees engaged in selling, advertising, sales promotion, credit, invoicing, installing and servicing of goods sold, as well as travelling expenses of salesmen, advertising, credit and collection expense, and the allocation of a portion of overhead cost. In a wider sense, the cost of transportation and storage may also be included in distribution costs.

[1] See M. Kalecki, *Studies in Economic Dynamics*, p. 62.

Now, theoretically, the cost of distribution may be divided into two parts. On the one hand there are the distributive costs proper, which have to be incurred for what may be called technical reasons, whoever in practice bears them, manufacturer, wholesaler or retailer. The goods have to be packed, consigned, stored, transported, and a whole apparatus necessary for an orderly distribution and collecting payment has to be maintained. The technique of this distribution may change, just as the technique of production. Distribution costs proper may thus vary, perhaps decrease with increasing efficiency of the technique; but their character as technically determined costs is thereby unimpaired. On the other hand there are distribution costs which are not technically necessary, but which are incurred by the individual firm for the purpose of enlarging its market. They may also be incurred by a group of firms, or an industry, to enlarge the market of this group or industry, but this case is probably of smaller importance. These are called selling costs. The peculiarity of these costs is at once obvious if we consider that in the case of all other costs like production cost, and distribution cost proper, the predominant endeavour of entrepreneurs is to reduce them, whereas in the case of selling cost this is not the overruling preoccupation of entrepreneurs. Rather do they seem, sometimes, to increase them intentionally.

The distinction which has been introduced by the authorities on the subject[1] is perhaps not as easy as it looks at first sight. Where selling costs of a certain type, *e.g.* advertising, have become the accepted practice in an industry, it may be as necessary for the individual firm to incur them as it is to incur production costs, because they could simply not exist without incurring them. It would probably be impossible, ordinarily, to sell cigarettes without advertising. We can get to the bottom of the problem only by realising that it is a matter of social organisation. Selling costs are bound up with the existence of competing individual firms, and competing private industries. They would not be necessary if there were no competing individual entrepreneurs, but socialised production, whereas distribution costs would be necessary even then. A great part of selling costs in an industry would become unnecessary already, if the industry were owned entirely by one single controlling agency, although the part of selling costs which is due to competition between industries would still remain.

The sense in which selling costs are not 'necessary' can thus be well understood from this point of view. It still remains a difficult matter to carry through the distinction in practice, quite apart from the inadequacy of statistical material. Some types of costs can be assigned without hesitation to selling costs: advertising is pure selling cost. More difficult is the case of commercial travellers and sales branches, which can in part be considered necessary distribution cost, but which in practice contain a very large element of selling cost. The characteristic of selling costs in all cases is that they are incurred not in order to render a service to the buyer, but in order to *persuade*

[1] Cf. Chamberlin, *Theory of Monopolistic Competition*, p. 117 *seq.*

him to buy from the particular source. The main forms of persuasion are either the impersonal mass appeal—advertisement—or the personal, individual persuasion—by agents, salesmen and demonstration.

2. The theory of selling costs can be based on the simplest possible considerations. Why are selling costs incurred at all? An entrepeneur who can afford an aggressive sales policy, having, for example, a sufficient margin of profit, has two alternative possibilities of 'pushing' his sales: he can either cut his price,[1] or he can incur selling costs. If he chooses the latter, it proves that he must regard it as the superior method of expanding his market in the circumstances. That is, an entrepreneur who incurs any selling cost at all must think that a certain percentage cut in prices is less efficient in promoting sales than the sacrifice of the same percentage, calculated on his expected sales, in the form of selling expenditure.

Now if we can assume that the reactions of buyers are, within a certain range, *symmetrical*, or to put it in the terminology of current theory, if the individual demand curve is continuous, then an important conclusion can be drawn at once: it must be possible for a firm to increase its price by a certain proportion and use the margin gained in this way for additional selling expenses with a resulting net advantage in the form of an increased sales volume. The extent of this resulting net effect on sales volume will depend on the degree to which selling expenditure is superior as a method of pushing sales to a price cut of the same extent.

It is plausible to assume that in the case of many commodities, a relatively small price cut will have little or no effect on sales volume, whereas a selling expenditure of the same magnitude in proportion to sales will have some effect. The superiority of the 'selling' method over the method of price cutting will be marked. It is equally plausible to assume that if we consider greater and greater selling cost ratios, the effect of corresponding price cuts is bound to become more important, and the superiority of the selling method over the price cutting method will thus decline with an increase in the ratio of selling expenditure; a point will sooner or later be reached where the superiority of selling methods over price cutting becomes doubtful, and beyond that, price cutting will be more effective than selling methods. In other words, the relative effectiveness of selling methods as compared with a corresponding price cut declines as the amount of selling expenditure in proportion to sales is increased. On the basis of this simple hypothesis we can understand how selling costs lead to an increase in prices, and where the limit to this increase is to be found. A firm may, theoretically, increase its selling cost, and finance this cost by a corresponding price increase, up to the point where selling methods cease to be superior to the price cutting method.

How is this *limit*, to which selling cost may raise prices, determined? Is it determined only by the business men's ideas and considerations, which may be arbitrary, or is it influenced also by actual reactions of the buyers?

[1] Provided that this possibility is not excluded by the peculiar form of the market—price agreements, etc.—a case to which we shall return later.

We can eliminate the arbitrary factor entirely in an abstract example: if there are a considerable number of competitors and all have just 'normal' profits, and if we may assume them to be sufficiently independent in their ideas, then they might start by all having different policies, *i.e.* incur different amounts of sales cost. With such a fairly large number of competitors the principle of natural selection will operate, and those who have incurred too much selling cost, and driven their prices up too much will find that they lose. The result will be that business men in this industry, by a process of trial and error, will find out the limit to which they can, with advantage, incur selling cost and raise prices. This limit is thus not arbitrary, but dependent on the reaction of the market.

In reality this mechanism works hardly as smoothly as that. In all industries where the number of competitors is limited, it does not apply at all, because the 'selection' cannot operate among a small number; the extent to which selling cost and prices will be raised in such industries will in fact very largely depend on the whim of the entrepreneurs. Only in industries with many firms can the actual market reactions have a strong influence. The most important qualification is here that the process of finding out about the limit mentioned is a very long run affair. Arbitrary elements will therefore no doubt have an influence. But it may be presumed that the influence of buyers' actual reactions is sufficiently important in those industries with large numbers of competitors, and we may then conclude that there exists a limit to which selling cost and prices can be raised.

What is the basis for the fundamental assumption of a superiority of 'selling methods' over price cutting? At the outset we have argued that this superiority must exist at least in the minds of business men, otherwise they would not incur any selling cost, but prefer price cutting except where this is impossible. But there is a valid argument that the superiority of the selling methods exists also *in fact*. It is based, as is well-known, on the imperfect knowledge of buyers about the alternative sources of supply and their relative incapacity of comparing the relative cheapness of the various competing products, in other words on the impossibility or impracticability of rational calculation on the side of the buyers. To this may be added, that apart from not being able to, buyers may even not want to calculate and compare rationally; they have irrational preferences.

This absence of rational comparison—within certain limits—on the side of the buyers is very largely assisted by differences in the products of the various firms. When different types and qualities of the goods exist it becomes impossible for the buyer to decide strictly which one is cheaper.[1] At the same time the existence of these qualitative differences favours the appearance of irrational buyers' preferences. Thus, quality differences will make the buyer insensitive against price competition, within certain limits. And these limits will be the wider, the less easy a rational comparison between

[1] Except where the quality difference can be reduced to a quantitative one which is easy to ascertain; this case is, in effect, the same as that of a homogeneous product.

the qualities becomes. Under these conditions the method of persuading the buyer of the relative advantages of a certain quality becomes obviously superior to the method of price competition. It then becomes possible within limits to increase selling cost and add this increase on to the price.

The limit of this process, the maximum amount of selling cost in proportion to sales which a marginal seller with no differential advantage can incur, will depend on the nature of the commodity. The greater the difficulty of rational comparison between the various qualities, the wider will be the limits within which price competition is inferior to selling methods, the greater therefore the extent to which selling cost can be incurred and financed out of increased prices. In the case of a commodity which is homogeneous, or where quality differences can be easily reduced to a measurable quantitative difference, the selling method should be superior only within very narrow limits and the selling cost incurred very small. Where a diversity of qualities and types exists, but their advantages can still be judged in rational terms, although it is rather difficult for the buyer to do so, the margin of selling costs will be much wider than in the first case. Machines, or various types of electrical equipment, for example, can be judged by their performance, but it is very difficult for the buyer to do so, and he will often find out about it only after it is too late. In those cases, finally, where the quality difference cannot be judged rationally, as with manufactured foods, beverages and cosmetics, or where the ignorance of buyers is necessarily very great, as with patent medicines, the extent to which selling cost may be increased will be greatest.

3. The limited ability of buyers to compare and judge the quality, as well as irrational preferences, lead to a phenomenon which has attracted much attention, the conscious endeavour of business men to offer types and qualities which are different from those of their competitors. This is called product differentiation. It is much the same as what business men call quality competition, if only we stretch this latter term far enough to include attempts to offer not technically better qualities, but goods which in some way or other at least appear to be of superior or preferable quality. We see, therefore, that once the buyers' competence to judge and compare qualities *rationally* is limited, diversity of types and qualities appears automatically. To produce a better, or seemingly 'better', quality at a given price, even if it costs more to produce, will commend itself to a firm, provided that it has a greater effect on the sales volume than a price cut of the same order would have. This condition will probably be realised, if buyers' judgment is defective in the way described. The consequence will be that in such an industry price competition will be, within certain limits, replaced by quality competition: firms will strive to create better, or supposedly 'better' qualities at a cost, and add this cost to the price. The limit of this process is again given by the defectiveness of buyers' judgment. This is, of course, not constant; in the case of machines or equipment, for example, the knowledge and ability to judge the performance may increase as the use of the

machine becomes more widespread, and price competition may then gain ground again.

It would be futile to treat the case of quality competition separately and apart from the case of selling methods such as advertising, dealt with before. In fact, the two not only arise from the same conditions, but they are in most cases very closely connected, so as to be practically only two aspects of one and the same thing. To create a different and superior quality, and to persuade buyers of the advantage of one's product—these are two things that logically go together. If selling costs are incurred to persuade the buyer, it is logical to help to this effect by differentiating the product; in fact, advertisement itself fulfils also the function of differentiating the product. If quality competition is used, its logical corrollary is the application of selling methods. This close connection should be kept in mind, because an artificial isolation of the two phenomena may result in misleading conclusions.[1]

4. To sum up the main argument: the superiority of selling methods and quality competition over a corresponding extent of price cutting decreases as the ratio of selling cost, or ' quality cost ', to sales increases, and it disappears at a certain point altogether. The ratio of selling cost, or ' quality cost ', at which selling methods, or quality competition cease to be superior is different according to the nature of the commodity: it is the higher, the greater the difficulty of rational comparison of qualities is for the buyers. One of the factors which will affect the difficulty of rational comparison for the buyers is, incidentally, the value of the individual purchase. Where a small sum is spent on the individual purchase, the price does not matter so much to the buyer, because he will not take the trouble of comparing it; where a big sum is spent in one lump it is more worth while for the buyer to get the necessary information for comparing different qualities and their relative cheapness, for example, in terms of performance.

Now the question obviously suggests itself whether the superiority of selling methods over price cutting depends also on the volume of sales, or in other words, on the size of the firm. It might be expected that in the case of advertising, for example, the effectiveness of a certain outlay depends not only on the ratio of selling cost to sales, but also on the *absolute* amount of the selling cost. This would amount to saying that selling costs are subject to ' increasing returns '. The question is of some importance. If selling expenditure is more effective ' in bulk ', and a large firm will therefore have more success with the same ratio of selling cost than a smaller one, it would seem to follow that selling methods increase the superiority of the bigger firm and favour concentration.

It is not easy to generalise on this question. First of all, we cannot decide

[1] Professor Chamberlin, for example, deals with the question of advertisement and excess capacity, and reaches the conclusion that, once a certain degree of product differentiation is given, advertisement will tend to reduce the amount of excess capacity. This appears to neglect the fact that advertisement itself leads to greater differentiation of product, and is in general part of a process of differentiation of product, so that its effects cannot be judged without taking this into account.

with great plausibility how far selling costs are subject to 'increasing returns'. With national advertising, the absolute amount spent is probably very important, and once national advertising has become a virtual condition for competing in an industry, it does favour large firms; in fact, it is probably an important element in establishing an oligopolistic situation in some cases where large advertising is required such as drugs and patent medicines.

If we compare national with local advertising the issue is more difficult to judge. It is not *a priori* obvious that the latter method must be always inferior. If we consider other selling methods which are based on individual persuasion, rather than 'mass appeal', for example sales agents, demonstrations, etc., then the importance of the *absolute* amount spent is much less obvious, if not altogether doubtful. The possibility of keeping more sales branches, depots, and facilities for servicing is one which favours the absolutely bigger selling expenditure; but in the case of travelling salesmen the advantage of the bigger selling expenditure is not so certain.

Whatever 'increasing returns' may be obtained in selling, another factor working in the opposite direction has to be considered as well. We have seen that selling methods cannot be considered apart from the differentiation of product. They themselves engender greater differentiation of product, or are part and parcel of a process of differentiation of product. But a greater differentiation of product means that a greater sales effort is required in order to gain an increasing share in the market, or in order to squeeze out competitors. The differentiation reduces the superiority of the bigger, or technically more efficient, firm, and thus makes concentration less easy. This effect of differentiation has to be set against the effects of 'increasing returns' in selling. It is hard to say in general, which one is the stronger. But there seem to be industries where high selling costs prevail without a remarkable tendency towards concentration.

5. We shall proceed now to give a plausible account of how selling methods are introduced in an industry, and how they bring about an increase in prices. We can imagine that these methods are introduced first by a few firms which have a differential profit advantage, and want to use it in order to gain ground at the expense of their competitors. Some of these, in good time, find out that they can apply the same selling methods, and can even finance their cost by an increase in prices, as there will still be a resulting net advantage, which will serve to counteract the sales effort of the first mentioned firms. In due course, the application of the selling methods will spread to all firms in the industry, leading to a general increase in prices. The firms which applied them first may retaliate by even greater selling expenditure, and be countered again in the same way.

This process may lead up to the point where selling methods cease to be superior over price cutting. In the end the firms which enjoy a differential profit advantage based on lower production cost are bound to make their superiority felt. But it must be realised that the process described will stretch over a considerable period, in fact, a good number of years. It resembles, in some way, the introduction of technical innovations, and has been called appropriately a ' commercial revolution '.[1] During all this period the selling cost ratio and the gross profit margins in the industry will gradually rise, until they reach the level at which price cutting, in its turn, becomes equally or more effective than further selling outlay. This maximum of selling cost is, of course, not a constant; it may change with the degree of defectiveness of buyers' judgment, on which it depends. If there are only a few firms, it may change simply with the policy of some of these firms. In the latter case we may therefore have periods of selling cost and quality competition alternating with periods of price competition.

6. We shall return now to a question which was pushed aside at the beginning of the chapter. Independently of the nature of the commodity, there may be quite another reason for practising selling methods. If price competition is excluded in an industry by tacit or open agreement, or price leadership, and if there is no sharing of the market between firms, would not this in itself result in selling costs ?[1] This may be the case. But if there is no irrationality involved on the side of the buyers, if the good is homogeneous and its price can easily be compared, then there would be little room for all the ingenious and manifold devices for persuading the buyer, which we are accustomed to associate with selling methods. The main trick would consist in trying to be the first on the spot when an order is given.

We might guess, therefore, that the impossibility of price competition, owing to agreement or price leadership, can be a reinforcing factor, but that, by itself, it should hardly give rise to substantial selling costs.

7. In the following some data on distribution costs of manufacturers will be presented. They are based on the U.S. Census of Business of 1935, the only one which contains such data. The distribution costs have been collected from manufacturers accounting for only about 40 per cent of the sales, but that is a larger sample than any of the private enquiries can offer. On the other hand, there are few details available; two parts of distribution costs only are given separately, ' pay roll ' and ' other expenses '. The data do not cover transport and storage. We have thus no way of separating selling costs even approximately. The differences in total distribution cost, as a ratio of sales, are due not only to different ratios of selling cost incurred, but also to different ratios of ' necessary distribution costs '. The latter are influenced by a variety of factors. The most important one is probably the value of the average individual order handled. The greater it is the smaller will be distribution cost as a ratio of sales. But selling costs should be sufficiently important to show their influence, if we compare a greater number of industries. To show their effect, and give at the same time a tentative confirmation of the theory, we shall try to select, out of all industries, those in which the products are of a fairly homogeneous

[1] M. Kalecki, *Studies in Economic Dynamics*.

[2] This point has been stressed—perhaps over-stressed—by Paul M. Sweezy, *The Theory of Capitalist Development*, p. 281.

character, approximately 'standardised' products. This selection is unfortunately somewhat arbitrary. There is no way of measuring *the degree* to which quality is standardised. But there are some rough criteria for our choice. Some goods are by nature fairly uniform and offer little technical

TABLE 7

MANUFACTURER'S DISTRIBUTION COSTS AS A RATIO OF SALES (1935)

(U.S. Census of Business)

'*Standardised Products*'

	Pay-roll	*Other Expense*	*Total*	*Note*
Flour	2.0	3.0	5.0	
Ice	14.4	10.9	25.3	
Liquors, distilled	3.5	4.8	8.3	
Malt	2.0	2.3	4.3	
Rice cleaning	1.4	5.2	6.6	
Sugar, beet	0.4	9.1	9.5	
Sugar, cane	1.7	3.0	4.7	
Cane sugar refining	0.4	1.2	1.6	
Woollen carpet yarn	1.3	0.5	1.8	
Cordage and twine	3.2	5.0	8.3	
Jute goods	1.9	2.1	4.0	
Cotton yarn and thread	3.0	3.4	6.4	
Timber n.e.c.	3.1	5.0	8.1	only very limited standardisation
Paper	2.7	3.9	6.6	,, ,, ,, ,,
Pulp	0.9	1.8	2.7	
Chemicals n.e.c.	2.7	6.1	8.8	Basic chemicals standardised, but not dyes
Compressed and liquified gases	5.0	10.2	15.2	
Drug grinding	1.3	0.5	1.8	
Explosives	5.5	6.7	12.2	
Salt	9.8	16.2	26.0	
Oil, cake and meal cottonseed	1.8	2.5	4.3	
Oil, cake and meal linseed	1.3	2.8	4.1	
Petrol refining	1.8	5.0	6.8	
Coke oven products	2.2	2.6	4.8	
Leather	2.4	4.5	6.9	very limited standardisation
Clay products n.e.c.	7.1	7.2	14.3	
Cement	4.8	7.7	12.6	
Graphite	6.0	8.7	14.7	
Lime	5.2	5.4	10.6	
Sound lime brick	5.8	5.2	11.0	
Gypsum	7.8	10.2	18.0	
Glass	3.6	3.4	7.c	
Blast furnace products	0.6	0.9	1.5	
Rolling mill products	2.0	2.4	4.4	
Cast iron pipe	4.5	3.1	7.6	
Wrought pipe	2.3	3.5	5.8	
Forgings	4.8	2.9	7.7	
Structural steel	6.5	4.8	11.3	
Steel barrels	2.8	4.3	7.1	
Wire	3.1	4.2	7.2	
Steel springs	2.9	4.0	6.9	
Bolts, nuts, etc.	5.3	3.6	8.9	
Nails, spikes	4.0	7.2	11.2	
Tin cans	2.1	2.2	4.3	
Aluminium products	3.7	3.7	7.4	Contains also differentiated products.
Non-ferrous metal alloys	3.7	3.1	6.8	
Sheet metal work	8.3	7.4	15.7	
Smelting and refining, copper	0.4	0.5	0.9	
Smelting and refining, lead	1.6	6.8	8.3	
Smelting and refining, zinc	2.0	2.0	4.0	
Smelting and refining, not from the ore	1.9	1.8	3.7	

TABLE 7 (*continued*)

	Pay-roll	*Other Expense*	*Total*	*Note*
Smelting and refining, gold, silver	1.9	1.6	3.5	
Tin foils	2.5	1.0	3.5	
Collapsible tubes	1.8	1.6	3.4	
Foundries	3.9	4.0	7.9	Mainly rough castings
'Non-standardised' Foods				
Beverages	11.0	11.9	22.9	
Bakery products	12.1	8.7	20.8	
Biscuits	7.0	10.0	17.0	
Butter	3.5	3.4	6.9	
Cheese	5.7	4.5	10.2	
Liquors, malt	4.1	9.8	13.9	
Liquors, rectified and blended	4.6	7.4	12.0	
Liquors, vinous	5.4	15.2	20.6	
Condensed milk	3.9	5.7	9.6	
Oleomargarine	2.2	8.8	11.0	
Canned and dried fruit and vegetables	4.3	7.7	12.0	
Canned fish	2.4	5.4	7.8	
Cereal preparations	3.9	9.8	13.7	
Corn syrup	2.2	5.7	7.9	
Flavouring extracts	10.4	12.8	23.2	
Confectionery	5.6	6.6	12.2	
Chocolate	3.2	4.0	7.2	
Chewing gum	3.6	20.2	23.8	
Ice cream	9.9	12.9	22.8	
Vinegar and cider	4.6	5.0	9.6	
Meat packing	1.7	2.7	4.4	
Poultry, etc.	3.3	3.5	6.8	
Sausages	6.6	5.0	11.6	
Shortenings	0.9	2.9	3.8	
Food preparations n.e.c.	6.3	11.7	18.0	
Maccaroni	5.2	7.9	13.1	
Feeds, prepared, for animals	3.1	4.1	7.2	
Chemicals, non-standardised				
Cleaning and polishing preparations	11.5	18.6	30.1	
Patent medicines	7.1	14.6	21.7	
Fertiliser	4.8	7.3	12.1	
Industrial and household chemical compounds	11.8	12.5	24.3	
Rayon	1.1	3.6	4.7	
Soap	6.0	13.6	19.6	
Paints and varnishes	8.7	8.9	17.6	
Perfumes and cosmetics	8.6	18.9	27.5	
Baking Powder	8.6	13.4	22.0	
Ammunition	5.1	7.8	12.9	
Blacking, etc.	11.7	12.8	24.5	
Bluing	18.0	11.7	29.7	
Bone black	2.0	5.8	7.8	
Candles	8.2	16.5	24.7	
Fireworks	3.3	4.8	8.1	
Glue and gelatine	7.8	8.3	16.1	
Grease and tallow	3.6	6.9	10.5	
Ink, printing	11.8	8.3	20.1	
Ink, writing	9.9	10.6	20.5	
Mucilage	10.8	9.4	20.2	
Tanning material	7.2	7.6	14.8	
Wood distillation	4.0	2.9	6.9	
Oil, essential	5.0	4.5	9.5	
Oil n.e.c.	2.3	5.1	7.4	

TABLE 8

FREQUENCY DISTRIBUTION OF DISTRIBUTION COSTS AS A PERCENTAGE OF SALES

	0—	% 2.5—	% 5.0—	% 7.5—	% 10.0—	% 12.5—	% 15.0—	% 17.5—	% 20.0—	% 22.5—	% 25.0—	% 27.5—	% 30.0—32.5	*Median*
All Industries	6	28	34	57	56	41	29	22	17	14	4	3	1	*11.7%*
'Standardised' products ..	5	14	13	10	5	3	2	1	—	—	2	—	—	*6.6%*
Non-standardised Foods ..	—	2	4	4	6	3	1	1	2	4	—	—	—	*11.5%*
Non-standardised Chemicals	—	1	2	3	2	2	1	2	5	3	—	2	1	*18.8%*
Machinery (all)	—	—	1	3	7	5	2	—	1	1	2	—	—	*12.5%*
Textiles (all)	2	9	9	16	16	2	5	4	1	3	—	—	—	*9.6%*

opportunity for differentiation—for example sugar, ice, metals and basic chemicals. For others, such as flour, cotton yarn, etc., rational methods of determining the quality have been developed. The selected 'standardised goods' and their distribution cost ratios are shown in Table 7. To reduce the comparison to a simple figure we have computed the median of distribution costs for all industries and for the group of standardised products (Table 8). For all industries the median of the distribution cost ratio is 11.7 per cent, for the standardised products it is 6.6 per cent. The result of the comparison seems fairly satisfactory, especially if we take into account that the cases of high distribution cost ratio among standardised products can be explained by special circumstances. Salt, for example, although technically fairly homogeneous, probably offers room for selling methods on account of the small amounts spent on it individually. Ice may have high 'necessary distribution costs' on account of its peculiar nature. A curious fact is the high distribution cost ratio for building materials, but in the year in question their sales were at an exceptionally low level (cement factories were working at about 30 per cent of capacity) and the distribution cost ratio may have been considerably higher than in normal times.

The value of the comparison is, however, considerably reduced by the fact that most of the standardised products chosen are handled in very large quantities. That is bound to reduce the 'necessary distribution cost' as a ratio of sales.[1] While it seems true that 'standardised products'—arbitrary though the definition may be—have a lower distribution cost ratio, we can only surmise that this is probably due both to low necessary distribution cost involved, and low selling cost.

Examination of some of the industrial groups shows that chemicals, excluding standardised products, have the highest distribution cost ratio. The median is 18.8 per cent. This is no doubt largely due to selling costs. For non-standardised foods, the median is about the same as for all industries, for machinery it is 12.5 per cent, for textiles 9.6 per cent, which is lower than the median for all industries.

VII. The Competition of Capital Between Industries

As shown above, the problem of prices and profit margins can be treated in the form of a modernised differential rent theory as long as there are marginal producers with normal profits in the industry concerned. But what about those industries where the marginal firms—the high cost producers—enjoy a profit themselves? It has to be shown whether and how this profit margin of high cost producers is determined.

As argued already this case will be of practical importance only where the marginal firms are not small firms in the usual sense of the term. It will be of the greatest importance in those industries where only a few firms exist and price policy is determined either by agreement or by price leadership. It

[1] It is this factor which should explain the low distribution cost ratio for some non-standardised products, such as in the case of meat-packing (4.4 per cent).

appears that traditional theory provides no satisfactory explanation of the formation of prices in this case. Its main answer is that competition between different industries, the possibility of substitution of the product of other industries, will set a limit to the exploitation of the market by a monopolistic price policy. This answer is unsatisfactory because the possibilities of competition between different industries have been over-estimated. Competition between industries which is of sufficient practical importance for price policy probably exists only in a minority of cases (an example is competition between rayon and other fibres). Ordinarily the elasticity of demand for the product of an industry is probably low (Chapter III) so that we must conclude that price policy is determined by some other factor.

Obviously this other factor can only be the potential competition of new entrants. This potential competition is weakened in those industries where small firms cannot compete; in fact, it is just due to this difficulty of entry that marginal producers can obtain a profit in those industries. But this does not mean that the threat of potential new entrants is completely eliminated.

In the classical, more exactly Ricardian, theory of prices the competitive effect of new entry played a paramount role in the form of the ' law of equalisation of the rate of profit '. The most important defect of this law is probably that it neglects the different degree of scarcity of entrepreneurial capital of various sizes, and the difference in technical opportunities open to them. It regards small units of capital as good as big ones, and assumes for all the same opportunities, thus neglecting one of the most important features of capitalism.

This defect could be easily remedied by assuming a law of equalisation of the profit rate for entrepreneurial capital of any given size. This law—valid only on the assumption of long-run mobility of capital—would indeed serve to determine the whole price structure. Imagine all enterprises cross-classified according to size of capital and to type of industry. In most types of industry not all size classes will actually be occupied by enterprises. In some lines enterprises will range from small to medium size, in others from medium to big. The size distribution of enterprises in various industries will thus be overlapping. Now in those industries where there are small firms with normal profits, the profit margin, and indirectly the profit rate, of medium firms is determined on the basis of cost differentials. In the industries where the marginal firms are medium, their profit rates, and indirectly their profit margins, are determined by the condition of equality of profit rate with that of equally big enterprises in the first mentioned industries. Thus the whole structure of profits can be determined, and is in the last resort based on cost differentials.

In its application the scheme proves to be an illusion, because its chief assumption, the long-run mobility of capital, does not hold. It is worth while, however, to discuss how far this assumption fails in practice. There are two reasons for the relative immobility of entrepreneurial capital, which must be clearly distinguished.

The first reason for immobility is that capital once invested in a certain industry can be freed only with great difficulty. Durable capital must be either depreciated first, which may take a considerable time, or it must be converted to other uses which probably involves a loss, if it is possible at all. Stocks must be liquidated slowly. Goodwill cannot be recovered at all. Of course, it was always maintained that capital can be 'unfrozen' only in the long run. The real objection is, however, that it is not possible to unfreeze the various parts of the capital at the same time. It is impossible to run production—or any business—smoothly and efficiently up to a certain date, and liquidate the next day. There will be a period of liquidation during which considerable loss is incurred. In practice, therefore, we may expect that capital once invested in an industry will hardly ever be withdrawn as long as any profit is to be gained from its use.

The first argument against mobility, the one which we have just discussed applies only to capital already invested. This leaves open the possibility that new savings may be 'mobile' in the sense that they can be invested in one or another industry. To the extent that new savings are formed in industry there would then be a tendency to *limit* inequalities of profit rates in different lines. Here we come up against the second reason against mobility of capital. It is a factor which has been mentioned already above (Chapter V): the free flow of newly-formed funds between industries would presuppose that entrepreneurs find it just as easy to enter an industry new to them, as to expand their business in their own industry. This is not the case. Entering a new industry will involve the acquisition of an entirely new market and goodwill, of new experience and new organisation. All this is more difficult than expanding an existing business within an industry. The conclusion is that the actual or potential flow of newly formed funds between industries will indeed do something to limit the inequality of profit rates between industries; but it will fulfil this function in a very imperfect way. We can only say that inequalities beyond a certain extent will induce this flow, *i.e.* attract new competitors from outside the industry.

We are now in a position to state in what way the 'law of equality of the profit rate' has to be qualified, and how far it will determine the profits of a marginal producer of medium or big size. As far as capital already invested is concerned it can be considered practically immobile. The possibility of withdrawal hardly exists, and if, therefore, the profit rate of a marginal producer falls, he must almost always resign himself to this position. There is thus no *lower limit* to the profit margin of the marginal producer. If strong competitive pressure arises within the industry, the marginal firms—even if they are absolutely big—will be reduced to the status of normal profit making firms.

On the other hand, if the profit rate of marginal producers in a particular industry rises considerably above the profit rate which capital of similar size earns in other lines, then at a certain point competition of newly entering capital will become effective. We might thus say that the profit rate of marginal producers is determined only within certain limits. The more closely we approach very high concentration, the more arbitrary the profit margins become. It might well be guessed that the element of arbitrariness in the determination of the system of prices and profit margins has increased with the development of capitalism towards higher and higher degrees of concentration.

That the limitation of profits by the entry of new capital is a factor of practical importance may be seen from a comparison of cases in which an absolute institutional monoply existed, and those where entry is only limited by the 'property qualification'. In the U.S. rayon industry there existed an absolute monoply, based on patent rights, up to 1920. The American Viscose Company was the only producer. After the patent expired in 1920 new producers came into the field. The average profits of all rayon companies between 1921 and 1929 seem to have been considerably lower, ranging between 18 per cent and 50 per cent in the various years, than the profits of the American Viscose Company between 1915 and 1920, which ranged between 26 per cent and 109 per cent of stockholders' investment.[1]

It should be recognised that the possibility of entry of new entrepreneurs with funds formed in other lines does set a limit to profits of even big producers, but it leaves most probably a considerable range of indeterminacy.

VIII. A Study of Profit Margins in U.S. Manufacturing Industry

In the present chapter an attempt will be made to assemble and compare some material on profit margins, or cost-price relations, and to analyse this material in the light of the theory of the preceding sections. Mr. Kalecki has shown that the gross profit margin, as a percentage of labour and raw material cost, in U.S. manufacturing industry increased remarkably between 1923 and 1931; and that the share of wages in the value added correspondingly decreased in the same period.[2] The analogous calculation of the share of wages has been carried through in the present study for the various industry groups separately, and as far as possible for individual industries. As we shall discover, this calculation reveals important differences in the behaviour of different industries. Most of the industries, it is true, share in the general decline of the share of wages in the 'New Era' (the 1920's), but the decline is not equally marked, and it proves merely temporary in some cases, and not in others. The industries which are highly concentrated and in which entry is difficult—we might call them somewhat vaguely 'oligopolistic industries' —show in most cases a stronger decline in the share of labour in value added (or, which means the same, an increase in the share of gross profits in value added) during the 1920's, and this movement is *not* (or only partly) reversed subsequently. In industries where entry is relatively easy and in which small and medium firms account for a considerable proportion of the output—we

[1] *Competition and Monopoly in American Industry*, p. 205.
[2] *Studies in Economic Dynamics*, p. 21, *seq*.

might call them, in this particular sense, ' competitive industries '—we find mostly that the tendency for the share of wages to decline in the 1920's is weaker and that it is subsequently reversed in the course of the 1930's.

The results bear a remarkable resemblance to those of a study by J. M. Blair[1] although the statistical method used is different, and there is also a difference in theoretical approach. Mr. Blair aims at comparing the development of labour productivity and of prices in different industries. Labour productivity is measured by physical output per man-hour; the reciprocal of this is the cost in man-hours of a unit of output. If we imagine this enquiry to be carried one step further by multiplying the cost in man-hours by an index of wage cost per hour of labour in the industry concerned, then the resulting comparison of wage cost per unit of output and price of the product should be comparable with the present study. The difference would be only in the statistical material used. Even though by taking into account wage per man-hour Mr. Blair's results would be somewhat modified especially in the case of the motor industry, the tendency which he uncovered would still be there. He shows that in non-concentrated industries, like textiles and furniture, the reduction in price has kept pace with the reduction in labour cost due to technical progress, whereas in concentrated industries (cement, steel, cigarettes) this has not been the case. With the qualification that we want to take account also of wage changes, the aim and results of the present enquiry are the same. It shows that wages in comparison to the value of output tended to decline in concentrated industries, but not in the non-concentrated industries, in the period 1923 to 1939.

We might well recall the outline of the theoretical argument of Chapter V. It has been argued that in ' competitive industries ' the net profit margin at given levels of capacity utilisation will be limited to a level which is determined by the rate of investment in the industry, in proportion to existing capital equipment. The net profit margin at given levels of utilisation will thus be kept within certain limits. In ' oligopolistic ' industries, on the other hand, there exists no such limit, and net profit margins at given levels of utilisation may therefore be expected to show an increase relatively to that in competitive industries. What has been said for net profit margins at given levels of utilisation should, broadly speaking, also apply to gross profit margins. There is one qualification to be made here, however. Selling costs may increase, and to this extent the gross profit margin will increase without an increase in net profit margins at given utilisation of capacity. Such an increase in selling costs may be very important in some ' competitive industries ' and, as we shall see, is in fact important in many cases. To this extent, the distinction between ' competitive ' and ' oligopolistic ' industries will not be clearly reflected in the behaviour of gross profit margins, because the latter will also reflect increases in selling costs. As to overhead costs in general, we shall discuss their possible influence later.

[1] Labour productivity and industrial prices. Appendix H of Monograph No. 22 of the *Temporary National Economic Committee.*

It will be noted that we do not calculate gross profit as a 'mark-up' *i.e.*, as a percentage of the sum of labour and raw material cost. The reason for this is, first, theoretical, because the 'mark-up' does not play in the present analysis the important role which it plays in Mr. Kalecki's theory. The 'mark-up' derives its theoretical importance from the concept of elasticity of demand which we have discarded altogether as a determinant of price policy. Second, there is a statistical reason: there may be changes in the degree of integration which would affect the mark-up, so that the latter would change without reflecting a real change in the cost-price relationship. We remain content, therefore, to calculate the percentage share of wages in the value added, the complement of which (100 minus percentage share of wages) is the share of gross profits in the value added. When we talk of gross profit margin, we always means, therefore, gross profits as a percentage of value added.

An analysis of the behaviour of profit margins in various industries on the basis of our theory requires, of course, some criteria according to which the character of the industry can be determined, viz. whether it is 'competitive' or not, and to what degree. This is considerably facilitated by the fact that a number of important industries in reality do represent extreme cases of either high concentration, with very big firms, and consequently great difficulty of entry, or else of low concentration, with small, or moderately big, firms accounting for a great part of the output. The classification of these industries into one or the other category can to a large extent be made on the basis of descriptive material alone. We shall draw on such descriptive material to a considerable extent.[1] Apart from that, however there exist strict statistical measures of the degree of concentration in various industries, and in relation to various products. These measures are represented by the proportion of output produced by the largest firms. In practice the largest four firms, and the largest eight firms are chosen. This material has been presented by the National Resources Committee[2] and by the Temporary National Economic Committee.[3] It makes it possible to classify industries according to a statistical criterion, but it must not be applied mechanically: there are industries where the degree of concentration for the whole national economy is not decisive, but it is rather *regional* concentration which determines the character of the industry e.g. cement.

The degree of concentration is, however, of only limited help in classifying industries for our purpose. What we want is to distinguish those industries in which the 'ideal' pattern of competition might be expected to work, and those in which it might not be expected to work. To the first class will belong the industries in which marginal firms can be squeezed out easily. This will be the case where the marginal firms are small, but it may also be the case with medium sized firms; we have seen that cost reductions of big

[1] For example, *T.N.E.C. Monograph No.* 21, Competition and Monopoly in American Industry.
[2] *The Structure of the American Economy, Part I.*
[3] *T.N.E.C. Monograph No.* 27, The Structure of Industry.

firms may reach such an extent that they will, by cutting prices, reduce even medium firms to the level of 'normal profits'. Thus, the ideal pattern of competition might work even in industries where the marginal firms are of considerable size; at least it may work so temporarily. Whether this will be the case will depend on the conditions of technical progress in the industry at the time. We can, however, say that the *bigger* the marginal firms become, the less likely is it that the ideal pattern of competition applies. In very highly concentrated industries, where four firms produce 80 per cent or more of the output, it is *a priori* most unlikely that the ideal pattern of competition applies. Further, in cases where the minimum capital requirements for a firm in the industry are fairly large, as in the steel industry, etc., we should not expect the ideal pattern to apply either. We may, therefore, attempt a rough classification, always remembering that the dividing line between the two types of industries is not rigid.

Technical Remarks

The share of wages in the value added has been calculated from the *Census of Manufactures* for the period 1899 to 1939. There are a number of technical difficulties involved in the calculation and interpretation of these data.

The coverage of the Census in this period has changed once. From 1899 to 1919 it included all establishments with a value of output in excess of $500 a year; from 1921 onwards it included only establishments with a value of output in excess of $5,000 a year. The relative weight of establishments which have thus been excluded is small; in terms of value added it amounted to 0.8 per cent in 1919. For manufacturing as a whole, the share of wages is reduced by 0.2 per cent by the exclusion of the small establishments. For the separate industries it is not possible to get overlapping series for the old and the new coverage, but we can guess that the error involved in the change in coverage is in most cases not greater than for total manufacturing. Only in some industries, printing, for example, is the relative importance of the small establishments somewhat greater and the error involved more serious.

Another difficulty arises from changes in classification of industries. In most of the important industries it was possible, by appropriate changes, to get a continuous series, on the basis of one and the same classification, for the greater part of the whole period. The classification is of course not always the one used in the last Census. Where it was impossible to adjust the classification, we have given overlapping series for the old and the new classification. Where the change in classification was small and did not result in any change of the share of wages, the series have been linked up directly. In a certain number of cases, however, the reclassification of industries has made it impossible to present any comparable series at all, and these industries have been omitted.

Another problem arises from the existence of contract work, that is work performed outside the establishment on raw material owned by the firm.

The cost of such contract work (work ' given out '), *i.e.* the sums paid for it, is treated from the 1935 Census onward in the same way as raw material cost, that is it is deducted from the value of the product in order to arrive at the value added. For the previous years, however, it is included in the value added. The figures for the cost of contract work for these earlier years are not always available: up to 1923 they are in general available, for the remaining years they are available for the industries where the cost of contract work is really important (that is, textiles and printing). For these industries the cost of contract work has been deducted from the value added for all years. For the majority of industries contract work is of minor importance; the change in its treatment in 1935 has been taken into account by presenting overlapping series, except where it did not affect the result at all and could therefore be neglected. The receipts for contract work performed are always included in the value added.

Indirect taxes should be, like material cost, deducted from the value of the product, in order to arrive at the proper ' value added '. For the tobacco tax this has been done in the Census only from 1931 onwards, whereas previously the tax was included in the value of products but not in materials. For these earlier years we have estimated the amount of tax from the internal revenue data, and deducted it from the value added as given by the Census. As the internal revenue figures are given for fiscal years, an estimate for calendar years had to be formed by interpolation. The result is thus not quite accurate but this has little importance in the case of tobacco, where the resulting changes in the share of wages are considerable. Alcoholic beverages where the tax is important need not trouble us, because we have excluded this industry anyhow from consideration on account of the prohibition which covered a great part of the period. As to other internal revenue taxes, the introduction to the 1937 Census says that they have been included both in value of products and value of materials. Nothing is said about the treatment of sales taxes of the States, but these are apparently very small (except for petroleum) and can in any case be neglected.[1] Some adjustment is, however required for pay-roll taxes. The social insurance contributions of the workers are included in the amount of wages, but the pay-roll taxes, payable for social insurance purposes by the employer, are apparently included in the value added but not in wages. As they are indirect taxes like sales taxes or excise, they should be deducted from the value added. The unemployment tax amounted to 2 per cent in 1937, and 3 per cent in 1938. The special tax for old age amounted to 1 per cent starting from 1937. The first of these taxes does not apply to enterprises with less than 8 employees, but the proportion of payrolls of these enterprises in sufficiently small to be neglected for our purposes. The taxes are levied on the total pay-roll, *i.e.* wages and salaries combined. As salaries are an overhead, we may consider that only the tax on the wages are prime cost and should be deducted from the value added. This can be very easily estimated by taking 3 per cent of the wage bill in 1937 and 4 per

[1] *T.N.E.C. Monograph No. 9.* Taxation of Corporate Enterprise, p. 104.

cent in 1939. The estimate of the tax on wages is then deducted from the value added, and the share of wages correspondingly increased in the two years mentioned.

An annoying defect appears in the Census figures for 1929, 1931 and 1933. In these three years the cost of 'shop and mill supplies,' which are rightly treated as raw material cost in all other years, are included in the value added. This defect cannot be satisfactorily remedied. In 1904 the cost of these shop and mill supplies amounted to 0.5 per cent of combined raw material and labour cost, or to 0.9 per cent of the value added, for manufacturing as a whole. This gives an idea of the order of magnitude of the correction which would be necessary. In some individual industries the correction would be greater. As it is difficult to guess the magnitude of this figure for 1929 to 1933, we have not attempted a correction. Fortunately the error is not of crucial importance for the results, because most of our conclusions depend on long run changes which manifest themselves in the series calculated, and are not much affected by relatively minor errors in the three years 1929, 1931 and 1933.

There remains the question how far the 'value of products' given in the Census for each industry, from which the value added is obtained, corresponds to the theoretical requirements. In principle the value of products is the value *ex factory*, exclusive of transportation cost. It can be presumed, therefore, that manufacturers who run their own wholesale departments, did not include the wholesale margin earned in this way in the value of products stated.[1] Thus, the possibility of an error of interpretation on this account can be, by and large, excluded. However, the value of products used in some industries is no doubt arbitrary. This is often the case where the products of the establishment are transferred to another establishment of the same firm, and where market prices for some reason cannot be or have not been used. The value given is here often a '*transfer* value', which in practice seems to be the cost of production. We shall probably avoid most difficulties arising on this account as long as we do not use too narrow industry classifications. To take an example, we have combined blast furnaces and rolling and steel mills. Where the product has a definite market price the danger of transfer values being used is smaller.

The share of wages in major industry groups

The peculiar development of various industry groups is seen more clearly against the background which the picture of manufacturing as a whole represents (Table 9). The share of wages here shows comparatively small fluctuations between 1899 and 1923, around a level of about 43 per cent. The one exception is the year 1921, in which a deep slump occurred; the share of wages increased to 45 per cent in that year. After 1923 a significant decline in the share of wages took place, which was partly reversed in 1935 and 1937, but apparently resumed again afterwards. The net effect was a

[1] This is expressly stated (see *Census of Manufactures*, 1939, p. 5).

decline from 43 per cent in 1923 to 38 per cent in 1939. The outstanding fact is that a significant change in the cost-price relation took place in the 1920's—in the so-called *New Era*—and that this change was not only temporary. We shall, therefore, have to concentrate our attention on this period.

A point of secondary importance is to explain the events of 1921. Two factors account for them. A minor one is the fact that in some industries (*e.g.* steel, cement) wages to a great extent behave like overhead cost, so that the unit wage costs are necessarily much higher when the utilisation of capacity is low. For this reason the share of wages tends to be higher in a slump in industries of this type. In most industries, however, wages vary more or less in proportion to output; yet we notice an extraordinary rise in 1921 also in the food and paper group. Secondly, it seems that there was in 1921 a particularly strong competitive struggle, leading to a big cut in profit margins in a number of industries. This might have been the consequence, on the one hand, of over-expansion during the war in some industries, and on the other hand, of considerable accumulation of funds out of war profits, with consequent aggressive policy on the part of these firms with the aim of gaining room for expansion, possibly also in new fields. These tendencies naturally made themselves felt first in the slump year. It is significant, however, that in the slump after 1929 the pattern was rather different. The tendency to cut profit margins appeared only very late in the depression.

Now consider the major industry groups (see Table 9). Their character, in so far as the pattern of competition is concerned, can in some cases be easily determined. Three of them, textiles, timber and leather, are typically ' competitive '. The degree of concentration is low in most of their branches, and entry is fairly easy which is also confirmed by the low level of profits common in these industries.[1] A further group, miscellaneous industries, seems to be composed very largely of competitive industries. The food group is to a large part competitive, but not exclusively so. It contains also highly concentrated industries such as sugar refining, chocolate, cereal preparations.

On the other hand, some groups have a clearly oligopolistic character which can be readily shown : the tobacco group is dominated by cigarettes, of which 90 per cent are produced by the four largest producers. The transportation group comprises the motor car industry where 87 per cent of output is produced by the four largest firms. The other industries in this group, locomotives, ship-building, aircraft, are obviously all industries where production must be carried on on a fairly large scale and free entry is therefore strongly impeded. The rubber group is dominated by rubber tyres, about 80 per cent of which are produced by the four largest firms. The non-ferrous metal group, for the greater part, is equally clearly a highly concentrated industry. In primary smelting and refining of copper three concerns are dominant, controlling about 80 per cent of refinery output and capacity,

[1] *Competition and Monopoly in American Industry.*

TABLE 9

THE SHARE OF WAGES IN % OF VALUE ADDED IN VARIOUS MANUFACTURING INDUSTRIES[1]

	Manufacturing industries total		Food and kindred products		Textiles and their products	Forest products		Paper and allied products		Printing publishing and allied ind.	Chemical industries	Products of petroleum and coal		Rubber products
	E_1	E_3	O	N	B	A	B	A	B	B		A	B	
1899 ..	44.3		30.0			48.4		39.5			21.9	37.2		38.9
1904 ..	43.7		30.3	30.8		47.5	50.1	41.7			21.7	33.5		29.6
1909 ..	42.2			28.2		48.8		39.7			19.5	36.2		33.6
1914 ..	43.2	43.0		28.8	50.0	52.8	55.0	43.5		33.0	22.6	33.0		32.0
1919 ..	42.2	42.1		31.4	41.5	49.4	50.5	40.2		32.3	25.8	27.6		35.7
1921 ..		45.0		35.4	50.5	53.5	55.0	50.2		33.3	25.8	31.6		37.8
1923 ..		43.0		32.0	47.0	49.2	50.4	43.3		32.3	23.6	28.5		39.8
1925 ..		40.4		29.8	48.0	50.0		42.0		30.9	21.6	23.9		35.6
1927 ..		39.9		29.0	47.5	51.2		38.7		30.5	20.6	30.4		35.0
1929[2] ..		36.9		27.0	45.5	47.0		36.8		28.6	20.0	21.8		38.4
1931[2] ..		36.9		27.5	48.0	49.8		38.2		30.4	18.9	33.4		31.2
1933[2] ..		36.5		26.6	48.7	46.7		33.4		28.4	19.2	29.1		38.0
1935 ..		39.9		30.6	54.2	49.6	50.5	37.0	37.1	28.8	20.6	30.8	31.0	43.2
1937 ..		41.1		30.7	53.1	50.0	51.0		36.4	30.1	21.4		30.4	47.1
1939 ..		37.8		27.3	50.0	46.7	48.0		36.1	28.3	19.2		26.1	40.5

TABLE 9 (*continued*)

	Leather and its products		Stone, Clay and Glass	Iron and Steel and their products		Non-ferrous metals and their products			Machinery			Transportation Equipment		Tobacco manu-facture	Miscellaneous industries	
	A	B		A	B	A	B O	B N	O	N	N_1	O	N		O	N
1899	54.5		55.4											41.8		
1904	49.4		55.3											39.2		
1909	48.0		54.3			41.7								37.6		
1914	48.1		54.5	51.1		41.8			44.5			46.3		38.4	38.2	
1919	40.5		48.3	50.3		46.0			44.0			52.0		44.5	37.9	
1921	51.6		50.7	55.5		49.0			44.2			48.7		68.4	41.7	
1923	48.9		45.8	49.5		45.0			44.2			49.7		57.1	39.6	
1925	47.3		45.0	47.1		42.5			40.4			44.0		36.4	36.2	
1927	46.7		45.6	47.7		42.5			38.9			45.0		29.5	36.2	
1929[2]	46.5		41.8	42.3		38.7			37.5	37.6		40.0		25.2	34.4	
1931[2]	50.0		40.8	47.9		40.4				36.3		40.4		18.7	33.8	
1933[2]	49.4		35.8	46.8		38.4				39.2		41.7		20.4	34.6	
1935	52.4	52.8	38.1	46.5	46.7	40.3	40.5			40.0		49.9		20.9	37.0	
1937		53.5	40.5		48.1		41.2	40.2		41.7	41.2	52.2	52.7	21.8	39.4	40.3
1939		51.4	36.6		45.0			36.9			38.1		50.4	19.8		36.0

[1] E_1 Establishments with value of products over $500.
E_2 Establishments with value of products over $5000.
O Older classification.
A Based on value added *including* cost of contract work given out.
B Based on value added *excluding* cost of contract work given out.
N Newer classification.
[2] In the years 1929, 1931, 1933 the cost of shop and mill supplies is included in the value added, whereas in all other years it is excluded.

according to the U.S. tariff commission.[1] Smelting and refining of lead and zinc is also highly concentrated. The same is true for a great part of the products of non-ferrous metals. The concentration figures (per cent produced by the four largest producers) are for aluminium products 76 per cent and for copper plates and sheets 90 per cent. There is no doubt that capital requirements in these industries are particularly great, and entry is correspondingly difficult.

Whereas in the case of the industries just mentioned their character can be judged directly from one concentration figure alone, we shall have to add some additional considerations in the following cases. In the iron and steel group the concentration does not seem as great as in the industries previously mentioned. In the case of steel works and rolling mills the four greatest producers account for 49 per cent of the output. In terms of output capacity of steel, however, the three largest concerns accounted for 60 per cent, and seven smaller concerns for 22 per cent. Now there is no doubt that capital requirements for any firm in the basic steel industry are very great. Similarly, large scale production and high capital requirements prevail in the case of many semi-finished and finished steel products *e.g.* sheets, plates, rails, structural steel. There are also industries with relatively small scale production, and low degree of concentration, but these weigh less heavily in the total group than the others. Thus iron and steel has much the same character as the industries dealt with before.

The stone, clay and glass group comprises to a great extent products which are very heavy, and in which producers cannot, therefore, compete on a national scale. The degree of concentration, on a national scale, is here misleading. The four greatest producers of cement account only for 30 per cent of the output, but if the geographical restriction of the market of a plant is taken into account, this concentration figure appears very high. We can only refer here to the verbal evidence of the T.N.E.C.[2] according to which regional concentration in the cement industry is very high. It is known that capital requirements per plant are very high. To a somewhat lesser extent similar considerations apply to bricks and tiles. With regard to glass the transport difficulties do not apply, and here the national concentration figures in any case are unambiguous. The four largest producers accounted for 85 per cent of the window glass, whereas one firm produced 95 per cent of the plate glass, and the glass container industry is also highly concentrated. We conclude that the *effective* degree of concentration in this group is very high indeed, the main exception being pottery.

In the chemical group the most important sector is the basic chemical industry. Concentration figures based on Census material do not tell us very much here because of the diversity of products. But mere verbal description offers a pretty clear picture of the character of the industry. Three big combines dominate the field, being highly integrated, and producing a great

[1] Quoted from *T.N.E.C. Monograph No. 22*: Technology in our Economy, p. 247.
[2] *The Structure of Industry.*

diversity of products. The high concentration in the industry was largely brought about after, and even during the first world war, by buying up and financial consolidations. Production is on a large scale and capital requirements are great. Patents and research are an important additional factor in strengthening the position of the few big concerns which dominate the field. According to the T.N.E.C. 'the bulk of the output of many chemicals is concentrated in the hands of a few firms.'[1] Apart from basic chemicals concentration is great also in rayon, soap, ammunition and explosives, etc. Some parts of the chemical group, it is true, are rather competitive (*e.g.* paints and varnishes). The chemical group as a whole is rather similar to the other oligopolistic industries.

In the 'petrol and coal' group the main industries are coke and petrol refining. In coke oven products the concentration as such is not of the highest—the four producers account for less than 50 per cent of output. But the minimum scale of production is no doubt so great as to make entry rather difficult. The position of the petrol refining industry is similar. The four largest producers account for only 38 per cent of output. However, it is known that the 20 major integrated companies which produce 84 per cent of the gasoline[2] are in perfect agreement about price policy. We should therefore expect, *a priori*, that the industry behaves as a typically oligopolistic one does, although we shall see later that very special circumstances have to be taken into account.

In the machinery group minimum capital requirements are high in some cases. This applies particularly to electrical machinery and apparatus. Here, concentration is sometimes very, and sometimes moderately high. In the production of machinery used in generation and distribution of power, for example, two firms accounted for 75 per cent of total output in 1923.[3] In electrical lamps, and in telephone apparatus, concentration is also very high. In other fields, for example electrical household appliances, the degree of concentration is more moderate. Amongst other machinery, a fairly high degree of concentration applies, for example in agricultural implements (4 producers having a share of 72 per cent), typewriters, and sewing machines. In machine tools on the other hand, concentration is low. The machinery group is thus not uniform, but oligopolistic industries form a considerable part of it.

In the paper group the secondary branch of the industry, conversion of paper or board into finished products, is highly competitive. The primary branch, production of pulp and paper, is not easy to judge. A fairly high degree of concentration obtains only in some branches, particularly newsprint. Apart from newsprint the degree of concentration would appear to be low. There is, however, much specialisation, and if concentration were measured for each type of paper, it might prove rather greater. Apart from

[1] *Competition and Monopoly in American Industry*, p. 201.
[2] Hearings before the T.N.E.C. Part 14, p. 7103.
[3] Federal Trade Commission, quoted from T.N.E.C. Monograph, Competition and Monopoly p. 198.

that the production of pulp and paper requires costly equipment and fairly high capital investment. Thus the pulp and paper industry, though not highly concentrated, is subject to considerable difficulty of entry.

Quite different from the industries treated just now is the case of the printing and publishing group. The degree of concentration in most of its branches is low. Printing as such is no doubt an industry where small scale production is easy, and which is therefore highly competitive. The same applies to some of the allied industries of the group (book binding). The case is rather different with publishing. The degree of concentration, it is true, is low here too. This applies even to newspapers, the reason being probably the great number of provincial and local newspapers, and national language papers. But it would be quite wrong to conclude from the low concentration that newspaper publishing is ' competitive '. The number of national newspapers is limited and the capital required for a big newspaper is exceedingly large. Local newspapers, on the other hand, have a very restricted field in which to compete. Thus conditions in newspaper publishing are very much the same as in highly concentrated industries. In book publishing, again, the capital requirements are an effective impediment to easy entry and concentration has become very high there too. The conclusion is that the printing and publishing sector is a sector in which entry is very difficult, and which shows considerable resemblance to a concentrated industry.

To sum up : the industry groups which are ' *competitive* ' are textiles, timber, leather, and miscellaneous, and to a considerable extent also food. Industries which are *very highly concentrated* are tobacco, transport equipment, rubber, non-ferrous metals, iron and steel, stone and glass, chemicals. Rather similar to these are products of petrol and coal, and partly also machinery. The paper group is not highly concentrated, but similar to the ones just mentioned, in so far as the difficulty of entry is concerned. A *mixed* group is printing and publishing.

How does the share of wages and profit move in these various groups ? It can be seen from Fig. 4 and Table 9 that in three of the competitive industries, *textiles*, *timber* and *leather*, there is no long run and persistent tendency for a decline in the share of wages. There is a temporary decline —a trough in the curves—mainly in the late 'twenties, but the share of wages returns to its former level in the late 'thirties. Thus in the long run the share of wages appears to have been fairly stable in these industries. In strong contrast to this picture is the development in *tobacco*, *stone and glass*, *non-ferrous metals*, *machinery* and *paper*. In these cases the share of wages shows a long run decline from 1923 onwards, which is not, or only partly, reversed in the later period. Fig. 4 depicts very vividly the divergence which developed after 1923 between the share of wages in these five industries, and that in the three ' competitive ' industries enumerated above. We have here what seems to be a fair illustration of the dictum that the ' ideal ' pattern of competition works in competitive industries, but in industries with high concentration, or difficult entry, the share of profit shows a long run tendency to increase. Two more of the 'concentrated industries' show the tendency to a declining share of wages : *iron and steel*, and *chemicals*. In iron and steel the development is rather irregular and the tendency is weaker than we might expect. This is due to the peculiar technical character of the basic iron and steel industry, where wages to a large extent have the character of overheads, so that the share of wages tends to fluctuate inversely with the degree of utilisation of capacity. If we could account for the changes in the degree of utilisation—by computing the hypothetical share of wages at a constant level of capacity utilisation throughout the period—we should obtain a more regular development. Moreover, the hypothetical share of wages at constant level of utilisation would show a stronger decrease than our figures in Table 9, because the degree of utilisation in the 'thirties was much lower, even in 1937, than in the 'twenties.

The chemical group also shows, starting from the early 'twenties, a decline in the share of wages. Here, as also in the case of non-ferrous metals, the share of wages seems, however, only to have regained, roughly speaking, the low level which prevailed already before the first world war. Thus it appears that in these industries, which were strongly oligopolistic already before, a temporary phase of competitive struggle set in after the first world war, after which the tendency of the declining share of wages set in again. There is nothing surprising in this. We have seen that even in industries with large marginal producers, where the 'ideal' pattern of competition has ceased to work, the cost differential between the various firms may after a time becomes so large that it leads to an explosive release of competitive forces, bringing the average profit margins down, and eliminating marginal firms at the same time. After this has happened, the tendency of the profit margin to increase must re-appear with even greater force, because the industry is now more concentrated. In the chemical industry the competitive post-war struggle is illustrated by the fact that in this period a large number of acquisitions took place, which were probably made possible simply by the pressure of competition. The industry underwent a strong concentration with a decline in number of establishments and concentration of ownership.

Three of the concentrated industries do not conform to the pattern which is followed by the others. In the *petroleum and coal* group the share of wages does show a conspicuous long run tendency to decline up to 1929. Afterwards, however, there is a strong increase. That this group should form an exception is due to the peculiar circumstances in the petrol refining industry. The major integrated oil concerns, which own the greater part of the refineries, and determine the price of crude and refined oil ex-factory, own also practically all the transport facilities, pipe lines and tankers which bring the crude oil to the refinery and take the refined petrol to the distribution centres. For these companies, the 'refinery margin', as reflected in the figure of share of profits in value added, has no material importance : a decrease in this margin may simply mean that the corresponding amount of profit appears in the accounting of the pipe line companies. On the other hand, the

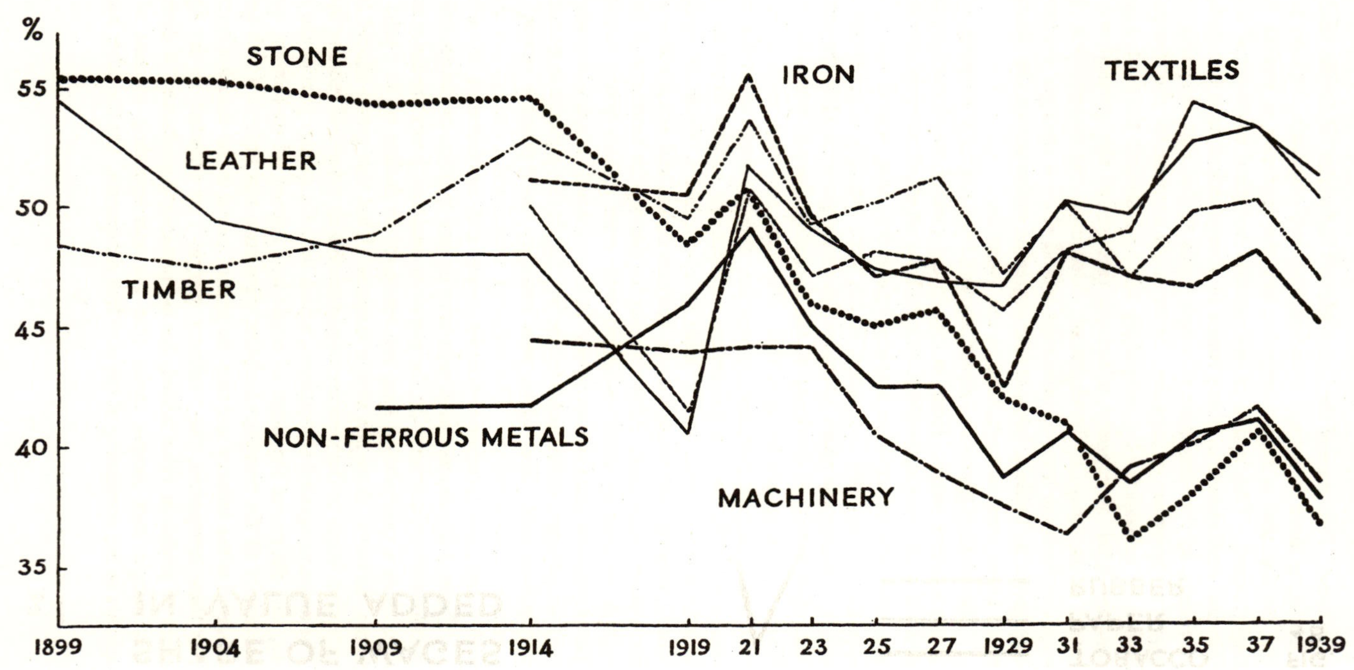
SHARE OF WAGES IN VALUE ADDED
FIG. 4A
%
55
50
45
40
35
STONE
LEATHER
TIMBER
NON-FERROUS METALS
IRON
TEXTILES
MACHINERY
1899
1904
1909
1914
1919
21
23
25
27
1929
31
33
35
37
1939

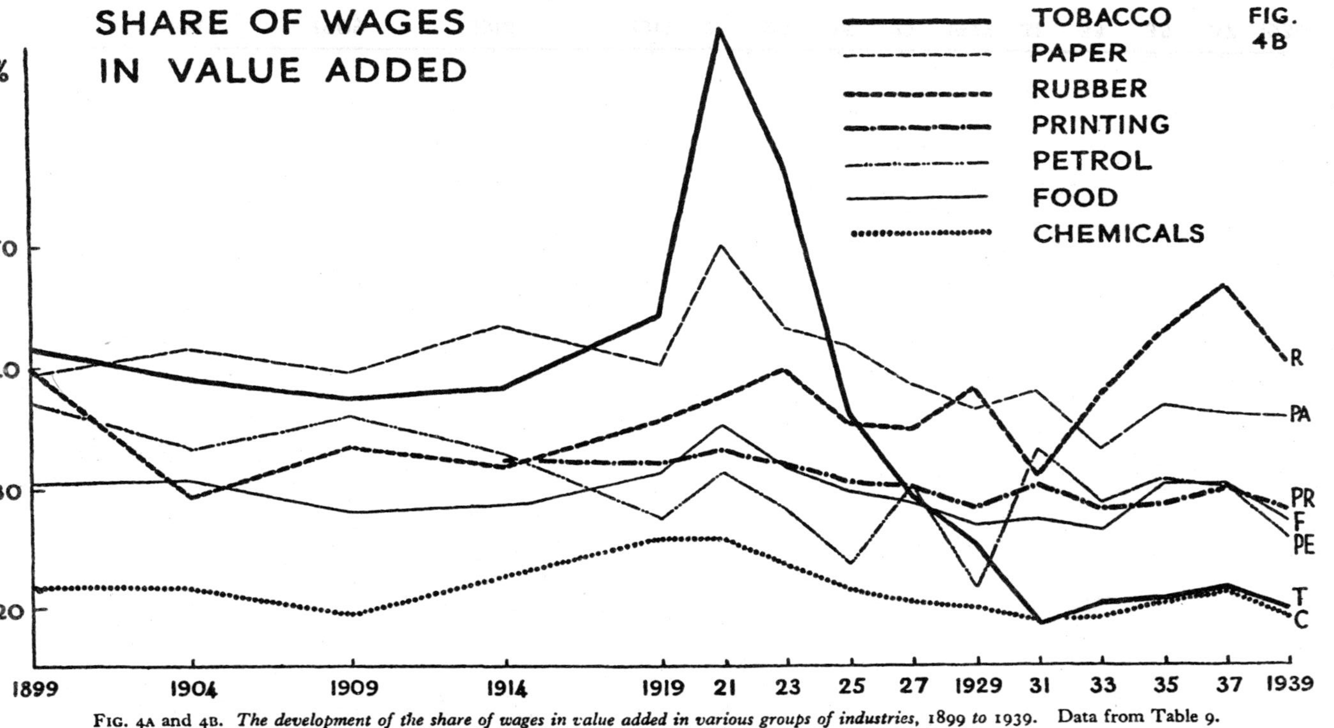

FIG. 4A and 4B. *The development of the share of wages in value added in various groups of industries, 1899 to 1939.* Data from Table 9.

squeezing of the refinery margin does have the effect of eliminating, or keeping in check, the independent refiners. That this is indeed the policy of the major integrated companies is confirmed by various accounts.[1] It may be concluded that this industry is only apparently an exception among concentrated industries.

The case of the *rubber industry* is different. This group shows no decline, but on the contrary even an increase in the share of wages, particularly in the late 'thirties. It behaves like an industry of small scale producers, although its main part, the production of rubber tyres and tubes, is highly concentrated. Descriptions of this industry confirm that there is very lively competition[2]—a most surprising feature in an industry where four firms produced 80 per cent of the output in 1937. There are some factors which go a long way in explaining this situation. Twenty-five per cent of the output of tyres is bought by the motor-car industry; a large part of the remaining output is handled by mass distributors (mail order houses, oil companies, auto supply chains). The oligopoly of the tyre manufacturers is thus faced with an oligopsony of car manufacturers and big dealers. The oligopsonistic buyers seem to have used their position ruthlessly, underselling the tyre manufacturers' own distributors, and thus making a discriminatory price policy impossible. The result of a profit squeeze in this industry can be well explained in this way. One result of it has been a very rapid elimination of smaller firms during the thirties.

The third exception among concentrated industries is the *transportation* group. This group does show a strong decline in the share of wages between 1923 and 1933, but the development is completely reversed afterwards. The peculiar development of the group is determined by the motor-car industry. It is difficult to explain the behaviour of this industry without taking into account the role of Ford. His insistence on price competition seems to give the industry a different character from other concentrated industries. This could not, however, prevent a relaxation of price competition in the period 1923 to 1933, when Ford had been losing ground owing to a shift in demand from standardised to quality cars. This industry must count as an exception, although even here the tendencies observed elsewhere are not altogether absent.

Among the partly competitive industries, the *food group* shows a declining tendency in the share of wages. Apart from the influence of concentrated industries in this group this may also be due to an increase in selling cost. It is plausible that in this group the development of modern selling methods and advertising—what Mr. Kalecki called the 'commercial revolution'—has proceeded during the 'New Era'. It is of course known that selling costs in manufactured foods play a very large role, probably more than in most other lines except such as medicines and cosmetics.

The *miscellaneous* industries group shows some declining tendency of the

[1] See *Competition and Monopoly*, etc., p. 167.
[2] *Competition and Monopoly*, etc., p. 48 *seq.*

share of wages too, but this group is very heterogeneous, composed of industries with widely different shares of wages, and with some shift in the proportion of different industries in favour of those which have a low share of wages. It will be better to judge these industries individually later on.

The *printing and publishing* group, a mixed group of industries, also shows a tendency for the share of wages to decline. The behaviour of individual industries in this group will be discussed later.

The conclusion may be drawn that the data for major industry groups can be interpreted fairly well on the basis of the theory. Before the individual industries within each group are surveyed, it is appropriate to deal with certain general objections which might be raised against our interpretation of the data.

Discussions of Objections

The first objection is that the development of the share of profits in different industries may vary because technical progress and cost reduction have played a bigger role in some than in others. This idea can be rejected out of hand. Productivity increase has been as important in textiles and furniture, as in the concentrated industries.

Another objection is that changes in the gross profit margin may be explained by changes in overhead cost per unit at given degrees of capacity utilisation. An increase of overhead cost might, for example, appear in the form of a greater *pay roll for salaries*. There is even an *a priori* likelihood of this: we should expect that technical progress which saves so much labour per unit of output does not reduce the cost of administration and distribution to quite the same extent. The salary bill should then be expected to rise in proportion to the wage bill, at given degree of utilisation. But there is no reason whatsoever why this relative increase in salary bill should be greater in concentrated industries than in others. Let us, however, examine the available data for salaries in total manufacturing (see Table 10). Expressed as a percentage of value added the salary bill shows a considerable rise between 1899 and 1914. We can hardly take the total increase as an indication of the rise in overheads, because in this time the incorporation of business has made its greatest progress, and part of what were formerly profits of independent business men became remuneration of the corporation's officers. This remuneration amounted to about a thousand million dollars in manufacturing corporations in 1920.[1] If we were to deduct it from salaries, the post-war ratio of salaries would probably be of the same order as at the beginning of the century. However that may be, we are not interested so much in the pre-war development because the rise in profit margins took place in the 1920's only. This is therefore the crucial period. It is found that the ratio of salaries to value added between 1923 and 1929 increased from 12.1 per cent to 13.6 per cent. These two years are chosen because they were

[1] The correct figure cannot be ascertained because corporations were 'consolidated' for tax purposes, and the figure thus includes corporations outside the manufactures field.

both years of high degree of utilisation. The increase was largely due to expansion of central office administration. In 1937, however, the ratio declined again to 12.5 per cent, not substantially above the level of 1923, though utilisation of capacity was lower in 1937. The increase in the salary ratio thus appears to have been temporary only; even this increase of

TABLE 10

SALARIES IN MANUFACTURING[1]

	Salary bill, including salaries paid in central administrative offices			*Salary bill excluding salaries paid in central administrative offices*		
	$ millions	*as % of wages*	*as % of value added*	*$ millions*	*as % of wages*	*as % of value added*
1899.. ..	366	19.4	8.7			
1904.. ..	550	22.6	10.0			
1909.. ..	901	28.2	12.2			
1914.. ..	1222	33.0	14.4			
1919.. ..	2763	28.7	12.2			
1921.. ..	2419	32.5	14.7			
1923.. ..	2848	28.1	12.1	2640	26.0	11.2
1925.. ..	2979	29.8	12.1	2753	27.6	11.1
1927.. ..	—	—	—	3024	30.0	11.9
1929.. ..	3999	36.8	13.6	3399	31.2	11.5
1931.. ..	—			—		
1933.. ..	—			—		
1935.. ..	—			2253	30.8	12.4
1937.. ..	3081	30.5	12.5	2717	26.8	11.0

1.5 per cent of the value added would account only for a part of the increase in the share of gross profits in value added. On the face of it the data do not support the idea that an increase in the salary ratio at given degree of utilisation could explain the increase in the gross profit margin.

Another plausible reason for a rise in overheads would be an increase in *depreciation quotas*. It might be possible that fixed capital in proportion to output capacity has been increased, particularly in the concentrated industries, and this might explain the divergent development in profit margins of different industries.

Data on depreciation are a rather tricky subject. Before 1919 there are no such data. But as the changes in the profit margins for the most part took place later, we may be content with depreciation figures for the period after the first world war.

The depreciation figures used are those given by Fabricant.[2] They are based on the statistics of income for corporations, and therefore include a certain amount of depreciation which does not relate to manufacturing, but relates to the properties of the respective corporations in other fields. Expressing this depreciation as a percentage of value added in manufacturing, we obtain the following series (Table 11).

The ratio of depreciation to value added is, of course, highly sensitive to changes in the degree of utilisation. Moreover, the depreciation is given as

[1] The value added, on which the calculation of percentages is based, excludes contract work and the tobacco tax. Figures for 1899 to 1909 include establishments with output valued at £500 or more, whereas the later figures include only those with output of $5000 or more.

[2] *Capital Consumption and Adjustment*. Table I, pp. 32–33.

it appears in the books. The 1919 figure is therefore almost useless because it is largely based on relatively low values of capital assets purchased before the great price increases took place. There occurred a considerable amount of revaluation in assets afterwards. The best we can do is to compare

TABLE 11

DEPRECIATION (BOOK VALUE) IN MANUFACTURING

	Depreciation, million $	*In % of value added in manufacturing*
1919	1006	4.4
1921	1168	7.1
1923	1387	5.9
1925	1493	6.1
1927	1718	6.8
1929	1879	6.4
1931	1849	10.2
1933	1631	12.1
1935	1510	8.3
1937	1610	6.5

the years 1923 and 1929, both years of high degree of utilisation. The depreciation ratio increased from 5.9 per cent to 6.4 per cent in this period and seems to have been roughly at the same level in 1937. The increase is thus fairly small. Even this is, however, almost certainly only an apparent increase, because it is based on *book values* of depreciation which increased in this period owing to replacement of capital assets at increased post-war prices. A proper correction of this is not possible. If we apply, *faute de mieux*, Fabricant's index of prices underlying book valuation, which is strictly applicable only to *all corporations*, to the depreciation in manufacturing, we get the following ratios of depreciation (at current values) to value added : 1923, 7.45 per cent; 1929, 7.15 per cent; 1937, 7.22 per cent. It would seem that, measured in current values (reproduction cost) the depreciation ratio did not rise at all, but probably even declined.

Depreciation in certain industry groups is given below as a percentage of ' gross income ' (sales) as reported in the statistics of income for corporations

TABLE 12

DEPRECIATION AS % OF ' GROSS INCOME ' OF CORPORATIONS

	Food and Tobacco	*Textiles and leather*	*Timber, Stone, Glass*	*Paper*	*Printing and publishing*	*Chemicals*	*Metals*	*All Manufacturing*
1923	1.95	1.95	3.48	3.25	2.47	3.39	2.45	2.46
1929	1.67	2.34	3.78	3.62	2.55	4.15	2.47	2.60

The increase shown in two groups is of the order of 10 per cent and is probably fully explained by a rise in book values of depreciation only. In chemicals there is a more substantial rise, but we have to remember that these corporation statistics include among chemicals the oil companies with their big investments in oil pipe lines, etc.

Though evidence on depreciation is very unsatisfactory, it does not appear that this factor can have played any appreciable role in offsetting the increase in gross profit margins during the New Era.

Much more important than the points discussed so far is the question of *selling costs*. Manufacturers' distribution costs in general are included in the value of products, except in so far as separate wholesale departments are kept to which the products are transferred at a price not including the costs of these wholesale departments. Except for this case the values given in the Census cover therefore also manufacturers' selling costs. The most important types of these selling costs are advertising and pay and travel allowances, etc., of agents, promoters, demonstrators, etc. Now if there was a general increase in selling costs, in proportion to sales, in the 1920's, and if this movement has not been reversed later, it might conceivably account for the increase in gross profit margins observed in total manufacturing. The question could only be satisfactorily answered if a time series showing the development of manufacturers' distribution costs over the crucial period were available. This is unfortunately not the case.

The most important aspect of our analysis of profit margins is, however, not the overall increase shown for manufacturing as a whole, but the divergent behaviour of ' concentrated ' and other industries. The question boils down to this: can an increase in selling costs be held responsible for the increase in profit margins in concentrated industries *relative* to those in other industries ?

It so happens that quite a number of the concentrated industries produce fairly *standardised* products: cement, glass and other building materials, steel and some important steel products (sheets, wire, etc.), non-ferrous metals and basic chemicals all seem to offer comparatively little room for the game of product differentiation. On a *priori* grounds we should thus expect that selling costs would play a relatively small role in these cases (see Chapter VI). It is therefore improbable that they should have increased to such an extent as to account for the rise in profit margins observed in these industries.

In the concentrated industries which produce non-standardised products—for example electrical machinery—an increase in selling costs may have played a role. There is little to be done to decide this question, except in those cases where we know something more about selling costs. In cigarette manufacture, where advertisement expenditure is known, the increase in the gross profit margin could not be explained in this way, because it is altogether too big in comparison to the advertisement costs.

The conclusion on this point of selling costs must necessarily be tentative. We should say that a possible increase in selling costs is not a plausible explanation of the rise in profit margins in a good number of cases. The evidence, as far as it goes, is at least compatible with the hypothesis that net profit margins at any given degree of utilisation have increased in concentrated industries relative to those in other industries.

The individual industries in the various groups will now be reviewed in detail.

Food Group

Among the 16 important food industries selected (Table 13), some have a fairly high degree of concentration. These show a tendency which is also clearly reflected in the total food group.

Concentration in Food industries (1935)

	% of output produced by the 4 largest producers
Chewing gum	92%
Oleomargarine (not made in meat packing establishments)	79%
Cane sugar refining	70%
Cereal preparations	68%
Chocolate and Cocoa	68%
Meat packing, wholesale	56%
Flavouring extracts	48%
Flour and Grain mill products	29%

Their share of wages is much greater in the years following the world war than it had been before. We have here an illustration of the case where competitive pressure becomes acute again in an industry where small scale producers have long been eliminated, and the profits had been considerable. The recurrence of competitive pressure in these industries may be partly due to their overexpansion during the war. In some cases it is connected with the instability of monopolistic positions acquired at a very early time. Cane sugar refining had been almost completely concentrated in the hands of one firm at the end of the last century, but this position did not prove stable. In general such recurring competitive pressure should, after it has led to further concentration, give way again to a relaxation of competition and increasing profit margins. This expectation is borne out in most cases: oleomargarine, cereal preparations, chewing gum, flavouring extracts, and cane sugar show the familiar pattern of a declining share of wages in the New Era, without a recurrence of competition in the thirties.[1] Only in chocolate and meat packing competitive pressure seems to have continued throughout this period. In meat packing a special technical development is responsible for that. The operation of medium sized packers in country districts proved technically advantageous and these newly established concerns competed strongly with the four big centralised meat packers of Chicago. This explains why the industry follows the 'competitive pattern'. In the long run this may prove again a temporary phase: the 'big four' have been buying up country meat packers and the process of concentration is renewed. An industry with rather moderate concentration, flour milling, also shows some decline of the share of wages after 1923.

Industries with low concentration are butter, ice cream, bread, beverages, confectionery, maccaroni, and manufactured ice. Canning is partly very concentrated, partly the opposite. Ice cream and beverages show a considerable increase in gross profit margins, which can be plausibly explained by a rise in selling cost. The case of butter and manufactured ice is more

[1] In all these cases, however, selling cost may have been responsible for all or part of the increase in gross profit margins.

TABLE 13

% SHARE OF WAGES IN VALUE ADDED: FOOD AND KINDRED PRODUCTS

	Butter, Cheese and condensed Milk	Ice Cream	Meat packing	Bread	Canning Fruit & vegetables	Cereal preparations	Chewing gum	Beverages	Chocolate and Cocoa	Confectionery	Flavouring extracts	Flour	Manufactured ice	Macaroni	Oleomargarine	Cane sugar & cane sugar refining
1899			32.8	34.8					17.9			22.3	32.4		10.2	
1904	33.2		37.2	38.1					17.0			21.3	31.0		25.0	
1909	28.5		30.7	37.4					18.9			18.5	31.0		23.6	23.7
1914	32.1	29.4	29.5	35.4	32.5	13.4	8.2		17.9	34.4	8.6	19.6	34.8	32.7	12.5	30.4
1919	27.1	29.7	45.2	36.0	30.0	20.5	10.4		24.8	27.9	11.3	20.1	36.2	35.3	23.2	32.4
1921	29.2	30.7	46.0	40.5	28.8	16.6	11.0	37.6	22.5	35.9	12.9	23.2	30.4	33.6	24.4	47.3
1923	27.8	28.3	40.9	39.1	26.4	16.4	8.7	29.2	22.2	33.6	11.7	25.6	29.7	33.4	18.6	42.8
1925	27.7	23.0	37.6	36.5	29.2	13.8	8.4	25.9	24.2	31.9	10.9	23.0	24.6	31.3	20.0	34.8
1927	24.8	21.9	41.1	33.7	28.7	13.2	7.8	24.5	22.6	32.9	12.7	21.4	22.6	28.5	19.0	38.1
1929	21.6	19.6	36.1	34.8	26.1	12.0	7.3	22.9	19.5	31.7	9.5	18.3	24.8	27.4	14.8	26.0
1931	23.9	16.1	39.4	34.9	28.3	12.5	7.2	22.0	17.7	30.3	9.8	19.9	21.5	28.4	18.7	26.5
1933	21.2	17.5	39.1	39.9	26.4	13.0	7.6	20.5	23.3	33.8	6.5	16.8	20.3	27.8	20.0	21.6
1935	22.3	17.6	41.1	44.1	29.4	13.3	7.3	17.8	30.1	37.0	7.0	19.8	20.5	33.5	14.3	31.4
1937	24.4	15.5	43.0	42.6	32.2	15.5	7.5	19.0	29.0	35.5	6.0	22.7	19.9	32.9	11.8	26.4
1939	25.8	12.5	39.0	38.8	28.1	14.3	7.6	9.6	21.8	32.8	4.2	19.8	17.1	28.5	10.5	28.6

difficult to explain, but the other non-concentrated industries, including canning, follow the competitive pattern.

Textile group

There is little to be said about the industries in this group (Table 14) except that they mostly follow the competitive pattern, which is in agreement with the low degree of concentration. Only carpets and rugs show a decline in the share of wages. This industry is rather more concentrated than the others, 4 producers accounting for 50 per cent in 1935. Cordage and twine shows a similar, though less marked tendency.

Linoleum, a very highly concentrated industry, shows a decline in the share of wages immediately after the world war, although the subsequent development is irregular.

It was not possible to get comparable series over a long period for the clothing industry. It is to be expected that these industries, like the others, follow the same pattern as the total textile group.

Timber group

The basic timber industry follows the competitive pattern. The series which is corrected for contract work shows in the long run a fairly stationary development. This is in agreement with the structure of this industry, in which small scale production prevails.

In the timber working industries (furniture, boxes, etc.) small scale production also plays a considerable role and the degree of concentration is low. On the whole these industries approximately follow the competitive pattern, although less closely than basic timber. In furniture a decline in the share of wages between 1923 and 1931 seems to have been temporary.

Paper and allied products

This group consists of two parts : the production of pulp and paper, and the conversion of paper into various products such as bags and boxes. The conversion is essentially small scale production. The pulp and paper production on the other hand, although not highly concentrated (except newsprint !) requires nevertheless great investment. It is therefore not surprising that the pulp and paper industry shows, after a period of strong competition immediately after the world war, a long term decline in the share of wages.

Among the converted products, envelopes and paper bags conform to the competitive pattern. A puzzling exception are paper boxes : although a highly competitive branch with small scale production, this industry nevertheless shows a marked long run decline in the share of wages.

The Printing and Publishing group

For the purpose of this study this group is rather difficult to deal with. Printing as such is a typically competitive industry with plenty of very small

TABLE 14

% SHARE OF WAGES IN VALUE ADDED: TEXTILE INDUSTRIES[1]

Year	Cotton Narrow Fabrics		Cotton Goods			Woollen Goods		Worsted Goods		Knit goods		Carpets and rugs	Lino-leum	Lace		Cord-age & twine	Corsets	
	A	B	OA	NA	NB	A	B	A	B	A	B			A	B		A	B
1899			53.4			52.3		46.5		54.6		52.9	45.1			36.6	44.5	
1904			58.8			53.0		46.9		52.4		58.1	47.9			42.3	41.4	
1909			51.7			54.5		45.1		49.7		49.1	40.4			42.1	36.9	
1914			59.2	59.7		60.3		55.7		53.2		54.9	41.0	46.6		43.2	38.1	
1919				42.0		45.3		40.2		43.8		43.2	29.2	37.4		33.6	35.7	
1921				57.5		57.0		45.7		48.4		53.3	31.4	42.2		44.7	35.7	
1923	46.2			52.7		53.8		49.0		46.2		47.5	25.6	38.2		43.6	33.6	
1925	47.1			55.6		58.0		55.7		47.3		51.9	22.8	43.5		41.7	31.6	
1927	47.0			54.8		56.3		54.3		47.9		51.7	29.0	47.8		41.4	29.7	
1929	48.9			51.8		52.8		49.2		47.6	49.1	44.3	25.6	40.3		34.7	30.4	
1931	52.0			54.7		57.9		52.0		49.7	51.7	48.8	24.2	48.4		37.1	28.6	
1933	47.4			56.3		54.4		49.6		50.7	53.0	44.0	20.8	48.7	50.4	36.3	32.3	
1935	50.7	51.4		62.0	83.8	54.1	54.5	56.6	59.1	59.3	63.4	46.9	28.4		49.7	39.2	33.7	34.9
1937		52.7			58.3		55.2		56.6		61.1	41.1	31.7		51.4	41.7		35.0
1939		47.0									58.0	38.6	25.3		54.2	35.6		35.8

[1] A Value added includes cost of contract work.
B Value added excludes cost of contract work.

O Old classification.
N New classification.

producers. Publishing is very different in nature ; big newspaper publishing approximates more to an oligopoly in the United States. Book publishing has become more and more concentrated. Quite part from this, publishing as such is really not a manufacturing industry. In practice printing and publishing are almost inextricably mixed. The latest census has done something in the way of giving more details, and there are now separate figures for newspapers, periodicals, and books. Each of these lines comprises to a large extent establishments which are active in both printing and publishing. A series for general commercial printing has been computed for the present purpose by deducting from the old series 'Book, music and job' the series 'Books, printing and publishing'.

We find that the newspaper, periodical, and book series show a decline in the share of wages since 1923. It is not completely certain whether this can be interpreted as a consequence of monopolistic elements and concentration; certainly it is not due, however, to a greater proportion of the printing for the publishing firms being done outside these groups, because the proportion of contract work does not show any secular increase.

The series for general commercial printing shows, contrary to expectations, also some declining tendency of the share of wages, although not very clearly. In one of the allied industries, bookbinding and blank book making, this tendency is marked. This case remains rather puzzling.

The Chemical group

Most of the series given for this group (Table 18) include heavily concentrated industries. 'Chemicals not elsewhere classified' is the basic sector of the industry, including acids, nitrogen compounds, potash, coal tar products, general organic compounds, etc. Production in all these lines is heavily concentrated and carried on in very large units. The figures for this and various other series (fertilisers, oils, drugs and medicines) indicate that a competitive struggle took place immediately after the world war (see above p. 81). From 1923 onwards the share of wages declined. If we exclude rayon from the series 'Chemicals n.e.c.' the decline in the share of wages is even more marked. The basic chemical industry thus behaves just as we should expect a heavily concentrated industry to behave. Rayon, itself very concentrated, is a special case. Its product is in relatively close competition with other fibres, and the industry has been continuously endeavouring to capture markets at their expense. The decline in profit margins can be plausibly explained by this factor.

Another instance of high concentration is soap, with a strongly declining share of wages. Drugs and medicines, similarly highly concentrated, show the same tendency from 1921 onwards. Fertilisers and oils show also some decline in the share of wages, although they are only in part concentrated: among oil, linseed oil and essential oils are concentrated industries, cottonseed oil is not.

A highly competitive industry is that of paints and varnishes, which

TABLE 15

% SHARE OF WAGES IN VALUE ADDED: FORESTRY PRODUCTS[1]

	Lumber and Timber basic products		Furniture and finished lumber group total	Furniture		Wooden boxes except cigar	Cooperage	Coffins
	A	B		A	B			
1899	47.4			49.5		50.7	54.0	44.3
1904	46.7	50.3		50.1		51.7	52.0	38.0
1909	49.0	51.7		48.9		53.0	51.5	36.6
1914	54.2	57.7	48.6	49.0		54.0	53.8	41.2
1919	52.2	54.0	44.5	44.7		49.2	47.5	35.0
1921	57.3	60.1	47.7	47.9		57.4	63.1	38.2
1923	50.2	52.2	46.0	46.0		53.1	53.2	39.1
1925	52.4		45.7	45.7		51.3	54.7	37.5
1927	55.1		45.8	47.3		50.4	56.0	34.6
1929	48.4		44.3	45.5		47.9	50.3	33.6
1931	54.6		45.1	46.2		50.3	52.0	34.4
1933	49.2	50.8	44.0	47.8		48.3	49.6	35.7
1935	52.3	54.1	46.5	49.0	49.3	48.3	48.3	38.1
1937	52.3	54.5	47.7		48.8	48.4	52.7	40.0
1939	49.0	51.0	44.6		46.5	47.0	48.6	35.3

[1] A. Based on value added including contract cost. B. Based on value added excluding contract cost.

TABLE 16

% SHARE OF WAGES IN VALUE ADDED : PAPER AND ALLIED PRODUCTS ; RUBBER PRODUCTS ; PETROL AND COKE [1]

	Pulp mills and paper mills	Converted paper products group total	Paper boxes	Envelopes	Paper bags	Rubber tyres and inner tubes	Rubber boots and shoes	Coke and by-products	Petrol refining A	Petrol refining B
1899	37.4	44.4	52.6	46.2	26.0		34.8	44.6	31.8	
1904	41.4	42.3	50.5	38.1	25.8		23.4	42.6	28.1	
1909	40.0	39.5	48.8	37.2	24.6		42.3	49.0	26.0	
1914	44.7	41.5	48.7	41.5	31.5		33.4	47.5	27.3	
1919	42.3	36.8	41.0	37.3	26.6		46.4	45.9	23.3	
1921	57.5	41.8	47.1	41.2	30.7	36.7	37.8	45.4	29.7	
1923	45.5	40.4	45.0	41.0	35.7	38.9	39.0	29.6	28.2	
1925	43.7	39.5	43.8	42.0	34.4	33.0	37.3	36.5	21.5	
1927	39.2	38.0	41.8	40.0	38.2	32.4	39.6	35.9	29.2	
1929	36.8	36.2	42.4	36.6	31.3	37.4	43.8	24.8	21.6	
1931	35.6	36.0	42.2	39.6	30.7	27.2	38.8	34.6	34.2	
1933	32.8	34.1	39.0	37.8	28.9	34.2	51.6	36.4	28.6	
1935	37.8	36.2	39.0	40.2	33.6	43.4	49.9	37.2	30.4	30.7
1937	36.7	35.9	39.1	40.6	34.2	46.8	56.0	39.8		29.4
1939	36.8	35.2	38.4	38.2	33.8	39.5	58.7	38.5		24.4

[1] A. Value added includes contract cost. B. Value added excludes contract cost.

TABLE 17

% SHARE OF WAGES IN VALUE ADDED: PRINTING AND PUBLISHING[1]

	Printing & Publishing Book, Music and Job	P. & P. Newspaper and Periodical	P. & P. News-papers	P. & P. Periodicals	P. & P. Books	General Commercial O	General Printing N	Bookbind-ing and related industries	Machine & hand-type setting	Electro-typing and stereo-typing
1899								51.9		50.0
1904								49.7		51.3
1909									52.0	50.0
1914	39.8	25.6						47.6	54.4	51.7
1919	39.2	25.2			10.9	45.3		44.3	50.0	43.1
1921	40.4	25.4			13.5	45.2		47.0	56.6	52.6
1923	41.0	23.8			14.1	46.1		47.5	54.1	50.0
1925	40.6	22.2	26.8	12.1	13.3	46.2		46.2	54.2	51.1
1927	39.6	21.6							52.0	
1929	36.8	20.4	25.0	10.6	10.0	42.4			50.7	
1931	39.4	22.0	26.8	11.6	12.9	45.2		44.3	54.6	52.5
1933	37.4	21.6	25.3	11.9	9.5	42.8		40.8	47.5	37.6
1935	36.4	21.7	26.0	11.1	8.4	41.9		42.5	50.0	36.6
1937	37.5	22.2	26.6	12.0	8.7	44.0	43.5	45.3	50.8	40.4
1939	—	20.5	24.4	11.4	8.5	—	41.7	41.0	48.2	41.1

[1] Value added is *net* of cost of contract work given out in all figures.

O. Old classification. N. New classification.

TABLE 18

% SHARE OF WAGES IN VALUE ADDED: CHEMICAL INDUSTRIES[1]

	Animal, Vegetable and Compound Oil	Soap	Paints and Varnishes	Fertilisers		Chemicals n.e.c. incl. Rayon & liquified gases	Rayon	Chemicals n.e.c. excl. Rayon and liquified gases	Drugs, Medicines, insecticides, etc.	Perfumes, cosmetics, toilet preparations		Cleaning & polishing preparations	Baking powders	Explosives
				O	N					O	N			
1899		—	19.8	26.8		33.9			11.9	14.5		16.7	9.5	35.3
1904		19.5	20.3	29.5		32.9			10.0	12.0		17.2	10.0	26.6
1909		15.8	18.1	21.8		26.8			10.7	11.6		13.4	8.8	24.9
1914	22.8	20.8	17.8	23.2		31.5			12.6	13.8		11.3	10.5	28.5
1919	20.8	27.1	19.6	26.4		33.6			14.2	12.0		13.8	18.4	26.8
1921	36.0	21.0	22.7	45.2		29.4			16.7	12.1		15.6	16.0	23.2
1923	23.4	20.2	19.3	29.8		31.7			13.4	11.3		12.4	16.4	25.6
1925	20.0	19.8	20.0	25.6		29.8	33.0		12.0	10.3		12.7	13.7	24.2
1927	23.4	17.2	19.0	33.7		28.0	34.0	28.5	10.9	10.1		11.5	15.4	22.8
1929	22.3	14.6	18.0	24.6		27.4	38.5	25.3	10.3	10.2		10.8	16.2	20.8
1931	22.8	13.0	18.7	25.3		26.1	39.6	23.2	9.9	9.3	8.9	9.7	18.3	21.0
1933	20.7	13.2	17.5	28.2		25.8	34.2	23.2	10.2		11.7	10.3	19.6	18.3
1935	20.2	15.4	17.4	23.4		27.6	42.0	23.8	10.7		11.5	12.0	24.0	23.6
1937	20.2	16.4	18.9	23.5	23.2	27.4	37.9	24.8	10.8		11.9	11.4	22.6	25.4
1939		13.3	17.4		24.3		36.2							

[1] O. Old classification. N. New classification.

shows very little decline in the share of wages. Perfumes and cosmetics, as well as cleaning and polishing preparations, seem to be influenced by the high selling costs prevailing in those lines.

Coke and Petrol

Production of coke must obviously be carried on in very large plants. The share of wages will be strongly influenced here by the degree of capacity use, because wage cost per unit will be greater with a low degree of utilisation. It appears that there is a definite downward trend in the share of wages up to 1929. The figures for the 1930's would have to be corrected downwards, if account could be taken of the lower degree of utilisation in that period.

In petrol refining the decline in the share of wages is obvious up to 1919. The later development is explained by a factor already mentioned above (p. 81). The dominating big oil companies own the pipe lines and tankers, and are able, by squeezing the refinery margin, to squeeze the independent refineries without harming themselves, because the reduced margin, for them, is compensated by increased earnings of the pipe line companies.

Rubber group

The main sectors of the rubber group, tyres and tubes, and rubber boots and shoes are both highly concentrated. They are nevertheless in fact very competitive. In the case of tyres this is due to the oligopsonistic position of the motor industry. In the case of shoes it may be that competition with leather shoes plays a part. The competitive struggle seems to have reached a pitch in the late thirties ; in the case of tyres it has subsided somewhat after 1937.

Leather group

All branches in the leather group are highly competitive; small scale production is possible in all leather working industries, and even leather tanning can be carried on on a moderate scale. The share of wages conforms to the competitive pattern in all cases. In leather tanning, etc., there is an increase in the share of wages in the whole post-war period as compared with the pre-war period. The competitive struggle in this industry is particularly sharp, because it is, since the world war, a declining industry.

Stone, clay and glass group

The most important industries in this group (Table 19) are highly ' oligopolistic '. Glass in all its branches (window glass, plate glass, containers) is highly concentrated. Cement is not highly concentrated on a national scale, but as the market of a plant is geographically limited, the effective concentration is in fact very high. By and large the same applies also to bricks, included in ' clay products '. Potteries, on the other hand, can be regarded as predominantly competitive.

Cement, clay products and glass show a most remarkable secular fall in the share of wages. In the case of cement the change is in reality even greater than appears from the figures, because the abnormally low degree of utilisation in the 1930's meant an increase in the wage cost per unit above the level which would have obtained with a more normal degree of utilisation.

Lime and concrete products follow a pattern similar to the above industries, although we should expect rather more competition here. Asbestos products are highly concentrated, but the figures give a rather irregular picture.

Potteries show much less of a decline in the share of wages than the other series. This is in conformity with the much greater competition obtaining in this industry, where transport costs do not limit the market.

Iron and Steel group

The concentration figures for industries in this group (Table 20) are given below:

	Proportion of output produced by the four largest concerns
Steel	49%
Tin cans	81%
Cast iron pipes and fittings	42%
Wire made from purchased rods	40%
Wire work n.e.c.	23%
Cutlery	36%
Tools (except edge tools, files and saws)	24%
Enamelled iron and sanitary ware	34%
Fabricated structural steel	25%
Bolts, nuts, rivets	34%
Forgings	21%
Wrought pipes	47%
Screw machine products	22%
Steel barrels, kegs, drums	37%
Stamped and pressed metals	12%

These figures do not give an adequate picture. In most cases the relevant degree of concentration is much higher, because various different products are combined in one and the same industry. Apart from this the scale of production and capital investment required in most of these industries is considerable. We should not expect, therefore, the competitive pattern to prevail (except in ' stamped and pressed metals '). In fact most of the series show a decline in the share of wages. It is very marked especially in the case of tin cans, wire, cast iron pipe, wrought pipe, where concentration is high, and in cutlery, bolts and rivets, forgings, etc. Among the concentrated industries only steel barrels make an exception. Stamped and pressed metals could be expected to follow the competitive pattern.

In the heavy sector of the industry (blast furnaces, steel works and rolling mills) the decline in the share of wages *at given level of utilisation* is partly masked by the abnormal degree of excess capacity in the 1930's, which, in this industry, raises strongly the wage cost per unit.

Non-ferrous metals

In this group (Table 21) again heavy concentration and large capital requirements predominate. Smelting and refining of copper, lead and zinc is one of the most concentrated lines of production altogether. Alloys and aluminium manufactures, too, are highly concentrated. The same is true of the main industries which compose the series 'sheet metal work', for example, copper plates. All these industries must be expected to conform to the 'monopolistic' pattern. In fact, since the end of the world war they show the familiar decline in the share of wages. It can be seen, however, especially in the case of smelting and refining, that the share of wages was much lower before the world war. It seems that there is here, again, a case of competitive pressure re-appearing in an industry where it has not been working since the turn of the century, and probably the over expansion of capacity during the first world war has contributed to this.

In the 'lighter' industries in this group the monopolistic pattern appears again in clocks and watches, silverware and lighting equipment. The degree of concentration in these cases is medium, and there are some additional factors limiting competition of new entrants: in clocks and watches old established firms have an advantage which is not easily reached by the new comer. Even the marginal producer may therefore earn a profit in this industry which explains why the competitive pattern is not followed.

Jewellery is an industry of extremely low concentration and small scale production. It conforms accordingly to the competitive pattern.

Machinery

Some of the industries in this group (Table 22) are highly concentrated, for example, electrical machinery and equipment, agricultural implements, sewing machines, cash registers and calculating machines.

Electrical machinery follows quite clearly the monopolistic pattern of a long run decline in the share of wages. Agricultural implements as well as engines and turbines show some decline in the share of wages since 1923. Textile machinery, sewing machines, washing machines and cash registers show no declining tendency, although they are highly concentrated.

The series for machine tools gives the impression of a competitive struggle after the world war, the share of wages subsequently returning to the pre-war level. The overall concentration in this industry is low and it conforms to the competitive pattern.

Transportation equipment

The series for motor cars (Table 23) suggests that in this industry periods of strong competition have been alternating with a slackening of competitive pressure. Up to 1923 competition seems to have been strong enough to prevent any fall in the share of wages. Subsequently competitive pressure relaxed, until in 1935 it was renewed. The intense competition up to 1923

TABLE 19

% SHARE OF WAGES IN VALUE ADDED: LEATHER GOODS; STONE, CLAY AND GLASS[1]

	Leather: tanned, curried and finished		Boot & shoe cut stock	Footwear	Suitcases, etc.	Leather gloves		Cement	Concrete products	Lime	Asbestos products	Clay products except pottery		Pottery incl. porcelain	Glass
	A	B				A	B					O	N		
1899	46.1		42.2	64.7	43.1	56.8									68.1
1904	44.0	44.6	41.3	56.4	43.2	49.5	52.0	49.7	51.9	49.5					69.7
1909	40.2	40.6	40.9	56.0	41.1	46.1	51.0	45.2	45.7	53.6					65.5
1914	38.4	39.0	44.3	55.2	43.0	49.0	54.1	36.5	48.5	55.5	35.7	58.9		67.1	63.2
1919	31.3	31.5	34.8	47.9	40.8	39.7	43.0	34.5	46.9	55.4	33.6	55.7		55.1	51.2
1921	54.6	55.5	44.4	52.7	45.4	52.8	54.7	33.9	47.5	58.4	27.2	58.4		60.0	53.5
1923	44.2	44.9	39.6	53.0	44.8	47.5	49.7	30.4	44.7	49.1	39.3	53.8		57.7	45.8
1925	42.4		44.8	50.9	44.3	44.5		28.9	43.8	45.6	45.3	54.5		60.7	47.5
1927	41.8		42.4	50.0	42.6	50.6		30.6	42.0	50.2	37.2	55.6		58.6	47.2
1929	44.2		40.7	49.4	42.8	48.8		28.4	38.5	43.4	35.1	50.2	50.0	52.3	43.8
1931	50.4		47.2	51.7	46.7	51.1		32.3	34.8	45.1	30.6		49.1	54.6	40.7
1933	43.5		44.4	53.3	46.3	52.9		23.2	32.2	42.2	35.2		42.6	56.8	35.2
1935	50.4	51.2	47.6	55.7	47.4	57.9	59.5	27.0	31.6	42.4	44.3		47.3	57.6	41.1
1937	53.8	54.8	49.2	55.4	47.5	58.7	61.0	30.4	34.2	44.7	41.8		50.8	57.0	41.6
1939	46.6	49.4	45.0	54.0	46.4	53.6	57.8	25.7	29.4	39.8	32.0		46.0	55.0	37.8

[1] A. Value added includes contract cost.
B. Value added excludes contract cost.

O. Old classification.
N. New classification.

TABLE 20

% SHARE OF WAGES IN VALUE ADDED: IRON AND STEEL

	Blast furnaces, steel works & rolling mills	Cast iron pipe & fittings	Tin cans, etc.	Wire from purchased rods	Wirework n.e.c.	Cutlery	Tools, except edge tools, files & saws	Enamelled iron sanitary ware	Fabricated structural steel	Bolts, nuts, rivets	Forgings	Wrought pipes	Screw machine products	Steel barrels, kegs & drums	Stamped and pressed metals A	Stamped and pressed metals B
1899	43.0			37.5	43.4	58.8			47.1	50.9	49.1	43.1	48.3			
1904	49.5		43.6	36.8	40.2	56.4			45.5	52.2	52.2	53.2	46.9			
1909	47.1	63.2	44.6	43.2	36.0	54.8			46.6	49.7	48.6	50.7	42.1			
1914	55.4	73.2	43.5	43.3	37.9	52.3			46.5	57.0	50.6	50.9	53.0		46.9	
1919	53.7	59.4	50.2	49.4	39.0	42.4			47.5	46.2	43.4	58.6	48.7	44.9	44.7	
1921	66.2	64.3	41.3	47.9	45.4	42.8			48.0	60.0	52.9	57.2	59.2	43.4	51.8	
1923	54.0	57.0	41.0	47.9	40.2	35.8		46.8	44.8	47.5	46.5	53.9	53.9	40.5	49.3	
1925	51.5	52.7	40.7	47.0	42.6	33.8		45.0	42.2	47.9	47.0	48.4	52.8	40.3	47.1	
1927	53.0	55.5	41.6	47.9	40.3	32.3	43.1	44.9	43.0	46.0	44.5	38.0	53.0	42.5	46.5	
1929	45.0	49.1	37.5	39.9	35.4	27.8	38.3	46.0	37.8	38.0	40.8	34.5	43.6	36.5	43.0	
1931	57.4	54.1	37.6	45.1	37.5	28.1	39.0	45.4	45.0	45.1	45.6	31.3	49.0	40.3	44.4	
1933	56.1	48.8	32.0	39.8	36.2	29.2	34.6	44.0	41.9	41.2	47.5	39.8	45.0	48.4	42.4	
1935	51.4	45.1	32.2	41.7	41.2	35.0	39.8	49.0	42.2	47.7	48.5	37.4	46.9	42.7	47.6	48.1
1937	51.1	51.5	33.0	42.1	46.2	38.0	43.5	48.7	44.4	41.6	47.3	43.6	47.4	41.8		50.9
1939	49.3	48.1	29.9	39.8	42.9	41.5	38.2	42.9	43.1	41.0	43.7	36.8	44.6	44.7		44.8

TABLE 21

% SHARE OF WAGES IN VALUE ADDED: NON-FERROUS METALS[1]

	Primary Smelting and refining (excluding Aluminium) O	N	Primary Smelting ing and refining (includg. Alumin-ium	Non-ferrous metal alloys A	B	Alumin-ium manu-factures	Sheet metal work	Lighting fixtures	Clocks & Watches	Silver-ware & plated ware	Jewellery A	B
1899	20.2			47.5				43.7	64.6	44.8		
1904	29.3			45.5			47.8	41.3	61.8	46.8		
1909	33.0			44.3			45.6	42.3	56.5	43.1		
1914	30.1			50.7		50.0	45.9	46.0	60.1	45.1	43.6	
1919	44.5	45.0		51.3		51.2	42.7	45.8	58.4	45.9	38.4	
1921		40.7		54.3		54.2	50.2	47.0	66.0	48.1	43.2	
1923		42.0		48.3		49.1	44.5	43.9	56.0	45.6	40.4	
1925		30.9		48.8		46.2	41.5	43.2	51.1	44.4	40.5	
1927		33.2		46.9		47.8	41.8	40.5	49.2	42.7	41.9	
1929		33.5		37.8		50.0	39.5	38.3	46.0	38.2	40.0	
1931		31.2		40.5		46.4	42.0	40.8	48.0	37.3	43.8	
1933		32.6		39.4		43.5	38.2	35.4	45.1	37.5	43.6	
1935		31.9		41.5	41.8	44.5	38.3	37.6	47.5	39.5	43.7	44.2
1937		33.6	29.9		42.2	46.5	40.5	42.3	47.0	41.0		44.5
1939			28.4		38.8	41.0	35.3	36.5	42.0	41.0		40.6

[1] A. Value added includes contract cost.
B. Value added excludes contract cost.

O. Old classification.
N. New classification.

TABLE 22

% SHARE OF WAGES IN VALUE ADDED: MACHINERY[1]

	Agricultural Implements exclusive of Tractors	Agricultural Implements inclusive of Tractors		Agricultural Implements, Tractors, Engines, Turbines and wheels (combined)		Machine tools		Textile machinery	Sewing machines	Washing machines	Cash registers and calculating machines		Electrical machinery & apparatus including radio and phonographs
		O	N	O	N	O	N				O	N	
1899										31.3			47.8
1904										43.8			41.9
1909										30.0			42.9
1914	38.2			42.7				47.7		34.4	23.0		40.0
1919	41.5			42.2		43.1		46.2		36.8	31.0		40.5
1921	52.1			55.7		57.6		50.6		36.0	30.0		39.5
1923	46.1			48.2		49.3		45.4		31.8	27.6		41.0
1925	39.1			42.1		46.5		45.2	53.4	27.2	24.2		36.0
1927	39.6			41.1		46.2		44.0	52.4	30.8	22.8		34.0
1929	36.0			37.6		42.4		44.5	62.5	29.1	30.0		34.2
1931	36.7	32.8		35.7		42.3		44.6	59.4	27.3	29.4		31.4
1933		51.8		48.5		41.2		46.4	54.8	31.7	36.0	34.6	36.0
1935		42.4		43.6		43.8		46.0	52.7	39.0		29.2	35.2
1937		44.2	44.5	45.2	45.5	43.5	44.3	46.8	54.0	41.3		32.3	37.5
1939			41.8		41.2		41.0			37.5			34.0

[1] O. Old classification. N. New classification.

TABLE 23

% SHARE OF WAGES IN VALUE ADDED: TRANSPORTATION EQUIPMENT AND MISCELLANEOUS[1]

	Motor vehicles	Motor vehicle bodies and parts	Motor vehicle combined total		Motor cycles and bicycles	Ship and boat building		Locomotives	Rail road cars	Photographic apparatus
			O	N						
1899					54.4	60.4			59.0	31.8
1904			42.6		80.0	64.5		49.8	56.4	20.2
1909			41.4		52.0	60.0		54.0	60.5	19.0
1914	31.8	53.1	36.8		41.6	65.8		56.1	65.8	20.0
1919	38.6	54.2	43.1		47.2	65.5		46.3	43.7	27.3
1921	39.4	50.0	42.0		39.1	67.5		44.0	55.2	28.9
1923	40.0	56.4	45.0		56.0	70.5		57.0	67.9	25.1
1925	31.3	56.5	40.7		47.1	67.9		77.0	62.0	25.2
1927	33.5	57.0	41.8		47.8	65.7		57.0	58.6	29.6
1929	27.8	54.0	36.6		50.0	60.7		57.9	60.7	28.3
1931	30.1	45.3	36.9		44.0	54.1		77.8	64.2	22.4
1933	31.6	46.5	38.9		44.1	55.1		70.5	78.2	24.4
1935	37.7	60.2	39.8		50.6	59.1	58.8	50.7	66.5	33.0
1937	45.6	55.7	51.0	51.8	51.1		64.0	45.6	55.5	36.9
1939				50.0	48.3		61.3	46.0	54.6	28.2

	Surgical equipment	Buttons	Brushes	Furs dressed and dyed	Fur goods		Advertising signs and displays	Toys		Musical Instruments excl. phonographs
					A	B		O	N	
1899	24.2	57.2		54.4	33.6					
1904	31.8	52.9		48.0	32.1					48.6
1909	30.0	51.5	40.0	51.0	32.3		35.3			49.0
1914	28.9	53.4	40.7	47.0	31.9		37.6	43.8		49.0
1919	29.0	55.0	36.6	50.7	35.7		35.6	45.7		49.5
1921	26.6	52.9	37.9	51.8	40.8		36.8	43.1		53.7
1923	27.1	57.2	37.0	46.0	38.8		36.8	43.2		52.1
1925	21.6	54.4	35.7	45.3	37.1		32.6	41.1		50.0
1927	28.2	52.5	32.4	50.3	36.1		35.5	40.6		51.9
1929	25.0	50.3	33.5	39.8	32.8		33.9	39.5		51.7
1931	26.0	50.8	36.2	36.8	40.0		34.6	38.6		52.4
1933	27.0	48.6	38.7	40.5	37.7		36.5	44.3		49.5
1935	24.6	48.8	25.9	51.5	38.1	39.8	37.8	42.9		52.8
1937	26.8	53.3	35.7	55.1		44.5	40.5	43.4	43.9	54.8
1939	22.0	50.9	35.9	52.9		39.4	38.0		43.5	54.6

[1] A. Value added includes contract cost. B. Value added excludes contract cost. O. Old classification. N. New classification.

was obviously due to the policy of Ford who was expanding his markets at that time and able to force his competitors to follow his policy of limited profit margins. It is known that subsequently his share in the market fell, owing to the success of other firms in producing quality cars. This seems to be the explanation of the relaxation of competitive pressure : Ford was no more able to limit the profit margins of his competitors by cutting prices, because he could not compete with their products. In the middle thirties it appears that the Ford company began to try again to gain additional markets by price competition.

Series for other transportation equipment have been given for the sake of completeness, but it is doubtful whether much inference can be drawn from them. The figures are very irregular, and it may be suspected that the valuation of product is not free from arbitrariness.

Miscellaneous Industries

With the exception of photographic apparatus and surgical equipment which are rather concentrated industries, the series given in this group (Table 23) are small scale industries which should be expected to follow the competitive pattern. Buttons, furs, fur goods, toys and musical instruments conform to this pattern. Brushes show some decline in the share of wages, which may be due to selling cost.

Photographic apparatus and surgical equipment give a rather irregular picture, and the decline of the share of wages in some periods is followed by a reverse tendency in other years. Competitive pressure seems to recur also in these industries at times, in spite of concentration.

PART II

THE ACCUMULATION OF CAPITAL

IX. THE INTERNAL ACCUMULATION OF FUNDS IN THE ECONOMY AS A WHOLE

1. *Profits and Accumulation of Capital*

Earlier on (Chapter V) the problem of long run growth has been analysed for a single industry in isolation. The same analysis of the relations between profit margins, internal accumulation and growth will now be applied to the economy as a whole. For this purpose we shall add up the equations (4) [p. 46] for all industries, and re-interpret the resulting relation. For the purpose of this analysis we shall assume that we deal with a closed system, *i.e.* that foreign investments do not come into the picture, and that there is no budget deficit or surplus. Moreover, we assume also that there is no government debt (public debt) nor any holding of foreign investments. The net debt held by individuals is thus exclusively owed by private business. We shall also, for simplicity's sake, ignore the problem of taxation of profits and income. As before, the analysis will apply to the long-run development, the changes taking place in the trend values of various factors.

The question what exactly is meant by 'trend' can be settled briefly. It is assumed that the cyclical fluctuations of capital accumulation are fluctuations round an average, and this average is the trend. There are of course various statistical methods of fitting such a trend ; but the method of fitting curves is excluded, because we do not know the shape of the trend *a priori*, but want rather to find out its variations from the data. The natural approach is therefore to fit a moving average over a series of years corresponding roughly to the length of the trade cycle. This method gives a rough definition of what we mean by trend of capital accumulation, and it can be equally applied to the other magnitudes, such as national income, profits, and so on.

Restating the relation (4) (p. 46) for the economy as a whole we have

$$s = \frac{s}{H} \cdot \frac{H}{Z} \cdot \frac{Z}{C} \cdot C = u \cdot \frac{1}{k} \cdot g \cdot C, \tag{9}$$

where s are sales, H is output capacity, Z the capital stock, C the entrepreneurs' own capital, u is the utilisation of capital, k capital intensity and g the gearing ratio. If we take the derivative of all these variables with respect to time, the resulting relation must also hold. For convenience we take logarithms first and rearrange the terms :

$$\log s + \log k - \log u = \log g + \log C$$

Taking the derivative with respect to time gives

$$\frac{ds}{dt}\Big/ s + \frac{dk}{dt}\Big/ k - \frac{du}{dt}\Big/ u = \frac{dg}{dt}\Big/ g + \frac{dC}{dt}\Big/ C. \tag{10}$$

The meaning of the terms on the left hand side can be further elucidated.

In fact, from the definitions implied in (9) the capital stock Z can be expressed as follows :

$$Z = s\frac{1}{u}k,$$

and by logarithmic differentiation we have

$$\log Z = \log s - \log u + \log k$$

$$\frac{dZ}{dt}\Big/Z = \frac{ds}{dt}\Big/s + \frac{dk}{dt}\Big/k - \frac{du}{dt}\Big/u. \qquad (11)$$

These relations, based merely on definitions, are the same as those used in Chapter V. Strictly speaking we should again consider as a complicating factor, the elimination of existing productive equipment by the process of price cutting and driving out of firms. But we shall neglect this complication in the following analysis.

It should be mentioned that the magnitude sales s in the above relations may be interpreted in various possible ways. We can interpret it as gross sales, but we can also interpret it as gross or as net national income. The meaning of the capacity output H and the meaning of capital intensity k will have to be different according to which interpretation of s is adopted.

This equation for the economy as a whole is obviously very closely related to the Keynesian equation of investment and savings. The left hand side of the equation (10) represents nothing else than *investment*, analysed into the following items : Proportionate growth of sales, proportionate capital intensification, and proportionate reduction in the degree of capital utilisation. It has been seen (11) that the sum of these items amounts to $\frac{dZ}{dt}\Big/Z$, the rate of growth of the stock of real capital.

The right hand side of equation (10), despite its unfamiliar form, represents nothing but *saving*. The item $\frac{dC}{dt}\Big/C$, the proportionate growth in entrepreneurs' capital, is familiar enough ; it is the internal saving of business, disregarding for the time being the possibility of new share issues. The other item, $\frac{dg}{dt}\Big/g$, the proportionate growth in the gearing ratio, requires rather more elucidation.

The *gearing ratio* appears now, in the economy as a whole, in a totally new light. For a single enterprise, it is the proportion of the entrepreneur's total assets to his own funds (entrepreneurial capital). For the economy as a whole, if we cancel out inter-indebtedness of business, it must be the proportion of the total stock of real (business) capital to the part of it owned by the entrepreneurs. As we have assumed that the saving of all individuals (non-entrepreneurs) is invested in claims against business, it follows that the total stock of real capital is equal to the sum of the claims of entrepreneurs (entrepreneurs' capital) and the claims of *outside savers* (non-entrepreneurs) against it. These two sets of claims between them exhaust the total of accumulated savings in the economy. The gearing ratio is thus the proportion of total accumulated saving to the entrepreneurs' capital. It follows that the gearing ratio will be *constant* $\left(\frac{dg}{dt} = 0\right)$, if the total saving (= total stock of capital) accumulates in the same proportion as entrepreneurs' funds, which implies that outside savings also accumulate in the same proportion as the other two. If we call the total accumulation of outside savers—which equals the debt of enterprises—D, then obviously

$$g = \frac{Z}{C} = \frac{C+D}{C} = 1 + \frac{D}{C}\,.$$

A constant gearing ratio clearly requires that C and D must change in the same proportion, *i.e.* entrepreneurs' capital and outside savings must accumulate at the same proportionate rate. Correspondingly an *increasing* gearing ratio (positive $\frac{dg}{dt}$) implies that outside savings (= debt) accumulate at a greater proportionate rate than entrepreneurs' funds. A *falling* gearing ratio means that outside savings accumulate at a smaller proportionate rate than entrepreneurs' capital. Thus, the item $\frac{dg}{dt}\Big/g$ in equation (10) indicates changes in the proportion of outside savings to internal accumulation of funds. We shall shortly come back to the problems arising from this definition of the gearing ratio.

Let us now analyse further the internal accumulation. As earlier on, we shall call the proportionate rate of internal accumulation $\frac{dC}{dt}\Big/C$ briefly α. It is very plausible to assume that it depends on p, the *net* rate of profit (exclusive of interest paid) on entrepreneurs' capital. Following Mr. Kalecki[1] we assume that entrepreneurs' saving is determined as a constant proportion $(1-\lambda)$ of the rate of profit in excess of a certain level. This follows from the idea that capitalist entrepreneurs have a certain basic standard of consumption depending on the amount of capital they possess, and that they consume, in addition, a certain proportion of the profits which they make in excess of this basic rate of consumption. Their consumption consists of a fixed percentage on their capital plus a proportion of the profits in excess of that. Thus

$$\alpha = (p-a)(1-\lambda) \tag{12}$$

where a is the basic standard of consumption expressed as a ratio of capital, and λ is the proportion of profits in excess of that which is consumed. The

[1] *Studies in Economic Dynamics*, p. 47.

magnitudes a and λ which describe the entrepreneurs' propensity to save, may of course change in the long run.

The *net* rate of profit p on entrepreneurs' capital is again determined by the *gross* rate of profit e (including interest paid on debt) on total capital assets, by the rate of interest r, paid on debt, and by the gearing ratio.[1] Thus

$$p = \frac{Z}{C}(e-r)+r. \tag{13}$$

One word should be added about the application of our definition to *corporate enterprise*. The entrepreneurs' capital C will be represented here by what is alternatively called 'equity' or 'net worth', *i.e.* the sum of share capital and reserves or 'surplus'. The internal accumulation can only comprise the retained profits ('corporate saving'), but not the saving out of dividends because the latter does not become available directly to the enterprise. Savings out of dividends are thus counted as outside savings. On the other hand, for a corporation there is a special way of increasing the entrepreneurial capital, namely by issuing new shares. The problems which arise from the possibility of issuing new shares are somewhat complex, and we shall, for reasons of exposition, assume in the present chapter that such a possibility does not exist. The only way of increasing entrepreneurs' capital which we consider for the present is, therefore, the retention of profits in the enterprise.

It remains to link up the gross rate of profit e with the *profit margin.* Consider first the simplified case where cost is divided into two parts κ_1, and κ_2, of which κ_1 is strictly proportionate to the volume of sales, whereas κ_2 is constant. The amount of profits E will then be determined as follows:

$$E = eZ = (1-\kappa_1)s-\kappa_2 \tag{14}$$

$(1-\kappa_1)$ will be the gross profit margin, which in our simplified case is constant; the amount of profit is obtained simply as the difference between this gross profit margin and the constant overhead costs κ_2. Dividing (14) by Z we get

$$e = (1-\kappa_1)\frac{s}{Z}-\frac{\kappa_2}{Z}. \tag{15}$$

Now we can regard $\frac{\kappa_2}{Z}$ as a constant, assuming thus that overhead costs are a constant ratio of the capital stock. From our definitions it follows that

$$\frac{sk}{Z} = u$$

so that we can write for (15) also

$$e = \frac{(1-\kappa_1)}{k}u-\frac{\kappa_2}{Z}. \tag{16}$$

[1] See my *Small and Big Business*, Chapter IV.

This shows that the gross profit rate e can be regarded as a function of utilisation. As $(1-\kappa_1)$ is positive, it will be an increasing function of utilisation. The gross profit margin $(1-\kappa_1)$ will be a parameter of this function; the greater this gross profit margin, the greater will be the profit rate e for any given degree of utilisation.

The above is a rather simplified case, although it may not be a bad approximation. In a more general case we must take into account that the gross profit margin $(1-\kappa_1)$, as well as the overhead cost κ_2 may vary with the degree of utilisation. We can then more generally regard the profit rate e as a function of utilisation, a function which will in general depend also on the capital intensity k, so that we can write

$$e = F(u, k). \tag{17}$$

We may, however, just as in the simplified case, assume that the profit rate will increase with increasing utilisation. The above function may be called the profit function.

It can be seen that the gross profit rate e can vary in two ways: either by a change in utilisation, or by a change in the parameters of the profit function. In the simplified case above, we can regard a change in the gross profit margin as an example of such a change in the parameter of the profit function.

We can now substitute the general expression for the gross profit rate in (13) and obtain

$$p = g\,(F(u, k)-r)+r. \tag{18}$$

This we can again substitute in (12) and obtain, for the proportionate internal accumulation, the expression

$$\frac{dC}{dt}\Big/C = \{g(F(u, k)-r)+r-a\}(1-\lambda). \tag{19}$$

The equation (10) can now be written as follows:

$$\frac{ds}{dt}\Big/s+\frac{dk}{dt}\Big/k-\frac{du}{dt}\Big/u = \frac{dg}{dt}\Big/g+\{g(F(u, k)-r)+r-a\}(1-\lambda). \tag{20}$$

The meaning of this equation is, again, that the rate of growth of the capital stock (being the sum of the terms on the left hand side) is equal to the proportionate rate of internal accumulation plus the proportionate change in the gearing ratio. But the internal accumulation is now shown as determined by various factors, such as the degree of utilisation, the profit function $F(u, k)$ and the saving habits of entrepreneurs.

What use can we make of this equation? It can obviously not help to explain directly a dynamic process. In fact, it embodies hardly much more than a few definitions. It will be useful, however, just for that reason: it will help to make the definitions clear, and we shall continuously refer to it in the verbal argument. We shall consider, in the first instance, that the rate of growth of capital is given, and the right hand side of equation (20) must be adjusted to it. In the further argument we shall also take into account that this process of adjustment of various magnitudes on the right hand side will react, in turn, on the left hand side of the equation.

The problems which we are discussing here, relating as they do to the economy as a whole, are considerably more complicated than the problem of an individual industry discussed in Chapter V. We could there assume that the growth of sales of the industry is determined from outside, and the question was merely one of the adjustment of the other factors. The growth of sales (or of national income) in the economy as a whole can, however, not be regarded in the same way as independently given. Our analysis will now start from a different idea. Let us imagine a self-perpetuating growth of capital at a certain rate. The possibility of such a self-perpetuating growth is based on an endogenous theory of investment. That is to say, certain economic circumstances, such as a given profit rate, will bring about a growth of capital at a certain rate. This growth of capital will in its turn cause the circumstances which produced it to continue. (We are all the time referring to moving averages of investment, etc., so that cyclical fluctuations do not enter the picture). That such a self-perpetuating growth of capital on the basis of an endogenous determination of investment is indeed possible, and how it comes about, can be fully demonstrated only by a mathematical treatment of the problem which is given in Chapter XIII. Within the scope of the present verbal argument it can only be explained in a less rigid fashion. We imagine that investment is not autonomous, but induced by various economic circumstances. These are, first, the internal accumulation of business, which after a time induces a certain investment. This influence on investment should be positive as long as internal accumulation is positive. Secondly, there is the degree of utilisation of capacity, which may have a positive or a negative influence on investment, according to whether utilisation is high or low. Thirdly, there is the gearing ratio, or relative indebtedness, which again may have an encouraging or discouraging effect on investment, depending on whether indebtedness is small or great. Finally, the rate of profit will also influence investment. These factors are all themselves influenced by the rate of growth of capital. If we imagine that they are at such a level as to induce a growth of capital which in turn keeps these various factors unchanged, then we have the picture of a self-perpetuating growth.

Supposing now something happens to the rate of growth, so that it declines. We leave it open how this modification comes about. (We do not necessarily need to think of an exogenous influence, but can imagine that some structural coefficient of the system changes). The growth rate of capital drops, for example, from 3 per cent to 2 per cent per annum. We shall now discuss the adjustments which can be expected as a consequence. In terms of equation (20) we can say that the left hand side has been reduced from 3 per cent to 2 per cent. We must expect that the right hand side of the equation will be adjusted. The first step to this adjustment is a reduction in internal accumulation. This should, in fact, be fairly easy. Given the propensity to save of entrepreneurs (the parameters λ and a) the rate of profit will have to fall so as to make entrepreneurs save less. The fall in the profit rate will be brought about automatically by the reduction in investment and the consequent pressure on effective demand.

But what about saving outside businesses? Will this be adjusted too, as a consequence of the fall in investment? The development of the gearing ratio will depend on the extent to which this adjustment of outside saving is possible. Moreover, the extent to which the profit rate has to fall will depend on how far outside savings are capable of adjustment. The next section will be devoted to these questions.

2. *Outside savings and gearing ratio*

The problem is this: the gearing ratio, for the economy as a whole, is, as we have seen, the proportion of total accumulated saving to the part of it owned by entrepreneurs. Its constancy, or change, therefore depends on the relative proportions in which outside savings and entrepreneurs' capital accumulate. On the other hand, the gearing ratio is the proportion which entrepreneurs, on the average, keep between their total capital assets and their own capital: it appears to depend, then, on the decisions of the entrepreneurs as to how far they want to indebt themselves. How are the relative rates of outside and internal accumulation brought into adjustment with the decisions of entrepreneurs with regard to the gearing ratio?

The problem is similar to the Keynesian problem of adjustment of savings to investment, but it is a more specific case: it is a question of adjusting the *proportions* in which savings are contributed by the two groups of savers, entrepreneurs and outside savers, to the proportion in which entrepreneurs wish to finance their total investment by own capital and debt. If the wishes of entrepreneurs with regard to the gearing ratio are to prevail, then the outside saving must be adjusted to internal accumulation. If, for example, the entrepreneurs wish to keep the gearing ratio constant, then the outside saving must accumulate in the same proportion as entrepreneurs' capital. If they wish to reduce the gearing ratio then outside savings must accumulate less quickly (in a smaller proportion) than entrepreneurs' capital. If the desired reduction in the gearing ratio is sufficiently strong to make an absolute reduction of entrepreneurs' existing debt necessary, then the outside saving must even become negative, with positive internal accumulation, so as to enable the entrepreneurs to repay debt.

Now let us resume the discussion begun above. The accumulation of real capital declines from 3 per cent to 2 per cent per annum, and as a first consequence the profit rate and the internal accumulation are reduced (a, λ and r are assumed constant). If a new 'moving equilibrium', with a constant rate of capital growth, constant rate of profit and gearing ratio, is to be attained, we must finally come to a state in which internal accumulation, accumulation of outside savings, and accumulation of total real capital proceed at the same proportionate rate (which need not necessarily be 2 per cent). In the intermediate period, however, an additional adjustment will be required. Owing to the decline in the rate of profit, the entrepreneurs will strive to reduce their gearing ratio, and in the final equilibrium it will have to be lower than it was at first, corresponding to the rate of profit finally established. Thus, in the intermediate period of adjustment, the accumulation of outside saving will have to be slower than internal accumulation ($\frac{dg}{dt}$ being negative), to enable the gearing ratio to be reduced. The period of adjustment might be either short and abrupt, the outside savings becoming negative, so that a part of entrepreneurs' debt can be quickly repaid, or the adjustment might be gradual and long-drawn out, in which case $\frac{dg}{dt}$ would be negative for a long time and the gearing ratio would slowly approximate to its new level.

This is how a smooth adjustment *might* proceed, but in reality events are likely to be quite different. We can take it for granted that outside savings are not very elastic, certainly they are less elastic than internal accumulation (see further below). If real capital accumulation drops from 3 per cent to 2 per cent per annum, then outside saving will be reduced *less* than internal accumulation : *i.e.* the former will remain above 2 per cent, and the latter must correspondingly fall below 2 per cent, with the consequence that $\frac{dg}{dt}$ will become *positive*, and the gearing ratio will *increase*. The entrepreneurs, even apart from their desire to reduce the initial gearing ratio, will soon be inclined to check this relative growth of their indebtedness, and their only possible reaction against it will be to reduce investment. This, however, will not put matters right. Assuming that outside savings are relatively inelastic, the further drop in the accumulation of real capital will not be accompanied by a corresponding drop in the accumulation of outside savings, and consequently internal accumulation must drop more than total capital accumulation, and the entrepreneurs will find that their relative indebtedness (gearing ratio) continues to grow. In other words, the impact of any reduction in investment, owing to the inelasticity of outside saving, must be mainly on internal accumulation.

The same process can, of course, take place in the opposite direction : if real capital accumulation increases, and if outside savings are relatively inelastic in the upward direction, then the gearing ratio will decline, encouraging the entrepreneurs to increase their investment, and an increasing upward trend will be established.

The upshot of these considerations is this : if outside savings are relatively inelastic, *i.e.* if their accumulation adjusts itself less readily than internal accumulation to a change of real capital accumulation, then any primary growth or decline in the latter will set up a further increase or decline in the rate of growth of real capital. The process might reach a limit, but this need not necessarily be the case. The matter has so far been discussed in the abstract and it is necessary to examine the question of *elasticity of outside savings* more closely.

Outside saving is of the following types: there is, first, the saving of rentiers, *i.e.* receivers of fixed interest on securities. Secondly, there is the saving out of dividends. Thirdly, there is the saving of professional people (doctors, lawyers, etc.) and of big salary earners (technicians, managers, actors, etc.). Finally there is the saving of small salary earners and manual workers.

Rentiers' saving is the least elastic of all. Changes of rentiers' income can take place with long term changes in the rate of interest—in so far as conversions, after a time, will adjust the actual interest payments received. A continuing secular depression may provide an abundance of liquidity and lead to a reduction in interest. But it is well known that the long term rate of interest can hardly be reduced below a certain level; besides, the interest paid in practice on corporate bonds is of course much higher than what is theoretically called the long term rate of interest (yield of government bonds on very long term), because it includes risk premiums which are themselves not very elastic. Thus rentiers' saving will change only very sluggishly, and will prove completely inelastic below a certain minimum. If the decline in capital accumulation brings with it a general price fall, the rentiers' real income and their money saving will even rise, so that there will be a negative elasticity of rentiers' saving.

Once the rate of interest has reached a practical minimum, we may well regard rentiers' saving, with good approximation, as completely inelastic. If all outside savings are rentiers' savings, then the model previously described will apply in a very obvious way: if real capital accumulation drops below a certain level, then the amount entrepreneurs wish to borrow will be insufficient to absorb the rentiers' saving. To the extent to which the (proportionate) accumulation of rentiers' savings is in excess of the proportionate accumulation of real capital, it will have to be offset by a corresponding reduction in internal accumulation. The internal accumulation will therefore proceed at a smaller (proportionate) rate than the accumulation of real capital, and the gearing ratio will rise. The consequent further reduction in investment will *pari passu* reduce internal accumulation, and further increase the gearing ratio. The process will lead to a stopping of real capital accumulation (internal accumulation being simultaneously negative so as to offset the fixed rentiers' saving), and beyond that to a growing decumulation of capital. This pernicious effect of the inelasticity of rentiers' savings has been fully described by Mr. Kalecki.[1] The present analysis merely provides

[1] *Studies in Economic Dynamics*, p. 85–6.

for an extension of his theory to take account of other types of 'outside saving'.

Saving out of dividends at first sight seems to promise sufficient elasticity, but an examination of existing data does not fulfil this expectation. The experience of the 1930's in the U.S. shows that dividend payments, although reduced, are kept at surprisingly high levels even in a time of severe and prolonged depression. Estimates of the saving out of dividends, although subject to some error, indicate that considerable positive savings out of dividends persisted throughout the 1930's (see Table 24), while at the same time internal accumulation of corporations was negative. It seems safe to conclude that savings out of dividends are considerably *less* elastic than internal savings of enterprises.

TABLE 24

SAVING OUT OF DIVIDENDS

	National Income	*Dividends*	*Saving out of Dividends*	*Corporate Savings*
	(1)	(2)	(3)	(4)
		(in thousand million $)		
1919–28	69.2	3.6	1.2	1.7
1929–37	59.0	3.9	1.1	—3.0

Sources. Col. (1): Department of Commerce.
Col. (2) to (4): M. Taitel, Profits, Productive Activities and New Investment (*Temporary National Economic Committee Monograph* 12)

There remain two types, savings of professional people and big salary earners on the one side, and workers and small salary earners' savings on the other. Both types of saving are presumably dependent on the degree of unemployment.

Of the net savings of *workers and small salary earners* it may reasonably be assumed that they are approximately zero, given a certain moderate degree of unemployment. To the extent, however, to which the economy approaches a state of full employment, these 'small savings' will presumably become positive. Thus there is a certain range between full employment and a certain moderate degree of unemployment, in which the savings are elastic. It might be thought that if the degree of unemployment increases above the level indicated, dissaving will take place. This, however, can only be a short run phenomenon: in a slump, following a boom, dissaving may take place for a limited time (not much more than a year perhaps), but as the liquid reserves of workers are not great, net dissaving can play no role as a long run phenomenon. Beyond a certain degree of unemployment workers' net saving will remain constant at zero value, if long periods are considered.

Saving of *professional people and big salary earners* will also be influenced by unemployment. A persistent high degree of unemployment will increase the competition in these groups, and tend to reduce their remuneration, as well as producing some unemployment among them. We must be careful, however, not to over-estimate the elasticity of savings in this group. To a large extent the savers in these groups are in relatively sheltered positions, and their income is not subject to very great pressure. The average money income in such independent professions, for example, as doctors and lawyers, did not seem to fall appreciably more between 1929 and the late 1930's than the cost of living.[1] Again, the need for dissaving will tend to arise mainly for those who have least liquid resources to draw on. Finally, there is the likelihood that greater insecurity will bring about an increase in the propensity to save in these groups. A not inconsiderable part of savings is in form of life insurance, and this part seems to be fairly resistant against the pressure of unemployment. It would seem to follow that the saving of this group may be adjusted by variations in the degree of unemployment, but that the elasticity is very limited. Almost certainly, considerable positive net savings will persist in this group even with a very high degree of long run unemployment.

The consideration of various types of individual savings confirms the assumption previously made, that outside savings are *relatively inelastic.* Let us render the meaning of this statement precise. Total saving is equal to entrepreneurs' saving plus outside saving (= change in business debt); thus (denoting by Δ the accumulation in a year):

$$\Delta Z = \Delta C + \Delta D$$

If the gearing ratio has to be constant the two types of saving must accumulate at the same rate:

$$\frac{\Delta Z}{Z} = \frac{\Delta C}{C} = \frac{\Delta D}{D}\,. \tag{21}$$

Expressing, alternatively, the two types of saving as percentage of total business capital Z we could write

$$\frac{\Delta Z}{Z} = \frac{\Delta C}{Z} + \frac{\Delta D}{Z} \tag{22}$$

and say that these ratios must change in the same proportion, if the gearing ratio is to be constant. Now the mechanism by which a reduction in saving is brought about is a reduction in incomes. Real incomes, with a given amount of real capital Z, may be reduced by a fall in the degree of utilisation of capacity. But the decisive point is this: in conformity with all that was said above, we may expect that outside savings, as a *proportion of the national income* (*or of total personal income*) will hardly be reduced much. Thus if the degree of utilisation falls by 50 per cent the ratio of outside saving to business capital $\frac{\Delta D}{Z}$ will hardly fall much more than 50 per cent. On the other hand, however, a reduction of utilisation by 50 per cent will certainly reduce profits

[1] See the data for income of professions in the *Survey of Current Business*, 1943 and 1944.

in a much greater proportion, and entrepreneurs' savings in an even greater proportion. Thus it follows that entrepreneurs' savings are more elastic than outside savings in relation to a change in income.[1]

This is in agreement with the surprising figures of S. Kuznets for individual savings.[2] According to his estimate, individual savings (at current prices) were $4.0 billions p.a. in the decade 1919–1928, and $3.7 billions p.a. in the decade 1929–1938, or 5.6 per cent and 6 per cent of the national income respectively. These estimates are subject to considerable error, but in so far as we can give credence to them, they suggest that even the high degree of secular unemployment of the great depression did little or nothing to reduce the rate of 'outside savings' in proportion to the national income.

Whatever elasticity of outside savings there *might* be (granting the possibility of errors in the figure just quoted) is dependent on unemployment. If therefore the real capital accumulation decreases, and it becomes necessary to reduce the rate at which outside savings accumulate in order to prevent a growing disequilibrium, then a considerable increase in the degree of secular unemployment is practically the only means to this end. The increased degree of unemployment can be brought about in two ways: either instantaneously, if the reduction in the rate of profit (consequent upon the fall in real capital accumulation) is caused by a reduced degree of utilisation of capital (because then, clearly, the national income must fall in relation to the existing capital stock, with the degree of unemployment increasing *pari passu*). Or, alternatively, if the rate of profit is reduced at constant degree of utilisation (see Chapter V), then the increased degree of unemployment can only come about by a slowing down of the rate of real capital accumulation in relation to the (natural) growth of the labour force.

If an increase in the degree of secular unemployment cannot bring about a sufficient reduction in the rate of outside saving—and on account of the considerations given above this is very unlikely—then, instead of leading to a new 'moving equilibrium' the sequence of events conforms to the disequilibrium described above. Internal accumulation is reduced proportionately more than outside saving, so that the gearing ratio increases. Further reduction of investment will fall more heavily on internal accumulation than on outside savings, so that the gearing ratio will continue to increase, in spite of entrepreneurs' endeavours to reduce it by reduction of investment. Real accumulation, internal accumulation, and the profit rate will thus continue to fall and the gearing ratio will continue to rise. The outstanding feature of this *disequilibrium* is that the gearing ratio *in fact* established is continuously out of harmony with the ratio entrepreneurs' *wish* to establish: this indeed is the reason for the continuing disequilibrium. There is a growing relative

[1] We do not forget that profit rates, and therefore accumulation of entrepreneurs' savings, can be reduced *without* a fall in utilisation of capacity. But in this case the personal incomes (except dividends) need not fall at all, and the relative inelasticity of outside savings is obvious.

[2] *National Income and its Composition*, Vol. I, p. 276, Table 39, and *National Income: A Summary of Findings*, p. 21.

indebtedness against the wish of entrepreneurs, one might say, an 'enforced indebtedness'.

How does this come about in practice? If we consider an accounting period τ, there will be, for a particular enterprise, a certain internal accumulation ΔC during this period. At the end of the period, the entrepreneur will, on the basis of internal accumulation and rate of profit during period τ, decide the investment ΔZ to be carried out in the next period τ. Provided this investment is actually carried out there will be the following changes during period τ: on the one hand total assets will increase by the amount of the investment ΔZ on the other hand there will be a new internal accumulation $(\Delta C)_1$. The *net* increase in indebtedness *during period* τ, will result from the balance of investment planned before and carried out during the period, and the internal accumulation taking place during the period. It can be seen that the control of the entrepreneur over the development of the gearing ratio during the period τ, depends on his correct anticipation of the internal accumulation taking place during the period. He may, for example, assume the internal accumulation to be the same as in the preceding period, and plan his investment so as to keep the gearing ratio constant. But if the actual internal accumulation falls short of the expected amount, his gearing ratio will have increased at the end of period τ, as compared with the beginning of period τ.

In practice this may well work as follows: The entrepreneur will provide long term finance (by issue of bonds) beforehand for the part of investment which, he anticipates, will not be offset by internal accumulation during period τ. The rest he will provide either by short term borrowing or by drawing on his liquid resources (cash, marketable securities), and expect that this temporary finance will be sufficient, because the internal accumulation realised during the period τ will take over the function of permanently financing this part of the investment programme. But if the internal accumulation in τ falls short of expectation, he will find that he cannot pay back the short term credits as expected (this is the well-known case of 'freezing of credits'), or else that the draft on his liquid reserves, instead of being temporary, has become permanent. In either of the two cases his 'relative indebtedness' will have increased against his wish.

The matter will be similar if the entrepreneur, on the basis of a certain dissaving $-\Delta C$ in period τ, plans a disinvestment (excess of depreciation over gross investment) $-\Delta Z$ in period τ. Expecting, for example, the dissaving to remain the same in period τ, he may plan to carry out a disinvestment in excess of the expected dissaving, which would give him the possibility of repaying debt or increasing his liquid reserves (a procedure which would be necessary for him if he wants to keep his gearing ratio constant). But if the actual dissaving in period τ turns out to be as great as the disinvestment, he will not be able to repay any debt, and if it is even greater, he will find either that his short term debt has increased or that his liquid reserves have been reduced. In each of these cases his relative indebtedness will have increased, because a constant gearing ratio would require that he reduces his debt in proportion to the decumulation of his own capital.

It has become clear from these considerations how a disequilibrium between the actual gearing ratio and the relative indebtedness desired and planned by the entrepreneur can come about. But it has been implied above that this disequilibrium can persist over a long series of years, causing the trend rate of capital accumulation to fall continuously. Is such a continuing increase in the gearing ratio possible? It would seem for one thing that creditors would not tolerate it. If the mechanism requires an absolute increase in debt, they would not consent to grant further credit; if it requires only a relative increase in indebtedness (in the case of decumulation of capital) they would from a point insist on withdrawing credit. Setting aside the objections of creditors, we find that even for the debtors a continuing increase in relative indebtedness would seem to lead to serious difficulties. The entrepreneurs who are hit most by the growing relative indebtedness (and we can suppose that the impact of it will be very unequally distributed) will get into serious financial difficulties and a growing number of them will come to the point of insolvency. It would seem that the process cannot continue very long, unless, on account of bankruptcies, a certain amount of the debt goes by default. The ancient law of Solon has little scope for application in modern capitalism, however. There is ordinarily a fairly strong tendency to protect individual savings.[1]

Nevertheless it is possible for the disequilibrium to continue for a long time. There will be great financial difficulties for a part of the debtors, and pressure of creditors on them, resulting in foreclosures and selling of their property and business.

The property (real estate, business premises) may be sold to an 'outside saver', who in this way might become an entrepreneur. The proceeds from the sale will serve to repay the debt. As the funds for the repayment come from outside savings, the net indebtedness of business will in this way be reduced. The incentive for the outside saver lies in the very low price at which the property will be offered if foreclosed or sold under pressure. We must not over-estimate this possibility of reducing business debt, but it may not be negligible.

If the property foreclosed or sold under pressure is not sold to an outside saver, it will be acquired by another entrepreneur. In an important case the creditor to whom the debt is due will himself acquire the whole business property of the debtor. With the merging of the debtor's business into that of the creditor the debt will disappear. Alternatively, the debtor's property will be sold to a third entrepreneur who presumably will have sufficient financial reserves to carry it without indebting himself on this account (or

[1] In the great depression in U.S. the government stepped in to prevent large scale defaults on debt by railways, etc. The figures for insolvencies do not seem to suggest that elimination of debt by default was a more important factor in the decade after 1929 than in the preceding decade.

at least not to the same extent as the former owner). Again the debt will therefore be eliminated, in this case by the simple device of transferring the property from an owner who is financially weak to an owner of greater financial strength.

It will be noted that in the above cases the elimination of the debt of one entrepreneur goes hand in hand with the elimination of an equivalent claim of another. There is thus no *net* reduction in the indebtedness of business as a whole, no reduction in the *net* gearing ratio. Accordingly, the simultaneous reduction of debts and claims also does not involve the use of any *net* funds. But it would be wrong to conclude that the change is therefore irrelevant for the risk position of entrepreneurs. In fact, from the point of view of an entrepreneur, the claims against another entrepreneur are by no means a simple *offset* to a corresponding amount of his own debt, so far as the risk position is concerned. What matters for the financial position of an entrepreneur is therefore not *only* his *net* indebtedness, his *net* gearing ratio, but he is equally well also concerned with his *gross* indebtedness, his *gross* gearing ratio (i.e. ratio of all assets, including claims against other entrepreneurs, to his own capital). The reduction of inter-business debt will therefore provide an improvement in the financial position of business. Beyond that one could say more generally that any merging of business into greater financial units, such as will come about by buying up, will strengthen the risk position. This is because financial reserves are more effective in concentrated form in fulfilling their function as a reserve against contingencies (' principle of massed reserves ').

The taking over of businesses by the creditors or by entrepreneurs with great financial resources, and the consequent reduction in inter-business debt therefore *ease* the pressure put on the business system by an increasing *net* gearing ratio. This would explain how a continuing disequilibrium with increasing *net* gearing ratio can persist at all over a longer period. It does not mean, of course, that the disequilibrium could be made to disappear on this account. The partial relief provided by reduction of inter-business debt is dependent on the very factors of foreclosures and financial difficulties of a part of entrepreneurs, and will therefore not operate to stop the declining trend of capital accumulation. The *net* gearing ratio remains a fundamental factor in the risk position of business, and it is clear that the reduction of inter-business debt has theoretical limits, and becomes more and more difficult long before these are reached.

At the conclusion of this paragraph it may be asked how far certain drastic simplifying assumptions made at the beginning impair the applicability of the conclusions. We have assumed that there is no budget deficit and no foreign investment. If we drop this assumption it is clear that any existing budget deficit or lending abroad will serve to absorb a corresponding amount of outside savings. Only the excess of outside savings over and above the budget deficit and foreign lending will play the role ascribed to outside savings in this paragraph.

3. *Profit margins and utilisation of capacity*

In considering the effects of a fall in the rate of growth of capital it has been rightly assumed that the internal accumulation of funds will be adjusted to it by a fall in the rate of profit [a, λ, and r in equation (20) are assumed constant]. The fall in the rate of profit will, of course, come about by a reduction of net profit margins, the profit made per unit of sales [$F(u, k)$ in equation (18)]. Now the net profit margin can be reduced in two distinct ways : either by a fall in the degree of utilisation of capacity u, the parameter of the function $F(u, k)$ remaining unchanged; or else by a change in the parameter of the function $F(u, k)$, with unchanged degree of utilisation, such as to reduce net profits per unit of sales. The latter case will be realised, for example, if gross profit margins are reduced, while supplementary costs remain unchanged (in the simple and presumably very frequent case where gross profit margins are constant at varying degrees of utilisation).

The distinction is familiar from the discussion in Chapter V. It has been shown there that in an industry where squeezing out of competitors is easy, the profit margin at given utilisation is elastic; if, for example, the proportionate growth of real capital in such an industry declines, the competitive pressure resulting will reduce the profit margin in this industry without a permanent decline in the degree of utilisation. On the other hand, in an industry which approximates to the oligopolistic type, where the driving out of competitors is difficult, the profit margin at given utilisation is inelastic. If the rate of growth of the capital stock in such an industry declines, the profit margins will remain at the former level; there is no mechanism to reduce them in the case of an individual industry. It is plausible that the first type of industries were predominant in earlier stages of capitalism, and the ' competitive pattern ', with elastic profit margins at given utilisation, was typical at that time. Certainly in modern times the second oligopolistic type of industry prevails, and correspondingly the profit margin at given utilisation is to a large extent inelastic.

In its application to the economy as a whole the distinction between the two patterns acquires a new significance. For the economy as a whole the net profit margin *must* necessarily be adjusted to a decline in the proportionate rate of capital accumulation. When the competitive pattern prevails, as it may have in earlier stages, the adjustment happens by a squeezing of profit margins with unchanged utilisation—a change in the parameter of the function $F(u, k)$. When the oligopolistic pattern prevails as it does in modern times, and the parameter of the function $F(u, k)$ has become inelastic, there must occur a reduction in the degree of utilisation sufficient to decrease the rate of profit to the required level.

An obvious disadvantage of the second type of adjustment to a reduced rate of capital accumulation is that it involves unemployment. To obtain the reduction in the degree of utilisation the national income must fall, and unemployment increase correspondingly. With the first type of adjustment this effect is absent.

Another disadvantage of the second type of adjustment is even more important, because it affects the further course of the trend. The reduced degree of utilisation will mean additional excess capacity, which is not desired and planned by entrepreneurs, but which is forced upon them from outside by the deficiency of effective demand. This undesired excess capacity will presumably have an unfavourable effect on investment.[1] If the entrepreneur finds himself with more excess capacity than he wants to hold in order to be able to take up an eventual increase in demand, then he will be strongly discouraged from undertaking any expansion. This discouragement will be even stronger if he knows that such an unusual degree of excess capacity is fairly general in his industry. Furthermore, he will be discouraged from replacing his equipment by new, technically more efficient and modern equipment, unless the old equipment has become definitely useless, or its performance is at least seriously impaired. It is often said with much justification, that the technical lifetime of equipment is practically always much longer than the time after which it is in fact replaced, in other words that replacement is in practice determined not by the process of physical wear and tear, but by technical obsolescence. If that is true, the above argument would affect a very great part of replacement demand. It is, of course, not suggested that the excess capacity will stop all modernisation of equipment, but only that it will discourage it. It may, for example, determine an entrepreneur to replace only a part of his existing output capacity by modern equipment, or it may make him hesitate for a longer time until he carries out the modernisation.[2]

The conclusion is that with the pattern of adjustment of the profit margin to be expected in modern times (owing to the predominance of oligopoly) a *primary* decline of capital accumulation will—via a reduced degree of utilisation—lead with a certain time lag to a further reduction in capital accumulation. This cannot easily lead to an equilibrium. The individual entrepreneur may think that by reducing investment he will cure his excess capacity, but in fact for industry as a whole this strategy has only the effect of making excess capacity even greater. The secondary fall in capital accumulation will again produce a fall in the degree of utilisation, and after a certain time lag this will reduce capital accumulation further.

The changes introduced into the economic system by the spread of oligopoly thus make it liable to react (in the absence of counteracting forces) to a *primary* decline of capital accumulation by a further retardation of growth.

The process described can even be obtained without assuming a primary reduction in capital accumulation. Supposing the growth of oligopoly in the modern economy leads to an increase of net profit margins at given utilisation

[1] This effect is separate from, and additional to, the unfavourable effects on investment which arise from the reduced rate of profit, and eventually from the increased gearing ratio, as discussed under the last sub-heading.

[2] That excess capacity has an unfavourable effect on investment is suggested by Mr. M. Taitel on the basis of his investigations of steel and oil corporations (*Temporary National Economic Committee Monograph No. 12*: Profits, Productive Activities and New Investment).

—to a change of the parameters of the function $F(u, k)$ so as to give higher profit margins for any given u. There is some degree of support for this assumption in the data for manufacturing after 1923, discussed in Chapter VIII. If the proportionate rate of capital accumulation remains constant in the first instance, then the change in the parameters of $F(u, k)$ must lead to a decreasing utilisation of capacity such as to keep the value of $F(u, k)$, the actually resulting net profit margin, unchanged. It is in this way only that the profit rate, and the resulting internal accumulation can be kept constant (assuming again, a, λ and r, as well as the outside saving unchanged). Thus the *tendency* of profit margins to increase under oligopoly must lead to a reduction in the degree of utilisation. With a certain time lag this will lead to a reduction in the rate of growth of capital, and the process of retardation of growth will continue as described before.

4. *The maldistribution of profits*

The preceding discussion of the growth of oligopoly and its consequences is in some ways over-simplified. Taking into account one important detail will yield further results.

In reality the growth of oligopoly in a modern economy does not affect all industries equally, and the inelasticity of profit margins at given utilisation will therefore be very different in different industries. To simplify matters we shall assume that the economy can be divided roughly into two sectors, an *oligopolistic* one where profit margins at given utilisation are inelastic, and a *competitive* one where the ideal pattern of competition still works with some approximation. In the oligopolistic sector there will be a tendency for profit margins at given utilisation to rise, because neither the competition within each of these industries, nor the possibility of new entry will be sufficiently strong to counteract this tendency. With unchanged degree of utilisation, this would, of course, lead to an increase in the rate of profit in the oligopolistic sector, and consequently to increased internal accumulation. But if the rate of growth of real capital remains constant, this cannot happen, because savings cannot outgrow investment. Consequently there will be a pressure on effective demand, and national income and output will be reduced in relation to the existing capital stock. The decisive point is that the pressure of reduced effective demand will by no means fall on the oligopolistic sector alone, but on all industries. In common economic terminology, the pressure of reduced effective demand will be distributed over the various industries in accordance with the income elasticity of demand for their respective products.

In the competitive sector the reduction in effective demand in relation to the capital stock will bring about a competitive pressure, resulting in the elimination of marginal firms, and a squeezing of the profit margins, and consequently reduction of the profit rate. The degree of utilisation will tend to be more or less maintained at its former level in the long run.

In the oligopolistic sector the reduction in effective demand in relation to the capital stock will simply reduce the degree of utilisation. As a consequence the profit rate will be lower than it would have been, if the degree of utilisation had remained at its former level.

Now let us assume that the marginal propensity to save [$(1-\lambda)$ in equation (20)] is the same in both sectors of the economy. As the profit rate in the competitive sector has been reduced, the internal accumulation must also have been reduced there. In order to maintain the proportionate rate of internal accumulation *in the economy as a whole* at its original level, the profit rate and the internal accumulation in the oligopolistic sector must therefore *rise*. As a net result of the increase in profit margins at given utilisation in the oligopolistic sector, and the consequent pressure of effective demand on the total economy, a certain amount of profits, and a corresponding amount of internal savings, have been shifted from the competitive to the oligopolistic sector.

The result is hardly surprising, because it only confirms the view—acceptable probably to most economists—that oligopolistic industries have the power, by raising prices in relation to cost, to attract to themselves a greater share in the total profits, and consequently also in the total internal savings.

If this conclusion is correct it must have an important bearing on the financial position and the development of the gearing ratio in different industries. It is worth while to trace the consequences in some detail.

If all industries increased their stock of real capital at the same proportionate rate, and all accumulated their entrepreneurial funds at the same proportionate rate, their gearing ratios would be :

$$\frac{Z_1}{C_1}, \quad \frac{Z_2}{C_2}, \quad \frac{Z_3}{C_3} \ldots,$$

and they would change in all industries in the same way, *i.e.* they would either be constant, or increase, or decrease in all industries in a parallel fashion.

Now assume we have only the two sectors above mentioned, the oligopolistic and the competitive sector. The gearing ratio will be $\frac{Z_1}{C_1}$ or g_1 in the first, and $\frac{Z_2}{C_2}$ or g_2 in the second. Let us assume that the rate of growth of real capital is equal in the two sectors; the rate of growth of internal funds, in accordance with our previous conclusions, is greater in the oligopolistic than in the competitive sector. Thus

$$\frac{dZ_1}{dt}\Big/Z_1 = \frac{dZ_2}{dt}\Big/Z_2, \tag{23}$$

$$\frac{dC_1}{dt}\Big/C_1 > \frac{dC_2}{dt}\Big/C_2. \tag{24}$$

From this follows immediately—subtracting the equation from the inequality and changing sign – that

$$\frac{dg_1}{dt}\bigg/ g_1 < \frac{dg_2}{dt}\bigg/ g_2, \tag{25}$$

i.e., the gearing ratio in the oligopolistic sector will *fall* relatively to that in the competitive sector (for example it will fall more than the latter, or it will rise less, as the case may be). In a special case, if the gearing ratio for both sectors combined is constant, it must necessarily fall in the oligopolistic sector and rise in the competitive sector.

In simple language, this means that oligopolistic industries will have relatively more abundant internal funds in comparison with competitive industries. There will be a maldistribution of profits and of internal accumulation between industries. This maldistribution could not be remedied by a lending of the funds from the oligopolistic to the competitive industries, because this would not correct the divergent development of the gearing ratios.

The only effective remedy in this situation would be for entrepreneurs in the oligopolistic sector themselves to enter the competitive sector, setting up new enterprises and carrying out real investment there. In this way the entrepreneurial capital could be redistributed between the two sectors. Some general considerations would, however, lead us to expect that this process is not without difficulties. In order to start a new business in a line different from his own, the entrepreneur must acquire the goodwill and the market, which is considerably more difficult than expanding in his own line. He must further acquire the knowledge necessary in the new line, or what comes to the same, an organisation with a proper staff of expert managers and technicians must be built up. All this involves costs and risks. Apart from that, however, it takes substantial time. The period can be shortened, if the entrepreneur takes over an existing firm in the competitive sector, giving it a time of trial, in order to expand later. In this case, however, no new real investment is undertaken immediately, only perhaps after a time of trial. It is true that the funds used for the purchase of the business accrue to the seller, or, if he uses them to repay his debts, perhaps to some other business in the competitive sector, and in this way they may stimulate investment somewhere. But the connection is very indirect. Broadly speaking, it would seem that the flow of entrepreneurs' funds from the oligopolistic to the competitive sector and the consequent encouragement of investment there does operate, but with difficulties and a very considerable time lag. The effects of the maldistribution of internal funds are therefore only partly offset on this account.

That these effects are equivalent to a reduction of investment is clear. The reduction of the rate of profit in the competitive sector will reduce investment there by a greater amount than the additional investment induced in the oligopolistic sector by a corresponding increase in the rate of profit. In view of the impossibility of increasing investment within the oligopolistic sector without reducing sharply the marginal rate of profit, and the difficulties of entering new lines, the stimulus to investment due to a certain increase in the profit rate in the oligopolistic sector will be very small indeed. The discouraging effect on investment of the corresponding reduction in the profit rate in the competitive sector is, on the other hand, not negligible.

The conclusion is that the maldistribution of profits and internal savings consequent on the growth of oligopoly will have a depressing effect on the rate of real capital accumulation.

This adds an important detail to the earlier result, according to which, in a sense, savings may be maldistributed between business and outside savers. This is, as can be seen now, perfectly compatible with a relative abundance of internal funds in a certain sector of business.

X. The Consequences of Undesired Excess Capacity

1. What follows is an analysis of the role which utilisation plays in the determination of investment.

What reasons are there to believe that undesired excess capacity discourages investment? In the first place this appears to be a natural implication of the idea of 'planned excess capacity'. If entrepreneurs regard a certain amount of excess capacity as desirable, this naturally implies that a greater or smaller excess capacity will not find their approval. It implies, in other words, that they are not indifferent about the degree of utilisation actually realised. Their response, if they desire an adjustment, can be only of two kinds: they can either try to influence the market, e.g. by a price cut, or else they can slow up or accelerate the pace of investment. The first type of response, we know, is often not practicable. The second is always possible (though not necessarily very adequate in the short run). We should expect it to occur at least in those cases where the first type of response must be absent, and quite likely we may expect it generally.

It may be interesting to note that the theory has a certain resemblance to the 'acceleration principle' which relates investment directly to the increase in demand. But whereas the acceleration principle implies that full utilisation is aimed at, the present theory postulates instead a certain degree of excess capacity as the aim of entrepreneurs. And whereas the acceleration principle implies that investment will be so determined that capacity expands *pro rata* with demand, the present theory attributes only a *partial* influence to demand. According to it, investment will be influenced by other factors as well, and demand, acting *via* utilisation, will only be a modifying factor.

The present theory, in other words, postulates that investment is a function of utilisation. The simplest expression of it will be obtained if we assume 'all other factors which influence investment' given and constant, and plot, in a system of co-ordinates, the amount of investment corresponding to various degrees of utilisation (Fig. 5a). The curve which shows investment as a function of utilisation is then supposed to rise from left to right.

This graphical representation still does not enable us to mark out one particular degree of utilisation as the planned one. But it enables us to distinguish between a change in the planned degree of utilisation, and a change in utilisation which is not desired. If the curve shifts upward, for example, we must say that the planned degree of utilisation has increased. Any given actual degree of utilisation will then call forth a greater amount of investment. If, on the contrary, the curve is stable, and we move along the curve,

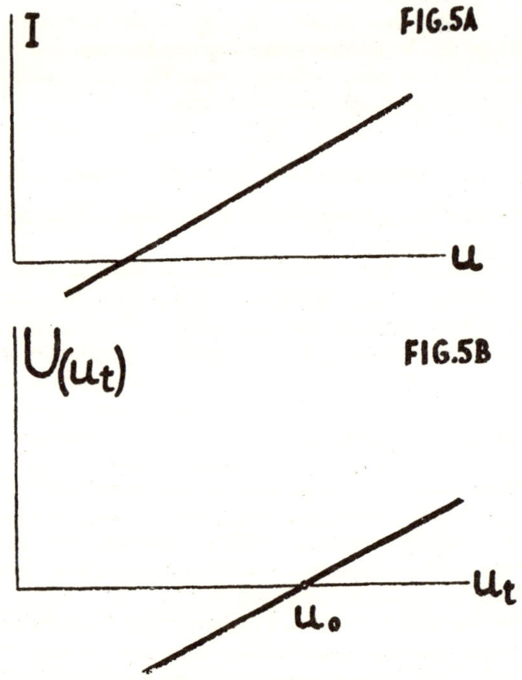

FIG. 5A and 5B. *The investment schedule.*

then we must say that investment changes as a result of a change in actual utilisation, with a given degree of planned utilisation.

A better expression of the theory is obtained if we take the other determinants of investment into account explicitly.

It is admitted that in practice investment will be influenced by innumerable circumstances and considerations. It should be possible, however, to explain it tolerably well by taking into account only the most important influences. As a reasonable judgment we suppose they are the following: (1) the internal accumulation which has taken place recently, (2) the degree of utilisation, (3) the degree of indebtedness, (4) the rate of profit, which may have a separate influence of its own in addition to the influence which it exerts *via* internal accumulation. We may assume that these influences are additive, and that investment can therefore be represented as the sum of various terms, each of them representing the 'influence' of one of the factors mentioned. Investment at a certain date will then be determined by an equation as follows:

$$I_{t+\theta} = \gamma \dot{C}_t + U(u_t) + G(g_t) + P(p_t). \tag{26}$$

The first term, $\gamma \dot{C}_t$, is simply a certain ratio of the internal accumulation at time t. The terms U, G, and P denote the influence of utilisation, gearing ratio and profit rate at time t respectively. The sum of these influences will determine the investment I after a time θ.

For the present purpose, we are interested only in the influence of utilisation, represented by the term $U(u_t)$ which we can now discuss in isolation. This term represents a certain amount of investment, which may be positive or negative, and which will be added to the amounts of investment as determined by the other influences. The investment represented by the influence $U(u_t)$ will be *an increasing function* of utilisation. If utilisation is very high, the term $U(u_t)$ will be positive, if it is very low, $U(u_t)$ will be negative. At a certain level of utilisation the term $U(u_t)$ will vanish and the 'influence' of utilisation will be zero. This level of utilisation at which $U(u_t)$ vanishes is the *planned degree of utilisation*.

In a graphical representation we can plot the 'influence' $U(u_t)$ on the ordinate and utilisation u_t on the abscissa (Fig. 5*b*). The 'influence' (representing a certain amount of investment attributable to a given utilisation) will rise with increasing utilisation. The curve will somewhere cut the abscissa, and the level of utilisation u_0 represented by this point is the planned degree of utilisation.

We have in this way obtained a general definition of the concept of 'planned excess capacity', which has been introduced in the first part of the book.

2. A theory of investment can be directly proved only by statistical tests. I cannot offer such tests to support the theory outlined above. Even so, it is a legitimate question to ask whether it would be possible, *in principle*, to test it. Similar questions have often been dealt with, in economics, by means of correlation of time series. This would be a particularly hazardous procedure in this case, since utilisation in practice is very closely correlated with profits. We should be bound to confuse the influence of the two factors, and I doubt whether there is a reliable safeguard against this danger. Quite apart from this the general objections against the use of correlation of time series would probably have a very strong weight in this case.

There exists, however, in principle a different approach. There is no reason why we should not compare different firms at the same time, and thus compare the investment materialising under different conditions of profit, utilisation, indebtedness, etc. This procedure would not be open to any fundamental statistical objections, and it could decide the question whether a particular factor has a significant influence or not.

The main difficulty of this approach is the provision of the requisite material which would have to consist of a sample investigation relating to data of individual firms.

3. In the absence of direct empirical tests, room will be given in the following to a plausible *a priori* argument to support the hypothesis of utilisation influencing investment. The argument will proceed as follows: we shall start by assuming the contrary, namely that investment is *not* influenced by utilisation, and we shall show that this leads to conclusions which are unplausible.

Let us then assume that investment is determined, on the simplest hypothesis, by the rate of profit alone. We cannot very well make the *absolute* amount of investment a function of the rate of profit, because the same amount of investment will have a different importance according to whether the stock of capital is large or small. We shall therefore take the investment per annum in proportion to the capital stock, that is the rate of growth of capital, and postulate that this is a function of the rate of profit.

The hypothesis should enable us, *inter alia*, to explain the relative amount of investment undertaken in different industries at the same time. On this basis we should expect that the growth of capital in different industries, relative to each other, is governed by the rates of profit in these different industries, in relation to each other. Comparing the various industries at a given time, the rate of growth of capital will be a function of the rate of profit.

Now let us presume that capital intensity is constant in all industries, so that a certain rate of growth of capital implies an identical rate of growth of capacity everywhere. Assume further that the rate of growth of the market in the various industries, relatively to each other, is also given. At any given rate of growth of the total system, the demand in the various industries will grow at certain rates, and if utilisation is everywhere to be kept at a constant level, the rate of growth of capital in the various industries will have to be adjusted to the rate of growth of demand. As the growth of capital, on our assumption, is governed by the rate of profit, there will be, for each industry, a certain rate of profit which will make utilisation constant. In other words, the relation between the profit rates in various industries will be determined by the requirement that the growth of capital in these various industries should be so regulated as to keep in step with the expansion of demand. From the point of view of a single industry, if the profit rates of other industries are given, there will be one and only one rate of profit which will induce it to expand its capacity in step with the given growth of its market. If a particular industry raises its rate of profit above the level so determined, it will be induced to expand capacity more quickly than its market expands, and it will experience a continuous fall in utilisation. The conclusion appears to be that an industry cannot, by monopolistic practices (open or tacit agreement, price leadership, etc.) increase its rate of profit without bringing about a continuous fall in its degree of utilisation. If we rule out the possibility that utilisation in ' monopolistic ' industries is continuously falling in comparison with other industries, it follows that ' monopoly ' cannot increase the rate of profit in an industry relatively to its level in other industries.

This conclusion I do not believe to be true, and I think there are many economists who will equally disbelieve it. I think that monopoly *can* increase the rate of profit in an industry, relatively to that in other industries, without bringing about a continuous fall in utilisation in that industry, relatively to others.

If this statement is accepted, then there must be something wrong in the assumption which led us to the unplausible conclusion. The faulty assumption is apparently that investment is governed solely by the rate of profit. There must be something which prevents investment in monopolistic industries from responding fully to the incentive of the higher profit rate. We get immediately a plausible picture of the situation if we take account of the effect of utilisation on investment. We may then argue as follows : if an industry, by monopolistic practices, raises its rate of profit, then it will in fact tend to a lower degree of utilisation, because the incentive of the higher profit rate will make it expand more quickly in the first instance. The reduced utilisation, however, will discourage investment, and at some point, this discouraging effect will outweigh the stimulating effect of the increased profit rate, so that the industry will again expand at its previous rate, and thus avoid a further fall in utilisation.

Another interpretation is equally plausible : it may be that the monopolistic industry never goes so far as to respond to the increased profit rate, and to bring about an actual reduction in utilisation at all. The reason would be that monopolistic industries, quite plausibly, may have a much greater fear and apprehension of excess capacity than others. This would mean that the discouraging effect of any given degree of utilisation would be greater in monopolistic industries than in others, in other words, the ' influence ' $U(u_t)$ would be smaller in monopolistic industries. Thus while monopolistic industries are subject to a greater incentive of profits, they will at the same time be more apprehensive of the danger of over-capacity, and this will prevent them from expanding too fast.

The two interpretations are equally plausible. They both require, of course, the hypothesis that investment is a function of utilisation. Once this hypothesis is accepted for the explanation of the comparative investment in different industries at the same time, it is logical to use it also for the explanaation of the development of investment in the course of time. The consequences of this hypothesis, in its application to long run development, are far-reaching. On its basis, the growth of monopoly can be shown to affect the course of capital accumulation. In fact, if the growth of monopoly power leads to an increase in the gross profit margins in industry as a whole, this will lower the degree of utilisation, and in this way discourage investment. The same effect may materialise, in conformity with the arguments used above, in a somewhat different way. If the transition of an industry from the competitive to the monopolistic form leads to a greater *fear* of excess capacity, then investment will be reduced even without any *actual* decline in utilisation. The 'influence' $U(u_t)$ of any given level of utilisation on investment will decrease as a mere consequence of the transition of industries from a competitive to a monopolistic structure.

The basic reason for the greater fear of excess capacity in 'monopolistic' industries is, of course, that the individual entrepreneur has much less chance (or perhaps often practically no chance) to expand at the expense of his competitors. This point has been laboured sufficiently in the first part of the book.

4. The theory of investment outlined in the previous pages does not make any mention of technical innovations. It differs in this respect from a view which has become strongly established in modern economics: namely that technical innovations are among the most important factors which cause net investment to be performed in the long run. Lord Keynes and many of his followers, as well as the adherents of the concept of economic maturity in America, all presume that technical progress in the form of innovations provides an important stimulus to investment. The prevailing view among these authors is that the relatively high level of investment in earlier periods of capitalist development was largely due to the emergence of innovations, whereas the low level of investment in more recent times was to a great extent due to the absence or comparative infrequency, or else to the different character, of innovations in this period.[1]

There is thus a strong traditional bias in favour of an exogenous theory of investment. Other determinants of net investment, such as for example population growth, are also recognised, but they are equally exogenous. The term exogenous signifies simply that investment in this explanation is dependent on certain variables—innovations, however they may be measured, or the rate of population growth—which themselves are unexplained and enter into the economic model as data. Corresponding to the exogenous character of the theory of investment, the explanations of economic maturity built on it are also of an exogenous nature. In fact, the advent of economic maturity, to the extent, at least, to which it is attributed to a decline in the rate of innovations, remains really unexplained and mysterious in the light of these theories. The doctrine of economic maturity has been very much weakened by this reliance on an exogenous theory of investment. It is difficult to find a relevant measure of innovations, to prove that their role has

[1] Mr. Kalecki, in a more refined analysis of these ideas, has remarked that technical innovations, if they stimulate investment on being introduced, must also depress it later when they become 'spread' over the economy (Essay on the trend in *Studies in Economic Dynamics*). In his analysis the role of innovations is therefore rather more complicated, but he too tends to believe that the frequency of innovations plays a decisive role in the explanation of the secular development of capital accumulation.

changed in the way presumed, and it is not even wholly plausible that it has so changed.

In contrast to these quasi-traditional views the present theory of investment is endogenous. On this view, net investment is called forth by the stimulus of economic factors, like internal accumulation of business, a high degree of utilisation, a high profit rate, or low indebtedness. Innovations, to express this view in its most extreme form, affect only the *form* which net investment takes. Innovations are applied, so runs the present argument, because business has money available, and demand is such as to produce a high level of utilisation. The stimulus of these economic factors produces additions to the capital stock, which usually, or very often, embody some innovation, simply because there is usually a stock of innovations and ideas waiting to be applied. Technological innovations accompany the process of investment like a shadow, they do not act on it as a propelling force. At the same time technological progress has of course a direct effect on cost, with manifold consequences. This effect, as distinct from its supposed effect on investment, can be empirically investigated and measured. It appears that it operates steadily and continuously. The rate at which cost (in man hours) per unit of product is reduced annually varies in different periods; it was, if anything, greater in the period of stagnation than in some of the preceding decades.[1] This aspect of technological progress is exceedingly important, but it is obviously altogether different from that considered in the theory of investment.

Like all extreme formulations, the above one may require qualifications.[2]

[1] Fabricant, *Output and Employment in Manufacturing*.

[2] Mr. J. R. Hicks suggested to me that my arguments against the ' technological innovations approach ' do not materially weaken one particular form of this theory: namely the view that it is *new industry development* which exerts a decisive influence on the long run level of the rate of investment. The outstanding example of a new industry which caused very great investments is the railways.

Now the railways, and to a lesser extent also other ' new industries ', were introduced, and net investment was undertaken in them, during a very long time. The pace at which they were introduced might certainly have been slower, perhaps it might have been quicker. The ' new industry approach ' does not tell us at what pace a new industry will be introduced, but it is this which matters above all for its influence on the rate of investment!

' New industries ' are only a particular form of innovation and most of my arguments apply to it. In particular, I think there is a 'stock' of new products and processes ready to be applied. Before they go into production, it is true, they must be developed. But this development is itself an investment; to go even further, the industrial research which creates the innovations is itself an investment. We may thus say without exaggeration that the innovations (inclusive of new products and processes) in modern capitalism are themselves generated and directed by a process of investment (which is largely private).

The prerequisite fundamental research is usually far ahead of the industrial applications, and the notion of an abundant ' stock ' applies to it. The idea that nothing remotely comparable to the railways could have been developed in mature capitalism is by no means as strong as it looks at first sight. The impression one gets from scientists is that twentieth century chemistry is capable of creating a revolution for the greater part of industrial production, and this would most probably involve heavy capital expenditure (cf. for example, J. D. Bernal, *The social function of science*, p. 386). We have seen in the last decade a small part of the tremendous potentialities of modern chemistry in the field of synthetic products, and the concomitant rise of a new chemical industry based on the by-products of the cracking process. That the industrial research which would bring about this revolution has not (or only to a small part) been undertaken can be explained in economic terms—it is just a case of lacking incentive to invest.

I believe, however, that it is a better basis for the understanding of long-run developments than the exogenous theory. In fact, I think that the great role attributed to innovations in the traditional view is due only to the absence of an endogenous theory of investment. Once such a theory is adopted, we can explain the secular change in the level of investment activity without relying on the *deus ex machina* of innovations. The following discussion will throw some light on the way in which, on the basis of the endogenous theory of investment, the differences in the secular level of investment activity in different stages of economic development can be explained.

We may start from an ideal case, in which the degree of utilisation is kept constant, not from year to year, but on the average of a series of years. This may result from two tendencies : on the one hand, we may suppose that there is a continuous tendency for gross profit margins to rise, because costs are continuously reduced by technical progress and prices are not automatically adjusted downwards. This rise in gross profit margins would tend to lower the degree of utilisation. On the other hand, we suppose the existence of strong competition, which by way of price cutting eliminates some productive equipment, and thus tends to prevent a fall in utilisation and at the same time an increase in the gross profit margin. We may suppose this competition just strong enough to keep the degree of utilisation at a constant level. This is merely an ideal case, which quite probably is not realised in any stage of economic development. But even so, it may be of use as an analytic device. We can regard it as a limiting case, and consider the more likely developments as deviations from this case.

In the ideal case of constant utilisation, the gross profit margin must be considered as *elastic*. It will always be adjusted, by the process of competition, in such a way as to keep utilisation constant. The rate of growth of capital will be determined by the various factors considered in our theory of investment, such as for example the investment induced by a certain internal accumulation, and so on. We can imagine that a constant rate of growth is established, and the system develops smoothly, with utilisation constant at a given level. If the rate of growth changes for some reason, then the gross profit margins will become adjusted so as to make the continuation of this new rate of growth possible without change in utilisation.

Now we have to consider that in reality deviations from this ideal case are to be expected for various reasons. In fact, the elasticity of gross profit margins at given degree of utilisation may become limited, both *upwards* and *downwards*, under certain circumstances. Whenever gross profit margins become thus inelastic, the system will become liable to deviation from the smooth path of a constant rate of growth either in the one or in the other direction. If gross profit margins are inelastic *upwards*, and if for some reason the rate of growth of capital experiences some long-term increase, then the degree of utilisation will rise above the previous level. As it is assumed, however, that the investment is influenced by the deviation of the degree of utilisation from the planned level, it follows that investment will rise further, and so on. In other words, the attempts of entrepreneurs to restore a given degree of utilisation will, given an inelastic gross profit margin, not only be doomed to failure, but they will necessarily lead to a further increase in utilisation. In the alternative case, if profit margins are inelastic *downwards*, and if a long run fall in the rate of growth of capital occurs for some reason, there will follow, *via* a reduction in utilisation, a further reduction in investment. The entrepreneurs' efforts to restore the former degree of utilisation will only lead to a further rise in excess capacity, with further adverse effects on investment, so that the rate of growth will decrease further. There may be thus a kind of ' cumulative process ', due to the interaction of investment and the degree of utilisation. This cumulative process may tend to a certain finite limit, in other words, the rate of growth may finally become established at a definite new level, from which it does not decrease further, but it is not certain whether this will be the case. The logic of the argument is clear : a given degree of capacity use can be restored adequately only by the method of eliminating existing capacity by price cutting, but never by the method of reducing investment, because this leads only to an even greater excess capacity. But the method of eliminating capacity by price cutting is *ex hypothesi* excluded—this is implicit in the assumption that gross profit margins are inelastic.

It is seen that inelasticity of gross profit margins may greatly influence the character of economic development. When and why should such inelasticity appear ? The reasons are quite different according to whether gross profit margins are inelastic in the one or in the other direction. The case of a limit, or impediment to an *increase* in profit margins will be treated first. This case is not of great practical importance in a fully developed capitalism, with plenty of capital equipment, and with a high and steadily increasing productivity of labour. Difficulties in the way of a shift of income to profits, with the aim of achieving the requisite rate of savings, appear here only in periods of war and of post-war reconstruction. In the early periods of capitalist development, however, the difficulties in the way of increasing the relative share of profits must have been of much greater importance. An increase in gross profit margins means a relative decrease in the income of other groups, amongst which labour is of primary importance. There is an absolute limit to the decrease in the income of labour which is vaguely indicated by the concept of a subsistence minimum. This limit is of great practical importance just in the early stages of capitalism, because productivity of labour is then absolutely low, and the possibilities of increasing it are very limited. We can have little doubt that during the period of industrial revolution in England, for example, wages were at, or even considerably below, what can reasonably be called a subsistence level. In stating that the subsistence level represents a limit to the possible increase in the share of profits we need not assume that entrepreneurs have any scruples which prevent a reduction of the real wage below the subsistence level. Most probably any such scruples were to a very large extent put aside in the early periods of frantic, and very brutal, capitalist expansion. But, whatever entrepreneurs might intend, the reduction of real wages below a point defeats its own purpose: it leads to a reduction in productivity of labour due to exhaustion, under-nourishment, etc. Thus it remains perfectly true to say that the increase in gross profit margins, for industry as a whole at least, is limited by the fact that the real income of labour cannot be reduced below a certain point. This consideration is obviously of overwhelming practical importance in those early stages of capitalist development when the productivity of labour was low, and its increase slow. Apart from the limit set by the subsistence minimum, the increase in profit margins may find a limit in the scarcity of labour. This does not apply to the industrial revolution in England (except with regard to skilled labour), but it was probably important in the industrial development of some overseas countries, especially the United States. There the scarcity of population and the relative abundance of land prevented a reduction of the real wage beyond a certain point.[1]

The factors which set a limit to an *increase* in profit margins are, as can be seen, of great practical importance in the first stages of industrial capitalism. They become less important later, owing to the increase in productivity and real wages, and to the abundance of labour created by population increase (only in great wars has the situation been different). Thus we have here a *prima facie* reason why in the early stages of capitalism a tendency to a cumulative process of expansion can easily come about, given only some primary increase in the rate of accumulation (or some equivalent change, such as a series of wars financed by budget deficits). In fact, we may be led to wonder how this early development of capitalism ever avoided plunging into headlong inflation. The answer is obvious: it was the increase in productivity through technical progress which prevented the cumulative process of expansion from becoming too wild, because it made a greater shift of income to profits possible. (Another factor may have been an increase in entrepreneurs' propensity to save.) The technical progress worked in practice mainly through the breaking of bottlenecks: bottlenecks in skilled labour and equipment and raw materials were successfully broken one by one, as they appeared, by appropriate inventions.[2]

It is very natural to surmise that the technical progress of this time, to a large extent, was the *consequence* of the tendency towards cumulative expansion: the bottlenecks which this process created, and the impossibility of increasing production in face of fully employed capacity and other bottleneck factors (like skilled labour) induced the entrepreneurs to find and introduce

[1] The objection that, according to Lord Keynes' theory, the scarcity of labour influences primarily money wages only, and not necessarily real wages, is not valid here. Given a relative abundance of land, so that the worker has the choice of either being independent or working for a wage, it will be the *real wage* which will influence his decision, and it will therefore be kept from falling below a certain level. For the importance of relative abundance of land in the industrial development of the U.S. see the posthumous paper of E. Rothbarth: Causes of the Superior Efficiency of U.S. Industry as compared with British Industry. *Economic Journal*, 1946.

[2] The process has been described by J. R. Hobson in his theory of inventions.

methods which would make the breaking of bottlenecks and the further expansion of production possible. This is not to say that other conditions are not necessary to explain the process of technical revolution in the early stages of capitalism. But the tendency to over-employment of capacity, and other bottleneck factors, was probably a very important necessary condition. Thus the expansion of early capitalism and the technical development itself were favoured by the relative inelasticity of profit margins prevailing under the circumstances.

Now let us turn to the question what limits may be set to a *decrease* in the profit margin. Under what circumstances will this type of inelasticity appear ? As has been explained, the squeezing of profit margins happens through the competition of entrepreneurs, which is essentially a process of squeezing out the weakest competitors. It is obvious that this mechanism works relatively well in a system where there are plenty of small producers, and plenty of competitors anyway. Thus, no difficulties of this type should appear in early capitalism, and even in fully developed capitalism for quite a time. In a mature capitalism, however, where large-scale production becomes the only possible form in many industries, and where, moreover, the number of competitors is reduced to a very few in a great number of cases, the profit margin becomes inelastic in the downward direction. Thus a new type of cumulative process becomes possible : any reduction of the rate of capital growth will reduce the degree of utilisation, and this will further reduce the rate of growth of capital. Thus, a given reduction in capital growth will lead to a further decrease in the rate of growth. This cumulative process may again tend to a definite limit, so that the rate of growth will settle down at a new lower level, but it is not certain whether it might not continue, theoretically, without limit.

The inelasticity of gross profit margins in an economy dominated by monopoly will thus reinforce any given fall in the rate of growth of capital. But, as pointed out earlier on, the effects of monopoly will not only be to make profit margins more rigid, it will be to raise them, and moreover, entrepreneurs will have a greater fear of excess capacity under a regime of monopoly. For both these reasons there will be a tendency for the rate of growth to fall. Utilisation will be lower than it was before monopoly became dominant, and moreover the investment attributable to the influence of any given level of utilisation will be lower owing to the fear of excess capacity.

The difference in the level of investment activity in different stages of the secular development can thus be explained in terms of an endogenous theory, taking account of well-known structural changes such as the development of monopoly. From the above discussion it appears likely that utilisation operates as an adverse influence on investment in the period of economic maturity in contrast to earlier periods, when it did not do so, and quite probably was high enough even to contribute a positive influence on the level of investment.

XI. THE JOINT STOCK SYSTEM AND THE MODERN CAPITAL MARKET

1. *Economic Principles of Share Issue*

The purpose of this chapter is to make good an omission: in the discussions of the gearing ratio and of 'outside savings' the essential features of the joint stock system have been left out of account. It was indeed assumed (p. 110) that joint stock companies[1] do exist, but do not issue any new shares (and that no new ones with an issue of shares to the public are formed). But the possibility of increasing the entrepreneurial capital by new share issues is obviously an important feature of the system, which must affect its working considerably, and has consequently to be taken into account.

Without joint stock companies, the problem of the gearing ratio is comparatively straightforward: all saving out of profits constitutes an accumulation of entrepreneurial funds; all other savings have to be borrowed by the entrepreneurs, and thus constitute an accumulation of entrepreneurs' debt (except in so far as they are absorbed by government borrowing or borrowing of foreign countries). The joint stock system modifies this state of affairs in two ways: on the one hand, a part of the profits is distributed as dividends, and the saving out of these dividends does not augment the funds at the disposal of the joint stock companies directly. On the other hand the joint stock companies possess the peculiar virtue of being able to draw on outside savings for the purpose of increasing their entrepreneurial funds, their 'risk-bearing capital'. They can employ outside savings without borrowing them, without increasing thus their gearing ratio, and thereby their risk. This they can do simply by issuing new shares, which is, we may say, a method of *merging a certain amount of outside savings into the equity*.

Mr. Kalecki deals with these difficulties in the following way: he assumes that dividend receivers are, roughly speaking, potential investors in new shares, and other savers are not. Therefore, a market for new shares will be created to the extent, and only to the extent, to which saving out of dividends takes place.[2] On this assumption, the existence of joint stock companies makes no difference at all to the analysis: just as in a system of 'individual' enterprise, all savings out of profits increase the entrepreneurial risk-bearing capital (the savings out of dividends being equal to the new share issues) and all other savings are accumulated in form of debt.

For a more elaborate treatment of the problem this assumption is not adequate. We cannot easily generalise about who will be ready to invest in shares. Under certain conditions—as for example in the 'New Era'—a great amount of saving from all possible sources is flowing into the share market, and the circle of investors in shares is widening. Under different circumstances—in the 'thirties for example—the market for shares shrinks so greatly that hardly any new shares can be issued at all; dividend earners themselves in those times are not prepared to reinvest their savings in shares.

[1] The term 'joint stock company' is used here in the English sense of the word. The American reader has to read for it 'corporation'.

[2] *Studies in Economic Dynamics*, p. 62. The assumption is not formulated as sharply there as it is above—it is clearly meant as a first approximation only—but it is implicitly made.

There is thus no necessary connection between share issues and saving out of dividends.

The conclusion to be drawn is that savings out of dividends are 'outside savings' as much as any other. They are not different in principle from rentiers' savings, and may play a similar role. This conclusion has been drawn already earlier on (p. 110).

There remains the question: What determines the amount of new share issues?

The City man will answer in one word: the market. His explanations will make it clear: first, that only under certain conditions will joint stock companies find it in their interest to issue new shares (these conditions have a lot to do with the price to be obtained for the shares); and secondly, that these conditions are determined in a very complicated way, so that it is only safe to describe them as the state of the market.

Logically we have to start with the considerations made on behalf of a joint stock company issuing new shares. The issue of a certain number of new (common) shares will mean, provided they carry equal rights with the existing stock, that the buyers of these shares acquire a proportionate claim to the profits of the company. At the same time the money realised from the issue will enable the company—by expanding production capacity, for example—to increase its profits. Whether the issue will be in the interest of the joint stock company—which is identical with the interests of the existing shareholders, amongst which are also the 'controlling interests' of the company—will depend on whether the proportionate increase in profits is greater than the proportionate increase in claims against them. Let the existing nominal share capital be Σ, the nominal value of the new issue $\Delta\Sigma$, the profits expected on the existing capital assets P and the profits expected from the investment of the receipts of the new issue ΔP.

The condition for the issue being advantageous is

$$\frac{\Delta\Sigma}{\Sigma} < \frac{\Delta P}{P},$$

or in different form

$$\frac{P}{\Sigma} < \frac{\Delta P}{\Delta\Sigma}. \qquad \text{(A. 1)}$$

This equation can be further modified if we consider that the net profit rate p on the old capital is the proportion of the expected profit P to the replacement value of the existing capital assets (after deduction of debt) C; and if we similarly define the marginal profit rate p' as the proportion of the expected additional profits ΔP to the net cash ΔC received from the issue. We have then

$$p = \frac{P}{C}; \quad p' = \frac{\Delta P}{\Delta C}.$$

Substituting in (A. 1) we get

$$\frac{C}{\Sigma}p < \frac{\Delta C}{\Delta\Sigma}p'. \qquad \text{(A. 2)}$$

In this inequality $\frac{C}{\Sigma}$ is the proportion of replacement value of the existing capital assets of the company, diminished by the amount of debt, to the nominal share capital. This proportion will be below 1.0, if and to the extent to which, the share capital is ' watered ' (in a new company this is usually the case). It may rise above 1.0 if the company has accumulated sufficient retained profits without taking new measures to water the capital again. The reciprocal of $\frac{C}{\Sigma}$ may be referred to as ' degree of capitalisation '.

The magnitude $\frac{\Delta C}{\Delta \Sigma}$, the amount of cash received for a certain nominal value of shares issued, depends obviously on ' the market '. If the market for shares were perfect, with an infinite elasticity of demand, and if the cost of flotation is neglected, this proportion would be equal to the price of the shares ruling in the market, $\frac{\Pi}{\Sigma}$. The inequality could then be written

$$\frac{C}{\Sigma}p \Big/ \frac{\Pi}{\Sigma} < p'.$$

The inequality has now taken a simple form easy to interpret: $\frac{C}{\Sigma}p$ is the profit rate on the nominal share capital, and divided by the price of the share this gives the *yield* (not in the sense of dividend yield, as usually given in financial statistics, but in the sense of ' earnings yield ', or earning-price ratio, which takes account of retained profits as well as of dividends). The condition thus becomes: the profit p' to be obtained from new investment must be higher than the earnings yield of the shares. It should be noted that not only the marginal profit rate p' but also the earnings are *expected* quantities, and not necessarily the same as current earnings.

We must now take account of the fact that the price obtained for the new shares will not be the same as the price which has been currently quoted in the market, but it will be lower, owing to the imperfection of the market. The price of shares will be more or less reduced, according to the amount of new shares issued, and we shall call this price actually received $\frac{\Pi'}{\Sigma}$. In addition there will be a certain cost of the issue, to be paid to underwriters, promoters, etc., which can be expressed as a proportion v of the net proceeds of the issue; the share price obtained $\frac{\Pi'}{\Sigma}$ has thus to be divided further by $(1+v)$ to get the net proceeds.

The final condition for share issue is then

$$\frac{C}{\Sigma}p \Big/ \frac{\Pi'}{\Sigma} < p' \Big/ (1+v). \qquad \text{(A. 3)}$$

That is, the marginal profit rate must exceed the *effective yield* by a proportion corresponding to the cost of the issue.[1] By 'effective yield' (the expression on the left-hand side of (A. 3) is meant the yield based not on the actual current market price of the shares, but on the price at which the shares can be sold. The effective share yield will in general be higher than the actual yield, and the discrepancy will depend on the amount of new shares issued. We can imagine a schedule which will show the increase in effective yield with the size of the issue. The increase will be more or less sharp according to the imperfection of the market.

The condition represented by (A. 3) shows that the earnings-yield on shares plays a role similar to the rate of interest. It limits the possibilities of new shares issues, just as the rate of interest is supposed to limit the amount of borrowing. There is, however, a major difference between the two. The rate of interest is separated from the marginal rate of profit by a very considerable gap, the marginal risk premium, which increases sharply with the amount borrowed. This gap is due to the fact that the rate of profit is uncertain and may fall below the interest, thus making a bad job out of the indebtedness. Is there any corresponding risk attached to the issue of shares? Looking at (A. 3) we see that the only uncertain quantities[2] are p and p'. Now it is quite obvious that if p and p' change in the same proportion, the relation of the two sides of the inequality remains the same. Thus if both p and p' were only half of what was expected, the considerations with regard to the advantage of the issue would remain unaffected. The only risk involved is therefore a change in the relation of p' to p, that is a change of the marginal rate of profit (on the new capital) *relative* to the rate of profit on the old capital. The marginal rate of profit will in general differ from the profit on the old capital, first because the new investment will embody technical improvements which will make it more productive than the old capital, and secondly because the expansion of the market necessary to employ the new capital will require price cuts, etc. The estimate made of the marginal rate of profit p' in relation to p is, of course, subject to error, and if it turns out to be wrong the considerations on which the share issue have been based may be invalidated. In other words, the issue may turn out to be disadvantageous to the old shareholders, if the increase in profits due to the new investment was over-estimated. It is quite certain, however, that this possible error in the estimate of p'/p is in practice much less serious than the errors which can be committed in an estimate of the *absolute* level of p' (this latter being the estimate which is relevant in the case of borrowing). The conclusion is that the risk involved (for the old shareholders) in a share issue are incomparably smaller than the risk involved in borrowing. We can expect therefore that a fairly modest gap between the marginal rate of profit and the effective share yield will suffice to make the issue worth while. The effective yield will be very closely related to the marginal rate of profit, whereas, it is fairly widely

[1] If the cost of the issue is for example 10 per cent of the net proceeds, and the effective share yield is 8 per cent, the marginal profit rate must be over 8.8 per cent to make the issue advantageous.

[2] Assuming that the price of the issue is guaranteed by the issuing house.

accepted by now, the rate of interest is only very loosely connected with it. Changes in the effective yield will be of much greater and more direct importance for investment than changes in the rate of interest.

The considerations affecting a potential issuer of shares have now been analysed. Without knowing anything in particular about the share market we can add an important principle. Supposing that the proportion of $p : p'$ is given and constant, what is the relevance of the absolute level of the profit rate for the opportunities of issuing shares ? If p is higher we can take it for granted that share prices will also be higher; we need not assume that the yield is necessarily the same with a higher rate of profit, but certainly it will not increase in the same proportion as the profit rate. Thus, if p and p' rise in the same proportion, the marginal profit rate p' will from a certain point on exceed the yield. That is, there is always a certain level of the profit rate at which share issues become advantageous. Below this profit level there will be no share issues in the given circumstances.

This principle is fundamental for the understanding of the joint stock system. It shows that while share issues are a new and additional method of increasing entrepreneurial funds, they are, just like internal accumulation, limited by the rate of profit earned.

2. *The Share Market*

The importance of the earnings-yield on shares is by now sufficiently clear. How is this yield determined and how is it related to the flow of savings ? The relevant considerations are here those of the share holding public.

The question of the public investor's willingness to hold shares can be treated as an extension of the well-known problem of the choice between different types of assets. The modern theory of money and interest starts from the consideration of an owner of wealth who distributes his assets between various types of holdings : money, short-term securities, long-term bonds. We have only to add to this the further alternative of holding common shares.

The nearest competing investment to shares are presumably long term bonds. The first and simplest consideration relating to the choice between the two is that common shares will be held only if the *expected* earnings-yield on them is considerably in excess of the yield on long term bonds. This must be the case because the earnings on shares are much more uncertain, at least as far as individual shares are concerned.[1] It is clear that the *expected* earnings are what matters. It may be plausibly assumed, however, that the expectation is very largely based on current earnings. It will deviate from this current value whenever something is known about changes in the

[1] The investor may distribute his holding between several shares and so reduce his risk, but if he goes far in this direction he can pay less and less attention to the fortunes of the individual companies concerned. The aim of holding a representative bunch of shares which *might* be theoretically as safe or safer than bonds is in practice impossible to achieve for the investor.

fortunes of the company. The expected earnings will deviate from the current ones especially if the latter are *temporarily* low or high—that is if it is likely that the current value of earnings is only temporary. Confirmation of this guess can be seen in the fact that in a sharp slump the yield based on current earnings is much lower than usual, while in the period of a war-time boom, for example, the yields are extraordinarily high. An additional fact is that in a comparison of different shares higher earnings seem to be associated with higher yields.[1] This also may be explained by the hypothesis that the expectation is influenced not only by the current earnings, but also by some estimate of ' normal earnings ', so that particularly high or particularly low earnings are less easily accepted as permanent. If this hypothesis is correct, it will nevertheless be safe to say that after a number of years a change in the current level of earnings will be fully reflected in the expectation of earnings. In another words, if we follow changes in the yield based on *current* earnings over a longer time, then the long term changes in the current yield will reflect in general also the movement in the expected yield. This conclusion is important for the interpretation of data.

Now if a certain yield on bonds and a certain (expected) yield on shares is given, the outside savers (whom we identify with the ' public investor ') will distribute their holdings between shares, bonds and other assets in certain proportions. If there happen to be more shares in the market than they want to hold, their price will fall and their yield increase until a substitution of share holdings for other assets is brought about.

With given yields there will be therefore a certain distribution of holdings between various assets. In the course of the year, however, new outside savings are accumulated, and these will be distributed again among the various types of assets in certain proportions. As far as the bond yields are concerned they will be hardly affected by this new saving, owing to the well-known factors which make for relative stability in bond yields (except over longer periods). The share prices, on the contrary, will be affected by the inflow of new savings, and the share yield will therefore decline. If the yield on shares was previously just below the marginal rate of profit, then the decline will stimulate new issues, theoretically just enough to absorb the flow of new savings into the share market. Thus a certain part of the outside savings will continuously flow into the share market, and make new issues of a corresponding amount possible.

If the marginal profit rate and the bond yield are constant, we can imagine that the proportion of outside saving flowing into the share market is constant every year. If outside savings are in constant proportion to the internal accumulation, we can see that a constant gearing ratio of companies will be possible. The condition is that the outside saving not absorbed by share issues accumulates in the same proportion as the real capital.

How will the finance of real investment in the joint stock companies

[1] See W. I. King, Analysing the relationship between stock prices, earnings and dividends. *Journal of the American Statistical Association*, 1931.

operate under these conditions? The joint stock companies will decide, on the basis of past data, on a certain amount of investment ΔZ to be carried out during the coming year. In the course of the year, owing to the investment carried out, there will be a certain amount of internal accumulation ΔC_1. In addition, outside savings will be generated, and part of it will go into the share market, so that the companies will find they can issue a certain amount ΔC_2, of new shares. At the end of the year it will appear that the net indebtedness of the companies has increased by $\Delta Z - \Delta C_1 - \Delta C_2$. The ability of the companies to manage their gearing ratio in a certain way will clearly depend on correct anticipation of the possibility of share issues. If they want to keep the gearing ratio constant, for example, their investment will be determined by the condition

$$\frac{\Delta Z}{Z} = \frac{\Delta C_1 + \Delta C_2}{C}$$

that is, the proportionate accumulation of real capital assets must proceed at the same rate as the proportionate accumulation of entrepreneurial funds, which is composed of internal accumulation *plus* new share issues.

The stable development described will be possible only if the rate of profit is constant. If it declines, the share issues will necessarily drop. The yield on shares may be reduced as a result of the smaller amounts of shares thrown into the market, but they cannot drop sufficiently to reverse the reduction in issues. Below a certain level of the rate of profit share issues will practically cease. On the other hand, an increase in the rate of profit (p and p' being assumed to change in the same proportion) will increase share issues; this will go hand in hand with an increase in yield to make possible the diversion of a greater amount of outside funds into the share market. It can be seen that changes in the rate of profit will have a doubly stimulating or depressing effect under the joint stock system of finance: they will not only increase or reduce the internal accumulation, but also increase or reduce the new share issues, and thus the proportion of outside savings which is 'merged into the equity', and need not therefore be borrowed. The amount of debt which can be incurred (with constant gearing ratio) on top of the increase in entrepreneurial funds will vary correspondingly more with any change in the rate of profit.

It can be easily seen that an inelasticity of outside saving will have even more drastic consequences than shown earlier on (p. 114ff.). A fall in the rate of profit which strongly reduces new share issues will not only reduce the amounts which the joint stock companies intend to borrow (assuming they want to keep their gearing ratio constant, or to reduce it), but it will at the same time *increase* the amount of outside saving which is not merged into the equity and is therefore available for borrowing. The instability due to inelastic outside saving, as discussed in Chapter IX, is therefore *reinforced* by the system of joint stock finance.

3. *A priori reasons for a decline in share yields*

Up to now the conditions of demand in the share market have been thought of as given. The actual yield then depends mainly on the relative amount of shares issued, and we can thus say that the effective yield is constant.

Demand conditions in the share market are of course liable to very violent changes in the short run, bound up with partly irrational changes in expectation and speculation. In so far as these upheavals affect the opportunities for share issue they influence the general economic situation.

There are, however, also long run changes in the demand conditions. For a number of reasons we should expect a long run tendency for the share market to widen and for the effective yield to decline, a tendency which accompanies the rise and development of the joint stock system.

(1) The development of *organised markets* for shares made them a much more acceptable investment, and widened the circle of shareholders. If a share is introduced, quoted and regularly dealt with at an official exchange market, its value increases considerably.

It would seem self-evident that the introduction of the joint stock system and its gradual spread to a great sector of enterprise must have meant a growth of the possibility of finance by share issue. In reality it was perhaps not so much the mere formation of joint stock companies, but the development of an organised market for their shares which widened the share market. The latter did not take place simultaneously with the former, but only after a time lag: a company might exist for a long time before its shares are introduced at the Exchange.

(2) The valuation of a share, or rather of the risk attached to it, depends very largely on the amount of information and experience people have with regard to the company in question. A new company will be considered a very risky venture, because one cannot know very much about it. After a long series of years a company may acquire reputation and standing, and a considerable experience with regard to its performance and financial position will have been gained. The ' effective yield ' on its shares will correspondingly decrease. As the joint stock system develops the proportion of established big companies presumably grows, so that for the whole system, the effective yield declines.

The bigness of the concern is also of some importance. Public investors will very often not unreasonably think that it is safest to throw in one's luck with those who in this world are likely to know best how to protect their interests. The development of big companies thus tends also to make shares more acceptable. This leads directly to the next point.

(3) One of the outstanding features in the development of the joint stock system is *financial concentration*, known as merger in the wider sense of the word. It is carried out for a variety of purposes, but one of them is almost always a purely finaneial gain. Some important examples are to be considered in turn.

(*a*) A company of good financial standing buys up one or several others. The shares of the latter are exchanged against shares of the former, and thus disappear from the scene. The exchange will presumably be made in proportions which are based primarily on the market value of the shares. As we suppose the buying company to be of better financial standing, the yield on its shares will be lower than the yield on the shares of the other companies. The process is essentially one of exchanging higher-risk shares against low-risk shares.

If we write Π_1, C_1, and p_1 for market value of share capital, real value of equity capital, and profit rate respectively of the buying company, and Π_2, C_2, p_2 for the corresponding magnitude relating to the company brought up, then

$$\frac{C_1 p_1}{\Pi_1} < \frac{C_2 p_2}{\Pi_2}.$$

After the purchase the market value of the total share capital of company (i) would be $\Pi_1 + \Pi_2$, if the market price of its shares remains unchanged. But as

$$\frac{C_1 p_1 + C_2 p_2}{\Pi_1 + \Pi_2} > \frac{C_1 p_1}{\Pi_1}$$

this would mean that the shares of the buying company now carry a higher yield. If the market values them in the same way as before, their price would tend to rise until the yield goes back to the former value. In view of this tendency the company can do one of two things: it can either water its capital without reducing the price of its shares (this could be done in such a way as to give an advantage to the old shareholders, e.g. in form of bonus shares), or else it can use the rising tendency of the market to issue new shares to finance real investment.

Apart from this there remains a permanent effect of the financial concentration. High yield shares have been exchanged for lower yield shares. The finance of the whole combined concern will from now on be done on the terms which the buying company can get in the market—and they are better than those at which the bought up companies could have financed. The result is thus a reduction of effective yields for the total joint stock system.

(*b*) A number of companies all exchange their shares into shares of a newly formed company. The identity of the old companies is lost and their shares disappear. This is the case of merger proper. We can again suppose that the new concern will be financially stronger and have a better market than at least some of the enterprises which are merged in it, that is, the yield on its shares will be lower than the yield of some or all of the former shares. That is, if we use the same notation as before, with the suffix 1 and 2 for two companies merged, and if Π_0 stands for the market value of the shares of the new company

$$\frac{C_1 p_1 + C_2 p_2}{\Pi_1 + \Pi_2} > \frac{C_1 p_1 + C_2 p_2}{\Pi_0},$$

i.e. the average yield of the old shares is greater than the yield of the new shares. From which follows that $\Pi_0 > \Pi_1 + \Pi_2$. The market value of the new shares will be greater than that of the old ones. The difference can obviously be made up by water, that is, shares can be issued in excess of the amounts which must be given in exchange for the old shares (the exchange being made at the prospective market value). These additional shares may be given, for example, to the promoters as a consideration for their services (they may be identical with the controlling interests of one or several of the merged companies, who in this way appropriate the financial gain of the merger).

The permanent effect is again a lowering of average effective yield.

(*c*) A new joint stock company may be formed for the sole purpose of holding shares in several existing companies. Usually it is called either a holding company or investment trust, according to whether or not the measure aims at controlling the companies in question. Financial gain is, however, almost always one of the aims and results of such a combination.

The shares of the existing companies are acquired at their market value (or somewhat above if the price is driven up by the procedure), and the necessary cash is obtained by the issue of shares of the holding company. The yield of the shares of the holding company will be lower than of the subsidiaries—again because of its greater financial strength. Just as before this gives an opportunity for watering the share capital of the holding company, and in this way realising a financial gain for the promoters.

Again the permanent effect will be to make it possible to finance the subsidiaries on cheaper terms than they could have done themselves. The holding company can issue new shares at a lower yield, and use the proceeds to take over a private placement of new shares of the subsidiaries. In this way the effective yield at which new capital can be indirectly procured by the subsidiaries is lowered.

In actual fact, the finance of holding companies is often based on different principles (issue of bonds, see below). The preceding example constitutes what may be regarded in a sense as ' sound practice '.

The conclusion is that all the cases of financial concentration involve not only an immediate financial gain, but in essence constitute an exchange of safer, more readily acceptable shares, which therefore carry a lower yield, against others. The consequence is a reduction in effective yield. There is no doubt that by this method of offering less risky shares to the public the market was considerably widened.

Taking all the factors together, it would seem that the development of the joint stock system must have meant a considerable widening of the market for shares, and correspondingly reduction in effective yield. This, taken by itself, would constitute a stimulating effect on real investment, comparable to a reduction in the rate of interest. It is surprising that economists have devoted hardly any attention to this circumstance, although it is bound to have a much more potent effect on investment than changes in the long term rate of interest.

4. *Data relating to the development of joint stock companies*

Joint stock companies ('corporations') were well established in the United States after the Civil War, especially in railroads. They grew in importance in the following decades and an increasing proportion of business, for example in manufacturing, became 'incorporated'. From 1904 on we can follow the development in manufacturing and mining on the basis of Census data, giving the proportion of businesses incorporated. In manufacturing the proportion of gross output accounted for by joint stock companies rose from 74 per cent in 1904 to 92 per cent in 1929. The increase appears to have been fairly gradual over this period (Table 25); it came virtually to an end after 1929. In this field a saturation point seems to have

TABLE 25

RELATIVE IMPORTANCE OF CORPORATIONS IN MANUFACTURING

	1904	1909	1914	1919	1929a[1]	1929b[2]	1939
Number of Establishments							
Total ('000)	216.2	268.5	275.8	290.1	211.0	206.7	184.2
Owned by Corporations ('000)	51.1	69.5	78.2	91.5	101.8	98.0	95.2
%	23.6	25.9	28.3	31.5	48.3	47.5	51.7
Wage Earners							
All Manufacturing ('000)	5,468.4	6,615.0	7.036.2	9,096.4	8.838.7	8,369.7	7,886.6
Owned by Corporations ('000)	3,862.7	5,002.4	5,649.9	7,875.1	7,945.5	7,481.3	7,050.7
%	70.6	75.6	80.3	86.6	89.9	89.4	89.5
Value of Products							
All Manufacturing ($ millions)	14,794	20,672	24,246	62,418	70,435	67,994	56,843
Owned by Corporations ($ millions)	10,904	16,341	20,183	54,745	64,901	62,520	52,661
%	73.7	79.0	83.2	87.7	92.2	92.0	92.7

been nearly reached—at any rate it would soon be reached with the complete incorporation of manufacturing—but in other fields where incorporation has proceeded less far (trade, services) this may not be so.

While incorporation as such had gone far already in the 19th century, the development of organised share markets lagged behind. In 1870 only 16 'industrials' and 21 'utilities', in all 37 common shares (excluding railroads) were quoted at the New York Stock Exchange, half of them irregularly.[3] The Cowles Commission index of common share prices which includes most shares regularly quoted at the New York Stock Exchange, embodies 12 industrial shares in 1871, 23 in 1897 and 157 in 1917. The

[1] Figures for 1929 and later include only establishments with products valued at $5,000 and more, whereas the figures for 1919 and earlier years include establishments with products valued at $500 and more. The comparability between 1929*a* and earlier years is thus somewhat impaired, but for a rough comparison of the proportion of wage earners and products at least the figures are sufficient.

[2] A number of industries (motion pictures, railroad repair shops, etc.) have been excluded from the Census after 1929, and the figures given under 1929*b* are adjusted to the scope of the Census in 1939.

[3] A. Cowles 3rd and Associates, *Common Stock Indices*, p. 4.

Standard Statistics index contained 146 'industrials' in 1918 and 351 in 1926. This gives a very good idea of the increase in number of shares quoted. It shows that the organised market for industrial shares developed really only from the turn of the century on. It was at that time also that important innovations in the technique of share issues took place. The practice of underwriting was developed and 'investment banking', the handling of flotations by specialised bankers employing active selling methods gained its real importance just at the turn of the century.[1] Parallel with the development of organised markets the circle of shareholders widened.

This development of share markets is closely bound up with the two so-called 'merger movements': the first in 1898–1902, the second in the decade 1919 to 1929 (the New Era). They were periods of wholesale financial concentration in the form of mergers, buying up of companies, and formation of holding companies, with prodigious issues of shares concentrated in a few years. For the first period data are given by Professor Myron W. Watkins.[2] According to this estimate there were in 1898–1902 168 industrial consolidations with a capitalisation of $4.9 billion, out of 237 consolidations with a capitalisation of $6 billion in the period 1890–1904 (public utility mergers not included). A considerable proportion of the capitalisation was water.

For the New Era it has been estimated by Thorp that the number of mergers (1919–1928) in manufacturing and mining alone was 1,268. The amount of capital involved by this second merger movement can only be guessed.

The most important effect of the widening of the market should, of course, be seen in the development of share issues (Table 26). Unfortunately the data do not quite tell us what we want to know. The question is how much the 'equity', the entrepreneurial capital of the corporate system has been enlarged by public share issues. But part of the share issues are used only to finance and hold other shares; this part does not form a new addition to the equity, and ought therefore to be subtracted.[3] The correction cannot be made. Even so it seems that new share issues were an important source, in addition to internal accumulation, of the expansion of entrepreneurial capital up to 1930.[4] After that time the share market seems to have contributed very little to this end.

[1] Atkins, Edwards and Moulton, *The Regulation of the Security Markets*, p. 25.

[2] *Industrial Combinations and Public Policy*.

[3] The question whether the receipts from the share issues are used for productive purposes (real investment) or not is irrelevant in this context. If they are used to repay debt or accumulate cash balances, they none the less increase the equity and reduce the gearing ratio. In this way they exert their influence on the readiness to invest in coming years.

[4] It will be seen from Table 26 that a considerable part of the share issues are preference shares. Preference shares involve a certain risk for the issuer, which is however much more limited than the risk of borrowing: preference dividends may have to be paid at the expense of the current *net* profit of the company, but never at the expense of its capital. They are economically, therefore, nearer to common shares than to bonds. In the calculation of the gearing ratio they must be reckoned as part of the equity, because their position vis-a-vis the bond holder is the same as those of common shares; they must be prepared to absorb the first shock of losses in order to secure the bond holders' fixed income. The issue of preference shares, like that of ordinary shares, therefore makes it possible to increase borrowing *pari passu* without increasing the risk.

TABLE 26

CAPITAL ISSUES

	Total share issues (including refunding)	New share issues. Total.	New Share issues Common Stock	New Share issues Preference Stock	Retained profits[1]	Total issues of bonds and notes (including refunding)	New issues of bonds and notes (domestic corporations)	Productive capital issues[2] (Moody)
1909	611				1032			
1910	405				1078	1113		
1911	352				665	1387		
1912	904				1475	1350		
1913	452				1180	1194		
1914	262				343	1175		
1915	325				2028	1111		
1916	782				4908	1405		
1917	455				4317	1076		
1918	298				1933	1047		
1919	1547	1436	710	726	3707	1174	810	
1920	1038	1002	540	462	1443	1895	1561	
1921	275	265	194	71	—2,606	2112	1435	864
1922	620	570	277	293	1746	2449	1642	1335
1923	736	659	324	335	2528	2497	1976	1624
1924	866	829	511	318	1574	2972	2200	1941
1925	1247	1153	558	594	2957	3427	2452	1824
1926	1220	1087	578	509	2335	3982	2667	1801
1927	1738	1474	600	874	1115	5546	3183	1781
1928	3491	2961	1812	1149	2400	4191	2385	1495
1929	6757	5924	4407	1517	2157	3105	2078	1787
1930	1527	1503	1091	412	—4247	3905	2980	1939
1931	343	311	195	116	—7327	2246	1239	796
1932	24	20	10	10	—8001	620	305	203
1933	153	120	105	15	—4480	229	40	106
1934	35	35	31	3	—2485	457	144	63
1935	151	69	15	54	—1253	2117	334	94
1936	553	352	262	90	— 799	4064	839	379
1937	760	408	199	204	— 960	1673	817	635
1938	98	67				2043	807	417
1939	234	97				1962	287	191

[1] T.N.E.C. Monograph No. 12.

[2] Productive issues are those issues (bond or stock) which are used to finance real *fixed* capital investment.

We have been led to expect, on general grounds, that the development and widening of the organised share market brought with it a tendency for yields to decline. How does this conclusion match with the facts ?

A series of earning yields (earnings-price ratios) of common shares computed by the *Cowles Commission* is available from 1871 onwards. The series is given for *all stocks*, and for separate industries ; these are classified into three big groups, railroads, utilities, and industrials (the latter containing everything which is not railroad or utility). The series relates to the great majority of shares for which regular quotations on the New York Stock Exchange are available in the particular year in question ; the number and identity of shares contained in it changes therefore continously. The weights are based on the share capital outstanding.

To interpret the series properly we have to remember that what matters are *expected* yields, not the current yields given (Table 27). On this account

TABLE 27

YIELDS OF BONDS AND COMMON SHARES

	Yield: Railroad Bonds	Earnings-Yields, Common Shares (Cowles Commission)			
		All Shares	Industrials	Railroads	Utilities
1871–78	6.59	8.83	10.50	8.79	9.65
1874–83	6.00	8.38	11.78	8.22	9.71
1879–88	5.34	7.00	12.20	6.82	8.02
1884–93	4.93	5.98	9.13	5.71	6.01
1889–98	4.64	5.75	10.32	5.20	6.80
1894–1903	4.27	6.44	11.35	5.81	6.18
1899–1908	4.04	7.48	11.91	6.71	5.69
1904–1913	4.11	7.50	10.47	6.60	7.14
1909–1918	4.35	9.83	13.07	7.90	8.48
1914–1923	4.77	10.60	12.31	9.40	10.01
1919–1928	4.80	9.09	8.51	10.08	10.10
1924–1933	4.68	6.44	5.99	5.70	7.36
1929–1937	4.52	4.35	4.24	0.50	5.58

we have to exclude at once the abnormally high yields of World War 1 and the equally low yields of the great depression after 1929. They are due to the fact that in both cases the rate of earnings has been considered temporary only.

Excluding these years we find for the 'All Shares' series a surprising picture. The yield does decline up to 1889–98, just before the first merger movement. From then on it increases and reaches its highest level in the decade 1919–1928—the New Era.

A part of the explanation lies in the composition of the series. It represents the shares *quoted* at the Stock Exchange, not the shares of all companies in existence. Just from the turn of the century on the number of shares quoted, especially ' industrials ', increased strongly. The proportion of industrials in the total index must have increased strongly since then. Now a glance at the figures shows that industrials carry a much higher yield than the average: they are more speculative. The inclusion of more speculative shares therefore increased the average yield of all shares. As these speculative shares, before they were introduced at the Exchange, presumably had a higher yield than afterwards, the picture is obviously distorted on this account.

A better picture is obtained if we consider 'industrials' by themselves. They too show some increase in yield with the advent of the first merger movement, which is presumably again due to the inclusion of more speculative shares. In any case the earlier figures are poor because so few shares were included. If, however, we follow the development since 1894–1903, the following picture of the yield emerges:

1894–1903	11.4 per cent
1904–1913	10.5 ,, ,,
1919–1928	8.5 ,, ,,

There was, thus, a decline in yield of industrials since the first merger movement, and in the New Era the yield was lower than ever before. The data thus confirm the *a priori* expectation of a decrease in yields in case of industrial shares.

The case of 'railroads' and 'utilities' is different: both show a considerable increase in yield concurrently with the decline in industrial share yields (and this is, in fact, the second reason why the 'all shares' series increased). Especially in the case of *utilities* it is at first sight quite unbelievable that such a rise should have occurred, especially that the yield should have been so extraordinarily high in the New Era (see Table 27). The explanation is, in fact, very simple. In the New Era there was a strong growth of public utility holding companies which followed a peculiar financial policy. They bought and held shares of operating companies, and financed them to a very considerable part, not by issue of shares, but by bonds (and preference shares). They could in this way obtain a much greater rate of profit on the equity than the operating companies. It is not unlikely that the profit rate might be doubled, or more than doubled, by the formation of a holding company 'of the first order', as shown by the Federal Trade Commission.[1] But there were holding companies of the second and of higher orders, that is, the common shares of the holding companies of the first order were held, and financed partly through bond issue, by holding companies of the second order, etc. In this way very high profit rates on the equity were obtained, while at the same time the risk was considerably increased. The practice amounts really to nothing else but an ***increase in the gearing ratio*** : a greater proportion of the real capital is (ultimately) financed by debt, with the consequence that the net profit rate is increased, while the risk at the same time grows. It is logical and reasonable that these high profit rates should not be 'capitalised' in the share market, just because

[1] Senate Document No. 213, 68th Congress 2nd Session, p. 173, quoted in W. Bayard Taylor, *Financial Policies of Business Enterprise*, p. 369.

they are associated with increased risk. The great increase in earnings yields of utility shares finds its explanation therefore in an increase in the gearing ratio.

A similar explanation would seem to apply in the case of railroads. The process of consolidation by which the big railway systems were created out of a merger of trunk lines began in the 1890's. These consolidations were effected by purchase of railway stock, which the purchasing company financed by issuing bonds. This again is clearly a case of an increase in the gearing ratio, and offers the most plausible explanation of the rise in the earnings-yield on railroads since the turn of the century.

In view of this explanation it appears that the increase in earnings-yield in the sphere of utilities and railroads did not mean, as it might be thought at first glance, a greater difficulty for the finance of investment in these fields. The yield did increase, but so did the net profit rate, owing to the increase in gearing ratio.[1] In any case, however, the policy was to finance mainly by bonds (and preference shares) and to keep the common shares as a means of control to a large extent closely held.

The practice of increasing the gearing ratio by the means described in those particular fields could not be expected on *a priori* grounds. It depends partly on irrational factors, as it involves the bearing of an increased risk. The practices especially of utility holding companies have been condemned as unsound (although it is hardly realised in this context that such unsound practice really represents an instance of the celebrated venturesomeness of entrepreneurs). The drawbacks become apparent in the depression. But while the increase in gearing ratio was being operated, the effect was doubtless to make a larger rate of investment possible.

The conclusion is that the development of the joint stock system exerted a stimulating effect on the economy in two different ways: in the field of industrials, it reduced the effective yields on shares, and therefore made growing share issues possible on more favourable terms. In the field of utilities and railroads, it led *via* the formation of holding companies and consolidations to an increase in the gearing ratio, which again meant a stimulus to investment.

5. *The net effect of the joint stock system*

What difference does the joint stock system, finally, make to the trend of capital accumulation? On the one hand, it makes it possible to merge a part of outside savings into the equity, by means of share issues. On the other hand, it distributes a part of the profit in form of dividends and salaries to executives, and the amount saved out of these increases the outside saving. If the share issues (subtracting the amount of share issues which are used only to acquire and hold other shares) are just equal to the amount of savings

[1] The yields may, however, have increased more than the net profit rate, because the share investors—theoretically quite rightly—may have put the increase in risk at a greater value than the increase in the profit rate. This probably was the case with railroads, which as a consequence were later *forced* to borrow because of unfavourable share yields.

out of dividends and executives salaries, the two forces balance each other. As the rate of profit is of primary importance for new share issues, it will also have an important bearing on the net effect resulting from the two forces.

It appears that up to 1929 the net effect of the joint stock system was stimulating. During this time, as has been shown, the system developed, making thus a growing amount of capital issues possible. It is true that a calculation by Mr. M. Taitel seems to show that even at that time the saving out of dividends in most years exceeded the amount of share issues.[1] However, we have to consider in addition also the effect on bond issues: the increase in gearing ratio bound up with the development of holding companies in public utilities is an additional stimulating factor which does not appear in the share issues.

The stimulation inherent in the development of the joint stock system played in practice the role of a counteracting force against certain other developments. There has been since the turn of the century a decline in the overall rate of profit (see below Chapter XII). Taken by itself this ought to have discouraged investment and reduced the rate of growth of capital. One might have expected that this should have led to stagnation much earlier than it did. That great prosperity was nevertheless possible, especially before the first world war and in the New Era, is at least partly due to the net stimulating effect of the joint stock development. The decline in yields on industrials offset the decline in the profit rate. An increasing amount of outside savings could therefore be merged into the equity in this field. In railways and utilities the development of consolidation was bound up with an increase in the gearing ratio, which made it possible to absorb an increasing proportion of outside saving in the form of bond issues.

It is clear that these stimulating effects are bound up with *the development* of the system, and there is therefore a limit to their action. The tendency to a decline in yield should almost certainly reach a limit sooner or later, because the excess of the share yield over the rate of interest can probably not be reduced below a certain level. Once the rate of profit drops further, share issues then diminish to a mere trickle. Even more limited is the effect of an increase in the 'propensity to borrow' (in the case of utilities); this is, in fact, purely temporary, and once enough bad experience has been made with it, there is likely to be a return to more conservative methods of finance.

From 1929 on the net effect of the joint stock system has certainly been depressing. Savings out of dividends were continuing at a considerable level, but share issues were very small, and the bold methods of holding company finance were out of fashion. The dwindling of share issues has a two-fold effect: on the one hand it decreases the rate of growth of entrepreneurial capital, and therefore the amounts which the companies can borrow if they wish to keep their gearing ratio constant. At the same time it increases the amounts of outside savings which must be *borrowed* in order to be used by business.

[1] *T.N.E.C. Monograph No.* 12. Profits, productive activities, and new investment, p. 75.

The joint stock system has served to delay the effects of the declining rate of profit considerably, but from a certain point on it could do so no more. The reverse of the medal then became exposed : there were no more share issues, but the creation of outside savings by sizeable dividends continued.

6. *Effects on the maldistribution of funds*

A detail of some interest remains to be added. The possibility of share issues depends on the relation between the effective yield and the marginal rate of profit. Now the rate of profit varies greatly from company to company, and from industry to industry. The rate of profit is in general greater in the oligopolistic industries; at the same time the yield of shares in big oligopolistic concerns is, if anything, likely to be lower than the average.[1] It follows that the big enterprises in oligopolistic industries will have much more ready access to the share market than the companies in competitive industries where profit rates are lower. If the overall rate of profit is not very high, it may happen that many or most of the competitive industries will have no access to the share market at all, while oligopolistic industries will absorb most of the cash obtained by share issues.

This factor reinforces the earlier conclusion that there tends to be maldistribution of entrepreneurial funds in favour of the oligopolistic sector of business : not only is the rate of internal accumulation greater in the oligopolistic sector, but the absorption of new funds by share issues is incomparably more easy there than in the sector of competitive industries.

XII. The Accumulation of Capital in the United States, 1869–1939

1. *The trend of capital accumulation*

A study of the trend of capital accumulation would be almost like groping in the dark, if it were not for the work of Mr. S. Kuznets and his collaborators who have recently provided us with estimates of national income, investment and capital for a period dating back almost to the Civil War.[2] It goes without saying that this is a bold statistical undertaking. This is not the place to discuss the technique and appreciate the validity of the estimates in detail. It seems, however, reasonable enough to say that the results of this elaborate work deserve to be taken seriously. We shall accept them, therefore, by and large, as they stand, and try to find plausible explanations for them.

The basis for the estimates may be briefly indicated. *Gross national income* and *gross capital formation* are estimated on the basis of output of finished goods from Census material.[3] Distribution costs are added to get the national product at ultimate cost to consumers. They are taken as a fixed percentage, corresponding to the proportion which distribution cost bears

[1] The cost of issuing shares may also be lower, in so far as the oligopolistic concerns are bigger.

[2] S. Kuznets, *National Product since* 1869.

[3] W. Shaw, *Commodity output since* 1869.

in more recent periods, for which fuller data are available. Services are estimated (for the earlier periods) on the basis of the proportion of services in workers' cost of living. The consumption of capital which is required to obtain *net capital formation* is estimated on the assumption of a given lifetime of capital goods. This lifetime is again based on estimates for the more recent decades made by S. Fabricant.[1] The resulting figures for national income and capital formation are given not yearly but for overlapping decades since 1869. In this form the figures are not at all badly adapted for a study of the trend.

The estimates of capital assets (reproduceable wealth) are mainly based on the Census of Wealth and given for the years in which this Census was made (1880, 1890, 1900, 1912, 1922). Capital assets are of four types: (1) real estate improvements (that is, capital which is the result of construction), (2) equipment, (3) inventories, and (4) net claims against other countries. The chief difficulty in estimating capital assets was naturally to reduce them to a comparable price level. From the resulting estimates of capital assets in 1929 prices a figure is obtained for the growth of reproduceable capital between 1880 and 1922. By and large this figure can be reconciled with the estimate of net capital formation for the corresponding period, as obtained by the first mentioned method. This check is, in fact, one of the most important props which support the confidence in the whole of the estimates. For individual decades, however, the two sets of figures (growth of capital assets and net capital formation) sometimes square very badly. It seems reasonable to give preference to the figures of net capital formation, as far as the development from decade to decade is concerned. Correspondingly, Kuznets has combined the estimate of wealth for 1880 with the decennial estimates of net capital formation to give a series for the growth of wealth from decade to decade.

It is on this series that our interest centres. We obtain from it easily the percentage accumulation per annum of total reproduceable capital (Table 28, Col 1). The features revealed are quite distinct: the accumulation of total capital is highest between 1879 and 1899, at approximately 5 per cent per annum. Before that period, in 1869 to 1879, the accumulation seems to have been lower, about 4 per cent. After the period of maximum accumulation at the end of the last century, a steady decline took place. The rate of accumulation dropped to less than 3 per cent in the 1920's. In the decade 1929–38 there was practically no accumulation of capital.

These then are the salient features: a rise in capital accumulation to a very high rate in the last two decades of the 19th century, and a steady fall of this rate of accumulation during the present century, which reached vanishing point during the decade 1929–1938.

We have here a concrete measure of what must be regarded as the most important variable in long run economic development: the rate of growth of capital. This will make it possible to continue the theoretical

[1] *Capital Consumption and Adjustment.*

discussion of capital accumulation (begun in Chapter IX) on the level of concrete application, with the aim of throwing some light on the most crucial stages in the development of American capitalism.

At first, it is necessary, however, to clear up the relation between Mr. Kuznets' data and the theoretical concept of capital accumulation used in Chapter IX. We have considered there only the accumulation of *private business capital* (reproduceable real assets owned by entrepreneurs and corporations) and assumed that other types of accumulation do not exist. Under these circumstances the total accumulation is exhausted by accumulation of entrepreneurs' funds C and accumulation of business debt D, which is equal to accumulation of outside savings. It can then be shown that with a constant gearing ratio these rates of accumulation must be equal :

$$\frac{\Delta Z}{Z} = \frac{\Delta C}{C} = \frac{\Delta D}{D}.$$

Or, if we express all types of savings as ratios of business capital

$$\frac{\Delta Z}{Z} = \frac{\Delta C}{Z} + \frac{\Delta D}{Z}$$

then these ratios must change in the same proportion to permit a constant gearing ratio. Assuming outside savings to be a constant ratio of capital it can be shown then that a fall in the rate of growth of capital must lead to an increase in the gearing ratio. Moreover, given the propensity to save of entrepreneurs, the fall in the growth rate of capital will also lead to a decline in the rate of profit.

These conclusions may have to be modified if there exist other types of accumulation, such as (1) budget deficits, (2) foreign investment, (3) residential housebuilding as far as it is not business investment. It is then conceivable that a fall in business accumulation is in some sense offset by the other items mentioned, so that the outside saving which is not borrowed by entrepreneurs will be borrowed for example by the government or by the rest of the world.

It would be useful to have some criterion by which we can decide how effective a given amount of this ' compensatory borrowing ' is. How much ' compensatory borrowing ' (budget deficit, etc.) is required to offset a given decline in the accumulation of business capital, or a certain *tendency* to a decline ? This depends on what we mean by offsetting. On a strict theoretical basis we could define it as follows : imagine the rate of growth of business capital *tends* to fall for inherent reasons, that is, owing to a change in the structural coefficients which determine its endogenous growth. We have had an example of such a change in the case of an increase of gross profit margins, which, by its effect on utilisation, might reduce the growth rate of business capital. Now we can conceive of an exogenous influence, in the form of ' compensatory borrowing ', which is just great enough to offset the tendency for the accumulation of business capital to fall, thus keeping the rate of growth of business capital unchanged. In this strict theoretical interpretation the concept of offsetting is, however, not useful for our present purposes. As we shall see, the growth rate of business capital has in fact declined, and the 'compensatory borrowing' thus obviously did not prevent its decline. But we still want to have some criterion which permits us to judge in a rough and ready fashion how important were the effects of such compensatory borrowing as there has been. We might ask how much of it is necessary to keep the gearing ratio stable in face of a given decline in the growth rate of business capital. Or we might ask how much compensatory borrowing is required to keep the rate of profit stable.

Let us now approach the question from the practical side and consider the significance of two ratios. Take, in the first instance, the sum of business accumulation and compensatory borrowing, and express it as a ratio of business capital. This is, in other words, the ratio of total savings to business capital. It is (denoting compensatory borrowing by ΔB)

$$\frac{\Delta Z+\Delta B}{Z}=\frac{\Delta C+\Delta D+\Delta B}{Z}.$$

What will it amount to if this ratio of total savings to business capital is kept stable in face of a declining growth of business capital?

Supposing the ratio of outside savings to business capital, that is, $\frac{\Delta D+\Delta B}{Z}$, is to be stable, then the ratio of internal accumulation to business capital $\frac{\Delta C}{Z}$ will also be constant. But as $\frac{\Delta Z}{Z}$ is falling, the proportion of internal accumulation to business accumulation must rise, and therefore the gearing ratio will be falling. At the same time the growth rate of entrepreneurs' capital must decline; for

$$\frac{\Delta C}{C}=\frac{\Delta C}{Z}\cdot\frac{Z}{C}$$

and, as before stated, $\frac{\Delta C}{Z}$ is constant, while the gearing ratio falls. But a falling growth rate of entrepreneurs' funds $\frac{\Delta C}{C}$ implies, if the saving propensities of entrepreneurs are unchanged, a falling rate of profit.

Thus if compensatory borrowing is large enough to keep the ratio of total saving to business capital constant in face of a declining growth rate of business capital, then this will prevent the gearing ratio from rising, and will even make it fall; it will, however, not prevent a fall in the rate of profit.

The conclusion is dependent on the constancy of outside savings as a ratio of business capital. It is therefore not general, but it serves well to give us an idea of what a constant ratio of savings to business capital may imply under simple conditions.

We may now consider an alternative ratio, namely the rate of growth of total savings. This is given by

$$\frac{\Delta Z+\Delta B}{Z+B}=\frac{\Delta C+\Delta D+\Delta B}{C+D+B}.$$

What will a constancy of this rate of growth of total savings imply? It should make it possible that the entrepreneurs' capital C and the stock of outside savings $D+B$ grow at the same rate, identical with the rate of growth of the total stock of savings. But if we suppose again that outside savings is a constant ratio of business capital, then the stock of outside savings will grow at a declining rate (because its proportion to business capital will increase). Consequently, the entrepreneneurs' capital C will have to grow at an increasing rate, to keep the growth rate of the total stock of savings constant. Assuming constant saving propensities of entrepreneurs, the rate of profit will therefore rise. Thus we find that a constant rate of growth of the total stock of savings (on the supposition that the rate of outside savings is a constant ratio of business capital) will imply a rising rate of profit.

The two ratios analysed, the ratio of total savings to business capital and the rate of growth of total savings, may serve to give us at least a rough idea as to the effectiveness of compensatory borrowing under simple conditions. If we regard the rate of profit as a criterion we should say that a *constant ratio of savings to business capital* will be insufficient to keep the rate of profit stable, while a *constant rate of growth of savings* will be more than sufficient to keep the rate of profit stable.

Stability of the rate of profit, in face of a declining rate of growth of business capital, will obtain in the case which is intermediate between the two above mentioned cases, namely where compensatory borrowing is big enough to make the ratio of savings to business capital increase, while it leaves the rate of growth of total savings declining.

At the same time we have seen that in both cases considered, the gearing ratio will fall. A constant ratio of savings to business capital (if the growth rate of the latter falls) is already more than sufficient to prevent a rise in the gearing ratio. Even a certain decline in the ratio of savings to business capital may therefore be reconciled with a stable gearing ratio. The preceding analysis is of course based on rather special assumptions: a constant ratio of outside savings to business capital at a given utilisation of capital, and constant propensities to save of entrepreneurs. Nevertheless the analysis may be of use in the interpretation of the data.

We have so far left out of account the issue of new shares. If we allow for it, we must recognise that the gearing ratio will be affected by it. In fact, any share issues will mean that a certain part of the outside saving is transformed into entrepreneurs' capital. Any share issues will therefore mean that the gearing ratio develops more favourably than would be expected on the basis of the preceding analysis. We might, for example, have no compensatory borrowing at all, and in spite of a decline in the growth rate of business capital the gearing ratio might be stable or even fall, if share issues absorb a growing proportion of the outside savings. On the other hand, the share issues contribute nothing to prevent a fall in the rate of profit. The total entrepreneurs' capital C will currently grow by two increments, internal accumulation ΔC_1 and share issues ΔC_2. The internal accumulation, as before, will be determined such as to make up the difference between total saving and outside saving, and the share issues do not change the amount of internal accumulation. The profit rate is related to internal accumulation by

$$p = a + \frac{1}{1-\lambda}\alpha.$$

Here α will be the ratio of internal accumulation ΔC_1 to entrepreneurs' capital C, and the latter grows now not only by the amount of internal accumulation but also by the amount of new share issues. The share issues will thus tend to reduce α slowly, and therefore also to reduce the rate of profit p. In practice this effect will be very slow, but after a long time, if the share issues have been sufficiently important, they should tend to make the profit rate lower than it would have been under the same circumstances, if the money had been borrowed by business instead of being provided by share issue.

After this discussion of the effects of compensatory borrowing we now return to the interpretation of Kuznets' figures. We are interested, first, in the accumulation of *business capital*, and second, in the extent of possible compensatory borrowing (which consists mainly of government deficit, foreign investment, and the part of housebuilding which cannot be included in business accumulation).

Kuznets' figures as given in Table 28, Col. 1, include, in addition to business capital, also the increase in net claims against foreign countries, the

TABLE 28

ACCUMULATION OF CAPITAL IN U.S.A.

Rates of growth in per cent per annum, based on $ values in prices of 1929

Jan. 1, Jan. 1	Total reproducible wealth % (1)	Real estate improvements, equipment & inventories % (2)	Business capital % (3)	Population % (4)	Gainfully occupied % (5)
1869—1879	4.1	4.4	3.9	2.3	3.0
1879—1889	4.9	5.2	4.8	2.2	3.0
1889—1899	4.9	4.7	4.5	2.0	2.2
1899—1909	4.2	4.0	3.9	1.9	2.5
1909—1919	3.5	3.0	2.8	1.4	1.3
1919—1929	2.8	2.6	2.2	1.5	1.4
1929—1939	0.2	0.3	—0.4	0.7	1.2

Column (1) and (2): Kuznets, Table IV, 10B.
Column (3): From Table 30.
Column (4) and (5): Bureau of Census, Comparative Occupation Statistics for the U.S., 1870–1940.

increase of capital assets owned by public authorities, and the part of building of dwelling houses which cannot be included in business investment. We have to see whether the subtraction of these items can make any fundamental change in the picture.

The net claims against foreign countries can be subtracted easily, because they are given separately by Kuznets. The remaining series (containing fixed capital and inventories) does not show a greatly different picture from the original one (Table 28, col. 2). The development of capital accumulation is much the same, except for the rather important difference that its decline begins already in the 1890's.

Government capital and residential housing cannot be directly subtracted in the same way, because the data for *net capital formation* do not permit a split-up of this kind. The estimates of wealth in the Census, however, do give these figures separately. The percentage share of industry, public utilities, residential housing and government in the total fixed capital (real estate improvements and equipment) has been calculated for the Census years (Table 29). The relative importance of these various sectors changes very little over the greater part of the period. The share of residential capital

TABLE 29

PERCENTAGE SHARE OF DIFFERENT SECTORS IN THE TOTAL CAPITAL (REAL ESTATE IMPROVEMENTS AND EQUIPMENT)

(Based on Kuznets' estimate of capital in 1929 prices (Method B)[1]

	June 1, 1880	June 1, 1890	June 1, 1900	Dec. 31, 1912	Dec. 31, 1922	Dec. 31, 1938
I. Private Industry	38.6	38.0	37.0	36.6	40.3	34.8
II. Public Utilities	31.4	29.6	30.8	30.0	27.0	30.6
III. Residential	24.6	26.4	25.1	26.2	24.4	21.5
IV. Government	5.5	6.0	7.2	7.4	8.3	13.2
	100.0	100.0	100.0	100.0	100.0	100.0

shows no trend whatsoever up to 1922, although after this date there is a decline. The share of government capital does show a continuous increase over the whole period. Up to 1922, however, this increase is too small to be of any importance for the problem in view (it amounts to only 3 per cent of the total capital for the whole period).

On the face of it, it would appear, then, that the exclusion of non-business capital from Kuznets' figures could effect very little change in the picture. We have to take into account, however, that the Census figures of wealth (on which the proportions of Table 29 are based) do not include public roads; the figures of capital formation on the other hand do include them, and they have therefore to be eliminated too.

It must be made clear at this point that the calculation of business capital which now follows is in the nature of an extremely crude estimate. A sober

[1] *National Product since* 1869, Table IV, 12.

weighing up of the magnitudes involved would, however, indicate that the vital conclusions cannot be invalidated on that account.

In trying to arrive at an estimate of *business capital* I have made no attempt to eliminate housing. The available evidence indicates that the proportion of residential capital did not change as much as to affect the result decisively. I have eliminated, however, all government capital including roads. After 1919 the data are fairly satisfactory. For the earlier periods, I had to rely upon the data derived by Kuznets from the Census of wealth, and, with regard to roads, on some plausible guess work. I have also eliminated the accumulation of monetary metals, which are included in Kuznets' inventory figures. The resulting modification of Kuznets' series of capital accumulation is given in Table 30, and Table 28, column 3. The development of accumulation of business capital, as represented in this series, is practically the same as it was before the elimination of government capital (only the decline in the last decades becomes stronger, with a slightly negative accumulation in the 1930's).

Next I have attempted to estimate the accumulation of non-business capital, or '*debt-capital*', as we may call it: that is, government debt and net claims against foreign countries. To these two items have to be added the increase in monetary stocks of metal, and also, for the modern period, the accumulation of consumers' debt (Table 31). Two separate things have to be considered here: the *rate* of foreign balance, government deficit, etc., in the periods concerned; and the amount of foreign claims, government debts, etc., at certain *dates*. Both series have to be deflated to make them comparable with the series of business capital which is in 1929 prices. Owing to the deflation the two series become, at first sight, irreconcilable; that is, the deficits do not square with the increase in debt in real terms, nor does the foreign balance square with the increase in net foreign claims plus gold imports.

This is not a freak of statistical procedure but economically quite correct. The increase in real government debt consists of two parts, the deficits incurred, and the change in its real value owing to price changes. Only the first part creates saving and should therefore be included in the accumulation of ' debt-capital '. Once we consider the *level* of existing debt, however, we must take account of the appreciation or depreciation of the debt in terms of goods, in order to evaluate correctly the relative importance of the debt-capital in comparison with business-capital.

The development of *debt-capital* is presented in Table 32. It is striking to see how its relative importance has changed. In 1889 it was about 1 per cent of business capital, in 1939 it amounted to 30 per cent of it. This is, of course, a consequence of the decline of business accumulation, and of the growth of ' compensatory borrowing ' for various reasons: increasing investment of local governments (roads, etc.), war, the emergence of large capital exports, the development of consumers' credit, and deficit finance by the federal government during the great depression.

TABLE 30

ESTIMATE OF BUSINESS CAPITAL (MILLIONS OF £ IN 1929 PRICES)

	Jan. 1, 1869	*Jan. 1, 1879*	*Jan. 1, 1889*	*Jan. 1, 1899*	*Jan. 1, 1909*	*Jan. 1, 1919*	*Jan. 1, 1929*	*Jan. 1, 1939*
1. Real Estate improvements, equipment, and inventories (Kuznets)	26,292	40,522	67,345	106,584	158,127	212,500	274,955	282,982
2. Tax-exempt capital	1,000	1,600	3,200	5,800	9,000	11,700	19,900	25,127
3. Additional improvements in Roads and Streets as compared with 1880	—1,000	—	1,500	4,000	7,500	14,000	23,000	33,000
4. Stock of monetary gold and silver	—60	400	800	1,160	1,870	2,400	2,600	3,860
5. *Business Capital* (1 −2 −3 −4)	26,350	38,522	61,845	95,624	139,757	184,400	229,455	220,995

Line 1. From Kuznets, Table IV, 10.

Line 2. The values for 1919 and 1939 are taken from Kuznets (N.P. since 1869) Table IV, 7 and IV, 9. 1929 is interpolated by the value of public construction and depreciation of government capital 1919–38. The earlier values are from the Census of Wealth, adjusted for the difference in date. For 1869 the value is assumed to be a similar proportion of total capital as in 1879.

Line 3. The total capital (line 1) in 1879 does not include roads and streets, because it is based on the Census of Wealth 1880. The other figures include the road construction *after* that date, because they are based on capital formation data. Value of existing improvements in roads and streets at the end of 1922 was 12.75 (estimate by the Federal Trade Commission), based on past cost. Kuznets estimates the improvements between 1880 and 1922 at $19 billions, which makes $16 billions for 1880–1919. This figure seems to be too high, and has been reduced to $14 billions. The total has been distributed over the period, having regard to some data on expenditure of local government for highways.

Line 4. The figure for 1879 is the actual stock in 1929 prices. The other figures are increase in stock *minus* net imports of gold, because it is this difference only which is included in Kuznets' figures of inventory accumulation.

TABLE 31

ESTIMATE OF TOTAL SAVINGS

($ *millions*)

	1869–78	*1879–88*	*1889–98*	*1899–1908*	*1909–18*	*1919–28*	*1929–38*
Current Prices							
1. Federal Government deficit	—470	—970	40	—220	12,700 }		
2. Local Government deficit	230	90	480	1,470	2,820 }	5,300	12,850
3. Export surplus	—1,160	—430	—8	—590	9,840	9,680	2,020
4. Consumers' Credit						5,200	—270
5. Accumulation of monetary metals	510	520	420	710	520	180	1,220
1929 Prices							
6. Federal Government deficit	—780	—1,960	90	—440	13,000 }		
7. Local Government deficit	380	180	1,100	2,930	4,360 }	5,300	15,300
8. Export surplus	—1,940	—870	—20	—1,180	11,170	8,700	2,200
9. Consumers' Credit						5,020	—220
10. Accumulation of monetary metals	850	1,050	970	1,410	740	170	1,380
11. Total 'compensatory borrowing'	—1,490	—1,600	2,140	2,720	29,270	19,190	18,660
12. Accumulation of business capital	12,170	23,320	33,780	44,130	44,640	45,060	—8,460
13. Total Saving	10,680	21,720	35,920	46,850	73,910	64,250	10,200

How far did this compensatory borrowing counteract the fall in business accumulation ? We shall calculate two series, the rate of growth per annum of *total savings*, and the ratio of total savings to business capital. Total savings consist, of course, of business capital and debt-capital, the latter being by definition savings which are not embodied in business capital.

Statistically the calculation of the rate of growth of savings is complicated by the fact that the accumulation of debt capital cannot be considered

TABLE 32

DEBT CAPITAL

	Beginning of year							
	1869	1879	1889	1899	1909	1919	1929	1939
1. Net Federal Debt						20.9	16.9	32.6
2. General Fund Balance						0.8	0.3	3.1
3. Federal debt minus General Fund	2,457	1,998	1,020	1,091	1,029	20,100	16,600	29,500
4. Net Local Debts	800	1,030	1,120	1,600	3,070	5,200	12,800	15,700
5. All Government debt, net	3,257	3,028	2,140	2,691	4,099	25,300	29,400	45,200
6. Consumers' Credit						2,000	7,196	6,926
7. Balance of Foreign Claims	—1,300	—1,100	—2,800	—2,800	—3,900	3,400	8,000	3,700
8. Stock of monetary gold and silver	200	400	1,000	1,200	2,150	3,680	4,540	9,400
9. Total Debt Capital	2,157	2,328	340	1,091	2,349	34,380	49,136	65,226
10. Total Debt Capital in 1929 prices	3,100	4,900	700	2,500	4,300	32,500	49,100	72,300

Line 1—5 : Net Government debt for 1919–39 : *Survey of Current Business*, July 1944. Federal debt before 1919 from Statistical Abstract (averaging debt at the end of two fiscal years). Local Government debt before 1919 derived from Census of Wealth Debt and Taxation by interpolation. The figures before 1919 are not quite comparable with the later ones in so far as they are gross debt.

Line 6 : *From T.N.E.C. Monograph No. 37*, Saving, Investment and National Income, p. 83. Before 1919 this item is neglected.

Line 7 : From Kuznets, *National product since 1869*.

Line 8 : Table 30, line 4, plus net imports of gold.

Line 10 : Deflated with the index of prices of business capital (construction, producers' durable goods and inventories) so as to make the debt capital comparable with business capital in 1929 prices.

identical with the changes in value of real debt from one date to the next : a part of this change is mere ' capital gain ' or ' loss ' and cannot be included in the accumulation of savings. We have therefore to resort to a statistical approximation to get the average rate of growth of savings per annum during a decade : we take the increase in business capital plus the amount of compensatory borrowing during a decade, and divide it by the average level of business capital and debt capital during the decade. The latter is approximated as the average of capital at the beginning and the end of the decade. (The procedure has been applied also to the accumulation of business capital alone. From a comparison of this series with the one obtained as the average logarithmic increase of business capital it can be seen that the errors due to the approximation are fairly moderate.)

The resulting data for the growth of savings are noteworthy (Table 33, col. 5). In spite of the growing importance of compensatory borrowing, the rate of growth of *total savings* has declined all the same from the high level of 4.5 per cent in 1889–98 to 3.9 per cent in 1899–1908, to 2.6 per cent in 1919–28, and to +0.3 per cent in 1929–38. Only in the decade which includes the world war, 1909–1918, did the high government deficit and foreign balance bring the growth rate of savings nearly back to its maximum level with 4.1 per cent. Consider now the other series, the ratio of total savings to business capital (Table 33, col. 6). This series, too, reaches its high level in 1889–98, and declines subsequently, except in the decade containing World War I. As compared with the level of 4.6 per cent in 1889–98, and 4 per cent in 1899–1908, the ratio was only 3.1 per cent in 1919–1928. The ratio was thus one-third lower in the 'twenties than it had been at the end of the last century.

We can now apply the general considerations which have occupied us a few pages earlier. It was shown there that a decline in the ratio of total savings to business capital, though it need not necessarily imply a rise in the gearing ratio, would under certain conditions indicate a fall in the rate of profit. In this sense we may say the series indicates that compensatory borrowing, although it may have prevented a rise in the gearing ratio, was not large enough to prevent adverse effects of the decline in business accumulation on the rate of profit. It does not look, broadly speaking, as if compensatory borrowing by itself has been a sufficiently strong offset to the powerful tendency of the rate of growth of business capital to decline.

At this point it is time to take a deep breath and look at the results. The accumulation of capital shows a definite pattern : *Rise—Decline—Stagnation.*

Is it really necessary to go back so far into history to understand the events which are still vivid in our memory ? Indeed, it is only after these data have become available that we can clearly appreciate even the meaning of stagnation. In terms of capital accumulation the decade of the great depression stands out from all the preceding ones as historically unique. In this period the system of highly developed capitalism worked under conditions to which it was never subject before. And it is only now that we can realise equally clearly how futile an attempt would be to deal with the events between the wars in isolation. Stagnation did not come over-night. Preceding it there had been a long process of secular change, which passed almost unnoticed, because memories are short and comparisons over long periods are difficult to make. Hardly anybody during the ' New Era ' was aware of the fact that the annual rate of growth of business capital then was only half of what it had been thirty years earlier !

These data, then, open up a new field in showing us the whole extent of the question of economic maturity and stagnation. They enable us to formulate precise and concrete questions :

(1) Why did the rate of growth of capital ever start to decline ? What was the reason for this ' primary ' fall in accumulation ?

This is the most difficult question of all, not least because the event took

TABLE 33

ACCUMULATION OF BUSINESS CAPITAL AND OF TOTAL SAVINGS

	(1)	(2)	(3)	(4)	(5)	(6)
	Average Business Capital	Average Debt Capital	Average Business and Debt Capital	Accumulation of Business Capital as percentage of average Business Capital	Total Savings as a percentage of average Business Capital plus av. Debt Capital	Total Savings as percentage of Business Capital
1869–78	32,436	4,000	36,436	3.75	2.94	3.29
1879–88	50,184	2,800	52,984	4.65	4.10	4.32
1889–98	78,735	1,600	80,335	4.30	4.47	4.55
1899–1908	117,690	3,400	121,090	3.75	3.88	3.98
1909–18	162,080	18,400	180,480	2.76	4.10	4.56
1919–28	206,928	40,800	247,728	2.18	2.60	3.11
1929–38	225,225	60,700	285,925	—0.38	0.36	0.45

place a long time ago, and statistics for this early period are particularly unsatisfactory.

The explanation which most easily hits the eye is the decline in population growth. We have to think of the growth of *working population* here, because it is this which is logically connected with the expansion of productive capacity. The critics of A. Hansen have poured ridicule on him for his attempt to connect the decline in investment opportunities with reduced growth of population (and the 'passing of the frontier'), taking it for granted that the former became apparent only in the great depression. But they were unaware of the fact (nor could even Hansen himself realise it) that for a very long time already a decline in growth of business capital was taking place *concurrently* with the decline in growth of the working population! (See Table 28). No mystic thread is needed to connect the two phenomena. The 'bogey' of economic maturity has been a reality for fifty years.

But the explanation hardly goes deep enough. It is not easy to dismiss the suggestion that the growth of the working population (especially since it was so largely determined by the extent of immigration) is at least as much an effect as a cause of the trend of capital accumulation. We had better admit that there exists no satisfactory explanation at present.

(2) The decline in the rate of growth of capital having started, why did it continue without interruption?

We separate this question from the first, because the reasons may not be the same in both cases. In fact, the second question is probably the easier to answer. *A priori* we have already a number of possible explanations in the 'cumulative processes' described in Chapter IX. Once a decline of the rate of growth has set in, it might lead, by its effects on the degree of utilisation, and on the rate of profit, to a further discouraging of investment.

There is still another factor to consider, which will be dealt with in one of the subsequent paragraphs, namely the fact that a declining rate of growth affects the age composition of capital in a way which is unfavourable to the inducement to invest.

(3) How is it possible that the decline in growth of business capital proceeded for a long time without producing any visible adverse results? There is surely some justification for the commonsense reaction of extreme surprise: the period before the first World War, say 1900–1914, and the 'New Era' of the 'twenties are reputed to be among the most prosperous times in American history!

To formulate the question more precisely: we should expect, on theoretical grounds, that the decline in the growth of business capital (since it was not adequately offset by compensatory borrowing) should have produced *much more quickly* a secondary fall in accumulation, resulting in noticeable excess capacity and unemployment. Particularly so, since we should expect as the most plausible result the rate of profit to have fallen with the decline in growth of total savings. And the coincidence of a declining rate of profit with periods of great prosperity remains, after all, a paradox!

(4) Why, on the other hand, was the fall in the rate of growth of capital so abrupt after 1929, as compared with the previous, more gradual, decline? And why did it now produce the adverse, visible results in the form of secular depression all at once, while previously nothing could be noticed of them? We should find it more natural, after all (and the critics of Hansen have laboured this point), if the great depression had cast its shadows before, and if the adverse effects of a decline in the rate of growth of capital had appeared *pro rata*, as it were, and simultaneously with it!

The two last questions (3) and (4) are intimately connected. In general terms, they themselves suggest the answer. There must have been compensating forces of some sort, which prevented the adverse effects from materialising up to a certain time. From this time on they became inoperative, or they were incapable of counteracting a further decline, and then the full force of the depression was unleashed.

The idea of compensating forces is not new, it is the main idea of Hansen's work on the mature economy. But it is another thing to identify these compensating forces. All the factors which Hansen mentions (e.g. motor car industry, road building, consumers' credit, capital export) are invalid as explanations of the problem as we put it. They could exert their influence only *via* the accumulation of business capital, or *via* the accumulation of debt-capital (compensatory borrowing), and, as we have seen, all these forms of accumulation together have declined in spite of the factors mentioned.

Some light will be thrown in the following on each of the above questions, although, needless to say, these explanations are not meant to be exhaustive. The order in which the subjects will be taken up is not necessarily the same as the order in which they have been put above.

2. *Did the rate of profit fall?*

One of the most striking features of the data is the decline in the rate of *growth of savings* since the end of the last century (Table 33). This is very conspicuous in particular in a comparison of the New Era (1919–28) with the first decade of the century (1899–1908). Generally speaking, one of three things must have happened: either *outside savings* have been accumulating at a slower pace, presumably because the outside saving as a proportion of income was declining. Alternatively the *propensity to save of entrepreneurs*, especially corporations, may have declined, so that, with an unchanged net rate of profit, corporations were accumulating funds at a slower pace. Or else, finally, the net *rate of profit* may have declined, so that even with unchanged propensity to save, the corporations would accumulate funds less quickly.

It will help the subsequent discussion, if we concentrate our attention on the ratio of total savings to business capital. This ratio is, of course, less likely to decline than the rate of growth of savings, but it so happens that, in fact, it too declines: it is 3.1 per cent in 1919–28, as compared with 4.0 per cent in 1899–1908 (Table 33, col. 6). Now this ratio of savings to business capital can be split up into outside savings and entrepreneurial savings according to the equation

$$\frac{\Delta Z+\Delta B}{Z}=\frac{\Delta D+\Delta B}{Z}+\frac{\Delta C}{Z}$$
$$=\frac{\Delta D+\Delta B}{Z}+\frac{\Delta C}{C}\cdot\frac{C}{Z}.$$

The three alternative possibilities can be analysed more precisely on the basis of this equation.

(1) Outside saving $\Delta B+\Delta D$ in relation to business capital might have declined. This would require either a decline of outside savings as a ratio of net national income, with the ratio of national income to business capital constant. Or it would require a constant ratio of savings to national income, with an increase in the ratio of business capital to national income.

The second possibility is definitely not realised. From Table 34 it can be

TABLE 34

RATIO OF BUSINESS CAPITAL TO NET NATIONAL INCOME

	Average Business Capital at current prices $ millions	Net National Product at current prices $ millions	Ratio of Business Capital to net national product
	(1)	(2)	(3)
1869—78	19,400	6,489	3.0
1879—88	24,850	9,941	2.5
1889—98	34,100	11,671	2.9
1899—1908	59,100	19,740	3.0
1909—18	114,500	36,341	3.2
1919—28	219,000	72,160	3.0
1929—38	199,000	61,274	3.2

Column (1): Average Business Capital in 1929 prices (Table 33) multiplied with price index of business capital.

Column (2): From Kuznets, *National Product since 1869.*

seen that the ratio of business capital to net national income did not increase; it remained constant between 1899–1908 and 1919–28. The first possibility, a fall in the ratio of outside savings to national income, is on general grounds very unlikely. As long as we have no evidence to the contrary, it is about the last thing we should expect. Some data of Lough (Table 35) would indicate that the ratio of personal savings to national income was lower before the first world war than afterwards. The value of this evidence may be doubted,

TABLE 35

SHARE OF PERSONAL SAVINGS IN 'CONSUMER'S OUTGO'[1]

1909	1914	1919	1921	1923	1925	1927	1929
9.6%	8.9%	14.3%	11.0%	11.1%	13.4%	12.5%	10.4%

[1] W. H. Lough, *High Level Consumption*, p. 22. 'Consumers' Outgo' is much the same as Income payments (personal incomes), including imputed incomes.

but the *a priori* reasons are strong. After all, nobody has so far found reasons for thinking that with an increasing standard of living the ratio of saving to income should actually *decline*.

(2) There remains a decline in entrepreneurs' saving as a ratio of business capital. This might have taken place with a constant rate of profit. Now it has been shown earlier that a constant rate of profit, with a declining rate of growth of business capital, must necessarily imply a fall in the gearing ratio $\frac{Z}{C}$. Therefore $\frac{\Delta C}{C}$, the proportionate accumulation of entrepreneurs' funds, must have fallen in this case. This means a decline in the propensity to save of entrepreneurs. Now, in principle, this is not at all impossible, but it is very unplausible that it should account for the full extent of the change shown by the data.

(3) As far as general reasoning goes, we have to lean very strongly towards the remaining alternative, a decline in the rate of profit. This would explain a fall in entrepreneurs' accumulation of funds even without any spectacular change in their propensity to save. The proportionate accumulation of funds is given as

$$\frac{\Delta C}{C} = \alpha = (p-a)(1-\lambda)$$

where a is the 'basic' consumption of entrepreneurs determined as a ratio of capital, and $(1-\lambda)$ the proportion saved of any excess of profits over a. A decline in the profit rate will obviously lead to a fall in proportionate accumulation of funds, if the saving habits (a and λ) are constant.

This is, then, what general argument leads us to believe. On such a vital question it is very important to have more direct evidence. The aim of getting statistical evidence in this field is necessarily restricted by the limitations of the data. Above all, we must restrict ourselves to corporations, to corporate profits, savings, and dividends. This is not such a bad restriction, for corporations accounted for a considerable share of total business in the whole period since 1900. Their share in total profits was certainly even bigger than their share in total capital. It is necessary to make another restriction and confine the enquiry, in the first instance, to dividends, that is from the point of view of corporations, the difference between profits and corporate saving $(p-\alpha)$. If it is found that dividends as a ratio of business capital have declined, then profits as a ratio of business capital have presumably declined too. This could be untrue only if the propensity to save of corporations actually *increased;* but that would mean that outside savings have fallen even more than the total savings, a possibility which we can dismiss as very unplausible. To choose dividends for measurement has great statistical advantages ; one does not have to bother, then, about the uncertainties of the undistributed profits and their economic meaning (distortion due to inventory valuation and to depreciation on the basis of book value).

The only data on dividends available from 1899 on are by R. F. Martin.[1]

[1] *The National Income of the United States* 1799–1938.

They are based on Treasury data from 1909 on, and on sample data for the preceding years. This dividend series has been deflated with the price index for business capital (described earlier on), so as to make it comparable with the figures of business capital in 1929 prices. The average of the deflated dividend for a decade has then been expressed as a ratio of the average business capital (in 1929 prices) in the same decade (Table 36, col. 2). This ratio of dividends to business capital dropped from 2 per cent in 1899–1908 to 1.7 per cent in 1919–28, or by 15 per cent. Now the dividends should of course be related to the *equity of corporations* only, which is but a proportion of total business capital. It is, however, quite safe to assume that the proportion of corporate capital in total business capital has *increased* in the period concerned. That equity has fallen in proportion to the real capital of corporations is not likely. It follows that the figures quoted *understate* the fall in the ratio of dividends to equity.[1] In appreciating the extent of the fall in the dividend ratio it must be borne in mind that, with a given propensity to save, a certain fall in the dividend is accompanied by a much stronger proportionate fall in the retained profits. The drop in the dividend ratio is therefore indicative of a much stronger fall in the profit rate.

The ratio of dividends of manufacturing concerns to fixed capital in manufacturing shows roughly similar tendencies (Table 36, col. 5). This series is rather imperfect, in so far as manufacturing concerns embody quite a lot of non-manufacturing activity.

How far the data on dividends are reliable is difficult to say. Two bits of evidence from other sources can be pieced together to give additional information. They relate not to dividends, but to net profits. Gordon and Epstein[2] have calculated the net rate of profit on equity for 24 identical manufacturing concerns in 1900–1914. This series shows a distinct downward trend, which is difficult to explain by any mere technical distortions, such as wrong valuation of capital, etc. The tendency seems to have been a real one at least for the concerns included. It agrees with the tendency shown by the dividend data. Further, there are estimates of the net profit of all corporations since 1909 based on treasury data.[3] Deflated and expressed as a ratio of business capital, these net profits show again a substantial fall: the ratio was 3.4 per cent in 1909–13 and 2.5 per cent in 1919–28 (Table 36, col. 7). The net profits given are those used in the Treasury statistics: to obtain an *economic* measure of profits they would have to be corrected for three factors: (1) capital gains and losses (on the sale of capital assets), (2) inventory valuation, (3) depreciation on the basis of cost value instead of reproduction value of capital. When correction for these factors is carried through for 1919 to 1928 (following Kuznets, *The National Income* 1919–38) it reduces the ratio

[1] The ratio of dividends to business capital shows a rise in 1909–13 and 1929–38. In both cases it is quite possible that the increase is due only to a rise in the proportion of corporate capital in total business capital.

[2] Profits of selected American industrial corporations 1900–1914. *Review of Economic Statistics*, Vol. XXI, 1939.

[3] M. Taitel, *Profits, Productive Activities and New Investments* (T.N.E.C. Monograph No. 12).

TABLE 36

DEVELOPMENT OF THE PROFIT RATE

	All Corporations				Manufacturing	24 Manufacturing Concerns	All Corporations	
	Dividends (Martin) in 1929 prices	Dividends as % of Business Capital	Dividends plus interest (Martin) originating in private business in 1929 Prices	Dividends plus interest as % of Business Capital	Dividends % of fixed capital	Profit as % of net worth	Net Corporate Profits (Taitel) as % of Business Capital	Net Corporate Profits *adjusted* (Kuznets) as % of Business Capital
	(1)	(2)	(3)	(4)	(5)	(6)	(7)	(8)
		%		%	%	%	%	%
1899–1908	2351	2.0	3873	3.3	6.2	7.5	—	—
1909–1913	3273	2.2	5190	3.4	5.4	6.7	3.4	—
1909–1918	3590	2.2	5484	3.4	5.3	—	3.7	—
1919–1928	3539	1.7	5543	2.7	5.5	—	2.5	2.2
1929–1938	4092	1.8	6390	2.8	6.2	—	0.4	1.0

slightly (Table 36, col. 8). For 1909–13 the correction can not be carried out, but it should be of relatively small importance : price changes were moderate then, and the correction of the depreciation could not have been very great. It follows that the profit rate in the decade 1919–28 was substantially lower than in 1909–13. If we take the sample of manufacturing companies of Gordon and Epstein as representative for the whole, *or* regard the dividend series as reliable, it follows that the profit rate in the 'twenties was also lower than in the 1900's.

The statistical evidence for the fall in the rate of profit is, taken by itself, not incontrovertible. It depends on the accuracy of the basic data, in particular the dividend series. The result gains significance, however, in so far as it is, on general grounds, the most plausible corollary to the fact of a fall in the rate of growth of capital and of savings. That the rate of profit has fallen in the period concerned can therefore be accepted, on the basis of the evidence available, as the best possible hypothesis.

There emerges, then, in its full extent, the problem already put before : we have, over the period concerned, a fall in the rate of growth of capital and of savings, leading to a fall of the profit rate. According to the theoretical deductions of Chapter IX this should involve a *cumulative* process, with the trend rate of accumulation decreasing more and more. The compensatory borrowing, as we have seen, probably could not have counteracted this effect. Now as the trend of accumulation has gradually been reduced in the period, it can be said that the theoretically expected course has been in a sense realised. But—although it is very difficult to give quantitative judgments in this field—it would seem very surprising that the effect of the falling profit rate was not much stronger at a rather earlier time. It looks, as has been said before already, as if a *compensatory factor* had been at work, which did not permit the adverse influence of the fall in the profit rate and in the internal accumulation *to work out to its full extent* ; and it seems that this compensatory factor must have proved incapable of further acting in this way from a certain point on, so that all the adverse effects materialised openly then, leading to a much stronger fall in accumulation than hitherto, and producing thus the *secular stagnation.* The compensating factor, as far as can be judged, has been the development of corporation finance by share issues to the public. The distortion of the proportion of outside savings to internal accumulation in favour of the former did not have to lead to any substantial increase in relative indebtedness because the innovation of share issues to the public permitted it to canalise a part of outside saving into the fund of entrepreneurial capital. This merging of outside savings into the equity must have played a considerable role in the 1920's and should therefore contribute much to an explanation of the great prosperity of this period in spite of the already fairly low rate of accumulation. At the same time the development of the share market led to a reduction of the *effective yield* at which shares could be marketed (see the demonstration in Chapter XI): this had the same effect as a decrease in the rate of interest would have had (the rate of interest itself in fact did *not* decrease, but was rather higher in the 1920's as compared with 1900-1914). That is, the *fall* in the profit rate was largely compensated by the cheapening of the terms on which share finance could be obtained. At the same time also certain practices bound up with the development of joint stock finance permitted or encouraged a virtual increase in the gearing ratio in certain sectors of industry: this is the development of holding companies in public utilities (electricity) in a form which meant financing of part of the equity of the operating companies by bond issues of the superimposed holding companies. This practice certainly also had a stimulating effect, because it permitted quicker expansion with a given rate of internal accumulation.

The stimulating effects of the developing joint stock finance were bound to reach a limit. The effective yield on shares *could* not easily fall below certain limits, just as the long term rate of interest is not easily reduced below certain levels. From a certain point on, a further fall in the profit rate could in any case not be further compensated by a cheapening of the terms of share finance, because the latter had reached its limits. At the same time the practice of holding companies financed to a considerable extent by bonds was bound to prove a merely temporary advantage: on ordinary business principles it was unsound and had to be given up. Now the gradual fall in the trend rate of accumulation and in the profit rate was apparently never held up completely, but only mitigated by the compensatory factor. In the very last years of the 'new era' the yield of shares was so low that it could not possibly remain on this level. It seems that an enormous optimism, completely detached from the underlying economic realities, contributed to the suddenness with which the compensatory factor of cheap finance ceased to act: the bow had been spanned to the utmost. As a consequence the reaction was complete: the finance by shares which had acted as a stimulating factor before stopped in practice *altogether*. The disproportion between outside savings and internal accumulation became then fully effective as an adverse element.

If the government had not borrowed the greater part of the outside savings in the 1930's, then—as business was not willing to borrow them for the purpose of investment—the system would almost certainly have been driven rapidly into strong decumulation of capital, with increasingly negative profit rates.

3. *Gross and Net Capital*

An entirely different problem has now to be faced. It is the problem of the age structure of capital. This problem has attracted attention from time to time in economic literature, but it always tended to get lost sight of again. The authors on the subject since Marx were fascinated by the idea of a certain irregularity of replacement, from which they sought to derive a theory of 'reinvestment cycles', with the aim of explaining either the business cycle (Marx) or at least some special cycles (J. Einarsen, the shipbuilding cycle).

This aspect of the problem is not treated explicitly here. The aim is rather to study changes in the age structure which take place over a rather longer time, and are relevant to the problems of secular development. It will become obvious that a somewhat different aspect arises from this treatment, which has hardly been sufficiently appreciated hitherto. The main reason for that is probably the lack of statistics. The work of Kuznets gives practically for the first time an opportunity to study the problem on the basis of empirical data, and to appreciate its significance for the secular development.

The starting point is the concept of gross and net capital. *Net capital* is the reproduction cost of the capital goods minus the depreciation already written off. It is this net capital and its accumulation which has been dealt with exclusively in these pages up to now. *Gross capital* is the reproduction value of the capital goods inclusive of depreciation already written off.

The significance of the concept of gross capital can be seen in a simple example. Imagine two similar machines with a life-time of 10 years, the one completely new and the other 9 years old. The net capital invested in the first machine is ten times as great as that embodied in the second one. Yet for the time being the productive capacity of the two machines is approximately equal. It may differ to some extent, if the machine deteriorates with age, but the difference will be nothing like the difference in the net capital value. Gross capital, measuring the number of machines in existence, will in general be much more nearly related to the productive capacity than net capital.

The ratio of net to gross capital will be the greater the 'younger' is the capital. In the above example it is 1.0 for the first machine and 0.1 for the second. The older the capital the more depreciation is already written off and the smaller the proportion of gross capital remaining. The ratio of net to gross capital is therefore an index of the *age structure of capital.*

A detailed picture of the age structure can be obtained if, at a certain date, an inventory of the capital is made, and it is classified into age groups. Let the age groups be, for example: capital not older than one year, capital aged between one and two years, etc. Let the gross value of capital J in these age groups be $b_1, b_2, b_3 \ldots b_n$.

Then the average age can be obtained as:

$$N = \frac{\frac{1}{2}b_1 + \frac{3}{2}b_2 + \frac{5}{2}b_3 \ldots \frac{2n-1}{2} b_n.}{b_1 + b_2 + \ldots + b_n} \qquad (27a)$$

The depreciation written off in each age group can be easily obtained, if we assume that the capital goods have all the same lifetime n, and the depreciation is uniformly distributed over the lifetime (straight line depreciation).[1] It is only necessary to choose between two conventions. According to the first convention, depreciation in a certain year is based on the average

[1] According to the enquiries of S. Fabricant (*Capital Consumption and Adjustment*) this method of depreciation is in practice the prevailing method, although in a minority of cases other methods are used.

value of gross capital during the year. The accumulated depreciation in the various age groups is then

$$\frac{1}{2}\frac{b_1}{n},\quad \frac{3}{2}\frac{b_2}{n},\quad \frac{5}{2}\frac{b_3}{n},\quad \ldots \frac{2n-1}{2}\frac{b_n}{n}.$$

Now the ratio of total depreciation to gross capital J is obviously the complement to 1.0 of the ratio of net to gross capital, i.e. it is $1-\frac{Z}{J}$. It can be easily seen that, multiplied by n, it equals the average age of the capital:

$$\left(1-\frac{Z}{J}\right)n = N. \tag{28}$$

In practical book-keeping another convention with regard to depreciation is more likely to apply: namely to calculate depreciation in a given year on the gross capital at the beginning of the year. The depreciation is then

$$0,\quad \frac{b_2}{n},\quad \frac{2b_3}{n},\quad \ldots \frac{(n-1)b_n}{n}.$$

To make the definition of average age square with this convention of depreciating, we have only to define capital of less than one year's age as being of age zero, capital of 1–2 years' age as being of age one, etc. The average age is then

$$N = \frac{0.b_1+1.b_2+2.b_3 \ldots (n-1)b_n}{b_1+b_2 \ldots +b_n} \tag{27b}$$

and this is again n times the ratio of depreciation to gross capital.

What is the age structure in a *stationary economy?* The gross output of capital goods is here a constant b_0, and the gross capital is

$$J = nb_0.$$

The annual depreciation is equal to the gross output b_0 and the annual replacement required is also equal to b_0. Both net and gross capital are constant.

The depreciation series, according to the first convention, is

$$\frac{1}{2}\frac{b_0}{n},\quad \frac{3}{2}\frac{b_0}{n},\quad \ldots \frac{2n-1}{2}\frac{b_0}{n}$$

and the depreciation is therefore the sum of an arithmetic series:

$$J-Z = b_0\left(\frac{1}{2n}+\frac{2n-1}{2n}\right)\frac{n}{2} = b_0\frac{n}{2}$$

$$1-\frac{Z}{J} = 0.5 = \frac{Z}{J}.$$

The ratio of net to gross capital is therefore 0.5. This implies, not very surprisingly, that the average age of the capital stock is half of its life time.

According to the alternative convention the depreciation is

$$J-Z = b_0\left(0+\frac{(n-1)}{n}\right)\frac{n}{2} = b_0\frac{n-1}{2}$$

$$Z = b_0\frac{n+1}{2}$$

and the ratio of net to cross capital is $\frac{Z}{J} = \frac{n+1}{2n}$.

If the life-time is fairly long, this ratio will not differ markedly from 0.5.

Now imagine that in this stationary economy a positive net capital accumulation suddenly starts. The gross output of capital goods rises above the former value b_0, and there is therefore an addition both to the net capital and to the gross capital (that is, to capacity). The replacement required and the depreciation being equal in the stationary economy, the additions to net capital and to gross capital are equal *absolute* amounts (given by the increase of b over b_0). As net capital is, however, roughly one half of gross capital, the proportionate accumulation of net capital is twice as great as that of gross capital: a disequilibrium has arisen between the growth of net capital and the growth of capacity.

As a consequence the ratio of net to gross capital is bound to increase: the capital becomes 'younger'. This process, as it goes on, should of course after a time reduce the discrepancy between the two rates of growth. The further idea suggests itself: the two rates of growth should come into equilibrium again, with a new appropriate age structure—provided of course that the pace of accumulation does not become quicker. More concretely, there should be an age structure appropriate to a particular pace of accumulation, which, once it is established, will be compatible with an equilibrium between the two rates of growth.

To demonstrate this we consider now the case of a *dynamic system*, where the output of capital goods is growing, and the capital stock in consequence is growing too. If the output in a given year is b_0, and it is growing at the ratio of j per annum, then after n years the gross capital will be

$$J = b_0(1+j+j^2 \dots +j^{n-1}),$$

$$J = b_0\frac{1-j^n}{1-j}.$$

It can be immediately seen from the formula that if output of capital goods increases all the time at the constant ratio j then the gross capital J will also increase at this ratio (because b_0 will grow at this ratio if we pass on in time).

The essential feature in a growing system is that the replacement required is always smaller than the depreciation. This is a consequence of the growth of output of capital goods. The replacement, that is the amount of capital that wears out and has to be replaced in the current year, is equal to the output of capital goods n years ago. The depreciation is the average output of capital goods over the past n years (or $1/n$ of gross capital), and that is necessarily bigger than the replacement.

The addition to net capital in a given year is the output of capital goods b minus depreciation d. The addition to gross capital is the output of capital goods minus the replacement b_0. If the ratio at which net capital grows annually is i and the ratio at which gross capital grows is j, then it is true that

$$b - d = Z(i-1)$$

$$b - b_0 = J(j-1)$$

and we obtain the relation between the two rates of growth :

$$j-1 = \frac{Z}{J}(i-1)+\frac{d}{J}-\frac{b_0}{J}. \tag{29}$$

The meaning of the equation is this : if *net* capital grows at a certain rate, then the addition to *gross* capital due to this net investment alone would make a smaller rate of growth; smaller, that is, in the proportion of net to gross capital. But in addition, gross capital grows also by the difference between depreciation and replacement. It all depends on whether this excess of depreciation over replacement is sufficient to offset the deficiency arising from the fact that the net accumulation does not apply to the part of gross capital already written off. If there is to be an equilibrium in the sense that net and gross capital grow at the same rate, then $j = i$, and it follows that

$$(i-1)\left(1-\frac{Z}{J}\right) = \frac{d}{J}-\frac{b_0}{J}.$$

Now $\frac{b_0}{J}$ is $\frac{1-j}{1-j^n}$. With regard to depreciation we have again the choice between the two conventions. According to the first one, $d = \frac{J+Ji}{2n}$. The equation becomes then

$$1-\frac{Z}{J} = \left(\frac{1+i}{2n}-\frac{1-i}{1-i^n}\right)\Big/(i-1). \tag{29a}$$

According to the second convention, $d = \frac{J}{n}$, therefore

$$1-\frac{Z}{J} = \left(\frac{1}{n}-\frac{1-i}{1-i^n}\right)\Big/i-1. \tag{29b}$$

These equations determine the ratio of net to gross capital which is appropriate to a certain rate of growth of capital, i.e. which will ensure equality of the growth of net and gross capital. In Table 37 the ratios corresponding to various rates of growth are calculated for a life-time of 50 years and 18 years.

The important argument can now be put into a more general form: starting from a situation in which the age structure is adapted to the existing rate of growth, if this rate of growth changes there will be disequilibrium. If the pace of accumulation quickens then the growth of net capital will exceed that of gross capital, and the capital stock will become 'younger'. If the pace

TABLE 37

Values of $\frac{Z}{y}$ *corresponding to given values of* i

$n = 50$

Formula: $1 - \frac{Z}{y} = \left(\frac{1+i}{2n} - \frac{1-i}{1-i^n}\right) \Big/ (i-1) \qquad (i \neq 1)$

i	$100\left(\frac{1+i}{2n} - \frac{1-i}{1-i^n}\right)$	$100\left(1 - \frac{Z}{y}\right)$	$100\left(\frac{Z}{y}\right)$
1.00	—	50.00	50.00
1.01	0.45875	45.88	54.13
1.02	0.83769	41.89	58.12
1.03	1.14345	38.12	61.89
1.04	1.38499	34.62	65.38
1.05	1.57233	31.45	68.55
1.06	1.71556	28.59	71.41

$n = 18$

Formula: $1 - \frac{Z}{y} = \left(\frac{1}{n} - \frac{1-i}{1-i^n}\right) \Big/ (1-i) \qquad (i \neq 1)$

i	$100\left(\frac{1}{n} - \frac{1-i}{1-i^n}\right)$	$100\left(1 - \frac{Z}{y}\right)$	$100\left(\frac{Z}{y}\right)$
1.00	—	47.22	52.78
1.01	0.45741	45.74	54.26
1.02	0.88538	44.27	55.73
1.03	1.28466	42.82	57.18
1.04	1.65619	41.41	58.60
1.05	2.00093	40.02	59.98
1.06	2.31990	38.67	61.34

of accumulation slows down, the rate of growth of net capital will fall below that of gross capital, and the capital stock will be ageing.

It would appear, if the economy is stabilised at the new rate of growth, that the disequilibrium will not continue for ever, but ultimately the age structure appropriate to the new rate of growth will be attained. The discrepancy between the two rates of growth should thus be gradually narrowed until it disappears. How long this process of adjustment takes will depend on the life-time of capital. With a life-time of 50 years the full adjustment should only be reached after a time as long as this, because only then the excess of depreciation over replacement will be adjusted to its new equilibrium level. Practically speaking the greater part of the adjustment is attained in a much shorter time. The discrepancy between the two rates of growth changes the net-to-gross capital ratio at first relatively quickly, the discrepancy being thereby itself reduced. Each subsequent step of the adjustment becomes then smaller and smaller, because a reduced discrepancy between the two rates of growth will also change the net-to-gross capital ratio at a smaller rate. It follows that the greater part of the adjustment must take place in the earlier part of the whole period, but with a life-time of 50 years the discrepancy will still be felt over a considerable number of years. In the case of very durable capital like buildings and all sorts of constructions, the problems discussed should therefore be practically relevant.

And now to the empirical data. Kuznets divides his capital into two parts, 'real estate improvements' (construction) and 'equipment' (producers' durable goods). As he assumes a certain constant life-time for each of these two types of capital, and assumes 'straight line depreciation', it would appear that we can immediately obtain the value of gross capital implicit in his calculations: either by multiplying the capital consumption with the life-time, or by cumulating the gross investment over a number of years corresponding to the life-time, for each of the two types of capital.

In reality, unfortunately, this proves to be less simple, because Kuznets has, by a purely statistical procedure, changed the economic assumptions from which he set out.

He starts off, in fact, by assuming a 50 years' life for construction, and 13 years' life for equipment, corresponding to depreciation rates of 2 per cent and 7.78 per cent respectively.[1] On this basis, capital consumption for a given year is obtained as the average gross construction or gross output of equipment in the 50 or 13 preceding years. This yields preliminary estimates of capital consumption for all the decades from 1869 to 1938. For the period after 1919, however, there exist more direct and presumably better estimates of capital consumption (based on the accounting records), made by S. Fabricant. These estimates are lower than the former ones. In the decade 1919–28, for example, they are 10.7 per cent lower than Kuznets' preliminary estimate. He proceeds now to reduce all his preliminary estimates of capital consumption by 10.7 per cent, and accepts this as the final estimates of capital consumption.

By this statistical procedure the life-time *implicitly* assumed is substantially altered. The implicit life-time is the number of years preceding over which we have to take the average of gross output in order to arrive at the final estimate of capital consumption. This is considerably greater than the 50 and 13 years initially assumed (even though the capital consumption is reduced by only 10.7 per cent). Moreover, this implicit life-time is no longer strictly constant over the whole period.

This raises, *inter alia*, the question of the trustworthiness of Kuznets' results as a whole. Can the implicit assumptions, broadly speaking, be

[1] This is ultimately based on depreciation rates collected by the Treasury (Depreciation Studies—Preliminary Report of the Bureau of Internal Revenue, 1931). The rates have been weighted by Fabricant according to the proportion of various types of equipment in the output in 1929 (*Capital Consumption and Adjustment*, p. 176 *seq.*).

justified, or is there any danger that the whole picture has been substantially distorted on their account? Now it is true that the estimates of capital consumption can in any case be only approximations which involve a certain element of speculation. It must be stressed, however, that the resulting estimates of net capital formation find some support in the data of wealth (from the Census of wealth and other material). Moreover, there are reasons to believe that the implicit assumptions of Kuznets are more realistic than the explicit ones from which he started. As far as can be judged on the basis of careful study of the data, it would not seem that the broad conclusions which we have drawn from them would be altered by such errors in the estimate of capital consumption as we can reasonably allow for.

For the specific purpose of studying gross capital we shall attempt in the following a reinterpretation of Kuznets' data.[1] In this reinterpretation we shall try to keep as close as possible to his own figures. At the same time we shall maintain the assumption of a constant life-time. On the most cautious view, the resulting picture might be regarded as a model which resembles the actual development at least in its most essential features.

For equipment we are assuming a constant life-time of 18 years throughout. The net capital formation, and therefore the figures of net capital have to be changed somewhat on this account, but the modification is comparatively minor. The constant 18 year life on the whole comes pretty close to Kuznets' own data. It will be asked how it can be reconciled with Fabricant's estimate of the average life of equipment, based on depreciation rates. Now the weights from which this estimate is derived are taken from the proportion of various types of equipment in the output in 1929. Strictly they should be based on the annual depreciation accruing for each type of equipment. It is likely that the weight of more durable equipment (locomotives, ships) in terms of depreciation was much greater than their weight in the output of 1929. The weighting is therefore biased in favour of shorter life-time. On this account alone it is reasonable that the average depreciation rate is considerably lower than the 7.78 per cent implied in Fabricant's life-time of equipment.

For construction Kuznets' figures have been merely reinterpreted in a simple, albeit somewhat arbitrary, way. A part of construction results in non-depreciable capital, which is kept serviceable by maintenance alone, and need never be replaced. (The maintenance is *not* included in the gross construction, and *not* included therefore in the capital consumption). This applies to roads as well as to a great part of public utilities (railways). It would appear that Kuznets, in arriving at his average life for construction, must have taken account of the non-depreciable part by assigning a very long life-time to it. The presumption is, however, that he made inadequate allowance for this non-depreciable construction. We assume that 11 per cent

[1] I am indebted to Mr. Kuznets for making available to me some of his basic data from his worksheets, which enabled me to make the recalculations strictly on his own data. Mr. Kuznets has, however, no responsibility for my interpretations.

of his gross construction is non-depreciable, and the 50 years' life-time is applied only to the remainder of gross construction. The resulting capital consumption and net capital formation is then exactly the same as obtained by Kuznets.[1]

Having given a consistent economic interpretation to Kuznets' data, we can calculate the *gross capital* implicit in these assumptions, separately for construction, equipment, and both combined. The corresponding net capital values have been given by Kuznets himself already (they are only slightly altered in the case of equipment to conform to the assumption of an 18 years' life-time).

From this is obtained the ratio of net to gross capital (Table 38), and the annual percentage growth of net and gross capital (Table 39). These figures have to be read in conjunction with the *a priori* values obtained in Table 37 for the ratio of net to gross capital appropriate to certain rates of growth.[2]

Consider the case of construction first. It appears that at the beginning of the whole period, in 1869, the ratio of net to gross capital was very low. We cannot place much reliance on this figure, partly because it is distorted on account of the non-depreciable assets, and partly because the estimates for the beginning of the period are necessarily the most precarious. There are, however, *prima facie* grounds for believing that in this year the age structure was not adjusted to the subsequent rate of growth. The decade preceding 1869 was deeply affected by the civil war, and accumulation should have been relatively slow then. In 1869–79 the growth of net capital amounted to 3.6 per cent per annum and it rose to 5.1 and 5.7 per cent in the two last decades of the century. It is very plausible that at the beginning of the period the age structure was not adjusted to such high rates of growth. As was to be expected on theoretical grounds, the growth of net capital per annum exceeds the growth of gross capital per annum in this period of accelerated accumulation (see Fig. 6). The discrepancy is quite formidable, amounting to about 1 per cent between 1879 and 1899. Correspondingly the capital stock in this period was getting 'younger', i.e. the ratio of net to gross capital increased (Table 38).

In the period of declining rate of growth during the present century the reverse phenomenon is observed. The rate of growth of gross capital exceeds that of net capital. In view of the continuous slowing down of accumulation, it is not surprising that the discrepancy persists over a considerable time. It is again sufficiently marked (from 0.6 to 0.8 per cent) to be of considerable practical consequence. Logically enough, the capital stock in this period is

[1] A fully satisfactory treatment would, of course, require the separation of non-depreciable construction from the rest on the basis of actual data. This is not possible at present. The total amount of non-depreciable assets up to 1919 allowed for in our calculation is somewhat greater than the value of roads.

[2] It should be noted that comparison between the *a priori* values and the empirical values is somewhat marred by the inclusion of non-depreciable assets in construction. This accounts for slight inconsistencies, as for example the fact that the ratio of net to gross capital is slightly rising from 1899 to 1909, although the rate of growth is declining.

TABLE 38

GROSS AND NET CAPITAL
(MILLIONS OF $ IN 1929 PRICES)

Year	Construction					
	New construction in preceding 50 years (1)	Depreciable (2)	Non-depreciable (3)	Total Gross Capital (4)	Net Capital (5)	Net capital as a percentage of Gross Capital (5 : 4) (6)
Jan. 1, 1869	34,846	31,117	3,729	34,846	18,006	51.7
1879	45,739	40,835	5,330	46,165	25,766	55.8
1889	67,138	59,954	8,197	68,151	42,470	62.3
1899	106,453	95,063	13,215	108,278	73,866	68.2
1909	154,322	137,810	19,472	157,282	109,052	69.4
1919	213,215	190,401	26,544	216,945	140,725	64.8
1929	281,353	251,248	35,436	286,684	175,164	61.1
1939	312,537	279,096	41,638	320,734	180,864	56.4
	Equipment			Equipment and Construction		
	Gross Value of Equipment (18 years' output) (7)	Net Equipment (corrected for the assumption of constant 18 years' life (8)	Net Capital as percentage of Gross Capital (9)	Gross Capital (10)	Net Capital (11)	Net Capital as a percentage of Gross Capital (12)
Jan. 1, 1869	3,619	2,122	58.5	38,465	20,128	52.2
1879	6,704	4,202	62.7	52,869	29,968	56.6
1889	14,362	8,882	62.0	82,513	51,352	62.3
1899	22,909	12,882	56.3	131,187	86,748	66.1
1909	37,263	22,872	61.4	194,545	131,924	67.8
1919	59,778	36,462	61.0	276,723	177,187	64.0
1929	86,917	51,692	59.5	373,601	226,856	60.7
1939	91,707	48,202	52.6	412,441	229,066	55.5

ageing, that is the ratio of net to gross capital declines from 69 per cent in 1909 to 56 per cent in 1939 (Table 38).

In the case of *equipment* the picture is not quite similar. We should expect that, because the life-time is much shorter, the development of the age structure would therefore be different on *a priori* grounds. The first thing which strikes the eye is that the ratio of net to gross capital is subject to much smaller changes than in the case of construction (Table 38). This agrees with the *a priori* figures of Table 37. The ratio, in fact, stays very much on the same level except in 1899 and 1939; in both these years it is rather low. It appears that the depression of the 1890's had a marked effect on the investment in equipment. [The level of 1869 is also low, but this cannot be considered very significant on account of the unreliability of the earliest figures.]

The discrepancies in the rates of growth should naturally also show a different picture as compared with construction. As the life-time is much shorter, the discrepancies should be adjusted much more quickly. In fact, we notice no discrepancy in the 1920's, although the rate of growth had by then fallen considerably as compared with the early part of the century. On the other hand the pattern of accumulation in the case of equipment is complicated by the existence of a temporary trough in the 1890's, which is followed by a partial recovery. Correspondingly the growth of gross capital in the 1890's exceeds that of net capital, while in 1899–1908 it falls short of it.

TABLE 39

RATE OF GROWTH OF NET AND GROSS CAPITAL
(IN PER CENT PER ANNUM)

	Real Estate Improvements		*Equipment*		*Total*	
	Net Capital	Gross Capital	Net Capital	Gross Capital	Net Capital	Gross Capital
Jan. 1 to Jan. 1	%	%	%	%	%	%
1869—1879	3.6	2.9	7.1	6.4	4.1	3.2
1879—1889	5.1	4.0	7.8	7.9	5.5	4.6
1889—1899	5.7	4.7	3.8	4.8	5.4	4.7
1899—1909	4.0	3.8	5.9	5.0	4.3	4.0
1909—1919	2.6	3.3	4.8	4.8	3.0	3.6
1919—1929	2.2	2.8	3.6	3.8	2.5	3.0
1929—1939	0.3	1.1	—0.7	0.5	0.1	0.9

The figures for the *total fixed capital* are naturally based on the sum of construction capital and equipment. As construction accounts for by far the major part of the total, we find that the pattern of construction is, by and large, repeated in this series without major modification (tables 38 and 39).

It is not difficult to discern the upshot of all this. The long-run changes in the rate of growth of capital involve discrepancies between the rates of growth of net and gross capital, and these discrepancies are large enough and persist over a sufficiently long time to be of practical significance.

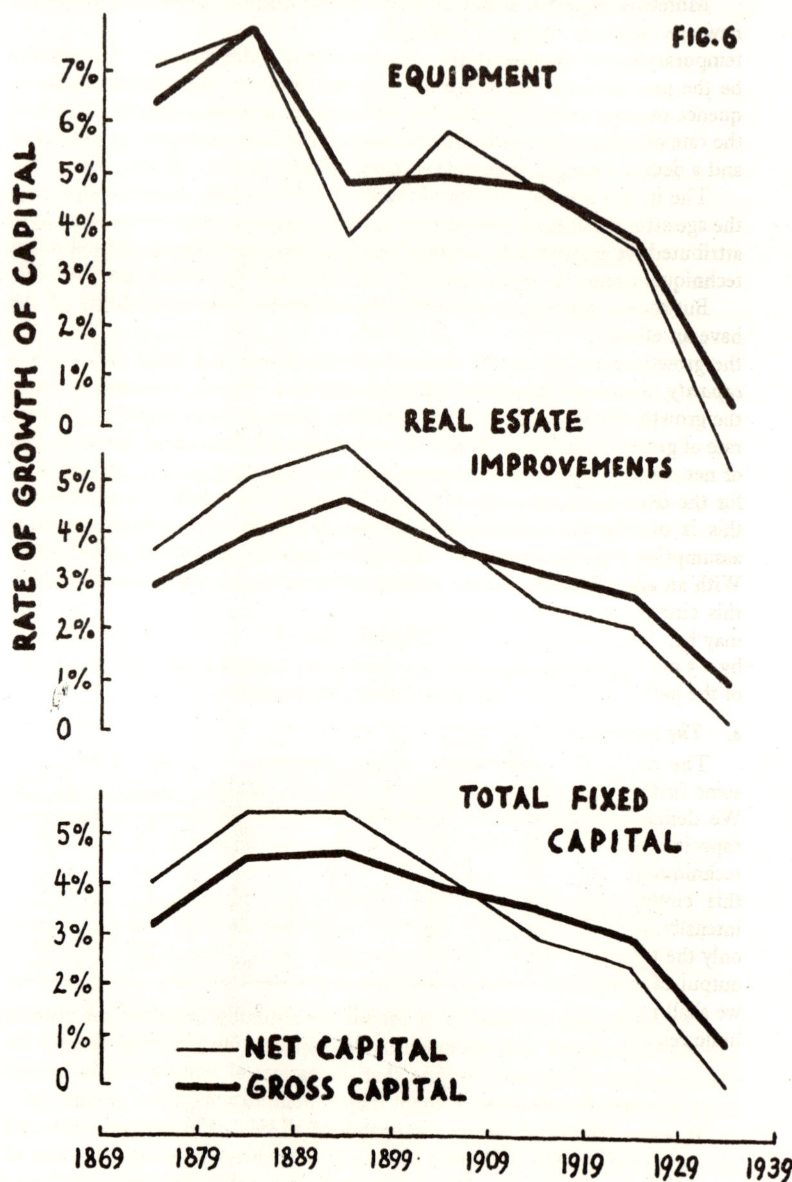

FIG. 6. *The rate of growth of net and gross capital.* Data from Table 39.

Moreover, these discrepancies give way gradually only by establishing a new age structure, that is, a new ratio of net to gross capital. Following the temporary effect of a discrepancy between the rates of growth, there will thus be the permanent effect of a changed ratio of net to gross capital, in consequence of any change in the rate of growth. That means that an increase in the rate of growth will have a *tendency* to raise the apparent capital intensity, and a decrease in the rate of growth will have a tendency to lower it.

The importance of this last mentioned effect is obvious. The change in the age structure has in principle the same consequences which are ordinarily attributed to a change in capital intensity arising from modifications of technique. They may, therefore, be ' stimulating ' or ' depressing '.

But the temporary discrepancy between the two rates of growth may also have an effect of its own. If the growth of gross capital is closely related to the growth of capacity, and if entrepreneurs intend to *control the growth of capacity*, then any change in the latter will be reflected in a *greater* change in the growth of net capital. The stimulating effect of a certain increase in the rate of growth of capacity will be increased by the fact that the rate of growth of net capital must rise even more, and the same is true, *mutatis mutandis*, for the depressing effect of a decrease in the growth of capacity. Whether this is of practical importance depends on the validity of the particular assumption that entrepreneurs aim at controlling the growth of capacity. With an age structure not in equilibrium with the particular rate of growth, this circumstance will exert a stimulating or depressing effect, as the case may be. The entrepreneurs may find, for example, that to increase capacity by 0.5 per cent per annum they need no net investment at all, just on account of the particular age structure established in the past.

4. *The ratio of capital to output*

The results of the preceding paragraph make it necessary to introduce some further complication in the definitions and the algebra of Chapter IX. We defined, there, capital intensity as the ratio of net capital to output capacity. But we have just seen that this ratio is not only determined by the technique of production, but in addition also by age structure. Ordinarily this circumstance receives scant attention in discussions about capital intensity. We clearly need a definition of capital intensity which embodies only the technical factors. This we get if we take the ratio of gross capital to output capacity; we shall call this ratio *true capital intensity* κ. In contrast we shall refer to the other concept as *apparent capital intensity* k. The algebraic relation of apparent and true capital intensity is easily obtained:

$$k = \frac{Z}{H}$$

$$\kappa = \frac{J}{H}$$

$$k = \kappa \frac{Z}{J}. \qquad (30)$$

The rate of growth of apparent capital intensity, as it appears in equation (20), p. 111, can now be split up as follows:

$$\frac{dk}{dt}\Big/k=\frac{d\kappa}{dt}\Big/\kappa+\frac{dZ}{dt}\Big/Z-\frac{dJ}{dt}\Big/J \qquad (31)$$

$$=\frac{d\kappa}{dt}\Big/\kappa+\eta.$$

The rate of growth of apparent capital intensity is thus the sum of the rate of growth of true capital intensity and of the discrepancy η between the rates of growth of net and gross capital. This discrepancy η, as we have seen in the last paragraph, arises through changes in the rate of growth.

The distinction of true and apparent capital intensity adds another complication to the analysis of the ratio of capital to output. Theoretically we are now clear that this ratio is composed of very different economic factors: change in true capital intensity, in age structure, in planned utilisation, and in undesired utilisation. Any empirical data of the capital-output ratio, and its historical development, can be satisfactorily explained only if we can trace its changes back to the various factors which are responsible for it. Unfortunately this is at present hardly possible, and what will be said in the following on this point is little more than vague guessing. Nevertheless, the theoretical analysis of the concept may at least prevent rather obvious misinterpretations of the data.

The first difficulty is, of course, that the estimates of capital are rather inadequate for the purpose in hand. In particular, to get an idea of the changes in true capital intensity, we want *gross capital.* Now we have obtained already in the last paragraph estimates of gross capital from the data given by Kuznets. But while these estimates are of interest in illustrating the changes in age structure, where we can compare them with certain *a priori* deductions based on plausible ideas, they are of little use in the present problem where no plausible *a priori* reasoning can guide us. We have hardly any general idea of what the development of true capital intensity has been, and the figures themselves are a little weak for the heavy task of deciding this question. We have nevertheless reproduced the figures for the ratio of gross capital to national product in Table 40. The reader is asked to bear in mind the rather speculative character of these estimates. Gross capital, as estimated, is based on the assumption of a certain life-time, and the capital equipment is supposed to have been replaced after the lapse of this given life-time, and not sooner nor later. This cuts out the whole question of variations in actual lifetime as a consequence of technical progress and competitive elimination of equipment. In addition there is a special element of arbitrariness in the estimates of gross capital: as mentioned in the last paragraph, a part of it is regarded as non-depreciable (permanent), and the rest is assumed to wear out after a given life-time. In the accounting practice of corporations and public authorities this distinction is also followed, but it seems that in their practice the proportion of capital that is non-depreciable is greater than we have assumed in the calculation of gross capital based on Kuznets' data.[1] On a different practice with regard to the classification of capital into depreciable and non-depreciable, such as is followed by corporations, the gross capital might show a greater increase than in our data, and the capital-output ratio would also rise more.

This arbitrariness in the definition of gross capital probably explains some of the fluctuations in the capital-output ratio in the first three decades covered (Table 40).[2] We can leave these early figures out of account. From the 1890's onwards the ratio of gross capital to gross national product shows at first little change, rises strongly in the 1920's and even more in the 'thirties. A part of this increase in the last two decades is due to the relative increase in government capital (especially roads). The increase in the 'thirties, moreover, is probably to a large part due to the reduction in utilisation which, on the average of the decade, was certainly considerably below the previous levels. As the construction capital is strongly influenced by the presence of public capital and, moreover, by the arbitrariness in the treatment of non-depreciable capital, it is of interest to consider separately the ratio of *gross equipment* to gross national product (Table 40, line 11). This, it may be seen, shows a fairly continuous increase. This would seem to lend support to the idea that a certain measure of capital intensification has taken place in the period considered. A certain part—certainly not all—of the increase in the capital output ratio should be due to the considerable reduction in the length of the normal working week which has taken place since the beginning of the century. The sharp increase in the ratio after 1929 is probably very largely due to a reduction in utilisation (not only because of the shorter normal working time, but also due to great 'undesired' excess capacity in the 1930's).

On the whole, the figures can be reconciled with the idea that true capital intensity has increased in the period of capitalist development under consideration, although this is by no means certain. It would seem, however—and this is a conclusion which can be fairly drawn in spite of all the limitations of the data—that true capital intensity has not experienced very spectacular changes (it is hardly likely that it has doubled in the whole period under consideration).

As the data of net capital are somewhat less ambiguous than the estimate of gross capital, the ratio of *net capital* to net national product (Table 34) constitutes, in itself, a better series of data. This ratio, it is true, is not related to true capital intensity but to apparent capital intensity : it must show the combined effects of technical changes in capital and changes in age structure (and, of course, the influence of utilisation). For many purposes, however, this series will be more directly relevant. It has also the advantage that it relates

[1] Gross capital as given in the balance sheets of corporations (*Statistics of Income, Part II*) bears a much greater proportion to net capital than in our estimates.

[2] It is not unplausible, however, that some of the fall of the capital-output ratio in the '80s, and the subsequent rise in the '90s was due to a high degree of utilisation in the '80s which subsequently declined.

TABLE 40

RATIO OF GROSS CAPITAL TO OUTPUT

	1869–78	*1879–88*	*1889–98*	*1899–08*	*1909–18*	*1919–28*	*1929–38*
1. Gross Construction Capital, 1929 prices	40,506	57,158	88,215	132,780	187,114	251,815	303,709
2. Gross Equipment, 1929 prices	4,875	10,062	18,402	28,463	45,401	71,266	92,218
3. Gross Construction Capital, current prices	19,000	24,800	35,020	61,480	107,200	258,360	276,380
4. Gross Equipment, current prices	3,680	5,390	7,990	14,170	32,370	73,480	84,100
5. Total gross fixed Capital, current prices	22,680	30,190	43,010	75,650	139,570	331,840	360,480
6. Gross national product, current prices	7,033	10,688	12,730	21,584	40,122	81,199	69,952
7. Net national product, current prices	6,489	9,941	11,671	19,740	36,341	72,160	61,274
8. Ratio of total gross fixed capital to gross national product, 5 ÷ 6	3.23	2.82	3.38	3.51	3.48	4.08	5.16
9. Ratio of total gross fixed capital to net national product, 5 ÷ 7	3.50	3.03	3.69	3.84	3.84	4.59	5.89
10. Ratio of gross construction capital to gross national product, 3 ÷ 6	2.70	2.32	2.75	2.85	2.68	3.18	3.96
11. Ratio of gross Equipment to gross national product, 4 ÷ 6	0.52	0.50	0.63	0.66	0.80	0.90	1.20

to business capital only, excluding government capital which is included in the gross capital figures. This ratio of net capital to net product shows surprisingly little tendency to change over the whole of the period covered. This should be directly relevant to the theory of the declining rate of profit of Marx, which for the modern period at least is not supported by these figures.[1]

5. *The turning point of capital accumulation*

Near the beginning of this chapter we formulated a series of questions which are suggested by the empirical data on capital accumulation. Something, however tentative, has been said in answer to these questions, with the exception of the first and most difficult one : what was the cause of the *primary* fall in capital accumulation which took place somewhere near the turn of the century ?

We can imagine two types of answer to this question. One would rely on historical accident, and indicate certain specific causes which just happened to occur. The other would try to explain the change as a ' natural ' and necessary outcome of the development of capitalism. This type of ' natural ' explanation is certainly suggested by the term *maturity*, although the authors who use this term in practice rather tend to apply the first type of explanation. In other words their theory is ' exogenous ', carrying the explanation—by and large—back to certain events like technological change which remain unexplained. This leaves us in doubt whether ' maturity ' is anything more than temporary and accidental, although these authors —like Professor Hansen—do give at the same time the impression that it is something more. We choose to take a clearly defined stand on this issue and to regard the decline in capital accumulation as a necessary consequence of the development of certain essential features of capitalism. The tentative explanation which will be suggested for it is admittedly of a very speculative character. It is clear that such an explanation requires an *endogenous* theory of long-run economic development, and very little has been done in this field on the purely theoretical level, not to speak of the difficulties of empirical testing. The attempt at such an endogenous theory will be elaborated in the next chapter. We shall here briefly anticipate this explanation of the decline in capital accumulation.

The theory is that already towards the end of the last century—in the 1890's—the American economy had undergone a transition which gave considerable weight to the oligopolistic pattern in the total economy. This transition had raised profit margins at that time (the statistics of profit margins given in Chapter VIII start only after this time—in 1899—and can therefore not confirm the hypothesis). As a consequence there should have been a fall in utilisation below the previous level. We might regard the big depression in the middle of the 'nineties as the signal of these difficulties arising from an increase in profit margins, and consequent fall in effective

[1] For the first two decades (Table 34) we may hesitate to attribute any significance to the figures, because the earliest estimates of capital are more unreliable than the later ones.

demand in relation to capacity. The decline in the average long-run level of utilisation would then be the explanation for the falling off in the rate of growth of capital.

One might prefer slightly more complicated explanations starting from the same point. The growth of oligopoly should have resulted in a redistribution of profits as between competitive and oligopolistic industries. This in itself should have tended to weaken the incentive to invest on the average, if we assume that a certain marginal volume of profits calls forth less addition to investment in an oligopolistic than it does in a competitive industry. This hypothesis is justified by the consideration that oligopolistic industries have to be much more afraid of excess capacity than others, as they cannot as easily hope to make room for themselves at the expense of competitors. The shift in profits to oligopolistic industries may thus equally well explain the primary decline in the growth of capital.

While the speculative character of this theory has been stressed, there is no reason to hide what it can claim as advantage. It does not, on the face of it, contradict any well-established facts. At the same time, the explanation does not lead back to causes which are in themselves puzzling and mysterious problems, like the development of technology and the trend of population, but it leads back to a very plain and well-known fact, the explanation of which is not too difficult: the growth of oligopoly at a certain stage of capitalist development.

XIII. The Long-run Theory of Investment

1. *The Trend and the Cycle*

All along this book has dealt only with the explanation of the trend. The problem of the trade cycle has been left aside, with the implication that it could be dealt with separately. This is admittedly a great weakness. A proper and fully adequate treatment should deal with trend and trade cycle at the same time, and should show how both are generated on the basis of certain assumptions embodied in a dynamic model. In principle this does not seem at all difficult. Difference equations, or differential equations can easily be constructed whose solutions will contain both trend and oscillatory components. In the concrete, however, the task is rather hard, not least because one is faced with a choice between various formulations, without having sufficient empirical knowledge for selecting the best approach. A fully satisfactory treatment of the problem is not attempted here. The following remarks about the relation of trend and cycle can do little else but to make clear just what the trend theory of this book means.

The most important feature of this explanation of the trend is that it is an *endogenous* theory. It starts from the conviction that in order to explain the historical phenomenon of growth of capital it is not necessary to have recourse to external influences, such as innovations, population growth, wars, etc. The growth of capital is, on the contrary, viewed as something inherent in the nature of capitalism, and to be explained by much simpler assumptions. The concrete hypothesis which explains growth is this : the mere fact that business concerns accumulate savings is sufficient to induce them (after a certain time) to invest. The internal accumulation, by itself, generates investment, and if there has been growth in the past sufficient to enable entrepreneurs to accumulate funds internally, then this will in itself produce a further growth. The growth of capital is in this sense self-perpetuating.

In the perfectly simple (but unrealistic) case where we do not take account at all of the existence of outside savings, the internal accumulation is equal to investment; this internal accumulation, after a time, generates again investment. Taking the total time lag as a unit of time we could determine investment I_t from the equation :

$$I_{t+1} = \gamma I_t.$$

The solution implies that there will be an exponential growth of investment : $I_t = I_0 e^{t \log \gamma}$. The structural constant which determines the rate of growth, γ, is the ratio of investment to recent internal accumulation.

This equation serves as an illustration of how an endogenous theory of growth can be based on our hypothesis. It has a straightforward and simple application, however, only in a model in which cycles as well as exogenous disturbances are absent. In a dynamic model which embodies these realistic features, the trend will presumably be determined in a more complicated fashion. Will our hypothesis then still retain its role as a predominant factor in the explanation of the trend, or might it perhaps be incapable altogether of explaining a trend under these circumstances ?

The question is pertinent in the light of economic literature. First of all, a great number of economists seem to favour, more or less clearly, an exogenous theory of the trend; they regard the stationary state as the norm, and one gets the impression that they cannot imagine how the phenomenon of long-run growth could be explained by simple endogenous factors, like investment and saving propensities of entrepreneurs. How could a straightforward explanation like the above one escape their notice ? More important still, the hypothesis of internal accumulation generating investment is not new; it has been fully used by Mr. Kalecki in his theory of the trade cycle.[1] He has assumed, it is true, that γ—in his notation : $(1-c)$—is necessarily smaller than unity, and this assumption is not made here, but that does not affect the main question. The hypothesis which we have made the cornerstone of the explanation of the trend is included in Mr. Kalecki's model of the trade cycle, and yet this model does not yield any trend : it is, according to the intention of the author, a theory of the 'pure business cycle' in which investment fluctuates round the zero level. Are we to conclude that the hypothesis mentioned is incapable of explaining the trend ?

We shall have to discuss the theory in broad outline. Mr. Kalecki's equation is as follows[2] (I am rendering it not in its final form, but before

[1] *Studies in Economic Dynamics*, p. 61. [2] *Op. cit.*, p. 66, *seq.*

certain adjustments, so as to bring out more clearly the hypothesis involved):

$$I_{t+2\epsilon} = (1-c)I_t + a\frac{d}{dt}P_t - bI_t, \tag{32}$$

where P is the volume of profits. On the assumption that only entrepreneurs save, the change in the volume of profit becomes a simple function of the change in the rate of investment, so that the equation is:

$$I_{t+2\epsilon} = (1-c)I_t + \frac{a}{1-\lambda}\ \frac{d}{dt}I_{t-\kappa} - bI_t. \tag{32a}$$

There are two principal hypotheses involved in this equation: the first is the one already mentioned, that investment, via internal accumulation, generates again investment. This is expressed in the first member on the right hand side. The second hypothesis is that a change in the *rate* of profit increases or decreases investment, according to whether it is positive or negative. The rate of profit is regarded as dependent on two things: the *volume* of profit, and the amount of capital over which this profit has to be spread. Correspondingly, an increase in the *volume* of profit will exert a positive influence on investment (this is embodied in the second member on the right side) and an increase in the amount of capital, which is identical with the rate of investment, will exert a negative influence on investment (this is embodied in the third member on the right hand side).

What are the solutions of the above difference-differential equation? For a simpler equation which embodied an earlier form of Mr. Kalecki's business cycle theory, the solutions have been investigated in great detail.[1] It has been shown that this earlier equation (with a practically unimportant qualification) can only yield, alternatively, *either* a trend solution or an oscillation (a ' pure cycle '). In the case of the present equation, which is much more complicated, it is by no means sure that the result will be the same. (We are leaving out of account that Mr. Kalecki makes the parameters in the equation vary in certain ways; for simplicity's sake we assume them to be constant).

We can imagine that the equation is approximated by a pure difference equation, replacing the differential by a difference. This can of course be done in more than one way and we cannot be sure how we find the best approximation. It is clear, however, that it will also depend on the relative magnitude of the lags κ and ϵ, what the order of the difference equation will be. If $\epsilon = \kappa$ the difference equation will at least be of the order three; it is thus, on the face of it, by no means impossible that the equation should yield a trend and an oscillation at the same time.

But this point is perhaps rather formal. It could be argued that whatever the possible richness of solutions, the parameters in practice are restricted to such a range of magnitudes that the solutions will give only a cycle (or perhaps several superimposed cycles). There is, however, another more

[1] See M. Kalecki, A macrodynamic theory of the trade cycle. Frisch and Holme, The solutions of a mixed difference-differential equation. *Econometrica*, 1935.

concrete point. It is curious to observe that in the above equation the re-investment hypothesis does not really play any *essential* role. (The two members with the coefficient $(1-c)$ and b combine, of course, into a single one.) That is to say, if we leave the re-investment hypothesis out altogether $(1-c=0)$, the general character of the equation would not be changed. It would merely affect the magnitude of a parameter. It is this which appears puzzling and which may mislead the observer to believe that the reinvestment hypothesis cannot play an important role in the trend theory.

However, it can be shown that this is only due to the peculiar mathematical formulation of Mr. Kalecki's underlying economic hypotheses. In fact, if these hypotheses are strictly formulated, the reinvestment hypothesis becomes clearly separated from the other main idea, the influence of changes in the profit rate on investment.

As we have seen, changes in the *rate of profit* are represented in the equation as depending, in a simple linear fashion, on (i) changes in the volume of profit, and (ii) changes in the capital stock over which these profits have to be spread. But the rate of profit, if we denote the capital stock by Z, is given as

$$p_t = \frac{P_t}{Z_t}.$$

If we differentiate this with respect to time we get for the change in the rate of profit

$$\dot{p}_t = \frac{\dot{P}_t Z_t - P_t I_t}{Z_t^2}.$$

It is this expression for the change in the rate of profit which we should insert, with an appropriate coefficient, into the equation in place of the second and third member. It is easily seen that the equation would then become non-linear.

One result, and a very unpleasant one, would be to make the mathematical solution a formidable problem. (At the same time, it may be mentioned that the problem of obtaining an undamped cycle would be solved in this way.) Now for the purpose of obtaining a model of the cycle it may be legitimate to cut out these mathematical difficulties and use a linear approximation, as Mr. Kalecki has done. But as soon as the long-run development is to be dealt with as well, the formulation cannot be adequate any more. An equation more generally valid as an expression of the underlying economic hypothesis would have to be formulated differently.

It is easy to criticize, but harder to mend. The critical points indicated will not be pursued further here, simply because the mathematical difficulties are great. But the purpose of this discussion was simply this : the Kaleckian business cycle equation gives the impression that the influence of internal accumulation on investment cannot in itself generate a trend. This impression may be misleading, because the equation is based on simplifications which make it applicable only in the short run.

There is still another point to consider. It seems to me that the inclusion of the *change* in the rate of profit among the determinants of investment, which brings with it such great difficulties, might well be reconsidered. There are no strong *a priori* or empirical reasons which force us to make this assumption. At least one can think of alternative assumptions which would be easier to handle mathematically. We might assume that the *deviation* of the rate of profit from a certain 'neutral' level in the one or the other direction exerts an influence on investment, which may be positive or negative. On the other hand it is a shortcoming of Kalecki's model that it does not take into account savings outside enterprises. These outside savings probably do play an important part in the trade cycle.

2. *A model of long-run growth*

To develop a theory of the trend it would seem the obvious thing to improve the model of the trade cycle by the various modifications outlined at the end of the last paragraph, and to obtain from it a trend as well as oscillations.[1] Here one comes up against a very fundamental difficulty, which concerns the determination of outside savings.

The long and short of the story is that we do not know very well how outside savings are determined. In the traditional short run theory, outside savings are a linear function of national income (or rather of personal incomes), and the ratio of savings to income increases as income increases. This traditional *savings function* is applicable only in the short run, and then only approximately, because we know for certain that this function shifts in the course of time. A crude way of accounting for this shift is to make one of the parameters into a function of time, thus postulating a certain shift of the savings function per year. This procedure has been rightly criticised, and it is indeed unsatisfactory.[2] The 'shifting of the savings function', if we put it that way, should be itself related to certain variables in an economic model, i.e. it should be 'explained'.

There are certain empirical indications which seem to warrant an explanation. It seems, by and large, that *in the long run* the savings ratio is constant. That is to say, if we take moving averages of outside savings and of income over a number of years, their ratio will be *approximately* constant. The long-run flow of savings thus behaves differently from the short-term flow. The statistical material on savings may not be very adequate, but by and large the above seems to be a reasonable approximation. Several modern economists have regarded it as such (for example, Modigliani, Duesenberry, etc.), and I agree with them. Assuming that the savings ratio is approximately constant in the long run, how can this be explained in terms of the behaviour, of the reactions of the individual savers ? We would like to have a generally valid savings function, which shows how annual savings are determined, and which

[1] The problem of damping may well be taken care of by a stochastic model where erratic shocks are operating.

[2] Franco Modigliani, *Fluctuations in the Savings-Income Ratio*. (Conference on Research in Income and Wealth : Studies in Income and Wealth, Vol. 11).

explains at the same time the short-run 'elasticity' of savings, and the long-run constancy of the savings ratio.

This problem has been neatly put by F. Modigliani, and he has suggested a solution for it.[1] He regards consumption as a function (1) of current income and (2) of the highest income reached in any previous year. The movements of the latter magnitude, the 'highest income reached in any previous year', will be an indicator of the secular growth of income. By means of empirical data he establishes the following relation (writing Y_t for current income per head, Y_t^0 for the highest income per head reached in any year preceding the given year, and C_t for consumption per head):

$$C_t = 2(\pm 32) + 0.773\, Y_t + 0.125\, Y_t^0$$

(± 32 being the standard error).

By means of the identity $S_t = Y_t - C_t$ (where S_t is savings) he renders the above equation in the following form:

$$S_t = -2 + 0.102\, Y_t + 0.125\, (Y_t - Y_t^0)$$

To use Modigliani's own words in the interpretation of this equation: 'Since the constant term is entirely negligible in comparison with the relevant values of Y, saving tends to represent approximately 10 per cent of income plus some 12 per cent of the increment of income. Because of the last term, the proportion of income saved will tend to vary somewhat in years of secular expansion, increasing as the rate of change in income accelerates. But since the normal secular growth is in the order of 2 to 3 per cent we may conclude that the savings-income ratio will tend to fluctuate around a level of about 10½ per cent'.[2]

We can see from this brief account that Modigliani has achieved his object: he gives an equation which determines the annual amount of savings and which explains at the same time two things: that the average savings ratio, taking the trend value of the variables, is approximately constant, and that the annual savings ratio fluctuates greatly (if current income falls greatly below Y_0, then the last term of the equation will have a relatively large influence). Thus we have here a theory of savings which explains what seem to be the essential empirical facts, but we cannot yet be entirely happy about it. For one thing it would be a trifle difficult to express this theory in the form of a difference equation.

Leontieff, in a critical note on Modigliani's paper, has put forward certain objections, and in his turn has proposed that consumption should be made a function not only of current income but also of a moving average of income over something like five years in the past.

The upshot of the discussion seems to be that a really satisfactory general-

[1] Ibid.

[2] *Ibid.*, p. 383. It should be noted that Modigliani's data are the *old* Department of Commerce estimates of saving, and that no importance should therefore be attached to the particular figure for the average saving ratio of 10½ per cent which is probably too high.

isation of the savings function is not yet available. One thing, however, seems to be almost sure: such a generalised theory of outside savings must be fairly complicated, in the sense that, if we put it into a difference equation, it will probably involve a good number of lags (see the above suggestion of Leontieff). If we should use such an equation to include it into a system of difference equations determining the course of investment, we should indeed get the only fully satisfactory model, which would include both trend and cyclical movements. But the system of equations would be fairly cumbrous.

I propose to by-pass these difficulties in a way which will immediately become obvious. Let us accept the hypothesis that outside saving is a constant proportion of income in the long run. That is only an approximation, of course, but it is, after all, the best we know about it. We accept this constancy, then, as a hypothesis with reasonable empirical basis, and do not worry how it comes about. Let us take then a number of n years, where n corresponds approximately to the length of a trade cycle, say perhaps 8 or 10 years. We assume that for moving averages over n years the savings ratio is constant.

Now we return to the determination of investment. Investment in every single year is determined by the preceding year's internal accumulation. We have therefore valid for every year the equation

$$I_{t+1} = \gamma \acute{C}$$

therefore also

$$I_{t+2} = \gamma \acute{C}_{t+1}$$

$$\cdots\cdots\cdots\cdots$$

$$I_{t+n} = \gamma \acute{C}_{t+n-1}.$$

If we add up the equations for n successive years we find that the moving averages are related in the same way as the annual values:

$$\sum_{t=1}^{t=n} I_t = \gamma \sum_{t=0}^{t=n-1} \acute{C}_t.$$

I want to indicate at this point that it might be possible to improve the theory embodied in the above equations by making investment, in addition, subject to an erratic influence ξ_t, so that $I_{t+1} = \gamma \acute{C}_t + \xi_t$. We could in this way obtain a more realistic picture of the determination of investment, which would take account, *inter alia*, of the 'lumpiness' of investment due to technological reasons. If we assume that this erratic component cancels out over a number of n successive years, the simple equation $I_{t+1} = \gamma \acute{C}_t$ would still hold good for the moving averages. The further consequences of the introduction of such an erratic component are, however, not so easy to judge, and I want to avoid the complications of a stochastic model. I shall therefore in the following assume that the above equations hold strictly, in other words I shall limit myself to a 'deterministic' model without erratic influences.

In the same way as for the above investment function we can derive from any relation between annual values the corresponding relation between the moving averages over n years. In one case, however, this will not be necessary. The (outside) savings function we assume to be given directly for the moving average, instead of deriving it from a relation determining annual values. Outside saving, if we have judged the problem rightly, has the peculiarity that the determination of its annual value is more complicated than that of its long-term flow. We thus achieve a decisive simplification if we use the simple relation determining the long-run flow of outside savings.

The purpose of our procedure has now become clear. Instead of dealing with annual flows, we are taking as variables for our system moving averages. One of our relations, the determination of outside savings, will be decisively simplified in this way. The other relations between moving averages will simply reflect the corresponding relations between annual values, from which we derive them. We shall obtain, then, a system of equations in which the variables are moving averages. The solution of these equations will tell us how these moving averages (of investment, income, etc.) develop in time; it will not tell us anything about the movement of the annual values from year to year.

The resulting model will exhibit any movements which are not eliminated by taking a moving average over n years. Thus it will certainly exhibit the trend, but also cyclical movements with a period of a greater order of magnitude than n years. It can therefore properly be regarded as a model of long-run economic development.

On the other hand our model will not exhibit the ordinary trade cycle, as n, the number of years over which the moving average is taken, is assumed to be about 8 or 10 years. The trade cycle could of course be explained only in a more general dynamic model which would apply to the development from year to year. To obtain such a general model we would have to replace the rough and ready assumption of a constant saving ratio by a savings function which explains the variability of savings in the short run. It is an open question whether other modifications and the inclusion of additional factors would not be necessary, as well, to account for the existence of a trade cycle with a fairly well defined period. This means, of course, that the model of long-run development which we are going to construct, is of a very tentative and preliminary character. But we could in any case not aim at anything much better, because of the absence of information about the numerical values of structural coefficients, and about the relative importance of various factors.

We shall, therefore, in the following leave aside the problem of the trade cycle, and concentrate entirely on the building of a model of long-run growth in which all the variables will be moving averages. We shall in the first instance construct a model of long-run growth in its simplest form. The mathematical treatment of this problem will detain us for a while.

Let us denote all the moving averages by a dash, writing I'_t for the moving average of investment over an n-year period terminating at time t. Similarly $\dot{C}'_t$ stands for the moving average of internal accumulation. We have then, assuming the lag between internal accumulation and investment to be one year :

$$I'_{t+1} = \gamma \dot{C}'_t. \tag{33}$$

The internal accumulation is the difference between investment and outside saving S'_t :

$$\dot{C}'_t = I'_t - S'_t.$$

The outside saving is a constant proportion of income. Strictly speaking, we should have to take personal income, but we shall simplify the problem by regarding outside saving as a certain constant proportion of national income. National income will be regarded in the present model as a constant proportion of the capital stock. This is a crude assumption which will be dropped when we construct a more complicated model. It implies constant capital intensity—which may well pass as a simplifying hypothesis. More seriously, it implies a constant utilisation of capital, a very special assumption indeed. On the basis of these rigid hypotheses the outside saving will be a constant proportion of national income Y'_t and of the capital stock Z'_t.

$$S'_t = \mu Y'_t = \nu Z'_t.$$

The equation determining investment then becomes

$$I'_{t+1} = \gamma I'_t - \gamma\nu Z'_t$$

or, seeing that the rate of investment is the derivative according to time of the capital stock,

$$\dot{Z}'_{t+1} = \gamma \dot{Z}'_t - \gamma\nu Z'_t. \tag{34}$$

We have thus a mixed difference-differential equation with the capital stock as the variable.

Putting $Z'_t = ce^{\rho t}$ we find the characteristic equation :

$$\rho e^{\rho} - \gamma\rho + \gamma\nu = 0. \tag{34 (i)}$$

We are interested in the real roots of this equation. We can get an idea of the conditions under which we shall obtain them by drawing the graph of the function $\rho(e^{\rho} - \gamma)$. [Fig. 7]. The curve will pass through the origin and cut the abscissa in its positive or its negative part according to whether $\gamma > 1$ or $\gamma < 1$. If we now imagine the abscissa to be lowered by $\gamma\nu$, then we shall obtain at the points of intersection of this lowered abscissa and the curve the roots ρ of the equation. It is easy to see that, *with* a *given* γ, it will depend on the magnitude of ν whether any real roots (which may be one or two) are obtained; ν must not surpass a certain value, if there is to be a real root. For this particular value of ν there will be a ' double ' real root, for any smaller value there will be two roots. Conversely, if we take ν as *given*, we can only get real roots, if γ takes certain values. In fact, with a given ν we can get real roots by making γ either sufficiently big or sufficiently small (which will give positive and negative roots respectively). Thus there is a certain minimum value of γ in excess of 1, and a certain maximum value of γ below 1, which will each give a double root (make the curve touch the abscissa). If γ is in the

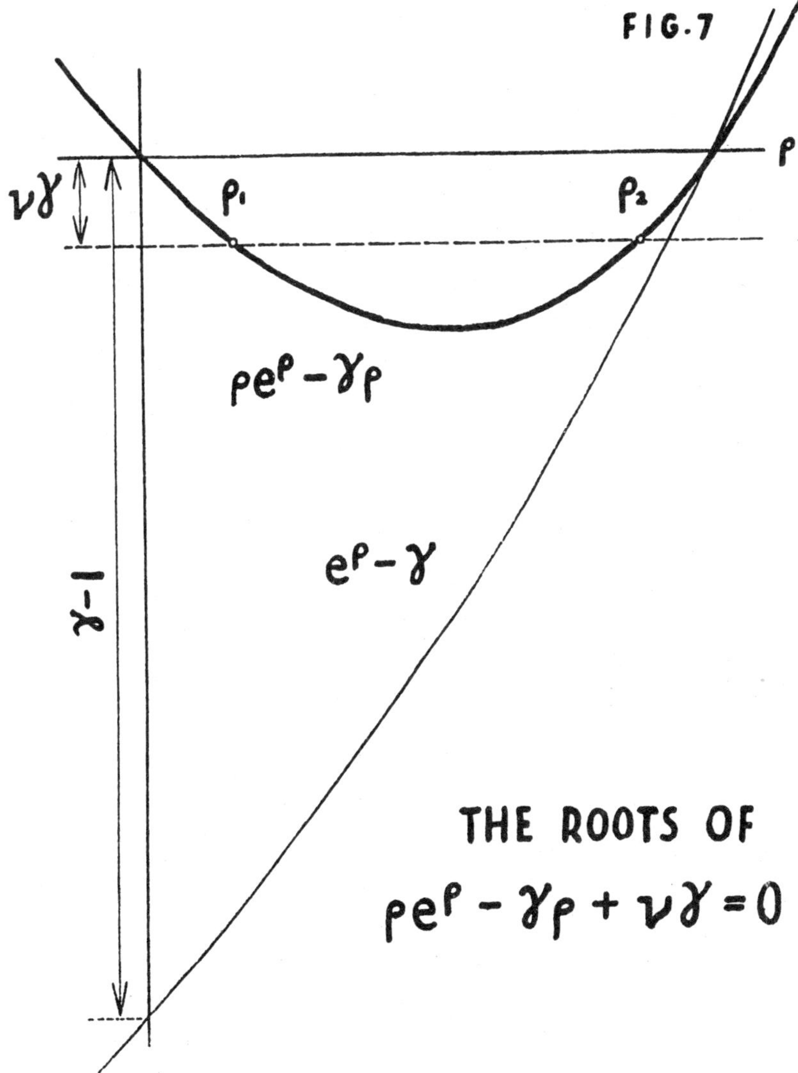

FIG. 7. *The real roots of the characteristic equation* $\rho e^{\rho} - \gamma\rho + \nu\gamma = 0$.

open interval between these values, there will be no real root, if it is outside the closed interval there will be two real roots.

The proof of these statements can be obtained as follows. If we take the derivative of the characteristic function with respect to ρ and put it equal to nought, then this equation together with the characteristic equation 34(i) will determine the relations which must hold between ρ, γ and ν if there is to be a double root. Thus

$$e^{\rho}+\rho e^{\rho}-\gamma = 0,$$

$$\rho e^{\rho}-\gamma\rho+\gamma\nu = 0,$$

from which follows that

$$\gamma = e^{\rho}(1+\rho),$$

$$\rho = \frac{\nu}{2} \pm \frac{1}{2}\sqrt{\nu^2+4\nu}.$$

The last two equations show that for any given value of ν we can always obtain a positive or a negative root ρ, which will be a double root, provided that γ is at a certain level above or below unity and this critical level of $|\gamma-1|$ is clearly the greater the greater is ν.

Each of the real roots obtained gives a possible rate of growth of capital. In addition to the real roots there will be an unlimited number of conjugate complex roots, giving oscillations with different periods. Under what conditions will there be a cyclical solution with a period greater than unity ?

Writing the characteristic equation in its complex form, where $\rho = \beta+i\alpha$, and separating real and imaginary parts, we obtain

$$\left.\begin{aligned} \beta e^{\beta}\cos\alpha-\alpha e^{\beta}\sin\alpha-\gamma\beta+\nu\gamma &= 0, \\ \alpha e^{\beta}\cos\alpha+\beta e^{\beta}\sin\alpha-\gamma\alpha &= 0. \end{aligned}\right\} \quad 34\text{ (ii)}$$

By simple means we can express from these equations β in terms of α. We find

$$\beta_{1,2} = \frac{\nu}{2} \pm \frac{1}{2}\sqrt{\nu^2+4\nu\frac{\alpha}{\tan\alpha}-4\alpha^2}. \qquad 34\text{ (iii)}$$

Now as the solution of β and α must be real, it is clear that the expression under the root sign must be positive or zero. If $|\alpha|$ is to be smaller than 2π (that is, if the period of the oscillation is to be bigger than unity), than we can at once see that $|\alpha|$ must be below a certain value in order to give a real solution. This can be found approximately, as we can assume that ν in practice is fairly small. We might, for example, take $\nu = 0.015$. ν^2 is then rather small and can be neglected for the purpose of an approximation. We must then have

$$4\nu\frac{\alpha}{\tan\alpha} > 4\alpha^2$$

or

$$\nu > \alpha\tan\alpha,$$

For $\nu = 0.015$, $|\alpha|$ will have to be approximately 0.12 or less. We can see then that $|\alpha|$ will have to be somewhere between zero and the limit indicated. If $|\alpha|$ reaches the permitted upper limit (the root expression becoming zero), then β according to (iii) will be $\frac{\nu}{2}$. Now if $|\alpha|$ decreases from this upper limit towards zero, then there will be two values of β, an upper and a lower one, and the discrepancy between the two will steadily increase until $|\alpha|$ reaches zero. We can therefore find the limits within which β must be, by considering its value for $\alpha = 0$. They are given by

$$\beta_{1,2} = \frac{\nu}{2} \pm \frac{1}{2}\sqrt{\nu^2+4\nu} \qquad (\alpha = 0) \qquad 34\ (\text{iv})$$

from which it appears that $\beta_1 > 0$ and $\beta_2 < 0$.
Thus for a cycle of period greater than unity β must be within these limits.

We can now determine what values the structural coefficient γ has to assume in order to give such a solution. γ is given by (ii) as

$$e^{\beta}\left\{\cos\alpha + \frac{\beta \sin\alpha}{\alpha}\right\} = \gamma.$$

Now if $|\alpha|$ has its maximum permitted value, and $\beta = \frac{\nu}{2}$ then γ will have one particular value. Some reflection will show that if $|\alpha|$ decreases from its maximum value towards zero, there will be two values of γ, and like those of β they will move further apart as $|\alpha|$ decreases and attain the maximum discrepancy if $\alpha = 0$. These extreme values of γ are given by

$$\gamma = e^{\beta}(1+\beta) \qquad (\alpha = 0) \qquad 34\ (\text{v})$$

and as the extreme values of β are positive and negative respectively those of γ will be above and below 1 ($\gamma_1 > 1$, $\gamma_2 < 1$). Now we have got the result that in order to give a cycle of period greater than unity the structural coefficient γ must be somewhere between two limits given by (v) and (iv), and these limits are ultimately determined by the value given to the other structural coefficient ν. If γ is outside these limits there can be no cycle of the requisite period. These limits, for which $\alpha = 0$, give the case of a cycle of infinite period, which is, in fact, the same as a trend.

Now by comparison with the previous investigation of the real roots of the characteristic equation (i) it appears that the solution for $\alpha = 0$ is identical with the double root found as a limiting case earlier on. Indeed, if we return to the graph of the characteristic equation, we see that the double root corresponds to the abscissa of the minimum point of the function. If we differentiate the characteristic function (i) we obtain

$$e^{\rho}+\rho e^{\rho}-\gamma = 0,$$
$$e^{\rho}(\rho+1) = \gamma.$$

If we obtain ρ from this equation (subject to the condition $e^{\rho}(2+\rho) > 0$)

it will give the abscissa of the minimum point on the characteristic function, which must be identical with the double root if there is one. Put it the other way round, if ν is given, and if there is to be a double root ρ_0, then γ must be such as to fulfil the equation $\gamma = e^{\rho_0}(\rho_0+1)$. But, putting β instead of ρ_0 we see that this is exactly the condition which γ must fulfil in the case $\alpha = 0$! The ultimate conclusion follows immediately: if ν is given there will be two values of γ such that $\gamma_1 > 1$, $\gamma_2 < 1$. If γ actually coincides with one of these values we shall obtain a single trend, and the rate of growth will be

$$\rho_{1,2} = \frac{\nu}{2} \pm \frac{1}{2}\sqrt{\nu^2+4\nu} \qquad (\rho_1 > 0, \quad \rho_2 > 0)$$

while the values γ_1 and γ_2 are given by

$$\gamma_1 = e^{\rho_1}(1+\rho_1),$$
$$\gamma_2 = e^{\rho_2}(1+\rho_2).$$

If γ is in the open interval (γ_1, γ_2), there will be a cyclical solution, but no trend. If γ is outside the closed interval (γ_1, γ_2) there will be two trend values, but no cyclical solution.

The nature of the solutions of (34) is now clear. We shall see now what influence the *initial conditions* will have in the concrete case. The initial conditions of the mixed difference-differential equation (34) must be specified over a whole interval of time, say from $t = -1$ to $t = 0$. They may be given as the shape of the time function Z'_t over this interval. Now, economically speaking, we must consider that as Z'_t is a moving average it will change slowly over this interval (which is of the order of a year). Generally speaking, we can only approximate the initial conditions by taking into account a certain number of the complex solutions and determine the respective arbitrary constants. But in order to demonstrate some very simple features we shall proceed as follows:

Let us assume the structural coefficients are such that there exist real roots. Further let us assume the initial conditions are such that we can approximate them by using the real roots only. We can then describe the initial conditions by fixing two values only, say the capital stock Z'_0 and the investment $\dot{Z}'_0$ at time $t = 0$. Taking the case of two real roots ρ_1 and ρ_2 the arbitrary coefficients c_1 and c_2 will be determined as follows:

$$Z'_0 = c_1+c_2$$
$$\dot{Z}'_0 = \rho_1 c_1+\rho_2 c_2$$

In different words, the rate of growth of the capital stock ρ_0 at time $t = 0$ is given, and from this the arbitrary coefficients are determined:

$$\rho_0 = \frac{\dot{Z}'_0}{Z'_0} = \frac{\rho_1 c_1+\rho_2 c_2}{c_1+c_2}.$$

What does this mean ? The initial rate of growth is a weighted average of the two 'theoretical' rates of growth which are the solutions of the equation; and the weights are the arbitrary coefficients, which must be so determined that the initial rate of growth is obtained as the average.

We can immediately deal with the case of a double real root. Remember that here we must write the two solutions $c_1 e^{\rho_1 t}$ and $c_2 t e^{\rho_1 t}$. We find

$$Z'_0 = c_1$$

$$\dot{Z}'_0 = \rho_1 c_1 + c_2$$

$$\rho_0 = \frac{\rho_1 c_1 + c_2}{c_1}.$$

Again the arbitrary coefficients have to be fixed at such a level that the initial rate of growth is obtained. We can easily put an economic interpretation on this mathematical procedure. The capital stock at time $t = 0$ can be imagined to consist of two parts c_1 and c_2 which accumulate at different rates ρ_1 and ρ_2. (In the case of the double root, however, we must imagine that the total capital is c_1 and the investment consists of an accumulation at the rate ρ_1 on this capital *plus* a constant rate of investment c_2.) The division into the two parts is determined in such a way that the average rate of growth of the total capital corresponds to that in the initial time. It becomes clear immediately that the average rate of growth of the total capital will change in time as we move away from the initial position, because the part which accumulates at a greater rate will necessarily increase its share.[1]

It becomes evident now—and that is the whole purpose of this demonstration—that the trend is jointly determined by the initial conditions and the theoretical values obtained as a solution of the equation. In the case of a double root, unless the value ρ_1 happens to coincide with the rate of growth in the initial time interval, the rate of growth will change as time goes on and approach more and more the theoretical value ρ_1. After a sufficiently long time it will coincide with it (because if t moves towards infinity, the constant part of investment c_2 will become negligible, and the growth rate of capital will become ρ_1).

If there are two roots ρ_1 and ρ_2 and the initial rate of growth ρ_0 is somewhere in between the two, then there will be a slowly increasing average rate of growth of capital which will approach the upper of the two values, ρ_2 as a limit.

What happens if the initial rate of growth is higher or lower than both ρ_1 and ρ_2 ? One of the coefficients c_1, c_2 must be negative then and the economic interpretation is slightly different. We must imagine that the actual capital stock is the *difference* between two (fictitious) capital stocks accumulating at different rates.

[1] We can see now what the initial conditions must be like in order to justify our procedure : there would have to be, strictly speaking, a changing exponential growth in the initial time interval. But as this time interval is short, we shall approximate the initial conditions roughly, provided there is a constant exponential growth in the initial interval.

The ratio of the two initial capital stocks is given as

$$\frac{c_1}{c_2} = \frac{\rho_0 - \rho_2}{\rho_0 - \rho_1}.$$

If $\rho_0 > \rho_2 > \rho_1$ then $c_2 > c_1$. That is, if the initial rate of growth is bigger than both theoretical values, the 'negative capital stock' c_1 will accumulate at a lower rate than the positive capital stock c_2.

The situation can be explained best by considering that ρ_2, the rate at which c_2 will grow, is simply the weighted average of ρ_1 and ρ_0, the growth rates of c_1 and Z_0' respectively. Formerly we have argued that the average growth rate of two capitals accumulating at different rates must increase. Now this average growth rate, ρ_2, is given and constant: it follows that ρ_0 must decrease. It can never fall below ρ_2 because ρ_2 is the average weighted growth rate of ρ_1 and ρ_0. Therefore, if the initial growth rate ρ_0 exceeds both the theoretical rates of growth, the resulting process will be a gradual fall of the rate of growth from the initial value, approaching the greater of the theoretical values ρ_2 as a limit.

Similarly, if the initial value is lower than both theoretical values, given $\rho_0 < \rho_1 < \rho_2$, it follows that $c_1 > c_2$. The (fictitious) capital c_2 will now have the negative sign, and will accumulate at a greater rate than the positive capital c_1. We can again understand the process by considering that here ρ_1 is simply the arithmetical weighted average of ρ_0 and ρ_2, the growth rates of the two capitals Z_0' and c_2 (taken both positive). The average growth ρ_1 of the two capitals growing at different rates cannot increase, because it is given; therefore ρ_0, the lower of the two rates of growth, must increase, in order to permit constancy of the average growth rate ρ_1. It seems at first that ρ_0 cannot increase to more than the value ρ_1. But if it reaches that value, then by dint of an earlier, simpler reasoning we can show that ρ_0 will continue to grow towards the value ρ_2. Thus, if we start with an initial rate of growth below both theoretical values, then the rate of growth ρ_0 will gradually increase, but never exceed ρ_2.

The reasoning which has been applied to the case of positive roots will be analogous in the case of negative roots. The value which the actual growth rate will approach as a limit is the *absolutely* greater of the two theoretical rates of growth.

The preceding discussion of the initial conditions is of some importance. In practice the initial conditions will often matter, because we shall not move very far away from the initial state. This is because the structural coefficients are liable to change, and when they change we should regard the actual situation at the time as new initial conditions, and see what happens then.

What will be, then, the importance of the theoretical values of growth obtained as solutions of the equation? They will, clearly, determine, together with the initial conditions, whether the rate of growth will be increasing, decreasing, or constant, and they will, moreover, determine the rate of change.

It is quite important to realise that we may have abrupt changes in the structural coefficients, and their effect on the rate of growth in practice will be gradual.

What happens now if the structural coefficients are such that there exist no real roots, therefore no trend ? As we have seen, there will be a cycle in this case. We can form a guess about the length of this cycle, because $|\alpha|$ will be determined entirely by ν and we have a very approximate idea of its possible order of magnitude (see p. 202 above). With $\nu = 0.02$, the period of the cycle would be 45 years at a minimum, with a lower ν its shortest possible length would be more. This would thus correspond to 'long waves' in investment. In reality such a cyclical solution can, of course, never be wholly realised, because our variable is the capital stock, and this cannot oscillate round a zero level. In itself this does not prove at all that the solution cannot be of importance in practice : we may realise, from certain initial conditions, a *part* of the wave.

Take the case where there has been a positive trend, and owing to some changes of structural coefficients the theoretical trend solution vanishes and there is only the cyclical solution. As there has been a positive growth at the beginning, the 'cyclical movement' of the capital stock will start in its ascending phase : the capital stock will continue to grow, but at an ever decreasing rate, it will reach a maximum, and will finally inevitably decline. There will thus sooner or later be a negative rate of growth.

3. *The theory of long-run growth : the case of constant utilisation*

The model of endogenous growth embodied in the difference-differential equation (34) uses only very few structural coefficients (γ and ν). This simplicity is partly due to the assumption of *constant utilisation.* (The utilisation is, of course, constant only for the average of a number of years, for it must be remembered that all the variables refer to moving averages). The assumption is unrealistic, although it may be thought that the model might approximate to a certain extent the features of an economy in which utilisation, though not constant, tends to be re-established at a certain level by the process of competition. A more complicated equation will be given later. If we deal with the present one in detail, it is because it serves as a preparation for the more complicated case, and because it is possible to explain certain problems even with this simple equation only.

It has been demonstrated just now that with given structural coefficients γ and ν the rate of growth of the system will approach a certain theoretical limit after a sufficiently long time. Let us assume this limit has been reached. What will happen to the gearing ratio ?

We can determine this from the equation together with the initial conditions. We need only remember that internal accumulation $\dot{C}t$ is the difference between investment and outside saving in our model. Thus

$$\dot{C}_t = \dot{Z}_t - \nu Z_t.$$

(Here and in the following we leave out the dashes in all the variables, remembering always that we are dealing with moving averages throughout and not with yearly values).

Now as we start from an initial state in which the theoretical limiting value of growth ρ has been reached the further development of the capital stock is given by $Z_t = Z_0 e^{\rho t}$. We therefore obtain

$$\dot{C}_t = Z_0 \rho e^{\rho t} - \nu Z_0 e^{\rho t} = Z_0 e^{\rho t}(\rho - \nu),$$

$$C_t = Z_0 \frac{\rho - \nu}{\rho} e^{\rho t} + K_c,$$

where K_c is a constant of integration the value of which can be determined as follows, if we know the initial value of extrepreneurs' capital C_0:

$$C_0 = Z_0 \frac{\rho - \nu}{\rho} + K_c,$$

$$K_c = C_0 - Z_0 \frac{\rho - \nu}{\rho}.$$

The value of the reciprocal gearing ratio g' at any point of time can thus be determined as follows:

$$g'_t = \frac{C_t}{Z_t} = \frac{\rho - \nu}{\rho} + e^{-\rho t}\left(\frac{C_0}{Z_0} - \frac{\rho - \nu}{\rho}\right). \tag{35}$$

It can be seen that the reciprocal gearing ratio will tend to a limit, provided ρ is positive:

$$\lim_{t \to \infty} g'_t = \frac{\rho - \nu}{\rho}. \qquad (\rho > 0)$$

The economic meaning of this can be readily understood. The limit $\frac{\rho - \nu}{\rho}$ is nothing else but the ratio of current internal accumulation to current investment—the proportion of investment which is financed internally. It is easy to see that if this proportion remains the same for a very long time, then the ratio of entrepreneurs' capital to the total capital will approach it more and more closely.

The limiting value to which the gearing ratio tends can equally well be given in a different form, for, from the characteristic equation

$$\frac{\rho - \nu}{\rho} = \frac{e^{\rho}}{\gamma}.$$

On economic grounds it can also be understood that there will be no limit to the gearing ratio if the rate of growth is negative: because the total capital is then decreasing while the debt, with positive outside savings, is increasing, so that the gearing ratio must increase without limit.

From (35) we can see also how the limit of the reciprocal gearing ratio will be approached: the difference between this limit and the initial value will decrease as an exponential function of time.

Further we can see that the change of the reciprocal gearing ratio over time will be given as

$$\dot{g}_t' = -\rho e^{-\rho t}\left(\frac{C_0}{Z_0} - \frac{\rho - \nu}{\rho}\right). \tag{36}$$

These results illustrate the general ideas about the gearing ratio which have been developed in Chapter IX. The development of the gearing ratio, with a constant rate of growth, depends on the proportion of internal accumulation to total savings $\left(\frac{\rho-\nu}{\rho}\right)$. Only if this proportion happens to coincide with the actual gearing ratio will the latter remain constant.

If ν, the outside saving in proportion to capital, is given, then there exists *one* particular rate of growth which will make the gearing ratio constant at a given level. Any higher rate of growth will lead to a declining gearing ratio, any lower one to an increasing gearing ratio. It can be seen that the case of a constant gearing ratio is a very specific one. At the same time, it follows from (35) that changes in the gearing ratio due to a change in the rate of growth (which may result from a change in γ) will usually be fairly slow.[1]

We may further illustrate the relations by a diagram (Fig. 8). This graph represents total saving and outside saving as functions of national income. It is convenient to plot on the ordinate the two types of saving as a ratio of total capital, so that the ordinate measures nothing else but ρ and ν. On the abscissa the national income is plotted as a ratio of capital.

As outside savings are assumed to be a constant proportion of national income, the ν curve will be a straight line passing through the origin, and in practice fairly flat. The ρ curve will be much steeper, because the difference between the two curves—the internal accumulation—is bound to rise appreciably more than outside savings with an increase in the ratio of national income to capital. We assume the ρ curve to be a straight line too. The position of the ρ curve in relation to the ν curve will depend on the profit margins and the propensity to save of entrepreneurs. That is to say, a greater rate of growth, with given ratio of national income to capital, is made possible by greater profit margins, or alternatively, greater saving propensity of entrepreneurs.

[1] A numerical example may illustrate this. Assume the reciprocal gearing ratio has become adjusted to a rate of growth of 0.05, with $\nu = 0.01$. It has thus reached its theoretical value 0.8. Now the rate of growth suddenly falls to 0.025, ν remaining at 0.01. The theoretical limit of the reciprocal gearing ratio corresponding to the new rate of growth will be 0.6. The initial value of the reciprocal gearing ratio $\frac{C_0}{Z_0}$ is 0.8, and the difference between the initial and the limiting value is 0.2. After ten years the reciprocal gearing ratio will be $0.6+0.78\times 0.2 = 0.756$. The effects of a fall in the rate of growth on the gearing ratio are thus slow, although they are not negligible. They will be much more marked, however, once the rate of growth falls to lower levels.

As the present model implies a constant ratio of national income to capital, we can mark off this given ratio on the abscissa, and we find, if the two curves are given, the proportion of internal to total saving from the ordinates. (The ρ is of course determined by the solution of the equation, and depends therefore on γ and ν). Now, to repeat, there will be one particular value of ρ (with given ν) which will make constancy of a given gearing ratio possible. Any greater or smaller rate of growth will lead to a changing gearing ratio.

As the solutions of our simple difference-differential equation, given certain initial conditions, may easily involve a changing gearing ratio, and as

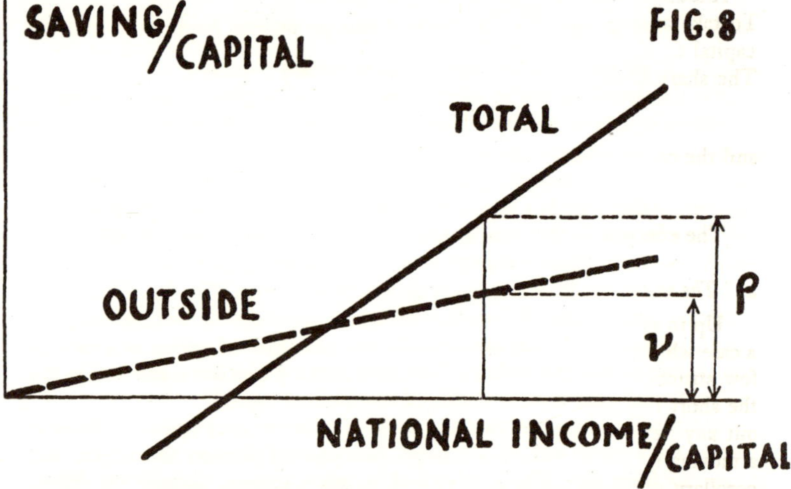

FIG. 8. *Total saving and outside saving in its relation to national income.* (Both savings and national income are expressed as a ratio of national capital).

this might again affect investment, the idea suggests itself to include this influence of the gearing ratio into the equation. This would mean making investment not only, as hitherto, a function of internal accumulation, but also a function of the gearing ratio. This extension of the theory will, however, be included in the next model which in addition embodies many other complications.

We shall, meanwhile, mention at this point a problem which can only be dealt with very briefly here. In its application to reality any model of endogenous development will, of course, have to take account of various circumstances which, at least from the point of the particular model, are exogenous. These factors will be given from outside, and in our equation they will appear as a historical element, a term which is given as a function of time. An important example of such exogenous factors are budget deficits.

A *budget deficit* may be regarded as dissaving which offsets a part of the outside saving. If the budget deficit is d_t then

$$\dot{Z}_t = \dot{C}_t + vZ_t - d_t$$

and the difference-differential equation (34) appears in the following modified form

$$\dot{Z}_{t+1} - \gamma\dot{Z}_t + \gamma v Z_t = \gamma d_t. \tag{37a}$$

The budget deficit enters the equation as a historical element, given as a function of time. In consequence the solution of the complete equation will contain an additional element, which will make for a greater rate of growth.

Another important modification are share issues of joint stock companies. To take account of them we must re-define the increase in entrepreneurs' capital $\dot{C}_t$ as consisting, now, of internal accumulation plus share issues s_t. The share issues are correspondingly deducted from outside saving. Thus

$$\dot{Z}_t = \dot{C}_t + vZ_t - s_t$$

and the complete equation becomes

$$\dot{Z}_{t+1} - \gamma\dot{Z}_t + \gamma v Z_t = \gamma s_t. \tag{37b}$$

The effect of share issues is thus comparable to that of the budget deficit.

4. *The theory of long-run growth: variable utilisation*

Up to now we have confined ourselves to the case of constant utilisation, a case which could be treated by means of equation (34) which involves very few structural coefficients. It presumes that utilisation, though variable in the short run, is re-established at a given level by the process of squeezing out any 'excess' capital equipment which may tend to appear. Taken as a moving average over *n* years utilisation may be considered constant. The corollary of this assumption is that the *profit function* is variable. (By profit function we mean the rate of profit as a function of the degree of utilisation.) In other words the profit rate at a given utilisation will adjust itself in response to changes in the rate of growth of capital.

But we can hardly maintain that this case is an adequate model embodying even the most essential features only, because the underlying hypothesis of a prompt re-establishment of a given degree of utilisation is not realistic. It is natural, then, to go a step further, to allow the degree of utilisation to vary and to set up a difference-differential equation appropriate to this case. The most obvious way is to go, as it were, to the other extreme : instead of taking utilisation constant, and the profit function variable, we shall make utilisation variable, and assume the profit function rigid.[1] This case is probably, strictly speaking, not realistic either : in reality, there may be *some* adjustment of the profit function in response to changes of the rate of growth of

[1] This rigidity implies only that the parameters of the profit function are treated as constants in our model. We shall, however, consider changes in these parameters (due to the development of monopoly) which from the point of view of our model are autonomous.

the system, and the actual behaviour of the system will probably be somewhere in between the two extreme cases. But if any adaptation of the profit function is rather sluggish, then the present case will doubtless be a more useful and adequate model than the first. It will force us to introduce more structural coefficients, but we shall have the opportunity then to analyse the effects of *autonomous changes* in these structural coefficients (which include the parameters of the profit function) on the growth of the system.

In addition we shall also introduce a further complication which the first, simple model did not include. We shall take into account that investment is not only influenced by internal accumulation, but also by the relative indebtedness (the gearing ratio) and the degree of utilisation. The 'investment function' which determines investment will thus appear in the following more general form.

$$I_{t+\theta} = \gamma \hat{C}_t + U(u_t) + G(g_t') \tag{38}$$

where $\hat{C}_t$ is as before, internal accumulation, $U(u_t)$ denotes the influence of a certain degree of utilisation, and $G(g_t')$ the influence of a certain reciprocal gearing ratio g'. The time lag between these various influences and the resulting investment is θ. We might make the investment function still more general by including also a certain influence of the profit rate: a higher profit rate may render entrepreneurs more willing to accept greater indebtedness, and it might thus have a separate influence, apart from the effect which profits in any case exert via internal accumulation. But in order to avoid complicating the model too much we shall not include this additional influence of the rate of profit.

To give concrete content to the theory we shall assume the functions U and G to be linear. The influence U on investment will thus be a linear function of utilisation u_t. At the same time we must consider that the influence of a certain degree of utilisation on investment should, logically, depend on the size of the capital stock: the greater the capital, the greater the absolute amount of investment induced by a certain degree of utilisation. Thus we shall write

$$U(u_t) = (mu_t - mu_0)\, Z_t$$

where m and u_0 are constants. The meaning of the constant u_0 becomes clear if we consider the case where $u_t = u_0$: the influence of utilisation on investment vanishes then. u_0 is thus what we call the planned degree of utilisation, that is the degree of utilisation which has *no* influence on investment. The parameter m, on the other hand, measures the response of investment to a certain 'excess utilisation' $(u_t - u_0)$.

We define now the degree of utilisation as

$$u_t = \frac{kY_t}{Z_t}$$

where Y_t is national income, and k is capital intensity, that is, the ratio of the stock of capital to productive capacity.

By using this definition of u_t we transform the above equation into the following :

$$U(u_t) = mkY_t - mu_0 Z_t$$

In the same way we can deal now with the influence of the reciprocal gearing ratio g'_t. It will again be a linear function, and it will again depend on the size of the capital stock. We thus write

$$G(g'_t) = (qg'_t - qg'_0)\, Z_t$$

where q and g'_0 are constants. The meaning of g'_0 is analogous to the meaning of u_0 : putting $g'_t = g'_0$ we find that the influence of the reciprocal gearing ratio becomes nought. g'_0 is thus the level of the reciprocal gearing ratio, at which its influence on investment vanishes. We might call g'_0 the 'neutral' reciprocal gearing ratio. The parameter q measures the response of investment to a given deviation of the reciprocal gearing ratio from its neutral level $(g'_t - g'_0)$.

The reciprocal gearing ratio is defined as the ratio of entrepreneurs' own capital to the total capital stock :

$$g'_t = \frac{C_t}{Z_t}.$$

Inserting this in the above equation we find the following expression for the influence of the reciprocal gearing ratio on investment :

$$G(g'_t) = qC_t - qg'_0 Z_t$$

Making use of the expressions obtained for the influences U and G we can now write the investment function (38) in the following form :

$$I_{t+\theta} = \gamma\dot{C}_t + qC_t + mkY_t - (mu_0 + qg'_0)Z_t \qquad (39)$$

We proceed now to the building of a model which will include this investment function, and in which the degree of utilisation will be variable. The present model, like the earlier one, relates to moving averages over n years of the different variables.

Investment is again equal to the sum of internal accumulation and outside savings. The way in which savings is adjusted to investment is, however, more complicated. With a rise in investment, national income will rise so as to produce greater profits, and therefore greater savings out of profits. At the same time the outside saving will rise as a consequence of the increase in national income. The national income will have to increase just enough to bring savings from the two sources, internal and outside, to the same level as investment. We shall therefore require a set of additional relations, linking internal accumulation to profits, and profits to national income. These relations will be assumed linear, and it may be noted that this assumption is all right, provided the functions are in reality approximately linear *within the range* in which the variables move in practice. Outside this range the relations are in reality certainly not linear, but this does not impair the usefulness of the theory.

Our system consists of seven equations in seven variables, namely investment, internal accumulation, outside savings, net profits, gross profits, dividends, and national income. It will be convenient in the first instance to write out all these equations one under the other, and to discuss them afterwards in turn. These are the equations :—

$$
\left.
\begin{aligned}
I_{t+\theta} &= \gamma\dot{C}_t + qC_t + mkY_t - (mu_0 + qg'_0)Z_t && \text{(i)}\\
I_t &= \dot{C}_t + S_t && \text{(ii)}\\
\dot{C}_t &= P_t - D_t && \text{(iii)}\\
D_t &= aC_t + \lambda(P_t - aC_t) && \text{(iv)}\\
P_t &= E_t - r(Z_t - C_t) && \text{(v)}\\
E_t &= vY_t + wZ_t && \text{(vi)}\\
S_t &= \mu(Y_t - \dot{C}_t) && \text{(vii)}
\end{aligned}
\right\} \quad (40)
$$

The notation is conveniently explained in the following 'vocabulary' :—

Variables

Z_t	Capital Stock
$\dot{Z}_t = I_t$	Rate of Investment
C_t	Entrepreneurs' Capital
$\dot{C}_t$	Internal Accumulation
S_t	Outside Savings (Personal Savings)
P_t	Profits net of Interest paid
E_t	Profits gross of Interest paid
D_t	Dividends
Y_t	National Income
$Y_t - \dot{C}_t$	Personal Income

Structural Coefficients

γ	'Reinvestment Factor'
a	'Basic Dividend rate'
λ	Proportion of marginal Profits going into Dividends
r	Interest Rate
v	Proportion of marginal National Income going into Profits
w	(Hypothetical) Gross Profit Rate obtaining with Zero National Income
μ	Ratio of Outside Savings to Personal Income
θ	Lag between Internal Accumulation and Investment
u_0	Planned degree of utilisation
g'_0	Neutral reciprocal gearing ratio
k	Ratio of capital to productive capacity
m	Response of Investment to excess utilisation
q	Response of Investment to deviations from the neutral reciprocal gearing ratio.

We are now going to discuss the economic meaning of the equations.

ad (i) This is the investment function which has been discussed already in detail.

ad (ii) Investment equals the sum of internal accumulation and outside saving.

ad (iii) Internal accumulation is the difference between net profits and dividends.

ad (iv) This equation determines dividends as a function of net profits and of the entrepreneurs' own capital. The dividend consists of two parts : one is the 'basic dividend' which is simply a certain proportion a of the entrepreneurs' capital C. The other part is a certain ratio λ of the excess of profits over the basic dividend. (Essentially this is Mr. Kalecki's theory).

An important question has to be considered here. In reality the payment of dividends undoubtedly follows the generation of profits with a lag, which is considerable (perhaps of the order of a year). It might be thought that this lag should be considered in the equation. This would indeed be necessary, if the internal accumulation were computed as the difference between profits and *dividends paid* in the same year. I think, however, that in reality the internal accumulation which matters for the determination of investment according to (i) is the difference between profits in a given year and the dividends which are declared on the basis of these profits, although they are paid out later. In other words the dividends which are determined on the basis of a given year's profits are set aside and treated as a debt. Internal accumulation is thus the difference between profits and *dividends owed;* correspondingly, the equation (iv) does not contain a lag, because it refers to dividends owed, not to dividends paid.

ad (v) This equation relates profits net of interest paid (P_t) to profits gross of interest paid (E_t). The difference between the two is simply the interest paid on the debt.

ad (vi) This is the profit function. It determines profits (gross of interest) as a function of national income Y_t and of capital Z_t. The equation may be interpreted as follows : if national income rises, then a certain proportion v of the increment of income will be added to profits. v is necessarily positive. Now it is practically certain that the average proportion of profits in national income will be lower than the proportion v of profits in the marginal income (broadly speaking, this is due to overhead cost). The second term in the equation wZ_t must therefore be negative, and w is thus negative on economic grounds. The term wZ_t signifies the amount of profits which would be realised if national income were zero. (This is, of course, a purely mathematical concept, based on the extrapolation of a linear function which empirically is only valid in a certain range of income). It will be noted that this second term wZ_t depends on capital. This is reasonable on economic grounds because the negative profits realised with zero output are related to the amount of overheads and should therefore grow in absolute magnitude with the increase in capital.

If we divide the equation (vi) by Z_t we obtain

$$e = v\frac{Y_t}{Z_t}+w$$

(where e is the gross rate of profit) or, if we define utilisation of capital u_t as $k\frac{Y_t}{Z_t}$ we have

$$e = \frac{v}{k}u_t+w.$$

In this form the equation shows that the rate of profit is a function of utilisation. w, which is negative, is the hypothetical rate of profit obtaining with zero utilisation.

ad (vii) This equation determines outside saving as a constant proportion μ of personal income. Personal income is defined as national income minus internal accumulation.

Owing to the definition of internal saving we adopted (profits minus dividends *owed*, not paid) personal income includes the difference between the dividends owing on the basis of current profits, and the dividends actually paid (which are related to earlier profits). This is no doubt unsatisfactory, but I feel that the point is not sufficiently important to justify complicating the model.

Having discussed the economic meaning of the equations we proceed now to reduce the system of equations (40) by successive elimination to a single difference-differential equation.

We first combine the equations (iii) to (vi). Substituting from (vi) into (v) gives

$$P_t = vY_t-(r-w)\,Z_t+rC_t.$$

Substituting this into (iv) gives

$$D_t = \lambda vY_t-\lambda(r-w)Z_t+\lambda rC_t+a(1-\lambda)C_t.$$

Substituting these expressions for D_t and P_t into (iii) gives then

$$\dot{C}_t = (1-\lambda)\{vY_t-(r-w)Z_t+(r-a)C_t\}. \quad (41a)$$

From equations (ii) and (vii) we have

$$I_t = (1-\mu)\dot{C}_t+\mu Y_t. \quad (41b)$$

In addition we have to consider (40 i), which we have not made use of yet:

$$I_{t+\theta} = \gamma\dot{C}_t+qC_t+mkY_t-(mu_0+qg_0')Z_t. \quad (41c)$$

From these three equations we have now to eliminate Y_t, $\dot{C}_t$ and C_t in order to get an equation in Z_t and its derivatives.

Now we shall greatly facilitate the further elimination, and the resulting equation, by assuming $(r-a) = 0$. This involves some loss of generality, but probably the loss is not of very great importance.[1] We shall therefore put $(r-a) = 0$, and deal with the simplified model only.

We obtain now Y_t from (41b) and substitute this expression in (41a):

$$\mu\dot{C}_t = v(1-\lambda)I_t - v(1-\lambda)(1-\mu)\dot{C}_t - \mu(1-\lambda)(r-w)Z_t$$

$$\dot{C}_t\{\mu + v(1-\lambda)(1-\mu)\} = v(1-\lambda)I_t - \mu(r-w)(1-\lambda)Z_t.$$

If we introduce a new constant by putting

$$R = \mu + v(1-\lambda)(1-\mu)$$

we obtain

$$\dot{C}_t = \frac{v(1-\lambda)}{R}I_t - \frac{\mu(r-w)(1-\lambda)}{R}Z_t.$$

Further, we substitute for Y_t in (41c):

$$I_{t+\theta} = \gamma\dot{C}_t + qC_t + \frac{mk}{\mu}I_t - \frac{mk(1-\mu)}{\mu}C_t - (mu_0 + qg_0')Z_t.$$

We take the derivative of this equation with respect to time:

$$\dot{I}_{t+\theta} = \gamma\ddot{C}_t + q\dot{C}_t + \frac{mk}{\mu}\dot{I}t - \frac{mk(1-\mu)}{\mu}\ddot{C}_t - (mu_0 + qg_0')\dot{Z}_t.$$

Now we can substitute both for $\dot{C}_t$ and $\ddot{C}_t$ in this equation (the value of $\ddot{C}_t$ is obtained simply by taking the derivative of $\dot{C}_t$) and we thus obtain

$$\dot{I}_{t+\theta} = \frac{qv(1-\lambda)}{R}I_t - \frac{q\mu(r-w)(1-\lambda)}{R}Z_t + \frac{\gamma v(1-\lambda)}{R}\dot{I}_t -$$

$$- \frac{\gamma\mu(1-\lambda)(r-w)}{R}\dot{Z}_t + \frac{mk}{\mu}\dot{I}_t - \frac{mkv(1-\lambda)(1-\mu)}{\mu R}\dot{I}_t +$$

$$+ \frac{mk(1-\lambda)(1-\mu)(r-w)}{R}\dot{Z}_t - (mu_0 + qg_0')\dot{Z}_t.$$

This equation contains only the capital stock Z_t and its derivatives as a variable, and we have thus arrived at the desired difference-differential equation, which, after cancelling and rearrangement, becomes:

$$\ddot{Z}_{t+\theta} - \frac{mk + \gamma v(1-\lambda)}{R}\ddot{Z}_t +$$

$$+ \left\{\frac{(1-\lambda)(r-w)\{\gamma\mu - mk(1-\mu)\} - qv(1-\lambda)}{R} + mu_0 + qg_0'\right\}\dot{Z}_t +$$

$$+ \frac{\mu q(1-\lambda)(r-w)}{R}Z_t = 0. \qquad (42)$$

[1] I have considered the more general case, and it appeared, in view of the plausible order of magnitude of the structural coefficients, that the influence of this factor is much less important than that of all the others.

The characteristic equation, obtained by putting $Z_t = e^{\rho t}$, will be

$$\rho^2 e^{\theta\rho} - L\rho^2 + M\rho + N = 0$$

where L, M, N denote the coefficients of the equation (42). We shall put $\rho\theta = \epsilon$, and the characteristic equation will then have the following form :

$$\epsilon^2 e^{\epsilon} - L\epsilon^2 + M\theta\epsilon + N\theta^2 = 0. \tag{43}$$

This characteristic equation is rather more complicated than the previous equation (34). We can, however, derive it from the previous equation by graphical means.

Let us, in the first instance, put the constant term in the above equation equal to zero, and divide through by ϵ. The equation becomes then

$$\epsilon e^{\epsilon} - L\epsilon + M\theta = 0$$

which is, essentially, the same as the previous equation (34). We know therefore the graphical picture of this simplified equation (Fig. 9). It is a curve which will cut the ordinate at a point whose distance from the origin is θM, and which will have a minimum, or a bulge in the downward direction.

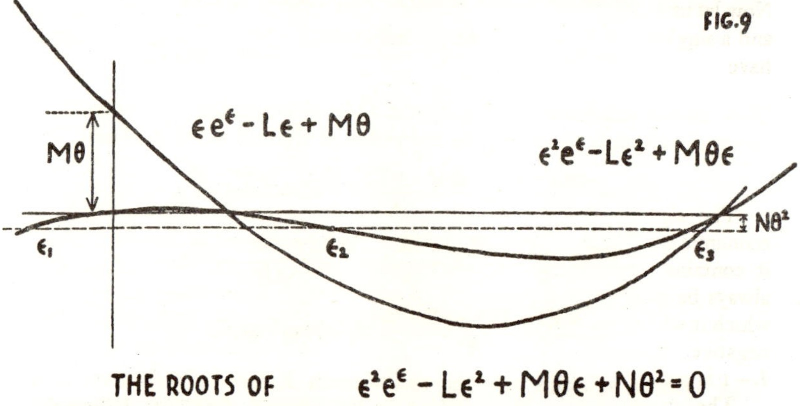

FIG. 9. *The real roots of the characteristic equation* $\epsilon^2 e^{\epsilon} - L\epsilon^2 + M\theta\epsilon + N\theta^2 = 0$.

According to whether L is bigger or smaller than one, the bulge will be in the positive or the negative part of the abscissa. The greater L, the greater will be the bulge, the more likely it will be, therefore, that the bulge reaches or cuts the abscissa, thus giving us real roots of the equation. We have assumed, in the graph, that $L > 1$, and the bulge sufficiently great to give us positive roots.

We can now obtain the picture of the more complicated equation (43), if we multiply, in the first instance, by ϵ. That is, each of the ordinates of the function drawn in the graph has to be multiplied by ϵ (the corresponding abscissa). The result is pictured in the graph. We obtain a curve which has again a bulge in the downward direction, but a very much flatter one than the former curve. In addition it has also a bulge in the upward direction—a maximum. The curve passes through the origin, and it falls off towards the left continuously in the negative half of the abscissa.

We need only shift the abscissa of our system downwards by an amount $N\theta^2$ and we have obtained the picture of the equation (43). As the graph shows, the equation may have three real roots, and it is bound to have at least one. If $L > 1$, as in our graph, then the one root which always obtains is *negative*, whereas the two other possible roots are *positive*.

If several real roots obtain it will be of considerable importance to know something about their absolute magnitude in relation to each other. On the basis of the graphical picture we should judge intuitively that, if positive roots obtain, the larger positive root will be *absolutely* greater than the negative root. That this is true can be demonstrated by a method of approximation. Let us put, as a rough approximation, $e^{\epsilon} = 1+\epsilon$. The characteristic equation then becomes

$$\epsilon^3-(L-1)\epsilon^2+M\theta\epsilon+N\theta^2 = 0.$$

Now let us suppose that this equation gives us a double root which we call ϵ_1, and a single one which we call ϵ_2. By virtue of a theorem of algebra we must have

$$\begin{aligned} 2\epsilon_1+\epsilon_2 &= (L-1) \\ 2\epsilon_1\epsilon_2+\epsilon_1^2 &= \epsilon_1(2\epsilon_2+\epsilon_1) = M\theta \\ \epsilon_1^2\epsilon_2 &= -N\theta^2. \end{aligned} \tag{44}$$

The sign of the coefficients can be determined on grounds of their economic meaning. $N\theta^2$ will certainly be *positive*, because all the coefficients it contains (including $r-w$) are definitely positive. $M\theta$ in practice will always be positive (some discussion of this follows in the later pages, from which it will appear that this statement is justified). $L-1$ may be positive or negative. We assume in the following, just as in the graph, the case where $L-1$ is positive.

The above relations show that the single root ϵ_2 must necessarily be *negative*, because $N\theta^2$ is positive. (We can, in fact, easily extend this statement to the case of three different roots ϵ_1, ϵ_2 and ϵ_3 : one of them at least must be negative, provided $N\theta^2$ is positive). They show further that, if $M\theta$ is positive, and the double root, as we assumed, is positive, then $|2\epsilon_2|<|\epsilon_1|$. That means the single negative root ϵ_2 must be less than half in absolute size of the positive root. But if that is true of a double positive root it must be *a fortiori* true of the larger of two positive roots, as a look at the graph will immediately show. We have therefore established that the larger of two positive roots will always be greater in absolute size than the negative root. We can further see from the relations that the condition $(L-1) > 0$ is *necessary* for positive roots to be obtained.

These results are important, if we are to interpret the economic meaning of the solutions of the difference-differential equation. In discussing the boundary conditions in connection with the previous difference-differential equation (p. 203), we found that of several real roots, it is always the one which is *absolutely* the greatest which matters most: it constitutes the limiting rate of growth to which the system tends as $t \to \infty$. What has been said there can be applied without modification in the present case. We find thus that if any positive roots obtain (which requires $(L-1) > 0$) the larger of the two positive roots (because it is necessarily absolutely the greatest of the three roots) will constitute the limiting rate of growth to which the system tends as $t \to \infty$. In other words, the existence of positive roots is sufficient to guarantee that there will be a positive growth of capital sooner or later.

To obtain positive roots, it is however not only necessary that $(L-1)$ be positive, but it must also be sufficiently large as compared with $M\theta$ and $N\theta^2$. Or, to put it the other way round, with a given positive $L-1$, $M\theta$ and $N\theta^2$ must be sufficiently small to give positive roots. If $M\theta$ or $N\theta^2$ rises, then the positive roots will at a certain point disappear, and will be replaced by a pair of conjugate complex roots, which will give a 'long cycle'. At the same time the negative root will persist. There will be, therefore, a combination of a negative trend and a 'long cycle'. The 'cycle' will be, in practice, very long, and, in economic terms, only a part of it will be of practical importance. The appearance of this 'cycle', in combination with the negative real root, will probably imply that the rate of growth of capital will fall. We shall, however, not discuss this case of complex roots in any detail, but confine ourselves largely to the case of real exponential solutions.

We have already indicated the limiting rate of growth of capital to which the system tends as $t \to \infty$. According to whether this limiting value is greater or smaller than the initial rate of growth given by the boundary conditions, the rate of growth will be increasing or declining, as we move on from the initial point of time. We may now determine also the limiting values of the gearing ratio and the degree of utilisation.

We start from the expression (p. 217)

$$\dot{C}_t = \frac{v(1-\lambda)}{R} I_t - \frac{\mu(r-w)(1-\lambda)}{R} Z_t.$$

Integrating this expression (which involves an arbitrary constant of integration) we obtain the value of entrepreneurs' capital C_t, and dividing by the capital stock Z_t we obtain the reciprocal gearing ratio. We then have to replace Z_t by its value obtained as a solution of the difference-differential equation, namely $ce^{\rho t}$; there will be three such expressions, i.e. $Z_t = c_1e^{\rho_1 t} + c_2e^{\rho_2 t} + c_3e^{\rho_3 t}$, but if $t \to \infty$ then two of them will become small as compared with the one which contains the greatest absolute ρ. We can therefore neglect them and write $Z_t = ce^{\rho t}$, where ρ is the greatest root. The constant of integration also becomes negligible. We obtain therefore the following value for the limit to which the reciprocal gearing ratio tends :

$$\lim_{t\to\infty} g_t' = \frac{v(1-\lambda)}{R} - \frac{\mu(r-w)(1-\lambda)}{\rho R}. \tag{45}$$

It can be seen that the limiting value of the reciprocal gearing ratio is the greater, the greater the limiting rate of growth ρ.

We can similarly find the limiting value of the degree of utilisation. We have (p. 216)

$$\mu Y_t = I_t - (1-\mu)\dot{C}_t,$$

$$Y_t = \frac{1}{\mu} I_t - \frac{(1-\mu)(1-\lambda)v}{\mu R} I_t + \frac{(1-\mu)(1-\lambda)(r-w)}{R} Z_t,$$

$$Y_t = \frac{1}{R} I_t + \frac{(1-\mu)(1-\lambda)(r-w)}{R} Z_t,$$

$$u_t = \frac{kY_t}{Z_t} = \frac{k}{R}\frac{I_t}{Z_t} + \frac{(1-\mu)(1-\lambda)(r-w)k}{R}.$$

If t is sufficiently large, the capital stock will grow at the limiting rate ρ, and we obtain therefore the following expression for the limit to which utilisation tends :

$$\lim_{t\to\infty} u_t = \frac{k}{R}\rho + \frac{k(1-\mu)(1-\lambda)(r-w)}{R}. \tag{46}$$

The limiting value of utilisation is the greater, the greater the limiting rate of growth of capital ρ.

We shall now investigate the role which various structural coefficients play in the equation (42). In the first place, it is of interest to know how the influence of the gearing ratio and of utilisation operate on investment. Do they stimulate growth or the opposite ? Economic intuition would tell us that this should depend on the level of the gearing ratio, or utilisation. The following analysis will make it clearer.

Let us take first the effect of q, which is the response to the reciprocal gearing ratio. We may regard the characteristic equation as an implicit function, which we denote by h, and we write h' for its derivative with respect to ϵ.

$$\epsilon^2 e^{\epsilon} - L\epsilon^2 + M\theta\epsilon + N\theta^2 \equiv h \tag{47}$$

where

$$L = \frac{mk + \gamma v(1-\lambda)}{R}$$

$$M = \frac{(1-\lambda)(r-w)\{\gamma\mu - mk(1-\mu)\} - qv(1-\lambda)}{R} + mu_0 + qg_0'$$

$$N = \frac{\mu q(1-\lambda)(r-w)}{R}.$$

We differentiate this function with respect to ϵ and to q in order to find the differential $d\epsilon/dq$, which will indicate the effects of a change in q on ϵ. We obtain

$$h'd\epsilon = \left\{\frac{v(1-\lambda)\theta\epsilon}{R} - g'_0\theta\epsilon - \frac{\mu(1-\lambda)(r-w)\theta^2}{R}\right\}dq. \tag{48}$$

Now we are interested in the case of a positive growth, we suppose therefore that there are positive roots ϵ. As the *limiting* rate of growth has the decisive importance, we are interested only in the greater of two positive roots. We can see from Fig. 9 (p. 218) that where the greater positive root obtains the characteristic function is necessarily *rising*, that means, h' is positive. The question whether $d\epsilon/dq$ is positive thus will be decided entirely by the sign of the coefficient of dq. The influence of q on the rate of growth will be positive provided that

$$\frac{v(1-\lambda)}{R} - \frac{\mu(1-\lambda)(r-w)\theta}{R\epsilon} > g'_0. \tag{49}$$

But as $\frac{\epsilon}{\theta} = \rho$, the expression on the left hand side of the inequality is identical with the limiting value of the reciprocal gearing ratio previously found. We can thus write

$$\lim_{t\to\infty} g'_t > g'_0. \tag{49a}$$

That means, if the limiting value of the reciprocal gearing ratio is greater than its 'neutral' value g'_0 (which is neutral with regard to investment) then the influence of the reciprocal gearing ratio will be stimulating. Whether this will be the case (whether the inequality will be satisfied) depends not only on the value of g'_0, but also on the rate of growth, as it is determined by the various other structural coefficients. The level of g'_0—the reciprocal gearing ratio which is neutral with regard to investment—depends on the attitude of business men towards indebtedness : the more they are inclined to accept high indebtedness, the lower will be g'_0.

We shall now analyse the effects of m, the response of investment to utilisation. In analogy to the previous procedure, we differentiate the characteristic function h with respect to ϵ and to m, and we obtain

$$h'd\epsilon = \left\{\frac{k}{R}\epsilon^2 + \frac{k(1-\mu)(1-\lambda)(r-w)}{R}\theta\epsilon - u_0\theta\epsilon\right\}dm. \tag{50}$$

If the ratio of the differentials $d\epsilon/dm$ is to be positive, then the coefficient of dm must be positive (seeing that h' is positive). As $\frac{\epsilon}{\theta} = \rho$ we obtain the condition

$$\frac{k}{R}\rho + \frac{k(1-\mu)(1-\lambda)(r-w)}{R} > u_0. \tag{51}$$

The left hand expression is the limiting value of utilisation so that

$$\lim_{t\to\infty} u_t > u_0$$

is the condition for m having a positive influence on the rate of growth. This means that the influence of utilisation on investment will have a stimulating effect, provided the 'planned utilisation' u_0 is smaller than the utilisation to which the system tends as a limit, which depends, of course, on the rate of growth as determined by the various other structural coefficients.

We can, however, say something more if we consider a more stringent condition. If

$$\frac{k(1-\mu)(1-\lambda)(r-w)}{R} \geqq u_0. \tag{52}$$

then the influence of utilisation will always play the role of a stimulating factor, provided only there is a *positive* limiting rate of growth ρ. This is because under these conditions the limit to which utilisation tends will necessarily be bigger than u_0.

If, on the other hand, we have

$$\frac{k}{R}\rho+\frac{k(1-\mu)(1-\lambda)(r-w)}{R}=u_0, \tag{53}$$

then this will mean that utilisation will always be *neutral* with regard to investment: the limiting value of utilisation, if this condition (53) is fulfilled, will be equal to u_0, and utilisation will therefore have neither a stimulating, nor a depressing effect. It can be seen that (53) can always be fulfilled, provided $(r-w)$ has a certain value; in other words, if the profit function (of which w is a parameter) is adjusted to a given planned utilisation u_0 and a given rate of growth ρ so as to make the condition (53) valid, then utilisation will tend to the level u_0, and it will consequently have no influence on investment. If, however, the parameter w of the profit function is increased, and $(r-w)$ therefore declines, then utilisation will tend to a level *below* u_0, and will therefore have an adverse influence on investment.

We turn now to the final problem. In earlier parts of this book the suggestion has been made that the *growth of monopoly* in the economy may have an adverse influence on investment, and that it may bring about a decline in the rate of growth. For this there are two arguments. First, the growth of monopoly should lead to an *upward shift* of the profit function, which means that the parameter w or v should increase. As a consequence of this, utilisation should fall, and the adverse effect of this fall of utilisation on investment might bring about a decline in the rate of growth. The other argument runs as follows: if competitive conditions in an industry are superseded by 'monopolistic' conditions, which means few large units, and impracticability of gaining markets at the expense of competitors, then the *fear* of excess capacity in such an industry becomes greater. This will express itself as a downward shift in the function $U(u_t)$ which represents the influence of various levels of utilisation on investment (p. 131). Correspondingly the planned degree of utilisation u_0 will *increase*. This should lead, again, to a fall in the rate of growth. We shall now analyse these two arguments in terms of the present model.

To find out about the influence of the parameter w on the limiting rate of growth ϵ we differentiate the characteristic function h with respect to ϵ and to w. We obtain.

$$h'\,d\epsilon = \left\{\frac{(1-\lambda)[\mu\gamma - mk(1-\mu)]\theta}{R}\epsilon + \frac{\mu q(1-\lambda)\theta^2}{R}\right\} dw.$$

The ratio $d\epsilon/dw$ will be negative, if the coefficient of dw is negative. An increase in the parameter w will thus lead to a decline in the limiting rate of growth, provided the following inequality is satisfied (writing ρ for ϵ/θ):

$$mk(1-\mu) > \mu\gamma + \frac{\mu q}{\rho}. \qquad (54)$$

The requirement is that m, the response of investment to utilisation, should be sufficiently large in comparison with γ, the reinvestment factor, and q, the response of investment to the reciprocal gearing ratio. If q is neglected the condition reduces to

$$m > \frac{\mu}{k(1-\mu)}\gamma.$$

If, for example, $k=2$, $\mu=0.05$, m would have to be 0.03γ, or more, to fulfil the condition. If q is taken into account, higher values are required for m. (The term q/ρ cannot, as it might seem at first sight, have arbitrarily high values, because the real root ρ must be at a certain minimum in relation to q.)

We have so far considered an increase in the parameter w. An upward shift in the profit function may, however, come about also by an increase in the parameter v, with w remaining constant. In fact, this case should correspond more nearly to the picture of an increase in gross profit margins. We can obtain the effect of an increase in v on the rate of growth by differentiating the characteristic function with respect to ϵ and v:

$$h'\,d\epsilon = \{-(1-\lambda)(1-\mu)\epsilon^2 e^{\epsilon} + \gamma(1-\lambda)\epsilon^2 - \\ -(mu_0 + qg'_0)(1-\lambda)(1-\mu)\theta\epsilon + (1-\lambda)q\theta\epsilon\} dv.$$

If an increase in v is to reduce the limiting rate of growth, then the coefficient of dv must be negative. The condition for this is given by the inequality

$$(1-\mu)\epsilon e^{\epsilon} + (mu_0 + qg'_0)(1-\mu)\theta > \gamma\epsilon + q\theta$$

or

$$(1-\mu)\epsilon e^{\epsilon} + (1-\mu)mu_0\theta > \gamma\epsilon + q\theta[1 - g'_0(1-\mu)].$$

This inequality, again, implies that m must be sufficiently big as compared with γ and q.

It appears thus that our first reason for expecting an adverse influence of monopoly requires a quantitative condition. Now let us turn to the second line of argument. What are the effects of an increase in u_0 on the rate of growth ? We differentiate the characteristic equation (47) with respect to ϵ and u_0 and obtain

$$h' d\epsilon = -m\theta\epsilon \, du_0.$$

The ratio $d\epsilon/du_0$ is undoubtedly negative as long as we have a positive root ϵ, seeing that m is positive. Our second line of argument therefore does not require any quantitative condition. An increased fear of excess capacity, due to the transition to monopoly, will always reduce the limiting rate of growth. If we imagine that we start from initial conditions in which the limiting rate of growth has been actually reached, then the transition to monopoly, operating via an increase in u_0, will reduce the actual rate of growth.

On the basis of the present model it is thus posible to demonstrate that the development of monopoly may bring about a decline in the rate of growth of capital. I believe that this is, in fact, the main explanation of the decline in the rate of growth which has been going on in the United States from the end of the last century. This is not to say that other factors not have played a role too, some of them accidental, some depending on inevitable structural changes; but the role of the monopoly factor seems to be the most essential in an explanation of this remarkable development.

It will be left open whether monopoly has operated only, according to our second line of argument, via a reduction in u_0, or whether it has acted on investment also via an upward shift in the profit function. We refer now briefly to a question which is of considerable importance, without attempting, however, an adequate analysis. It appears from our model that the effect of a given change in u_0, or in w (supposing the inequality (54) holds) on the rate of growth is in general *limited* : that is, the rate of growth will after a time settle down to a new, lower level. In a merely verbal analysis, we would say that a fall in the rate of growth must reduce utilisation, and this should again reduce the rate of growth and so on. All these cumulative effects are, however, included in our system of equations, and are therefore taken account of in the result. It appears thus that, in general, this ' cumulative process " has a limit, and this limit is the new rate of growth at which the system settles down. This is not, however, necessarily the case. We can imagine that the increase in u_0 and in w goes far enough to make the positive real roots disappear. We are then left with a ' long cycle ', combined with a negative trend. Intuitively (without going into a rigid proof) we should say that the cyclical solution will imply a decline in the rate of growth of capital. The rate of growth will sooner or later fall to nought and then become negative. A limit to this process is only reached when the capital stock vanishes. There is thus a possibility that a given increase in u_0 and/or w will lead to a *continuing* decline in the rate of growth. If this pattern is realised, it means, in concrete terms, that the structural changes following from the development of monopoly have made an exponential growth of capital impossible, bringing about in its place an ever-slowing growth and finally decline of the capital stock. This may be the pattern of economic maturity, and it would mean that the causes which have brought about the decline of the growth rate of capital to zero in the decade before the second world war may largely have operated a considerable time ago.

This chapter may best be concluded by an indication of the limits of the present method of analysis. It is evident that the model presented cannot be much more than a beginning in the theory of endogenous long-run economic development. There exists so little sound empirical knowledge about economic relationships, that it would be futile to expect too much of it. We could, for example, not hope to explain the actual values of the rate of growth which have been observed in reality. On the other hand, however, the mathematical formulation of the underlying theories has considerable advantages in checking the logic of the argument, and making the assumptions explicit. It draws attention, above all, to the type of empirical questions which need to be answered.

Having experimented with my model quite a lot, I am aware of its defects, and I shall not try to hide them from the readers. One of the difficulties is this. It is fairly difficult to explain, on the basis of my model, moderate rates of growth, such as have been observed in reality in the history of capitalism, that is, annual rates of growth not exceeding about 5 per cent. If plausible values are given to the structural coefficients, in so far as their values can be guessed (for example for μ, λ, k), and the value of the others (γ, m) fixed in such a way that *real* roots can be obtained from the equation, than it appears that the limiting rate of growth thus obtained is very big. Two alternative conclusions may be drawn from this : either the model requires modifications in important respects in order to be realistic, or else, it follows that an exponential trend in the strict mathematical sense is not a proper description of long-run growth. Long run development would be described, then, by a ' long wave ' (corresponding to the complex roots obtained as solutions of the equation), or rather by *parts* of a long wave. Owing to the changes in structural coefficients occurring in the course of time, and the intervention of exogenous factors, the long wave is not likely to be realised in recognisable form. (The empirical long waves which Kondratiev found, or thought he found, may be pure accident, and have no relation to the present question; certainly they could not be accepted as a proof of the hypothesis discussed here). Long run development would, then, consist of a succession of parts of ' long waves '. If this hypothesis is correct, it does not discredit the main ideas of this book. The long run development will not be a ' trend ' in the mathematical sense, but it will still be *endogenous* long run growth. Nor do I think that in this case my attempts to explain maturity would become superfluous. The changes in structural coefficients are, quite probably, more important for the actual development of maturity than the wave character of long run development. I would be necessary, however, to extend my analysis which to a great part was confined to real roots of the equations, to the case of complex solutions, which presents formidable difficulties owing to the complicated role of the boundary conditions.

The second of the main difficulties of my model concerns the reconciliation of the trend, or long wave, with the existence of the ordinary business cycle. A satisfactory theory should explain both phenomena from a set of consistent assumptions.

The following remarks may at least indicate the direction in which the solution of this problem might be sought.

In order to show that the assumptions of the long-run model of moving averages (as embodied in the system of equations (40)) can be reconciled with the existence of a trade cycle with a period of less than ten years, let us proceed as follows. Let us consider a model in which the variables are the yearly values (not moving averages) and which is to be applied only to a relatively short stretch of time (one trade cycle). We may then use the traditional savings function, that is, we may write

$$S_t = l(Y_t - C_t) - m_t,$$

where l is the short-run marginal propensity to save, and m_t is a function of time, indicating the shift of the savings function over time; for the purposes of this model we assume this rate of shift of the savings function as given *a priori*. If we now substitute the above savings function in the system of equations (40) instead of the equation (40 vii), then we get a model, represented by a difference-differential equation, which will differ from the long-run model (equation 42) only in two respects: (1) the equation will contain a *particular solution*, depending on the function m_t and this solution will represent an induced trend. (2) Instead of the average long-run propensity to save μ we have the marginal short-run propensity to save l. Now, leaving aside the *particular solution*, which gives the induced (exogenous) trend, as uninteresting for our present purposes, we may deal with the *reduced* difference-differential equation only. This *reduced* equation will differ from equation (42) only in so far as l, the short-run marginal propensity to save, takes the place of μ, the long-run average propensity to save. We may be sure that l is considerably greater (perhaps 0.20 to 0.25) than μ (which may be 0.05 to 0.1). How will the general solution of the equation be affected by this quantitative change? In practice it will make the coefficients M and N greater, and L smaller. Now if the equation yielded a trend solution or a long wave with the low value μ, then it should yield a shorter cycle as soon as μ is replaced by the higher value of l. In other words, the difference in the savings function in the short-run and long-run model may explain the simultaneous existence of a cycle in the short-run model, and a trend or long wave in the long-run model, under otherwise equal assumptions in both cases.

A considerable amount of experimenting on the basis of simplified models (putting $q = 0$, and using pure difference equations) has shown me, however, that the numerical difference between l and μ is not sufficient to account for the simultaneous existence of a short cycle of less than ten years in the short run model, and a long wave, or trend in the case of the long run model. It seems that there should exist also other differences between the short run and the long run model.

One of them is most probably the following: The profit function which I assumed constant in my long run model should not really be so. In reality there will be a certain elasticity of the profit margins, that is the profit function will depend on the degree of utilisation (a high utilisation shifting it upwards, and a low utilisation downwards). My mathematical model does not include this complication, and it is in this respect poorer than the verbal exposition of the theory in earlier chapters. On the other hand the rigidity of the profit function is probably realistic for the short run model. Thus there will be an important difference in the behaviour of the profit function between the short run and the long run model. This should, intuitively speaking, help to reconcile the trade cycle and the long run development. Perhaps there are still other differences which ought to be taken into account in the comparison of short run and long run models.

I have indicated, in my concluding remarks, the problems which I had to leave open. That I have not been able to resolve them is to a large extent due to our great ignorance with regard to the empirical value of the structural coefficients, in particular to the almost complete absence of any sound empirical knowledge about the investment function.

XIV. Karl Marx and the Accumulation of Capital

1. *General Observations*

It is not altogether out of place in the context of this book to discuss various ideas of Marx which are closely related to the subject matter. This is not only interesting in itself, but may also help to clarify the ideas which have been presented here. The remarks which follow should not be taken, however, as a study in economic doctrine, an exhaustive appreciation, and perhaps not even as a correct interpretation, but rather only as a sequence of ideas stimulated by Marx's work.

Two broad considerations which have not invariably inspired the literature on Marx are to be given due weight. The work of Marx deals seriously with problems which more than one generation of economists—for the greater part—have neglected and ignored. Its greatness has only begun to be recognised, willingly or unwillingly, wittingly or unwittingly, in modern economics. His method of looking at the economy as a whole, analysing the relation of aggregates, and building models, has become an essential part of modern economics. His problems, unemployment, technical progress, underconsumption, concentration of capital, are the problems which occupy at least the more realistic economists of to-day.

At the same time, economics is not made in the brain alone, not even in a very exceptional one. How Marx himself felt about this can be seen from his never tiring appeal to empirical data and information. But the data at his disposal were defective for his own time. Since then much more information has been collected, referring to his own time and to the time which passed since he wrote. This information is still defective. In fact, economists have constantly to exercise their judgment in relation to the given information which is always inadequate. This involves errors of judgment. The rule of the game, as we conceive it, is to judge on the best available evidence, and to revise judgment when new evidence becomes available. This is hardly in contradiction to the teaching of Marx. In fact the essence of Marxian thinking implies that economics cannot be fixed to a rigid pattern established on the basis of the limited experience available at a certain historical date. The work of Marx is unfinished in more than one sense, and it could not be otherwise. It is not surprising that Marx committed errors of judgment in the light of to-day's evidence. Regrettably enough, the writers who stand up for Marx sometimes cling with peculiar stubbornness just to these errors of judgment, as if *they* were the essence, and not his approach, his method, his problems.

2. *The law of accumulation*

In her critical appreciation of Marx Mrs. Robinson concludes that his work contains really no solution of the problem how the product is divided between wage-earners and capitalists. '. . . as soon as the rigid subsistence level theory is abandoned, it provides no definite answer to the central question—what determines the division of the total product between capital and labour ?'[1]

This conclusion is somewhat too negative. The subsistence-level theory is, if we look at it closely, much less rigid and much more complicated than it appears. It calls for a detailed analysis of its logic and its assumptions, part of which may be invalid without necessarily destroying the usefulness of the whole of the arguments. Such an analysis is attempted in the following.

The 'subsistence-theory' is at first introduced by Marx in a rather formal way. 'The value of labour power' (labour power is what the worker sells and the capitalist buys for a wage) 'is determined by the value of the necessaries of life habitually required by the average worker'.[2] This is a formal statement, satisfying the general rule that commodities have a 'value' corresponding to their production cost in hours of labour, a rule which is here extended to the 'commodity' called labour-power. We are still in the sphere of definition here. The theory becomes more concrete by the additional statement that the *price* of *labour power* (that is, the wage) in the long run should tend to approximate to its *value*[3], but even then it remains still rather

[1] J. Robinson, *An Essay on Marxian Economics*, p. 39–40.

[2] *Das Kapital.* Volksausgabe besorgt vom Marx-Engels-Lenin Institut. I. Band XV. p. 544. *Capital* (Everyman), p. 563. (The quotations given in the text are partly the author's own free translation from the German.)

[3] *Das Kapital* I. XV.

formal on account of the very cautious definition of the 'subsistence-level', which is *historically* determined.

Marx becomes, however, quite concrete when he analyses the effects of increasing productivity on real wages. There is no possible doubt whatever that he expected the *relative share of labour* in the product to *decline* with increasing productivity. Even though real wages may rise, he says 'they never rise proportionately to the increase in the productivity of labour'.[1] It should be noted that, time and again, Marx considers and admits the possibility of an *absolute* increase in real wages. This is clear from the passages in which he argues that this absolute increase in real wages does not change the fundamental relations of capitalism. 'An increase in the price of labour power in consequence of the accumulation of capital means in fact only that the golden chain which the workers have forged by their own work has become so long and heavy that it can be stretched a little more loosely.'[2] And in another place there is the comparison of the small hut and the palace: they may both grow, but if the *relative* discrepancy in size and convenience of the hut and the palace remains or even grows, the owner of the hut remains, in a very relevant sense, as poor as ever, or becomes even poorer. 'Even though the consumption of the worker has risen, the social satisfaction which it grants has diminished in comparison with the greater enjoyments of the capitalist in which the worker has no part, and in relation to the stage of development reached by society in general.'[3]

Marx thus did not deny that the increase in productivity may raise the level of real wages. What he most definitely expected, however, was a diminution of the *relative share* of labour in the product, taking place as a result of the historical process of increasing productivity which is bound up with the development of capitalism. Only in this very qualified sense can we speak of a 'subsistence-level theory'.

This broad expectation of Marx is, however, a result rather than a starting point of his analysis. How exactly did he arrive at this result? The skeleton of his theory is contained in Chapter XXIII of Volume I. We can best start by considering the basic difference between Marx and other writers who held that real wages are in some sense tied to a subsistence level. These other writers, in particular Malthus, and later Lassalle, based their view on the 'law of population': an increase in real wages above subsistence level, they held, would lead to an increase in population which, owing to the decreasing returns to land, would lower the real wage again until it reached the 'equilibrium'— the subsistence level. Now it is perfectly clear that this is not the reasoning on which Marx based his own conclusions. In fact some of his most venomous attacks are directed against the law of Malthus. He perceived in the reasoning in question—probably rightly—the hidden intention of offering a general apology for all the ills of capitalism, by

[1] *Das Kapital* I. XXII, p. 635. Everyman ed. p. 665.

[2] *Das Kapital* I. XXIII, p. 649–650. Everyman, p. 682.

[3] Lohnarbeit und Kapital (Verlag Neuer Weg GMBH 1946), p. 30. Selected Works (Lawrence and Wishart), p. 269.

making out that poverty was a law of nature.[1] He did not believe (any more than we do now !) that an improved standard of life has a positive effect on the rate of population increase; as far as fertility is concerned the effect is more likely to be negative.[2] He did not believe in the law of decreasing returns on land as a historical, long-term law. And he finally makes the very appropriate point against Malthus' law that its mechanism is much too slow to have practical importance.[3]

If this is not the reason for expecting real wages to remain behind as compared with the increase in productivity, what then is it ? What is the specific Marxian theory of real wages ?

In Chapter XXIII Marx puts the question squarely before us and analyses it.[4] Is an increase in real wages possible ? What are its consequences ? Yes, he says, an increase is possible, *if it does not interfere with the continuation of the process of accumulation*. If, on the other hand, it *does* interfere with the continued accumulation, then the accumulation is temporarily reduced, and this leads to greater unemployment, and this again brings about a pressure on real wages, which are thus in the long run brought back to a sort of equilibrium level.

This is the starting point of the analysis. It is to be noted that *a certain long-run rate of accumulation* has to be assumed as given here: 'The magnitude of accumulation is the independent variable, that of the wage is the dependent one, not the other way round.'[5] It follows then that the real wages in the long run must be *limited* in such a way as to leave over, out of the net product, enough for the capitalist to enable him (after allowing for his own consumption) to accumulate at the given long-term rate. 'The . . . law of capitalist accumulation says in fact only that *by its nature* accumulation excludes any decrease in the degree of exploitation, or any rise in the price of labour, such as could endanger seriously the steady reproduction of capital and its reproduction on a continuously expanding scale.'[6] In other words, the real wage must be low enough to enable the capitalists not only to reproduce their capital (to leave over a sufficient amount for depreciation) but also to enlarge it steadily. Again *a certain* (proportionate) *rate* of this enlargement has to be assumed, although this is not explicit in the last quotation.

We can see that Marx, after all, *has* a theory of the determination of real wages. It is based on the implicit assumption of a somehow given long-term rate of accumulation. This is in no way an illegitimate assumption. The

[1] Critique of the Gotha Programme. Selected Works, Vol. II. p. 573. See also Engels' letter, *ibid.*, p. 589.

[2] *Das Kapital* I. XXIII, p. 678. Everyman, p. 711.

[3] *Das Kapital* I. XXIII, p. 672. Everyman, p. 704.

[4] *Das Kapital* I. XXIII, p. 651. Everyman, p. 683.

[5] *Das Kapital* I, p. 652. Everyman, p. 684. It is clear from the context that this sentence refers to the long-run (trend) rate of accumulation, and the (average) long-run level of real wages.

[6] *Das Kapital* I, p. 6523. Everyman, p. 684. To the 'degree of exploitation' corresponds, in modern literature, the concept of 'relative share of labour in the net product'. Reproduction on an expanding scale means simply positive net accumulation of capital. 'Kapital verhältnis' is here rendered as 'capital'.

question how this trend rate of accumulation is determined, can be left open (as Marx does leave it) as long as we may assume that it is to a large part determined by factors acting in the past. The assumption, of course, in no way implies that the trend rate of accumulation is constant, but only that it changes relatively slowly. In a modern interpretation, we would say that it is to a large extent determined by the trend of capital accumulation in the past, which conveys a certain momentum to the present trend rate of accumulation, while other modifying factors act on it as well.[1]

What is the *mechanism* by which the long-run level of real wages is adjusted to the requirements of the given trend rate of accumulation? According to Marx the *actual* level of real wages deviates in the short run from the ' equilibrium level ' which is compatible with the given trend rate of accumulation. These deviations lead to fluctuations of the *actual* rate of accumulation round the given trend level. (These are, in fact, identified by Marx with the trade cycle, although he gives also another, entirely unconnected explanation of the trade cycle—the re-investment theory). We can see that for the *short run* Marx postulates a relation which is completely contrary to that prevailing in the *long run*: namely that the real wage is the primary factor, and the rate of accumulation is determined by it. Real wages, in the short run, are determined by the degree of unemployment; the rate of capital accumulation, in turn, is determined by what is left over to the capitalist out of the net product at the given real wage.

The mechanism, then, works as follows: when real wages rise above the ' equilibrium ' level, the rate of accumulation falls below its trend level: accumulation is slowed down. This leads to an increase in the degree of unemployment. The greater unemployment depresses the level of real wages; their fall leads to an increase in capital accumulation, which now rises above its trend level. At this stage we must suppose the fall in unemployment to raise the real wages again above their ' equilibrium ' level, etc.

We are still far from a full explanation of the mechanism. But it should be stressed at this stage, that the *short run* relations are of completely different type from the long run relation postulated initially by Marx. Without disentangling the two it is impossible to get a clear understanding of Marx.

As we have seen, the mechanism depends on the influence of unemployment on real wages. We disregard for the moment the question whether this connection is realistic. To get the concept clear: what influences real wages according to Marx is the proportionate unemployment—the ratio of unemployed to employed.[2] The real wage is a function of the degree of unemployment. The question immediately arises whether we have to imagine this function to remain constant in the long run. Marx does not say anything about it. It would be plausible that, for example with the develop-

[1] It may be suggested that all this means reading more into Marx's Chapter XXIII than there is. And that Marx only meant real wages must be such as to permit of *some* positive capital accumulation, without thinking of a certain rate of it. The further analysis will show that the more specific interpretation makes sense.

[2] *Das Kapital* I, XXIII, p. 671. Everyman, p. 703–704.

ment of trade union strength, the real wage which corresponds to a certain relative unemployment might rise. We must leave the question open, but for simplication of the discussion we shall for the time being have to assume that the function remains constant.

If that is the case, it would seem that the above mechanism cannot work with every arbitrarily assumed trend rate of accumulation, but that the latter must bear a certain relation to the rate of population increase. To take the simplest case dealt with by Marx : the productivity of labour, the length of the working day and the intensity of labour are constant. The organic composition of capital (the ratio of capital invested to the wage bill) is also constant, and so is the division of the capitalist's share in saving and consumption. Then a constant proportionate rate of accumulation would require that the division of the product and therefore the real wage remains constant. But if the long-run average of the real wage is to remain unaltered, the relative unemployment—again, on the average—must also remain constant. It follows then that the proportionate rate of accumulation must be the same as the rate of population growth ! And it would appear that the growth of population is the final datum in the system !

This impression is at once thoroughly corrected by Marx. First of all, it is not the growth of population which is relevant, but the growth of the industrial labour force. This is itself largely influenced by the process of accumulation. In a developing capitalist system, the rate of accumulation can easily exceed the growth of population, because the very process of accumulation will lead to dispossession of small proprietors, and bring new recruits into the army of industrial workers.

Moreover, there is another even more important factor : *technological progress*. This implies that capital can grow at a greater rate than the labour force. Capital accumulation is in this way freed from the limitations of the available labour. Marx shows again that the process of technological improvements is itself influenced by the pace of accumulation of capital : if this exceeds the growth of the labour force, and relative unemployment therefore declines, a tendency for real wages to rise will set in. This brings about an endeavour on the side of capitalists to introduce labour-saving innovations. The accumulation of capital therefore creates by itself the relative abundance of labour necessary for its own continuation.

There is one special point to be cleared up in this context : a continuing process of technological progress, according to the above, would presuppose that the level of real wages is permanently higher than it would be otherwise. The corollary of this is a permanent decrease in the relative amount of unemployment; the industrial reserve army would thus have to be permanently smaller in a system with technical progress, because this is the very condition for the progress being kept going. But Marx, on the contrary, in one passage even maintains that relative unemployment will (or at least may) be *increased* owing to technological progress.[1] We are led to the con-

[1] *Das Kapital* I, XXIII, p. 679. Everyman, p. 712.

clusion that Marx did not think of technological progress as entirely regulated by the level of real wages. Once the process of innovations has started, it acquires its own momentum, becomes independent of the actual conditions of scarcity or abundance of labour, and sets free even more workers than necessary for the undisturbed continuation of the growth of capital.

It is now clear that the growth of population is not a primary force in the dynamic process envisaged by Marx : if the population growth does not keep pace with the growth of capital, the necessary labour is provided by dispropriation of small owners or by technological progress. The accumulation of capital remains the primary motive force. This is explicitly confirmed by Marx when he talks of ' the law which always keeps the relative surplus population or industrial reserve army in equilibrium with the extent and energy of accumulation.'[1] Now we are able to vindicate the earlier statement, that the rate of capital accumulation *in the long run analysis* is the primary factor, which is assumed as given : the real wages are determined by it. It is of the utmost importance to disentangle this fundamental long-run relation from the short-run analysis, in which, as we have seen, the connection is the other way round.

And now back to the original question : how does Marx arrive at the conclusion that the relative share of labour in the net product is bound to fall with the development of capitalism and the progress of technology ?

We shall show that this conclusion is entirely dependent on the assumed increase in the ' organic composition of capital '. In the process of technological improvements two things have to be distinguished : the one is the increase in productivity, which displaces labour, the other is the increase in the ratio of capital invested to net product, or to wage bill. (What Marx calls ' organic composition of capital corresponds to the ratio of capital invested to wage bill ; but in the following discussion we prefer to work with the ratio of capital invested to net product.)

On a superficial reading it would seem that the productivity effect of technical progress is alone sufficient for Marx to demonstrate the necessity for a constant pressure on real wages which prevents them from sharing proportionately in the increase of the net product. Take, however, a simple model : assume that technological progress proceeds, involving a continuous increase in net real output per worker employed, and that the ratio of capital invested to net output remains constant. Net output and capital invested therefore grow at the same rate, and this rate is, on our assumptions, greater than the rate of growth of the labour force employed (because net output per worker increases). Thus, if we assume *a given trend rate of growth of capital*, the rate of growth of employment must fall short of it; the difference will be simply determined by the increase in productivity per unit of time. This is the simple demonstration of the displacement effect of technological progress,

[1] *Das Kapital* I. XXIII, p. 680. Everyman, p. 714.

and it is based solely on the assumption of a given trend rate of accumulation.[1]

The displacement of labour will first of all act so as to make it possible for capital accumulation, in the heyday of capitalism, to proceed much quicker than the growth of population. As has been said already, the technical progress acquires momentum and is carried on even though the industrial reserve army is more than abundant, thus producing increasing relative unemployment.

Marx argues that this displacement, by increasing the competition among workers and weakening their bargaining position, will press on real wages, thus preventing labour from sharing proportionately in the increase in real income per head. It can easily be seen, however, that this cannot be the whole argument. The increasing share of capital in the net product would necessarily have to go hand in hand with an increasing rate of accumulation—as long as the ratio of capital invested to net product is constant.[2] The increased rate of growth of capital—contradicting the initial assumption—would counteract the displacement, and destroy the validity of the whole argument.

It is thus essential to assume an increase in the ratio of capital invested to net product. If this is done, then the share of capital in the net product not only can, but must, increase *in order to permit the continuation of the given rate of accumulation*. We arrive at the final conclusion that Marx's prediction with regard to the course of real wages is in the last resort dependent on one crucial assumption : the increase in the ratio of capital to net output.

Marx has put this assumption in a slightly different form : his organic composition of capital, or ratio of constant to variable capital, seems to correspond really to the ratio of capital invested to the wage bill.[3] In this form the assumption is really not strict enough, because an increasing ratio of capital to wage bill need not imply an increasing ratio to net product (if the share of wages in the product declines). But in spite of this awkwardness of definition—to which we come back in another context—the sense which Marx wanted to convey is almost certainly correctly interpreted in our formulation.

It is not without interest to note that the famous conclusion of Marx with regard to the secular development of the share of labour is dependent on this particular assumption. Modify this assumption, and the conclusion is different. It so happens that—as far as our evidence goes—both the assumption and the conclusion are not valid for the modern period of capitalism (that is, in America for example, since about 1900). The ratio of net business

[1] It may be argued that technical progress itself stimulates the rate of accumulation, in so far as innovations raise the prospective rate of profit for the firms which first introduce them (M. Kalecki, The Trend, in *Studies in Economic Dynamics*). But technical progress is not necessarily of this type (as Kalecki points out). An example is the situation in the 1930's when a stimulating effect on investment was not at all apparent, while technical progress nevertheless expressed itself in a very marked increase in productivity.

[2] We are assuming, for simplicity's sake, that the division of capitalists' share in consumption and accumulation is constant.

[3] *Das Kapital* I. XXIII, p. 643. Everyman, p. 675.

capital to national product does not seem to have increased at all since the first decade of the century (see above Chapter XII, 4). The data, it is true, are not at all reliable. But Marx certainly expected *very marked* changes, such as could not fail to show themselves even in fairly inaccurate statistics. Changes of this order of magnitude can be with some confidence excluded, as far as concerns the period covered by the data.

That the share of labour in the product does not show any marked tendency to fall in the later stages of capitalism has been shown by various statisticians. To take the case of American manufacturing industries: the share of wages in value added did not show any *spectacular* decline between 1899 and 1939 and, moreover, most of the decline occurred after 1923. The number of workers employed per unit of output decreased from 1899 to 1937 by 50 per cent (1.8 per cent per annum), that is, the cost in working days of a given output was halved.[1] In comparison with this increase in productivity, the decline in the share of wages in value added from 44 per cent in 1899 to 41 per cent in 1937 and 38 per cent in 1939 is certainly much smaller (only about 15 per cent). By and large it is true to say that the expectation of a *marked* fall in the share of labour is not realised in the ' mature ' stage of capitalism. But it may have been quite different in earlier stages, especially in the period of hectic development during the ' industrial revolution '.

That the concrete conclusion of Marx is not applicable to the whole of the history of capitalism does not, however, necessarily reflect on his entire analysis. This has still to be examined on its own merits.

From the point of view of modern theory we run up against a formidable difficulty here. Keynesians have never had much use for this part of Marx's reasoning (the ' law of accumulation ' contained in Chapter XXIII), because it assumes, at least for the short run mechanism, a dependence of real wages on the degree of unemployment. This assumption might perhaps be applicable in an open system. In a closed system, however, most economists would nowadays think it unrealistic. The degree of unemployment may well influence *money wages* here (although this relation is subject to considerable long-run changes, money wages becoming more resistant against the pressure of unemployment as trade union organisation develops). But a general rise or fall in money wages would not necessarily and regularly affect the share of profits, because it is the capitalists who decide the ' mark-up ' which is added on to wage costs in order to arrive at the price; it is quite plausible, at the least, that this percentage mark-up remains unaffected by changes in the general level of money wages. The best support for this modern view is the fact that the share of wages in the course of the trade cycle does not develop according to the pattern expected by Marx. The percentage gross profit margins show no cyclical dependence at all in American manufacturing as a whole,[2] even though money wages did rise in the boom and fall in the

[1] S. Fabricant, *Employment in Manufacturing*.
[2] M. Kalecki, *Studies in Economic Dynamics*, p. 23.

slump. The share of wages in the *net* income produced in manufacturing depends indeed on the cycle, but in a way quite contrary to Marx: it falls in the upswing and increases in the downswing.[1]

But the worst about the short-run analysis of Marx is this. By assuming that the degree of unemployment influences not only *gross profit margins*, but also net profits, and thus the *rate of profit*, he has run counter to the best established truth of Keynesian economics: namely that a given amount of profits can only materialise (assuming capitalists alone to be net savers) if there is a corresponding amount of net investment and capitalists' consumption. Marx assumed that the upward pressure of wages in the boom reduces the rate of profit and therefore discourages accumulation; and that the lowering of wages in the depression raises the profit rate and therefore gives a stimulus to accumulation. This is, of course, straightforward 'classical economics', a faulty reasoning from which Marx did not manage to detach himself completely, and which most other economists got rid of only in the comparatively recent past. The increase in wages could never reduce profits as long as investment (and capitalists' consumption) remain high; a fall in wages could never increase profits, unless investment first increased. In Marxian terms, we should say that surplus value (profits) in order to be obtained, must not only be 'produced' but also 'realised'.[2] And the realisation, as the Marxian reproduction schemes show, can only take place if there is a corresponding amount of investment and capitalists' consumption.

The short-run analysis of Marx is therefore a relic of views which Marx would probably have completely discarded had he had the time to develop the under-consumption approach which is implicit in the later parts of his work.[3] But does the failure of the short-run analysis invalidate his long-run theory? This, as we have seen, is of a very different kind. Its basic idea shows a remarkable family resemblance to the type of thought which Keynesians apply to the short run: capital accumulation (investment) is here the primary motive force. Other factors are adjusted so as to make the given rate of capital accumulation possible. In the Keynesian short run theory, these 'other factors' are incomes, which rise or fall so as to provide just enough saving to finance the investment. In the Marxian long-run analysis the adjustment concerns the distribution of income between workers and capitalists (of which the former save nothing and the latter quite a lot): this distribution of incomes in the long run is adjusted in such a way as to provide just the necessary saving to finance the given trend rate of accumulation.

When Marx comes to demonstrate how this long-run adjustment works, he does however apparently rely on the unacceptable elements of his short-run analysis. His basic reasoning, as we have seen, is this: the capitalists always manage to create enough unemployment (through technical progress) to keep real wages low enough to make the given rate of accumulation

[1] Kuznets, *National Income and its Composition*, 1919–38. Vol. I. Table 74, p. 358.
[2] *Das Kapital* III, p. 272.
[3] See P. Sweezy, *The Theory of Capitalist Development*, Chapter X, 2, p. 162 *seq.*

possible. The influence of unemployment on the distribution of the net product seems to be an unavoidable condition !

It is, however, possible to base the long-run theory of Marx on a different and firmer foundation. The alternative line of reasoning can be found in certain parts of Marx's own work, although he has never made it quite explicit.

When he discusses the question of real wages and of the distribution of the product, Marx says that it should be influenced by two factors : competition between workers, and competition between capitalists.[1] In the version analysed above, it is the competition between workers which does all the tricks. This version is not satisfactory. But what about the competition between capitalists ? Is there a possible version which makes use of this idea ?

It might look somewhat like this. Imagine there is a given trend rate of growth of capital. If the percentage gross profit margin is arbitrarily determined, then the requisite level of the rate of profit, which enables the capitalists to accumulate at the given rate, will be obtained by an adjustment of the degree of utilisation of capacity.[2] If the gross profit margin is relatively low, for example, then the degree of utilisation will be high. This high utilisation, on the average over a longer period, might lead to a slackening of the competitive struggle between capitalists, who are always to a greater or lesser degree trying to push each other out by price cutting. Owing to the lessening of the intensity of this struggle for markets, gross profit margins will increase. If on the other hand, the gross profit margin is relatively high, then the degree of utilisation must be low, that is, excess capacity will be great. This should lead to an intensified competition between capitalists, who are now more than usually intent on pushing each other out by price cutting. This will lead to a reduction of gross profit margins.

It is by no means fantastic to suggest that Marx has actually thought on these lines or at least come very near to it. A passage in ' Wage Labour and Capital ' (an early work) shows it fairly clearly. In this passage Marx tries to explain how capital accumulation affects real wages. In dealing with the same question in ' Kapital ' (Vol. I) he would argue that accumulation might increase the demand for labour, and by reducing unemployment, might raise real wages, although this conclusion is considerably qualified by taking into account the displacement owing to technical progress. This is, then, the version of ' competition between workers '. In the passage in ' Wage Labour and Capital ' we get a glimpse of the alternative version :

' *How does the growth of productive capital affect wages ?* '

If on the whole the productive capital of bourgeois society grows, then *a more varied* accumulation of labour takes place. The capitals grow in number and extent. *The increase* in capitals increases the *competition among capitalists*.'[3]

[1] Lohnarbeit und Kapital, p. 23. Selected Works, p. 262.

[2] This works only as long as it does not involve full use of capacity; in this case the gross profit margins even in the short run could not be assumed any more independently of the rate of investment (Kalecki).

[3] Lohnarbeit und Kapital, p. 35. Selected Works, Vol. I, p. 274 (Italics by Marx).

And in the following passages Marx proceeds to describe this competition among capitalists as a struggle, in which some (those who have acquired cost advantages through introduction of new methods) endeavour to throw out others. He shows, further, that this struggle for markets can be carried out only by price cutting, and that it affects therefore the cost-price relation, the gross profit margin.

The result of this competitive struggle, according to Marx, is that the *increase* in (gross) *profit margins* acquired by certain capitalists, thanks to the introduction of new methods which cheapen production, *is counteracted*, and the level of profit margins is therefore reduced again.[1]

The idea of 'competition between capitalists' as a factor influencing the distribution of the product is clearly visible in these passages. It is clearly said that this competition is bound up with the process of concentration, the driving out of capitals which are in some sense 'surplus capital', in order to make room for the growth of the remaining capital.

The idea, it is true, has never been followed up by Marx. We get a glimpse of a theory *in statu nascendi* but we are left with a great intellectual difficulty. The competition between capitalists is regulated by the relative abundance of capital. If there are more 'capitals', then they push each other harder for there is apparently some sort of restricted room in which they have to operate. But the long-run growth of capital, we know, does at the same time create the markets: the greater the investment, the capital accumulation, the greater the effective demand, the market. How can the growth of capitals then lead to greater competition of capitalists?

The riddle is only solved, if we think of the 'growth of capital' in the context of this sentence as a *potential*, not an *actual* one. The *actual* trend rate of growth of capital is determined by factors acting in the past, and it is this actual rate of growth which (given the capitalists' propensity to save) determines the growth of the market. This is therefore given. But if the gross profit margin rises, there is a *potential* growth of capital which cannot materialise and which expresses itself in reduced utilisation: in this specific sense there is then a relative abundance of capital, which does not find sufficient room to operate. In Marxian terms: if the rate of exploitation rises, then there is more surplus value 'produced'. But without an increase in capital accumulation, this increased surplus value cannot be *realised* (as can be seen from the reproduction schemes). It is this *unrealised surplus value*, this merely *potential* accumulation, which brings about the competitive struggle between capitalists, and thus reduces again the rate of exploitation.

It is quite another story that the whole mechanism of competition between capitalists, as described by Marx, is not an absolute law of capitalism, equally valid at all times. Its importance, on the contrary, changes in the course of historical development. The growth of oligopoly in the 'mature' stage of capitalism restricts the validity of this mechanism of competition more and more, because oligopolists are less keen to push each other out. It

[1] See also *Kapital* I, X, p. 331–334. *Capital*, p. 330–333.

requires consequently a modification of the analysis, if the later stages of capitalism are to be dealt with realistically. To this we shall soon come back.

3. *The declining rate of profit*

It is an inherent law of capitalism, according to Marx, that the rate of profit should have a tendency to decline. This tendency depends entirely on one assumption, the rise in *organic composition of capital.* This can best be defined, in accounting terms, as the ratio of capital invested to the wage bill. Marx shows, in the first stage, that if, in relation to a given wage bill, capitalists' profits do not rise, but the invested capital does increase, then the rate of profit falls. In the subsequent pages, Marx fully admits that the profits made in relation to a given wage bill can rise (and even will rise) with the increase in productivity in the course of development of capitalism. He nevertheless asserts fairly definitely that this rise in the share of capitalists cannot hold up the tendency for the rate of profit to fall.

Critics have pointed out that Marx has not given any logical proof to justify his position. Strictly speaking this is true. The ratio of capital invested to the wage bill can theoretically rise without limits, but so can the ratio of profits to the wage bill. It is not without interest, however, to point out that Marx could have obtained a logical proof without difficulty if he had chosen a different concept of the 'organic composition'. If, instead of his definition, we take the *ratio of capital invested to the net product*, then the matter becomes immediately obvious: this ratio can, theoretically, still increase without limits. The ratio of profits in the net product, however, can rise only by a certain maximum factor: assuming for example that it was originally 50 per cent, it could at best only be doubled. As the rate of profit is the ratio of profits in the net product divided by the ratio of capital to the net product, the proposition follows: with the increase of capital in relation to a given net product, the profit rate must necessarily decline sooner or later.

With Marx this reasoning must have been at the back of his mind and explains the tenacity of his conviction. It becomes clear only in the following quotation (which is badly worded, and like the whole part of the work shows all the signs of being a mere sketchy draft):

'In so far as the development of productivity diminishes the portion of labour which is paid, it increases the surplus value, because it increases its rate; in so far, however, as it reduces the *total quantity of labour employed by a given capital,* it reduces the factor by which you have to multiply the rate of surplus value, in order to obtain its mass. Two workers who work twelve hours each cannot, even if they could live on nothing and therefore did not have to work for themselves at all, produce the same mass of surplus value as 24 workers who work only 2 hours each. In this respect, then, the compensation of a diminished number of workers by an increased rate of exploitation of labour has certain limits beyond which it cannot go; it can therefore retard the fall of the profit rate, but it cannot stop it.'[1]

[1] *Das Kapital* III, 15, p. 275–276. *Capital*, Vol. III (Kerr), p. 290. (Italics by myself).

The concrete example given has only one interpretation : a given amount of capital[1] employs at first 24 workers (who presumably work twelve hours a day) and produce each 2 hours surplus value a day. After a fundamental change in technical methods, the same amount of capital employs only 2 workers; even if these 2 workers, working 12 hours a day, require no payment at all, and thus produce 12 hours surplus value a day, their total mass of urplus value—24 hours—is less than the mass of surplus value produced formerly for the same capital, namely 48 hours.

It is obvious that Marx has inadvertently changed his definitions here : for the rate of surplus value, in the above passage, we have to read ' ratio of unpaid labour time to total labour time ' (as opposed to his usual definition : ratio of unpaid to paid labour time). And instead of the usual ' organic composition of capital ' (ratio of capital invested to paid labour) we are plainly referred to the ratio of capital invested to the *total* hours of living labour used together with this capital. It follows then logically that an increase in capital in relation to labour employed cannot be compensated beyond a certain point by an increase in the amount of unpaid labour per worker.

Thus for the logic of the argument. The empirical hypothesis on which it is built is not as realistic as Marx doubtless expected. In mature capitalism the ratio of capital to net product quite probably does not increase at all. This is partly because the ratio of *net* capital (which is what matters for the computation of the rate of profit) is not only influenced by the technique of production, and the relative cheapness of capital goods, but also by the *age structure* (see Chapter XII, 3). But even apart from that there seem to be new tendencies in the development of the technical structure which operate in a direction quite opposite to the increase in ' organic composition ': in certain cases, at least, the tendency to employ less (gross) capital in proportion to a given output has been demonstrated.[2] Whatever the uncertainty and doubt about the evidence concerning the development of the capital-output ratio, one conclusion seems safe : the increase, if any, cannot have been of the order of magnitude required to make the law practically relevant. This applies fully to the modern stage of capitalism. But even for the earlier stages it is doubtful whether the increase in the capital-output ratio was of such an order of magnitude as to be important in this context.

The chief question about the law of the declining rate of profit, however, is this : do we have to conceive of this tendency as an *actual* fall in the rate of profit, which *in fact* takes place as a consequence of the change in capital-structure ? If the law is understood that way, then it is in contradiction to the best modern economics (and with that also to the whole underconsumption approach which, as Sweezy showed, is contained in the work of Marx itself). The amount of profits realised is entirely determined by the amount which capitalists invest and consume (assuming that wage earners do not save, but

[1] This is measured, of course, in terms of *labour hours* used up in its production (' frozen labour ').

[2] D. Weintraub, Effects of Current and Prospective Technological Developments upon Capital Formation. *American Economic Review*, 1939.

only capitalists save). As long as the sum of capitalists' consumption and investment, as a ratio of their capital, does not decrease, the rate of profit *can never decrease*. The consequence of a steadily increasing ratio of capital to (planned) output, under these circumstances, will be simply this: the degree of utilisation will continuously rise, and the system will finally plunge headlong into inflation. Needless to say, in peace-time capitalism there has never been any sign of that.

The alternative interpretation of the law of the declining rate of profit is this: we may conceive it as a *potential* tendency, which is never realised, but may none the less be important. We should say then that the capitalists do not, in fact, carry out certain possible changes in the capital structure, because they would lead to a decline in the rate of profit. By thus refraining from making production more capital-intensive, they do of course invest less than they otherwise might, and this is obviously of practical consequence.

It has been demonstrated that individual capitalists, when they consider the introduction of new methods which cheapen production, but raise the ratio of capital to output, may find that the use of these methods would involve a reduction in their rate of profit. This result is the more likely, the greater their net profit margin is to start with.[1] (In a popular fashion this may be expressed simply as follows: if the net profit or the surplus value happens to be a small proportion of the output or value produced, say 10 per cent, there is more room for the proportionate increase in this fraction, than there is if the proportion is, say, 50 per cent to start with. An increase in the ratio of capital to output with constant profit rate is relatively easier in the first case than in the second. A doubling of this capital-output ratio, for example, in the first case would require an increase of the share of net profit in the output to 20 per cent to leave the rate of profit unchanged. In the second case the same result could hardly be achieved at all, because the profit would have to swallow up the whole product.)

The law of the declining rate of profit may therefore be of great practical relevance for the individual capitalist, as long as he considers at all capital-intensive methods of cheapening production. It is true to say that a decline of the rate of profit on this account may easily prevent him from adopting such methods. This is, firstly, because he will not invest at all at a rate of profit below a certain level. And secondly, because there may be other possibilities for investment which do not involve a decline in the profit rate; he may, for example, use technical methods of cheapening production which do not involve greater relative use of capital, or he may concentrate on cheapening purchase or distribution by large-scale methods, or use all his means to acquire quasi-monopolistic positions, etc.

How far the law of the declining profit rate, in the sense just explained, has operated in the course of capitalist history to restrict the adoption of capital-intensive methods which would theoretically have been available, it is hard to judge. The problem might be relevant for the question of the

[1] Cf. *Big and Small Business*. Economic Problems of the Size of Firms. Chapter III.

mature economy, if it could be shown that ' capital-intensification ' had been of great importance in earlier stages of capitalism. But it may be thought that other more obvious factors are of much greater importance for the problems of economic maturity.

4. *Underconsumption and the crisis of capitalism*

Marx foresaw that, in one way or another, but for reasons inevitably bound up with its own inherent development, capitalism would function less and less well as it developed. Its disadvantages would grow and more and more outweigh its positive achievements (which Marx never denied). The troubles, or illnesses, which it would develop would finally lead, or at least contribute, to its downfall.

What precisely the nature of these troubles are, and why they should inevitably develop, Marx did not satisfactorily explain. He had various ideas on this score, but they remained in an unfinished state. P. Sweezy has admirably shown that there are two main alternative explanations of the ' capitalist crisis ' in Marx, the law of the declining rate of profit and the under-consumption approach. What Sweezy has to say on this subject makes it superfluous to add anything more here.[1] Briefly speaking he regards the first approach—via the ' declining rate of profit '—as not promising, and sees in the second—the under-consumption approach—the basis from which a satisfactory explanation could be developed. His reasons for this view are only too convincing.

Sweezy has also attempted to construct himself the rough outlines of a logically consistent explanation of the capitalist crisis, based on the under-consumption idea. It is this explanation which calls for comment.

His basic assumptions can be easily seen from the rigid mathematical demonstration of the argument.[2] In his simple model the national income is defined as the sum of (1) wages (which are equal to workers' consumption), (2) capitalists' consumption, and (3) investment. It is assumed that while the national income rises steadily, both wages and capitalists' consumption increase less quickly than investment. The consequence is that investment in relation to total consumption must rise continuously.

This result is based on the following reasons: the first reason is that capitalists will tend to accumulate a greater and greater proportion of their surplus, and consume a correspondingly lesser and lesser proportion (Sweezy, *op. cit.*, p. 181). The second reason is logically confused.[3] The third reason

[1] Cf. *The Theory of Capitalist Development*, Chapter X.

[2] Sweezy, *op. cit.* Appendix to Chapter X, p. 186, *seq.*

[3] Sweezy introduces here an exceedingly puzzling distinction between *investment* and *accumulation*: ' accumulation ' is the part of the surplus value which is not consumed by the capitalists. *A part of accumulation* is laid out by the capitalist in the purchase of additional raw materials and capital goods and therefore adds to the stock of constant capital (machines, buildings, inventories). This is called ' investment '. The other part of accumulation is laid out in additional wages (and therefore consumed by the workers). This part, according to Sweezy, is not ' investment ', although it is ' accumulation ', and Sweezy blames the Keynesians for not appreciating this distinction.

The reproach is hardly fair, because Sweezy's distinction is illogical. It implies that

is not stated explicitly, although one has the feeling that it is somehow present in the background. In any case it is a *necessary* reason : namely that surplus value is rising, or at least constant as a proportion of the national income.

Disregarding the second reason, we find that the first and the third yield the result in a perfectly natural way : if we define the sum of investment and capitalists' consumption (contrary to Sweezy, but correctly) as *profits*, or *surplus value*, and assume (a) that investment as a proportion of surplus value increases, and (b) that the surplus value as a proportion of national income *does not decrease*, then it follows at once that investment increases in proportion to national income and total consumption. Sweezy does not choose to put the argument that way, but it is in point of fact a reasonable interpretation of his algebraically defined assumption.

The further hypothesis which is needed to complete the model is this : if consumption increases by a given amount, then the capital stock must increase by a given and constant amount, assuming full utilisation. This amounts to the same as the well-known ' acceleration principle '.

On the basis of these assumptions Sweezy is able to demonstrate ' under-consumption ' in the case of a constant or declining rate of increase of national income. The gist of this demonstration might perhaps be rendered verbally as follows : as long as the national income rises at a constant rate, or a declining one, the capital stock should also rise at a constant rate, or even only at a declining rate, to assure full utilisation. But a continuous rise in national income involves a rise in surplus value, and *a fortiori* a rise in the rate of investment. Now a rise in the rate of investment, of course, implies that the capital stock will not grow in a linear fashion, but *at an increasing rate :* which clearly cannot be reconciled with the requirement of full utilisation. The argument shows that a discrepancy between consumption and the production capacity must necessarily arise, a discrepancy which most probably would show itself in under-utilisation of capacity.

The demonstration of Sweezy, as he himself stresses, does not necessarily hold in the case where the national income rises at an increasing rate. It should be possible, however, to prove it also for the case of a constant

some part of his national income flow is *wages*, and at the same time is also *surplus value* (profits) *in the same period*; that some part of the value created *in a given year* is unpaid labour and at the same time also paid labour ! No doubt, this unfortunate terminology has its roots in Marx. In fact, it is nothing but a relic of that weird old monster, the wages fund doctrine, which Marx killed in a brilliant attack, only to permit its ghost to muddle up his terminology ! There is no reason nowadays, even for a Marxist, to preserve the remains of that fossil out of mere piety.

The assumption in which Sweezy uses the distinction is this : that ' investment ' increases in proportion to total ' accumulation '. Together with the first assumption, that accumulation rises as a proportion of surplus value, this should lead to the result that investment rises in proportion to national income (according to the argument in the text, p. 181). It does not yield this result, however, unless we assume something about the proportion of surplus value in the national income ! The text (p. 181) gives almost the impression that Sweezy did assume surplus value to rise in proportion to national income (' making as much profit as possible '), but he does not state it explicitly. Once we make this assumption of increasing or even constant surplus value in relation to wages, the whole of the argument about accumulation and investment becomes superfluous !

logarithmic growth of the capital stock, and thus make it yield a more widely applicable conclusion.

As the theory stands, there is, however, a snag in it. It presupposes a secular increase in the ratio of investment to consumption. The evidence of Kuznets' data does not confirm this assumption, and it is almost certainly not realistic. It is also very unlikely that capitalists' saving as a ratio of their income actually increased in the later stages of capitalist development. It is again unlikely that capitalists' income in relation to wages actually increased. The decrease in the rate of growth of capital in the mature economy and the concomitant decrease in the rate of profit tend to bring about a decline in the share of profits in incomes, and a decline in the share of capitalists' savings in profits.

To take account of the realities of the situation the under-consumption theory needs a different re-interpretation. If we think of it, the tendency for the capitalists' share in the product to increase does, after all, exist *potentially*. It is a consequence of the growth of oligopoly. The expression of this tendency can only be an *increase in the gross profit margins*. That means that the actual share of *net* incomes of capitalists need not increase at all. The increased gross profit margins may be compensated by a reduced degree of utilisation, so that there is not a shift of actual income from wages to profits, but a shift of potential income of workers to wastage in excess capacity.

This could be very easily represented in Marxian terms. We should have to say that as a consequence of the rise of oligopoly, the rate of *surplus value produced* tends to increase : the rate of exploitation rises. But as Marx explained, producing surplus value does not necessarily mean realising it, and the realisation depends on the existence of a sufficient market. We should now say that surplus value can be realised only to the extent to which there is a corresponding amount of investment and capitalists' consumption. If this amount does not increase, then the rise in the rate of surplus value *produced* will not lead to any increase in surplus value *realised*, but only to excess capacity.

This has been described already above in connection with the ' law of accumulation '. It was shown there that the excess capacity might lead to an intensified competition between capitalists, and that should tend to bring the the rate of ' surplus value produced " down again. To this a modification has to be added now : with the growth of oligopoly, the competition between capitalists works less and less well, and the excess capacity can persist long without leading to the forcible ejection of superfluous capital. The excess capacity remaining, it exerts then a depressing influence on the investment decisions of capitalists, and the rate of growth of capital slows down.

We can see that the appearance of a ' *surplus value produced* ' which is not correspondingly ' *realised* ' is capable of fulfilling the function of an under-consumption theory. It is not open to objections on realistic grounds. It can be perfectly well reconciled with the fact that ' surplus value realised ', or net profits, actually decline as a ratio of wages. It does not even require that surplus value produced, which we might tentatively identify with the gross profit margin, should continuously rise : because the mechanism of competition between capitalists, which tends to reduce this margin, may still be working, although with much delay. It is then possible that, as the decline in capital accumulation is set in motion and proceeds, the pressure of excess capacity will bring about subsequently some reduction in gross profit margins, but this reduction will be sluggish, just enough perhaps to prevent a continuous rise in excess capacity, but not enough to eliminate the excess capacity created at the outset by the original rise in profit margins.

We may, then, observe a constancy or even fall of gross profit margins in a mature economy, and nevertheless, with the decline in the growth of capital, the gross profit margins may all the time be too high to permit a ' normal ' utilisation of capacity. There will therefore all the time be underconsumption, expressed solely in an abnormal degree of excess capacity which will continuously react on capital accumulation in an adverse way.

The details of this theory do not need to be gone into here, as they have been discussed in earlier sections of this book. It is of interest, however, to show that this theory can be organically developed out of the underconsumption approach of Marx. It requires a few additional concepts and hypotheses, especially the effect of excess capacity on accumulation, but basically it rests on the idea of a production of surplus value which is not realised, and this happens to be the way in which Marx literally formulated the underconsumption approach

INDEX